The Growth of
British Industry

The Growth of
British Industry

A. E. MUSSON

Professor of Economic History,
University of Manchester

Batsford Academic and Educational Ltd

TO MY WIFE, ANNE

© A. E. Musson 1978
First published 1978
Reprinted in this paperback edition 1981

ISBN 0 7134 1243 7

Reproduced from copy supplied, printed and bound in Great Britain
by Billing and Sons Limited, Guildford, London, Oxford, Worcester

Contents

Preface

Britain's industrial growth and prosperity depend fundamentally upon her industrial-technological skills—more than ever today, when she is no longer the centre of an empire, when her overseas investments have largely disappeared in two world wars and when she relies so heavily on imported food and raw materials. This dependence is the result of historical development, especially since the Industrial Revolution, but, although industries figure prominently in general economic histories of Britain, there has been no study focused particularly on industrial-technological growth, though there are numerous specialized works on agriculture, trade and transport. The *History of Technology*, edited by Charles Singer and others, is essentially a history of techniques, by numerous authors, and is universal in scope; though its massive volumes are useful for reference, they do not provide a unified account of the growth of British industry in its broader economic aspects. The aim of this book therefore is to provide such an account, in one volume, including not only technological changes but also such related economic factors as industrial structure, business organization, entrepreneurial innovation, capital investment and markets. It includes all manufacturing and extractive industries but not agriculture, trade and transport, though these are frequently referred to in their marketing and other relationships.

This book also emphasizes the immense industrial achievements of capitalist enterprise, and its equally enormous social benefits in increasing wealth and income, in providing an ever-widening range of consumer goods, in mechanizing production, lightening labour, reducing working hours, lengthening human life and providing the whole material framework of modern urban industrial society, with living standards beyond the wildest dreams of earlier centuries. Too often nowadays, the views of social critics on the misery and exploitation of industrialization are taken as simple truths, regardless of the enormous mass of contrary evidence on its benefits. These social aspects can only be referred to briefly in this work, but, centred as it is on the productive achievements of British industry, it demonstrates their fundamental contributions to improving social welfare.

It begins around the year 1500 and ends in 1939. Both these dates are somewhat arbitrary but justifiable. Industrial development, of course, goes back far earlier than 1500, but over previous centuries and millennia it had been comparatively slow: from 1500 onwards there are clear signs of quickening and more fundamental changes, though Nef's views have attracted much criticism. These changes certainly became more dramatic in the 'first industrial revolution', from the late eighteenth century onwards, but their roots go back into the earlier period. On the other hand, the extent of industrial changes before the mid-nineteenth century have been greatly exaggerated: only in a few industries, such as textiles and iron, had the steam-powered factory system been developed on a large scale, and most manufactures were still predominantly handicrafts, organized in small workshops or on a 'domestic' basis, or else in small water-powered mills; earlier forms of industrial technology and organization long remained widespread and were still to be found even in the twentieth century. For these reasons it was considered necessary to start this book in the so-called 'pre-industrial' era of the sixteenth and seventeenth centuries. These earlier centuries, when industries were fewer, more primitive and of relatively minor importance within the whole economy, have been accorded much less space than the more recent periods, in which technological changes were revolutionizing old industries and creating new ones, transforming Britain into a predominantly industrial society, but it is hoped that the processes of industrial evolution and revolution will be more clearly evident from this long-term viewpoint.

The terminal date presented greater difficulties, but 1939 was eventually chosen, for various reasons. Firstly, by that time there had been a considerable restructuring of British industry necessitated by the 'second industrial revolution', based on electricity, motor transport and new chemicals, and by Britain's loss of world industrial leadership. Secondly, the Second World War and post-war period witnessed a massive growth of State intervention, demonstrated most notably by the growth of socialism and nationalization, as well as by Keynesian economic controls; although governmental intervention had been growing in the inter-war period and the free-enterprise system had been considerably changed by the growth of large-scale business and cartels, Britain clearly entered a new phase in the post-1939 period, which could not be adequately dealt with here. Moreover, there is a very considerable literature dealing with this recent period, which has naturally attracted much attention from industrial economists. It was therefore considered best to concentrate on the period up to 1939, to provide an historical dimension for these modern studies.

Over this vast range, covering nearly four and a half centuries and all industries, I have, of course, drawn heavily on the works of innumerable other scholars, though my own academic interests have always been mainly in the industrial field and I have been able to bring together the fruits of my previous more specialized researches. Footnotes have, as far as possible, been excluded, so as to provide a continuously readable text, but I have made numerous references to authors from whom I have drawn quotations, factual statements and statistics, while a lengthy, though select, bibliography is provided at the end of the book.

There is, in fact, an enormous literature relating to particular industries, areas and firms in different periods, with which students and even academic staff cannot familiarize themselves without prolonged study, and it is the main object of this work to present a general synthesis and interpretation. It surveys British industrial development as a whole, within the world economy, and also traces the growth of particular industries, including not only the great basic industries that have attracted most historical attention but the whole range of manufactures, thus providing a comprehensive view of the country's industrial evolution.

I wish to express thanks to my colleagues, Colin Phillips and Andy Marrison, for having read the typescript, the former in part, the latter in whole, and for having made many helpful suggestions towards its improvement. I am also very grateful to our departmental secretaries, Liz Dyckhoff, Maggie Chawner, Jane Crawford, Hilda Graham and Tina Reid, for their labours in typing my manuscript. Above all, I thank my wife—to whom this book is dedicated—for all that I owe to her over many years.

May 1977   A. E. MUSSON

PART I

THE PRE-INDUSTRIAL ECONOMY, 1500–1700

1

Industry in Town
and Country

Writing at the beginning of the twentieth century, in his famous study of *Industrial Organization in the Sixteenth and Seventeenth Centuries*, George Unwin emphasized the prolonged survival of successive but overlapping stages of industrial organization, still strongly evident in modern urban society. There was still some production in the home, with home-made clothing, home-baked bread, domestic shoe repairs, etc.—'survivals from the domestic economy of the primitive village community in which every household supplied almost all its own wants'. There were still also numerous examples of small-scale handicraft production, which had evolved with the growth of trade and industry and the development of towns, with their markets and specialized crafts, organized in small workshops and gilds: many small independent tradesmen—butchers and bakers, tailors and cobblers, blacksmiths and carpenters—still produced directly for local consumers, though the former craft gilds had long previously decayed and disappeared.

In many industries, however, larger-scale capitalist organization had developed with the more widespread growth of regional, national and international trade. But many of these trades were still, in Unwin's day, conducted on the 'domestic or commission system', or what is often called alternatively the 'putting-out system', with mercantile capitalist middlemen distributing materials to wage-earners still working in their homes or in larger workshops under small masters. There were still, in the early twentieth century, considerable numbers of such domestic workers, frequently exploited under the 'sweating' system. In fact this domestic system was still 'the predominant method of employment in the East End of London', in 'the tailoring of Whitechapel, the silk-weaving of Bethnal Green, and the cabinet-making of Shoreditch'. It still survived widely also in other towns and trades, 'including the cutlery trades of Sheffield, the pottery and the chain and nail-making of the Black Country, the lace-making and hosiery of Nottingham, the straw-plaiting of Bedford, the glove industry of Worcester and Oxfordshire, the smallware trades of Birmingham and the silk-weaving of Macclesfield'. In some cases, as in the Nottingham and Birmingham trades, there was a transitional arrangement, half-way between domestic workshop and factory, of a kind that had earlier existed in Lancashire cotton-spinning, in which small masters hired rooms or floors, together with mechanical power, in a factory building.

In many industries, of course, by that time, the factory system had fully developed, in which large amounts of fixed-capital equipment were required, in the form of buildings, machinery and engines, and in which large numbers of wage-earners were employed, not only in factories in the narrow sense but also in large collieries, shipyards and building works. But there is a strong tendency in many if not most general economic and industrial histories to exaggerate the pace at which the factory system developed, to over-emphasize the early growth and spread of power-driven mechanization and to underestimate or to neglect almost entirely the long survival of earlier forms of industrial organization and technology. Sir John Clapham's shrewd observations—that, in the second quarter of the nineteenth century, factory workers were still a small minority and that there were still more shoe-makers and cobblers than coal-miners—have been inadequately appreciated, in the general emphasis upon the more striking aspects of the Industrial Revolution.

When one delves much further back, into the centuries before the Industrial Revolution—into what has in recent years been increasingly but rather misleadingly referred to as 'the pre-industrial economy'—the more striking is the very gradual rate of change, the more widespread the persistence of traditional industrial techniques and organization. Undoubtedly this was an economy based overwhelmingly upon agriculture rather than upon industry: in that sense it was 'pre-industrial'. The great bulk of the then much smaller population—less than 3 million in the England and Wales of 1500—lived in the countryside and derived their livelihood from the land. Towns, trade and industry had certainly been developing over earlier centuries: the Middle Ages, it has become increasingly evident, were not static industrially and technologically; numerous handicrafts had developed, manufacturing textiles, making clothes, working in wood and metals, producing pottery and glass, building houses, etc., and the power of water and wind had been employed for grinding corn and fulling cloth. And these industrial developments were to be continued and extended, as we shall see, in the early modern period. But even at the end of the seventeenth century, according to Gregory King's contemporary estimates, out of a total population by that time of about $5\frac{1}{2}$ million less than a quarter-million were numbered among the families of artisans and handicraftsmen, though other groups such as shopkeepers and tradesmen, and labourers and cottagers, were also involved to some extent in manufactures.

Many manufacturing operations were closely related to the land and agriculture and were located in rural areas as well as in towns. Cities and towns drew not only their food supplies but also their industrial raw materials from the surrounding countryside. Spinners and weavers in the woollen manufactures, together with tailors, hatters and cappers in the clothing trades, were dependent on growing flocks of sheep and enclosures; the linen trade similarly required flax, rope-making hemp, and dyeing was based on other agricultural crops such as woad, weld, madder and saffron. The food and drink trades, of course, were similarly supplied, millers with grain and bakers with flour, butchers with meat, and brewers with barley and hops. Tanners, shoe-makers, saddlers and other leather workers used animal hides, while soap-boilers and candle-makers consumed the animal fats for their tallow. The building trades drew their requirements from rural lime-kilns, quarries and clay pits; carpenters and wheelwrights were likewise dependent on rural woodlands, which also provided the charcoal for iron-smelting furnaces and forges, from which smiths and other iron workers were supplied with their raw materials. Potteries were similarly provided with clay, and glassworks with sand and vegetable potash.

Manufactures may thus be regarded throughout this period as appendant to the land and agriculture, which supplied the organic raw materials for satisfying the basic human needs of food, clothing and housing. Many of these trades, in fact, were located in the countryside, often combined with agriculture as subsidiary or even primary occupations. Rural textile manufactures, as we shall see, were widespread, especially (as Joan Thirsk and others have demonstrated) in areas unsuited to intensive arable cultivation, such as poorer, hilly, pastoral or woodland regions. This combination of agricultural smallholdings with spinning and weaving of wool or linen is well known; but similar 'dual economies', though much less familiar, were very numerous. Stocking-knitting, lace-making, glove-making, straw-plaiting and basket-making were common rural crafts in which women and children as well as men were widely employed; yeomen farmers often operated corn or fulling mills, agriculture was also combined with the mining of coal or metallic ores, with quarrying, brick-making, lime-burning and charcoal-burning, with metals, glass and pottery manufactures and with fishing. Dr Thirsk has suggested indeed that during the seventeenth century 'somewhere near half the farming population' were part-time craftsmen. Seasonal inactivity in agriculture could be balanced by industrial work, which could be temporarily abandoned when labour was urgently required on the land, when even town artisans often left their trades to get in the harvest. In the countryside more commonly than in the towns, many commodities long continued to be home-made, not only in such essentially rural activities as butter- and cheese-making, but also in making clothes and brewing. Many articles, moreover, were made by rural craftsmen such as weavers, tailors, smiths, tinkers and carpenters, who long remained numerous and widespread, often with small agricultural holdings.

The increasing use of water and wind power also tended to locate various manufacturing operations in the countryside. There were, of course, countless thousands of corn-mills—over 5,000 water-mills had been recorded in the Domesday Book—and in the later Middle Ages the introduction of fulling mills had brought about a migration of the woollen industry into the countryside. Water-wheels had similarly come into use in the iron industry, for working the bellows of bloom-smithies, and from the late fifteenth century onwards they were to be further employed at blast-furnaces and for operating forge tilt-hammers and rolling and slitting mills. Their uses were also extended into other industrial processes, such as pulping rags in paper mills, driving grinders' wheels in the cutlery trade, grinding flints for pottery manufacture and crushing seed in oil mills, and these mills were generally situated in rural areas, where water power was available. Mills built for one purpose were, not uncommonly, later applied to another: many fulling mills were converted corn-mills, corn-milling and fulling were often combined, and both types were utilized for paper mills, etc.

Trade and industry, of course, had long been developing in towns, dating back to the early Middle Ages and Roman times. A distinctive urban commercial and manufacturing sector had been evolving over the centuries, with increasing division and specialization of labour. Towns had developed primarily as centres of trade and industry, with markets and fairs, merchant and craft gilds. Some of the larger towns, above all London and to a lesser extent Bristol, Norwich and Exeter, had developed widespread trading relationships, extending far beyond local markets into national and international trade. Not merely did they act as commercial and administrative capitals for their regions—London as the great national trading metropolis—but were also busy manufacturing centres. In London, for example, one hundred and eleven crafts were listed in 1422, and there were scores in other large towns. London had a population of about 60,000 in the early 1520s and was beginning to grow rapidly. Other towns were of considerably less importance: Norwich, the largest provincial city, had little more than 12,000 inhabitants, Bristol less than 10,000, while the next biggest, such as Exeter, Salisbury, York and Newcastle, had around 8,000, followed by sizeable towns, such as Coventry and Worcester with around 6,000, middle-sized towns, like Leeds, Leicester, Derby and Northampton, with from 3,000 to 4,000, while the great majority of market towns had only one or two thousand inhabitants or less; many had only a few hundred and were little more than large villages.

In all these towns there were industrial crafts, organized into gilds, which were numerous and highly specialized in London and the larger cities, with weavers, fullers, dyers, shearmen and drapers in the textile trades; skinners, tanners, curriers, whittawyers, cordwainers, shoe-makers, pursers, glovers and saddlers in the leather trades; founders, blacksmiths, armourers, cutlers, pin-makers, pewterers, etc., in the metal trades, and a host of other crafts in clothing, wood-working, building and the food and drink trades. In the small towns the gilds were less numerous, craftsmen often being organized into broader manufacturing groups.

In some towns there were already, by the early sixteenth century and perhaps previously, clearly discernible tendencies towards local industrial specialization. As Hoskins has shown, for example, Coventry was by that time specializing in textiles and to a lesser extent in metal manufactures, while Northampton and Leicester were becoming centres of the leather, shoe-making and allied trades. Birmingham was already notable for its metal manufactures, as Leland observed in his *Itinerary* in 1538: 'There be many Smithes in the Towne that use to make Knives and all mannour of cutting tooles, and many Lorimers that make Bittes, and a great many Naylors, soe that a great part of the Towne is maintained by Smithes who have theire Iron and Sea Cole out of Staffordshire.' Later on, brass and copper manufactures of buttons, buckles, locks, etc., were developed there and were flourishing by the late seventeenth century. The Sheffield and Rotherham manufactures were similarly remarked on by Leland, with 'many smithes and cuttelars', producing knives and 'all cutting tools'. In the Birmingham and Sheffield areas, this industrial development was based on local resources of iron ore, wood, coal, limestone, sandstone, fire-clay and water power, while metal manufactures and farming were often combined in the surrounding countryside, especially in the pastoral areas. Similar geological and geographical factors, local raw materials such as wool, metallic ores, clay and salt, availability of water for power and transport and access to markets, were bringing about localization of industry in other areas.

In all these towns, however, it appears that a considerable proportion of tradesmen were occupied in providing for basic consumer needs. In Leicester, for instance, according to Hoskins, 'well over half ... were engaged in the clothing, food and drink, household goods (cutlers, chandlers, ironmongers, etc.) and building trades. If we include the distributive trades, just about three persons in five were engaged in providing for the consumer.' Similar findings have been made in other towns. Norwich, for example, though clearly specializing in textiles, which occupied about 30 per cent of the tradesmen in the 1520s, had sizeable proportions in the distributive, food and drink, leather, building and clothing trades. This appears to have been the pattern in all provincial towns, though with varying industrial specializations. Even in Birmingham, the wealthiest tradesmen were not the smiths, lorimers and nailers but those in the tanning, leather-working and woollen manufactures, as in many other midland towns; the metal trades in that area appear to have developed originally in response to local rural demand for saddler's ironmongery, nails, scythes, etc., as Court says, in 'a district dominated by the grazier', and many of these midlands craftsmen were also smallholding farmers. The leather crafts, as Clarkson has shown, were of much greater importance than economic historians had previously recognized, second only to textiles, in fact, and extensively occupied in making not only boots, shoes, belts, gloves, purses and pouches but also clothing, drinking vessels, buckets and saddlery, as well as industrial requirements such as bellows for blast-furnaces and smiths' forges.

In all provincial towns there was a high degree of dependence upon the surrounding countryside. Whilst supplied with foodstuffs and raw materials from the land, they reciprocated by providing the neighbouring countryfolk with all kinds of manufactured articles. The weekly town markets and annual fairs served as centres of exchange, frequented by hundreds and even thousands of people, while craftsmen's shops were beginning to carry on more continuous trade. The butchers, bakers and brewers of the town, the shoe-makers, tailors and drapers, carpenters, masons and slaters, smiths, wheelwrights and saddlers were not catering merely for the urban inhabitants. To quote Hoskins, 'We can hardly envisage three people in every five [in Leicester, for example] selling consumer goods and services to the other two in the town.' At the same time, the Leicester butchers, tanners, curriers, whittawyers, saddlers, shoe-makers and glovers in the growing leather trades were dependent upon the neighbouring cattle pastures. Indeed, the town itself, like most others, still had its surrounding open fields, meadow and common, in which the burgesses had holdings and grazing rights. In many towns the inhabitants were still obliged to grind their corn at the town mill and bake their bread in the common ovens; in non-corporate towns, such as Manchester, these feudal obligations were still due, together with market tolls and water mill rights, to a lord of the manor, right down to the nineteenth century. The average market town long remained not much more than an enlarged village. In Oakham (Rutland), for example, there was only a handful of craftsmen, most of whom were also described as yeomen or husbandmen, and, according to Cornwall, farming was 'the first and foremost occupation of the townsmen'. As Hoskins says, 'Elizabethan Leicester kept a country air about it. Orchards, barns and stables, and large gardens lay among the streets; windmills stood silhouetted ... against the southern skyline; the streets petered out in ten minutes' walk into lanes redolent of cow dung and hay.' Down such country lanes, as late as the 1820s, it was still said to be possible to walk round Manchester on a Sunday afternoon.

One must not, however, go too far in stressing the rural characteristics of provincial towns in this period. As the Tawneys perceptively observed many years ago, in using a muster roll as an occupational census of Gloucestershire in 1608, these features were no doubt strongly marked in the small boroughs, such as Chipping Campden and Winchcombe, in which 30 to 40 per cent of the men were stated to be engaged in agriculture, but the larger towns of Gloucester, Tewkesbury and Cirencester 'had an economic character of their own, which made them something other than large villages'. They contained few farmers or farm labourers but had distinctively mercantile and industrial characteristics. But, whilst the proportion of their inhabitants engaged in such industrial occupations as metal, wood, leather and clothing manufactures and in the building trades was significantly higher than in the rural areas, these towns were not, in the Tawneys' view, primarily industrial centres. Urban predominance was most strongly marked in wholesale dealing and retailing, in food and drink and in the leather trades: the towns were 'primarily . . . not manufacturing, but finishing and distributing centres'.

This conclusion is broadly in agreement with the subsequent findings of Hoskins and other scholars, who have also stressed the importance of trade and the dominance of mercantile wealth in the towns. But it must be pointed out that the Tawneys' own Gloucestershire figures show that the number engaged in manufacturing occupations (textiles, leather, clothing, woodwork, building, metal work and making of food and drink) comprised nearly 52 per cent of the urban total. They were undoubtedly right, however, in stressing that the economic basis of provincial town life was 'to serve as a market and source of supply for the agricultural districts'.

'They handled such products of the surrounding region as required to be worked up, supplied the agricultural districts with wares that could not be produced locally, and served as a link between them and the distant world of London. Thus Gloucester . . . contained 9 brewers, 15 maltsters, 18 tanners and curriers, and 10 saddlers, who offered a market for barley, hops and hides; while its 34 mercers, 16 drapers, 20 tailors, 23 shoemakers, 11 glovers, and 5 haberdashers . . . can hardly have made a living by clothing [only] its own population.'

Gloucester was clearly much like Leicester and other towns in its general manufacturing and trading characteristics. In the important case of textile manufactures, however, there was not the same urban predominance in the county generally; nor were other manufactures concentrated exclusively in the towns. Whilst agriculture was certainly the main occupation, especially, of course, in rural areas, it employed only about half the total adult population (and not much more, apparently, in Northamptonshire at that same time). Industrial occupations were, in fact, widely dispersed not only in textiles—most notably by this time a rural domestic industry—but also in most other trades: smiths, carpenters, building workers, millers, butchers, tailors and shoe-makers were found scattered throughout the country areas. There were, however, marked tendencies towards regional concentration even in rural industries: the woollen industry, for example, was concentrated on the steep western escarpment and in the valleys of the Cotswolds, where swift-running streams provided power and water for fulling and dyeing, though weaving was more widely dispersed; similarly, miners, iron smelters and nailers were concentrated in the Forest of Dean and Kingswood Forest, where coal, iron ore and charcoal were available, whereas smiths were more scattered, to be found in most villages of any size. The Tawneys therefore concluded that, although Gloucestershire was predominantly rural, it was by no means overwhelmingly agricultural:

'... some conventional pictures of what is called pre-industrial England may require to be modified. Parts of it, at least, would appear to have been more industrialised than such accounts suggest. In reality, rural society in the early seventeenth century was, at any rate in Gloucestershire, somewhat highly differentiated. It was by no means exclusively, and in certain areas was not even predominantly, an agricultural society. Agriculture and industry were inextricably intertwined. Not only corn and cattle, but corn, wool and cloth, and even, in some districts, corn, coal and iron, were almost joint products. Many families, from the gentry to the humblest peasant, were almost equally interested in farming and manufacturing ... rural society and agricultural society were by no means equivalent expressions.'

Subsequent local studies based on taxation returns, wills, probate inventories, parish registers, lists of freemen, etc., have borne out these conclusions in other areas. (See, for example, the works by Chalklin, Chambers, Court, Hey, Hoskins, Jones, Laslett, Mendels and Thirsk referred to in the Bibliography.) They have shown how numerous and widespread rural manufactures and peasant craftsmen were, in many parts of the country and in many industries, not only in textiles but also in metal manufactures and other trades, as in the rural areas around Birmingham and Sheffield, in the Vale of Trent, in south-west Lancashire and elsewhere: agricultural communities were by no means 'pre-industrial'—indeed marked industrial concentrations and specializations existed in rural areas long before the Industrial Revolution. These researches have also supported, to some extent, the Tawneys' findings in regard to the widespread existence of small independent or semi-independent producers, and the relatively minor importance of a purely wage-earning class in this period. Even in textiles, where there were some considerable capitalist clothiers, especially in the West Country, these were much less numerous than the small master weavers, fullers and dyers who were working on their own, helped by their families, or in some cases employing one or two servants. Indeed, both in textiles and in other manufactures, it is difficult to distinguish a purely proletarian class, when agricultural and industrial occupations, independent production and wage earning were so often combined; even those supplied with working materials by a clothier or some other

merchant employer tended to be regarded not as wage workers but as independent producers, and it is also difficult to differentiate between those who were
working for such employers and those who were producing directly for local
customers or for the market.

On the other hand, evidence has accumulated that in towns, at any rate, the
Tawneys' findings exaggerated 'the smallness of the proletarian elements in the
population compared with the large numbers of the *petite bourgeoisie*'. Not only in
London but also in provincial towns, such as Leicester, Northampton, Coventry,
Norwich and Exeter, as well as in the smaller country towns of Buckinghamshire,
Rutland and Sussex—indeed apparently in all towns—there was a very high
concentration of mercantile and industrial wealth, a 'social pyramid', with a
small number of wealthy families at the top and a relatively large number of poor
at the bottom. From the subsidy returns in the first half of the sixteenth century, it
is evident that a considerable proportion of the adult population, as much as a
third or even a half in some towns, had no assessable goods or income—were too
poor to be taxed—and nearly half of those who were taxed belonged to the
wage-earning or small master class, paying only at the minimum rate. 'Above
this wide base', as Hoskins has observed, 'the pyramid rose through a middle
class of prosperous artificers, merchants and professional men, to a needle-like
point.' In Leicester, for example, twenty-five persons, or 6 per cent of the taxable
population, owned nearly three-fifths of the wealth; in Coventry and Exeter 7 per
cent owned about two-thirds; in Norwich about 6 per cent owned approximately
60 per cent. The wealthiest individuals, moreover, were mostly merchants—
grocers, drapers, wool merchants, clothiers, etc.—rather than manufacturers,
though there was no sharp distinction between mercantile and manufacturing
activities, and mercantile employers, as we shall see, often had economic control
over small craftsmen, both small masters and wage-earning journeymen, not only
in the towns but increasingly also in the countryside.

In all these developments there was no sharp division between the medieval
and early modern economy and society. Towns had been growing, trade and
industry had been expanding, a monetary economy and system of mercantile
credit had been developing over earlier centuries, and as markets
expanded—long before Adam Smith enunciated his famous obser-
vation—industrial specialization and division of labour had been increasing,
tending to produce distinctions between agriculture and industry, between town
and country, between mercantile and handicraft functions, between capital and
labour and between the increasingly numerous manufacturing operations into
which major industries such as textiles, leather manufactures and the building
trades had become subdivided. At the same time, especially in the smaller towns
and rural areas, these distinctions were by no means clearly marked: various

combinations of industry, trade and agriculture, of independent production and wage earning, remained very common.

The growth of towns, with their markets, fairs and shops is in itself evidence of expanding internal trade. In the later Middle Ages this was accompanied by vigorous expansion of English overseas trade, as evidenced most notably by the rise of the Merchant Staplers and Merchant Adventurers, trading in wool and cloth and in a variety of other goods, mainly with north-west Europe, and challenging the former predominance of Hanseatic and Italian merchants. This commercial expansion was associated with industrial growth and changes in industrial organization. In particular, it greatly increased the importance of mercantile capital and credit, since production was now for wider markets, both internal and external, especially in the textile trades but also in metals, leather and other manufactures. Not all trades were affected—many, as Unwin observed, such as butchers and bakers, tailors and shoe-makers, smiths and carpenters, long continued to produce on a small scale for limited local markets—but, where markets were becoming regional, national or international, changes inevitably occurred. As the distance between producer and consumer increased in space and time, as more raw materials were required and as the number of specialized manufacturing operations became more complex, there was need for more commercial capital and co-ordinating control.

The craft gilds, into which most urban manufactures had been organized, gradually underwent a metamorphosis. These were essentially urban institutions, each organizing and controlling all craftsmen—masters, journeymen and apprentices—in a particular trade in a particular town: each craft in the woollen industry, for example, such as weaving, fulling, shearing and dyeing, would have its separate gild in each town where this industry existed. The main purpose was to maintain monopoly control over entry into the local trade and over production and marketing of its products. Entry was generally by apprenticeship, the period of which (commonly seven years) and the number of apprentices being under strict gild regulation, though entry could also be obtained by patrimony—son usually following father in the trade—and could also be purchased; 'illegal' men were not permitted to practise the craft in the town, and 'foreigners', including outsiders from elsewhere in the country and not simply aliens, were also kept out. Apprenticeship provided, of course, a system of industrial training, to ensure that workmen were properly qualified, and gild 'searchers' were appointed to see that shoddy goods were not produced, thus protecting consumers; night work was generally prohibited. Bans on such trading abuses as engrossing, forestalling and regrating also gave consumers some protection against cornering of the market but were perhaps primarily intended to share out local trade fairly among gild members; under the town corporation, the gilds also regulated markets and prices. Production, being mainly for the local market, was on a small scale, using hand tools or simple machinery, in small domestic workshops. Capital requirements were therefore limited, and it was possible for many journeymen to become small masters; there was no impassable gulf between capital and labour.

It is easy, however, to overidealize craft gild organization, forgetting its petty, local, narrowly exclusive, monopolizing characteristics and its prime aim of protecting producers rather than consumers; gilds were also very sectional and prone to demarcation disputes. It is very doubtful, indeed, whether the idealized gild ever actually existed; in any case it cannot have survived long, because trade expansion and mercantile capitalism began to transform gild organization in the later Middle Ages. The more enterprising masters, acquiring wealth and influence, began to form an exclusive clique of 'liverymen', controlling the gild, separated by a widening gulf from the smaller masters and journeymen who began to form a separate 'yeomanry', though usually still within the gild. The journeymen tended to become either lifelong wage earners or, if they were permitted to become masters, remained mostly subordinate and dependent, excluded from the livery, whose members usually ceased to practise the craft and concentrated on control of trading operations. Thus were created the livery companies, especially in London, many of which, in fact, such as the mercers, grocers, drapers, haberdashers, etc., were purely trading companies, controlling the subordinate handicraft gilds: the haberdashers, for example, found employment for and controlled the trades of hatters, cappers, felt-makers and pinners; the leather-sellers similarly controlled the whittawyers, glovers, pursers and pouch-makers. In each case the manufacturing element was subjected to mercantile capitalist control, either by the livery within a particular gild or by a trading company controlling and often absorbing several handicraft gilds.

The wealthier traders had little interest in maintaining petty local trading restrictions. They began to take on more apprentices and journeymen or even to employ 'illegal' men, and they tended to allow the system of 'searching' to fall into disuse. At the same time, especially in London, they expanded the area of their trading operations, in both home and overseas markets, employing larger quantities of capital in stocks of raw materials and finished goods. Thus in these trades gild monopolies and regulations were gradually broken, especially as workers were increasingly employed outside the town boundaries and in rural areas, where labour was cheaper and beyond gild control. In this way such industries came to be organized on the domestic or putting-out system, merchant employers distributing materials—raw wool or yarn, rod iron, leather, etc.—to craftsmen working in their own homes or small workshops, in both town and country but increasingly in the countryside. These merchant middlemen would be engaged in buying and selling, at the same time co-ordinating the various manufacturing processes: the clothiers in the woollen industry, for example, bought raw wool from fellmongers or wool merchants, put it out to spinners and weavers—or had depots from which these workers collected it—and then arranged for the cloth to be fulled and perhaps also dressed and dyed, before selling it to cloth mechants, drapers or merchant adventurers, either in local markets or in Blackwell Hall, London, for sale either at home or overseas.

These changes were not, for the most part, accompanied by technological developments but were mainly in mercantile organization, resulting from expanding trade, capitalist enterprise and competition, breaking down the barriers of gild monopolies and corporate town controls. In London particularly, the merchants who engaged in these larger commercial operations frequently had little or no real connection with the trades of the companies to which they belonged, as a result of entry by patrimony rather than by craft apprenticeship, and through the 'custom of London', whereby a freeman of one trade was free of all. A member of the Skinners' or the Merchant Taylors' Company, for example, would most likely never have had any training in tanning or tailoring. They were mercantile rather than industrial capitalists, and their efforts were directed mainly towards enlarging markets and output by increasing the scale of their commercial operations and by employing more workers. The craft gild did not generally decline on account of technological changes: for the most part the handicraftsmen still continued to use the same simple equipment in their homes or small workshops—hand spinning wheel or distaff and spindle, together with hand loom, in textiles; needle and thread in tailoring and shoe-making; hammer and anvil in the metal trades; hand saw, chisel and plane in wood-working; adze and hammer in coopering; hand wheel in pottery and similar hand tools in a host of other trades.

One notable exception, however, occurred in the woollen industry, where water-powered fulling mills produced what Professor Carus-Wilson has called 'an industrial revolution of the thirteenth century'. This technological change not only required more fixed capital but stimulated migration of this industry into the countryside, as in the Cotswolds, near sources of water power, and tended to bring about the decline of some of the existing urban manufactures. Combined with the domestic system of spinning and weaving in rural areas, it accentuated the role of the capitalist clothiers, some of whom, like the Springs of Lavenham or the Paycockes of Coggeshall in East Anglia, or John Tame of Fairford or Thomas Horton of Bradford-on-Avon in the West Country, had by the end of the medieval period become very wealthy men, employing hundreds of domestic rural outworkers. This growth in trade and capitalist organization perhaps also accounted for the widespread adoption of the spinning wheel, displacing the distaff and spindle, and of the horizontal frame loom in the later Middle Ages.

One must not, however, exaggerate the revolutionary effect of these changes. In the woollen industry, for instance, urban manufactures still continued in the early modern period, fulling mills were to be found in towns as well as in the country, and small clothiers and independent weavers remained very numerous.

The craft gilds, as we shall see, were a long time dying, new gilds and companies continued to be formed, and some of them survived into the eighteenth and even the nineteenth century, still endeavouring to maintain their traditional regulations. The widespread complaints of the decay of industry in ancient corporate towns in the sixteenth century, and the undoubted evidence of the widespread development of manufactures on a more capitalist basis in the countryside, must not obscure the fact that many of those towns continued to grow as centres of trade and industry in the early modern period. In Wiltshire, for example, as Ramsay has shown, towns such as 'Salisbury, Devizes, Chippenham, Calne, Bradford, Trowbridge, Westbury and certain other centres were always of particular importance as homes of the woollen industry', and the same was true of Exeter, Tiverton, Witney, Norwich and Colchester in other woollen-manufacturing areas; many towns, such as York and Chester, retained their importance and their gilds, despite the decline of their textile trades, and, though others certainly declined as centres of industry, they often remained important as trading, social and administrative centres.

Gilds survived longest in those trades in which production was still manual and on a small scale, with numerous independent craftsmen, whose trade was mainly local. Some industries, however, never appear to have been under gild organization. By their very nature they required relatively greater concentrations of capital and labour, as in coal-mining, iron-smelting, shipbuilding and large building constructions. But these industries had not developed to any great extent before the sixteenth century, and production units were mostly small, with handfuls of men, using simple hand tools and equipment, such as picks, shovels and windlasses in mining, saws, adzes and hammers in shipbuilding and stonemasons' chisels, mallets and trowels in building, though water-driven bellows and hammers had been introduced into bloom-smithies. Cathedrals, churches, castles and large mansions required relatively large numbers of skilled masons, etc., who tended to be migratory and outside gild organization (though having their own masonic lodges); but most houses were small and more primitively built of timber and clay by local workers, often part-time and rural, though many carpenters were small town tradesmen, organized in gilds; so, too, were plasterers and tilers. Many of those engaged in the mining of coal and metallic ores in the early sixteenth century were also independent or semi-independent producers, such as the free miners of the Forest of Dean, the tin miners of Cornwall and Devon and the lead miners of the Mendips and the Pennines. Mining and smelting operations were mostly rural, often combined with small farming, but in the sixteenth and seventeenth centuries they were to experience some striking changes, which Nef has seen as the basis of 'an early industrial revolution'.

2

An Early Industrial Revolution?

During the sixteenth and seventeenth centuries new forces tended to accelerate commercial and industrial development. Though overseas trade had become increasingly significant in the English economy of the later Middle Ages, as evidenced by the rise of the Merchant Staplers and Adventurers, the geographical discoveries of the late fifteenth and early sixteenth centuries brought about more fundamental changes in England's world trading position. Trade gradually began to develop with the Americas, Africa and India, and by the mid-eighteenth century Britain was well on the way to establishing a large colonial empire, which not only provided a widening range of imports, especially of tropical products such as sugar, tobacco, tea, etc.—leading to the establishment of refining, blending and manufacturing processes in this country, especially in London and other ports—but also greatly stimulated exports of woollen, metal and other manufactured goods and led eventually to the development of new industries such as those of cotton and silk, in imitation of eastern fabrics. And at the same time as the Africa, East India, Virginia, Hudson's Bay and other companies were opening up trade with new lands, English merchants were penetrating into European markets: the Muscovy (Russia) and Eastland (Baltic) companies were entering former Hanseatic preserves, while the Levant and Barbary companies were challenging Italian merchants in the Mediterranean. Moreover, increasing numbers of independent merchants were engaging in general European trade: we must remember Unwin's warning that the new trading companies, like the old, were restrictive monopolies and that the growth of English overseas trade in the seventeenth and eighteenth centuries was associated with the breakdown of their exclusive privileges under free-trade attacks. This trade expansion gave an immense stimulus to industry: by the late seventeenth century, Davis has estimated, 'a quarter of all manufacturing production, a half of the production of woollen goods, was exported'. This increasing production for overseas markets led to growing manufacturing concentration in particular areas, under mercantile capitalist control, with increasing subdivision and specialization of labour. Shipbuilding and allied trades were also greatly expanded.

Equally if not more important, however, was the expansion in internal trade, stimulating and stimulated by improvements in road and river transport and growth of coastal shipping, with increasing numbers of merchant middlemen, larger-scale wholesaling and more retail shops, developments so impressive to Defoe by the early eighteenth century and further emphasized by the modern researches of Westerfield, Willan and other scholars. Population growth and rising prices were probably the main driving forces behind this trade expansion. From less than 3 million in 1500, the population of England and Wales grew to about 5½ million by 1700. This increased population, as we have seen, was still overwhelmingly rural; though London had grown prodigiously, to about half a million inhabitants, provincial towns had expanded much less rapidly, the largest such as Norwich and Bristol having risen to between 25,000 and 30,000 but no other, apart from York and Exeter, having more than 10,000. The metropolitan market, however, as Defoe observed and as Fisher has emphasized, was of immense importance, drawing in foodstuffs and raw materials, dominating the export trade and also acting as a great distribution centre both for imports and for its own manufactures. Provincial towns also continued to grow, though less strikingly, as centres of trade and industry, the bigger ones sharing in national and international trade, the smaller ones still serving regional and local market areas.

It is not clear, however, whether domestic demand was stimulated by rising living standards, as well as by the growing population, because of the complicated effects of the 'price revolution' of the sixteenth and early seventeenth centuries. This remarkable rise in prices—by about seven times for foodstuffs apparently and by three times for industrial products between 1500 and 1640, though with considerable variations between different commodities—has been attributed to various factors, such as debasement of the coinage, the influx of silver bullion from Spanish America and the pressure of rising population. Its effects have also been considerably debated. Some economic historians and economists, such as Hamilton and Keynes, have argued that it resulted in 'profit-inflation', because prices rose faster than costs—wages lagging especially—and that this stimulated capitalist enterprise among landowners, merchants and industrialists. In agriculture, for example, enclosures and agricultural improvements were encouraged by rising prices not only of foodstuffs but also of wool and other farm products; some historians, particularly Kerridge, have even discerned an 'agricultural revolution' in this period. Others, notably Nef, have observed an 'early industrial revolution' as a result either of greater profit opportunities or of rises in the prices of raw materials such as timber, which together tended to stimulate technological innovations, more industrial investment, greater output and larger-scale capitalist organization. But, since food prices rose more rapidly than wages and industrial prices, it would seem—as Brenner, for example, has argued—that agricultural production was not keeping pace with the rising population or that wages lagged because of surplus labour and unemployment, so that living standards of large sections of the community tended to fall, a greater proportion of their incomes had to be spent on food and demand for industrial products was thus relatively reduced or grew more slowly; or it may be argued that industrial supply was more elastic than agricultural, adjusting more flexibly to growing demand, so that industrial prices rose less sharply than those of foodstuffs. It may also be pointed out that, as the pressure of increasing population was mainly on agriculture, rising food prices gave increased incomes to the farming community—the greater part of the population—whose demand for manufactured goods was thus increased; this would apply particularly to farmers who held their land freehold or on fixed copyhold rents and who either employed no labour or whose wages bills were increasing less rapidly than the prices of their produce. On the other hand, the growth of population created more landless wage earners and pressed down wage rates, thus providing cheap labour for industrial growth. As Phelps-Brown and Hopkins have emphasized, however, 'industrialism did not create that [wage-earning] class, it found jobs for it'.

In all this controversy there is danger of circular argument, for the growth of population has itself been attributed to increasing agricultural and industrial production and employment. It seems clear, however, that the rising population and the price revolution together did stimulate industrial development. At the same time there were other forces at work. The Renaissance is said by some scholars to have resulted in a more rationalist secular outlook, a more materialist and calculating attitude—double-entry book-keeping dates from that period—whilst also leading through scientific enquiry to technological innovation. The socio-economic effects of the Reformation have been similarly emphasized, particularly by Weber, who discerned close links between the 'Protestant ethic' and the 'spirit of capitalism', encouraging individual enterprise, the profit motive and commercial competition, and leading to the removal of controls on usury (interest) and prices and of corporate restrictions such as those of the gilds; the dissolution of the monasteries, moreover, led to large transfers of land to lay owners, more interested in the profitable exploitation of their agricultural and mineral resources.

Here again, however, there have been conflicting arguments. Economic individualism, capitalist enterprise and technological innovation, it has been pointed out, were not new nor confined to Protestant countries; ecclesiastical and gild controls on economic development had long been disintegrating; science likewise was not unknown in the Middle Ages, and in any case had little influence in the early modern period. Scholars holding these views place more emphasis on purely economic factors such as overseas trade expansion, population growth and rising prices, while some, notably Nef, have attempted to combine economic, technological, socio-cultural and religious factors in broader interpretations.

Indeed there are additional factors to be considered. The decline of feudalism and manorial structure in the later Middle Ages, together with the development of a more purely monetary economy, a freer land market, the growth of trade and industry and educational expansion, produced greater economic and social mobility. The nobility and gentry, or their younger sons, were now more commonly involved in industry and trade, exploiting their mineral resources and developing urban property; in a period of rising prices, many of them were eager to exploit all possible sources of income and, as Stone has emphasized, played an important entrepreneurial role, especially in the iron industry. At the same time, prosperous merchants and industrialists were acquiring landed estates, being knighted or ennobled, and marrying into the upper ranks; while yeomen farmers, craftsmen and shopkeepers were similarly thriving and rising and intermingling. It is also true, of course, as Stone says, that 'downward mobility was the lot of those who were improvident or incompetent, extravagant or unlucky', though these have attracted comparatively little historical attention; but while increasing economic and social competition involved falls as well as rises, opportunity for the latter encouraged risk-taking enterprise.

Another problematical factor is the role of the State. Some historians have emphasized the significance of Mercantilist policy, a 'policy of power', aimed at increasing national economic strength by means of protective tariffs and navigation laws, by fostering the development of new industries and processes, especially those of strategic significance such as the manufacture of gunpowder and armaments, and by encouraging foreign immigrants and capital to come here to develop the metallurgical, textile and other industries, so that this country could catch up with more advanced German, Dutch, French and Italian technology and achieve economic self-sufficiency; the granting of exclusive manufacturing and trading rights, by patents of monopoly—the origin of the patent system for protecting inventions—became a common method of encouraging these new developments, though it tended to be exploited for fiscal purposes. On the other hand, governmental policy was in many ways conservative and restrictive in endeavouring, for example, to preserve town and gild monopolies, to check the growth of capitalist enterprise in rural areas, to regulate wages, hours and apprenticeship, to impose manufacturing regulations, to ban certain labour-saving machines and to place many industries and trades in the hands of monopolists. Other historians therefore have stressed the weakening of central government as a result of the Civil War and constitutional changes of the seventeenth century, which resulted in the abolition or decay of such restrictions and the development of a *laissez-faire* policy in industry, giving free play to private capitalist enterprise.

With all these new forces at work, it might well be expected that major changes would occur in the industrial life of the country at the end of the Middle Ages. Indeed, Nef has powerfully argued that there was 'an early industrial revolution' in Britain, between about 1540 and 1640, and, although his views have aroused considerable controversy, they merit our first consideration. Whilst recognizing, in his celebrated study of the rise of the British coal industry in 1932, that this 'early industrial revolution' was 'less important than that which began towards the end of the eighteenth century', he pointed out that these earlier develop-ments—hitherto comparatively neglected by economic historians—were of great significance in laying the foundations for Britain's later industrialization. The sixteenth and seventeenth centuries, he went on to argue, witnessed remarkable technological innovations and growth of large-scale capitalist organization in many industries, old and new, so that by the end of this period Britain had established a clear industrial lead over other countries.

Coal-mining

The most striking feature of these developments was the rapid increase in the production and consumption of coal. Mining had been developed to only a very limited extent in the late medieval period; coal appears to have been used by smiths and lime-burners but hardly ever as a domestic fuel, except by the very poor, near outcrops. Wood and charcoal were the almost universal fuels. But from the mid-sixteenth century onwards a remarkable expansion in the output and uses of coal occurred: Nef's estimates show British production rising from just over 200,000 tons per annum in the 1550s to nearly 3 million tons in the 1680s, rising to over 10 million by the 1780s and over 240 million by the early 1900s. The percentage rate of increase in the sixteenth and seventeenth centuries was thus comparable with that in the later period, though the absolute amounts were much smaller. The most striking expansion occurred in the North-umberland and Durham coalfield, especially in the lower Tyne and Wear valleys, centring on Newcastle and Sunderland: by the 1680s this coalfield was producing nearly 1¼ million tons, over 40 per cent of total British output. This was because of its access to cheap water transport, by river and sea, and the development of the coastal trade in 'sea coal' to the rapidly growing London market and other eastern and south-eastern ports. Land transport was much dearer, trebling or quadrupling the price of coal in ten miles, so that it was not economic to market it overland at a distance of more than ten to fifteen miles from the pithead. Coastal coalfields were therefore the most developed, above all that of Northumberland and Durham but also the south-west Lancashire, north and south Wales, Cumberland, Firth of Forth and Ayrshire fields, which also had easy access to sea transport. Some inland coalfields had river transport, for example Shropshire (Severn), Forest of Dean (Wye) and Nottinghamshire (Trent), but there were also considerable land sales, by carts and packhorses, from the widely scattered coalfields of the midlands and north, with markets in the growing towns near the collieries.

Coal exports also increased, mainly to northern Europe, rising from an estimated 12,000 tons annually in the 1550s to about 150,000 tons by the 1680s. But the entire foreign market appears to have absorbed only about a fifth as much coal as was shipped coastwise to eastern and south-eastern England. British coal production vastly surpassed that of Europe, being perhaps six times that of the whole Continent by the end of the seventeenth century, a crucial factor in Britain's early industrial lead.

This remarkable expansion in Britain, by comparison with other countries and with preceding centuries, Nef ascribed to several causes. In the first place, this country had great natural advantages in the location of numerous coal seams near to cheap river and sea transport. Moreover, there was a 'timber crisis' from the mid-sixteenth century onward, caused by growing demand for timber as domestic and industrial fuel and for constructional use in building and shipping, as a result of growing population, towns, industry and trade; woodlands were also being converted to arable and pasture to produce more food and wool. Deforestation resulted in sharply rising prices for timber and charcoal: prices of firewood apparently increased seven- or eight-fold between the late fifteenth century and 1640, rising more than prices generally. This timber shortage—much more serious than on the Continent, except in Holland—stimulated technological innovations to make possible the substitution of coal or coke for wood and charcoal in furnace-using industries, as well as its increasing use as a domestic fuel. Thus more and deeper mines were sunk, as it became economic to transport coal over greater distances. The shift to coal may also have been stimulated by governmental restrictions on the use of timber, especially of oak, required for naval shipbuilding. Parliament passed legislation to protect woodland from the ravages of ironworks, etc., as early as 1543, and further statutes and proclamations followed, restricting the cutting down of timber. But more important was the rising cost of timber, resulting from the pressure of demand and diminishing supply. This, according to Nef, was the main factor causing stagnation in the iron industry and growing imports of pig and bar iron from Sweden, Russia, Spain and the American colonies, where timber resources were more abundant and cheaper.

The more extensive exploitation of coal resources, Nef considers, was facilitated by the dissolution of the monasteries and the confiscation and sale of Church lands. Ecclesiastical landowners, many of whose estates were on the richest coalfields, especially in Northumberland and Durham, had previously been very conservative and restrictive, imposing short leases, high rents or royalties and output limitations. But the new lay landowners were keen to exploit their coal resources, either directly themselves or by granting more favourable terms to capitalist lessees and mining 'adventurers'. This more commercial capitalistic enterprising spirit—perhaps associated with the 'Protestant ethic' or stimulated by rising prices and pressure on incomes—led to the more vigorous development of coal mining and marketing. At the same time, these developments were encouraged by enclosures, which, though mainly for improved arable and pastoral farming, led to the decline of small copyholders and freeholders and the growth of large estates, whose owners were also interested in exploiting their mineral resources.

Among all these factors, however, Nef placed most emphasis on the links between the expanding coal industry and the widespread changes in technology and business organization that constituted, in his view, 'an early industrial revolution'. The increasing output of coal itself was made possible by technological improvements in sinking shafts; by drainage channels (adits) and pumping engines, mostly of the 'rag-and-chain' type, powered by horses or water wheels, thus making deeper pits possible; by horse gins for winding up the coal; by the introduction of furnace ventilation; and by improvements in transport, such as the development of tramways, on which trams or corves were moved by human labour or, eventually, by pit ponies. These developments required large amounts of capital, many thousands of pounds in larger pits, provided by landowners, merchants and co-partnerships or companies of 'adventurers'.

The size of mines varied greatly. The biggest, on Tyneside, were 300 to 400 feet deep, extending up to 200 yards from the pit bottom, and with annual outputs of up to 30,000 tons. But there were many smaller pits in inland coalfields, many only a few fathoms deep and producing only a few hundred tons annually. In most mines the coal was got by pillar-and-stall (or bord) working, leaving standing pillars to support the roof, but the longwall system using pit-props originated in Shropshire in the seventeenth century. The tendency was towards large-scale organization. Sometimes landowners exploited the mines directly, appointing an agent or 'viewer', but others leased them to mercantile industrial capitalists employing managers or overmen, with subordinate foremen to supervise the working colliers; in many areas, especially in the midlands, contracting was common, under the butty or charter system, with partnerships or gangs of colliers. The average pit at the beginning of the eighteenth century probably had no more than a dozen miners—many were smaller—but in Northumberland and Durham and in Cumberland there were bigger pits and a few collieries, including a number of pits, with several hundred workers above and below ground.

Coal fuel and industrial development

The biggest market for the growing output of coal was as domestic fuel, for heating and cooking. By the end of the seventeenth century, as Nef remarked, coal 'had come to supply the great majority of the population with its necessary firing', especially in London and other towns, though it was also widely used in rural areas. Houses were now increasingly built with chimneys, and there were already complaints of urban smoke pollution.

Coal or coke also came to be used in a wide range of industries, instead of wood or charcoal. Some of these were long established, but others were either newly introduced or very greatly developed; they included many new processes and technological advances, especially new types of furnaces, kilns and ovens for utilizing coal or coke. At the same time, as we shall see, other new industries and processes were established, some brought in from abroad. In fact, 'the period from 1560 to 1700 was one of unprecedented growth in many industries besides coal. By 1700 Britain had already become a country of "manufactures".'

Coal became the general fuel in smith's work, in a wide range of small metal manufactures in iron, copper, tin, bronze and brass, producing nails, pins, knives, razors, scissors, tools, swords, guns, locks and keys, hinges, horse-shoes, stirrups and bits, pans and boilers. All these trades expanded considerably in this period, especially in coalfield areas such as Birmingham and the Black Country, south-west Lancashire, Sheffield and the north-east, in the towns and surrounding countryside. By the eighteenth century a considerable degree of local specialization had developed, as Ashton emphasized:

'In the metal area of the West Midlands, Birmingham specialised in guns, swords, buttons, buckles, and other "toys" made of steel or brass. Wolverhampton and Willenhall made locks, Walsall bridles and bits, Dudley and Tipton nails, and so on. Sheffield concentrated on knives, razors, and files; scythes and sickles were made in the adjoining villages, and nails in the nearby parts of Derbyshire.'

In the small smithies and forges producing these finished manufactures (as distinct from the primary processes of ore smelting, etc.), coal could be substituted for wood fuel without any technical problems. Similarly, its use was also extended in lime-burning, for making building mortar and agricultural fertilizer.

Coal was also used instead of wood without any serious technical difficulties in various industries in which liquids had to be boiled. It was consumed in great quantities in the production of salt, by boiling sea water in lead or (increasingly) iron pans, on the north-east coast, the Firth of Forth, etc., and similarly at brine springs in Cheshire and at Droitwich; also in refining rock salt mined in Cheshire from the late seventeenth century onwards. Salt production thus greatly increased in this period, using several hundred thousand tons of coal annually (several tons being required to produce one ton of salt). Coal also came to be extensively used in brewing, for firing the coppers in which 'liquor' (water) was heated for the malt mash tuns, and the resultant wort was boiled with hops, prior to the yeast-fermentation process; it was similarly employed in the distilling of spirits; it was also used in soap boiling, heating the pans containing tallow or oils and alkali; and likewise in making candles; sugar boiling and refining also needed coal; it was used to heat the cauldrons for scouring wool, etc., in textile manufactures, and similarly in bleaching yarn and cloth; it was also required for roasting and boiling the minerals, alumina and iron pyrites, to produce alum and copperas that were used as mordants or fixing agents in dyeing, as well as for heating the dyeing vats themselves; the manufacture of saltpetre for making gunpowder, another mineral-boiling process similar to that for making alum and copperas, also utilized coal.

In these processes coal fuel could be used with little or no danger of spoiling the product, but there were many others in which the quality or taste would be affected, and it was therefore necessary either to free the coal from its noxious elements or to invent new furnaces protecting the raw materials from the smoke and fumes. Coke could be made from coal in much the same way as charcoal from wood, and various patents for 'charking' coal were taken out from 1620 onwards. Thus, from about the mid-seventeenth century, coke came into use for drying malt for brewing. In glass-making, on the other hand, originally a woodlands industry, improved by French, Flemish and Italian immigrants in the later sixteenth century, a new enclosed type of fire-clay pot was developed in the early 1600s, in which the sand and alkali (potash or soda) were fused in coal-fired reverberatory furnaces, tall and cone-shaped to obtain increased draught and heat. Despite the restrictions of Sir Robert Mansell's prolonged patent monopoly, this led eventually to more rapid expansion of glass-making for windows, bottles, drinking glasses, etc., and encouraged migration of the industry from the Sussex and Surrey Weald to the coalfields of the west midlands (Stourbridge) and the north-east (Newcastle), where glass-making techniques were further advanced by Huguenot immigrants later in the century. In pottery manufacture likewise, the wares were enclosed in saggars for firing in conical kilns using coal fuel, which also came to be used for drying clays; the early development of the north Staffordshire potteries was based on local resources of coal as well as clay. Coal fuel was similarly used for making bricks and tiles. The smelting of metallic ores, however, presented greater difficulties, which were not finally overcome until the late seventeenth and early eighteenth centuries, by utilizing coke and developing the reverberatory furnace, firstly for smelting lead, copper and tin, and finally for iron: the famous inventions of Darby and Cort in the eighteenth-century iron industry were the culmination of these earlier developments (see pp. 98–99).

The increasing use of coal as an industrial fuel was already resulting, before the eighteenth-century Industrial Revolution, in a marked shift of industry towards the coalfield areas of the midlands and the north. Even in textiles, it was a significant factor, because of its use in scouring, bleaching and dyeing. Defoe, for example, on visiting Halifax in the early eighteenth century, remarked on two factors particularly favourable to the development of the woollen industry there: 'Coals and running Water'. Other industries were similarly attracted to the coalfields: salt-boiling, glass-making, pottery manufacture, miscellaneous metals trades, copper refining and tinplating. Coal, of course, was not the only locational factor: proximity to consumer markets was also important, especially in London, still the main centre of trade and industry; but 'sea coal' was also vital to many metropolitan manufactures.

Nef emphasized this early development of the coal industry and coal fuel in the origins of the later and greater Industrial Revolution of the eighteenth and nineteenth centuries. Not only was the use of coal fuel much earlier and more widespread than had previousy been thought, but it stimulated many technological innovations, some of which were to become of far wider importance. The growing problems of mine drainage, for example, led ultimately to the development of the steam pumping engine, while colliery wagonways or tramways were the beginnings of railways.

In subsequent publications Nef enlarged upon these themes. Whilst continuing to stress the central importance of coal, he widened his survey to include new industries and technological processes introduced in the late fifteenth and sixteenth centuries, generally with State encouragement, requiring greater amounts of fixed capital and leading to 'the growth of large-scale industry', that is bigger plants and firms. Some of the industries in which coal fuel was used were new industries or had previously been very little developed in this country, for example the manufactures of alum, copperas and sugar. Other new industries were also introduced, mostly from the Continent, such as printing and paper-making, brass-making and 'battery work' and the manufactures of saltpetre, gunpowder and firearms. Most of these industries, Nef pointed out, were established on a capitalist basis each works requiring the expenditure of 'hundreds, and in many cases thousands, of pounds' on buildings, plant and raw materials and also employing a relatively large number of hands; some of the processes were water-powered. The alum houses at Whitby, for example, containing furnaces, cisterns, pans, etc., each cost 'many thousands of pounds' and employed about sixty workmen, as well as others required for maintenance and transport; alum was also produced on the Isle of Wight, and the copperas works at Queenborough in Kent were on a similar scale. John Browne's cannon foundry at Brenchley in Kent employed two hundred men early in the seventeenth century. John Spilman's famous paper mill, established at Dartford in the same county, in the late sixteenth century, with water-powered stampers for pulping the rag raw materials, 'certainly employed scores of hands', if not the six hundred spoken of in Thomas Churchyard's poem about it. Water-powered gunpowder mills and battery works were probably no less costly. Sugar-refining, brass-founding and saltpetre manufacture apparently required less capital outlay but were similarly carried on in factories. In fact they all demonstrated 'the growth of industrial capitalism'. Many of these new industries, because of the risky capital investment involved or because of their importance to the economy or security of the country, were encouraged by royal patents of monopoly.

A much greater number of workpeople, however, and much more capital were drawn into large-scale enterprise in old industries than in these new manufactures. In some of these, too, such as salt, glass, starch and soap, monopolies were granted, generally for allegedly new processes, but usually with less worthy underlying motives. In all of them, however, capitalist features were becoming more pronounced: breweries, soaperies, glassworks, brickworks, saltworks, dyeworks and lime-kilns, in which coal fuel was being increasingly used, were all tending to grow in size, with more and bigger furnaces, kilns, boilers, vats and pans and with horse- or water-powered mills for grinding materials, working pumps, etc.; Nef refers, for example to saltworks and breweries in the sixteenth and seventeenth centuries in which thousands of pounds were invested and considerable numbers of men were employed. Large-scale production in these industries, he emphasizes, was of cheaper-quality goods for wider markets. Shipyards were also becoming bigger, with the growth of the navy and mercantile marine, and with increasing size of ships—the total English mercantile tonnage rose from 50,000 tons in 1572 to 340,000 tons by 1686, according to Davis— and they were not only employing more men but were also introducing labour-saving saw-mills and cranes; allied trades were also stimulated, making sails, ropes, blocks and ironware.

Equally striking were developments in the metallurgical industries, which were strongly encouraged by the Government because of their national importance in the manufacture of armaments. Though the finishing processes—the making of metal manufactures—remained almost entirely in small smithies and forges, technical progress in primary production necessitated greater capital investment, and small 'free miners' tended to lose their independence. In the mining of tin, copper, lead and iron ores, as of coal, large quantities of capital were invested in sinking shafts to greater depths, in cutting adits and in installing horse- or water-powered drainage pumps and 'whims' or winding engines for raising the minerals; water wheels were also used in stamping and grist mills for crushing and grinding ores, in operating the bellows of blast furnaces and refineries, in working tilt-hammers in forges, and in rolling and slitting mills. These larger-scale enterprises were established with the aid of capital, technology, entrepreneurs and skilled workers from south Germany, where the metallurgical industries were then the most advanced in Europe.

Tin-mining, of course, was of ancient origins in Cornwall and Devon, originally in 'stream' or alluvial workings but now increasingly in underground mining of the lodes or veins of ore. It was used in the manufacture of pewter, mainly in London, and was combined with copper in making bronze; there was also a long-established export trade. But in the sixteenth and seventeenth centuries production tended to stagnate, as pottery and glass were displacing pewter, and bronze was being displaced by brass. Smelting of the ore in local 'blowing houses', with charcoal furnaces and water-powered bellows, required transport of fuel over considerable distances; after repeated attempts at using coal, the coke-fired reverberatory furnace was successfully introduced at the end of the seventeenth century. Many new smelting works were then built in the area, but tinplating was established in south Wales, where coal and iron were available.

Lead, which had also long been mined in many areas, was now increasingly in demand for roofing, pumps and ammunition, and mining and smelting therefore expanded in the Mendips, Derbyshire, Wales and the northern Pennines. The ancient bole or wind furnaces and hand- or foot-operated bellows were being replaced by larger water-powered installations. But, again, it was not until the late seventeenth century that coke was successfully substituted for charcoal in the smelting process, using a reverberatory furnace.

Copper-mining and smelting also developed considerably from the 1560s onwards, as it came increasingly into use for making domestic utensils such as kettles and pans and also for industrial boilers, etc. The discovery of the mineral calamine, the ore of zinc, in the Mendips in the 1560s and later in Gloucestershire and Nottinghamshire led to the establishment of brass (copper and zinc) foundries and brassware factories or battery works, where brass ingots were hammered by water-powered tilt-hammers and small hand hammers into plates or sheets and various kinds of manufactured articles; brass was also required for the making of cannon.

These metallurgical industries were encouraged by the Crown, partly to obtain increased revenue from royalties but mainly because of their increasing importance for armaments and the need to reduce dependence on imports (hence, also, governmental encouragement of the iron industry and the saltpetre and gunpowder manufacture). Thus the Society of Mines Royal was established in the 1560s, a joint-stock company with exclusive rights to mine metallic ores in the northern and western counties of England and Wales, aided by German entrepreneurs, capital and technical expertise and by a considerable number of German workers. They had little success in prospecting for gold and silver but started mining and smelting copper near Keswick in Cumberland, in Devon and in Wales, with another smelting plant at Neath, though they eventually abandoned these latter operations. Another company, the Society of Mineral and Battery Works, was set up at the same time, also with the aid of German technology and workmen and with similarly exclusive privileges in the mining of calamine and also of copper ore in counties outside those reserved for the Mines Royal, together with a monopoly of the manufacture of brass and battery ware and wire-drawing. They began mining calamine in the Mendips and built works at Tintern in Monmouthshire for the manufacture of iron and brass and for wire-drawing, using water power; the wire went mainly into making cards for the woollen industry, previously imported, and also into pin-making; battery works were also established in London and Nottinghamshire and lead furnaces in Derbyshire. These monopolistic concerns, though significant as the first industrial joint-stock companies in this country, did not prove very successful, however, gradually declining during the seventeenth century, despite German business and technological expertise, including early use of coal and even coke fuel, as Hammersley has shown; they had little success in establishing the manufacture of brass from native ores, and the country remained largely dependent on imports of Swedish copper and of brass made in Germany and the Low Countries. It was not until towards the end of that century, when these monopolies were abolished, that copper mining began to be vigorously developed in Cornwall and Devon. Even more important was the successful introduction of coke-smelting with a reverberatory furnace, in the 1680s and 1690s; this was established at first near Bristol and in the Forest of Dean but later developed mainly in the Swansea district. Whereas tin was smelted locally, copper required far more fuel for its reduction, so it was more economic to transport the ore to south Wales than to bring coal to Cornwall.

Developments in the iron industry during this period were of more fundamental long-term importance. The blast-furnace, developed on the Continent in the late Middle Ages, appears to have been introduced into this country from France towards the end of the fifteenth century. With its greater height and water-powered bellows, though still fuelled with charcoal, it had a considerably greater smelting capacity than the medieval bloomeries and bloom-smithies, which therefore gradually disappeared. The pig-iron product could be used in cast-iron manufactures—cannon, firebacks, pots and pans, etc.—which now began to be developed. But to make bar- or wrought-iron, still the main requirement, the blast-furnace pig-iron had to be refined (freed of carbon and other impurities) in a forge, with finery and chafery hearths and water-powered tilt-hammers; rolling and slitting mills were also introduced from the late sixteenth century onwards, similarly driven by water-wheels, to make bars, rods and sheets of iron, for smiths, nailers, etc.; water power also came to be used, as in other metallurgical industries, in ore-stamping mills.

Thus iron smelting and forging became increasingly capitalist in organization.

On account of its requirements of ore, charcoal, limestone and water power, however, the industry was closely associated with the land: the landowning aristocracy and gentry—notably the Sydneys in Sussex, Glamorgan and Shropshire, the Pagets, Talbots (Earls of Shrewsbury) Willoughbys and Dudleys in the midlands, and many others, during the later sixteenth and early seventeenth centuries—either directly exploited their own mineral and timber resources or granted leases, often of furnaces and forges as well as of mines, etc., to capitalist ironmasters and merchants, many originally of yeoman stock. The industry was also encouraged by the Crown, especially for casting cannon and shot, which developed rapidly from the mid-sixteenth century onwards, though iron was also used in an increasingly wider range of products, of both cast- and wrought-iron.

The early iron industry was concentrated in the Weald of Sussex, Kent and Surrey, where there was a conjunction of ore and charcoal resources, but later developed in other areas such as south Wales, Monmouth, the Forest of Dean, the west midlands, Cheshire and north Wales, Yorkshire, Derbyshire and the Lakeland counties, where ore, charcoal and water power were also available, and generally in closer proximity to the finishing trades, the miscellaneous iron manufactures in which coal fuel could be used; forges and slitting mills were often located separately from the furnaces, moving particularly to the midland ironworking areas of Birmingham, the Black Country and Sheffield. Consequently, the Wealden industry, with its dwindling ore resources, began to stagnate and ultimately to decline in the seventeenth and eighteenth centuries. In the expanding areas, however, some very large integrated businesses came to be established by the late seventeenth century, like the Foley partnerships, owning furnaces, forges and slitting mills in the Forest of Dean, the west midlands and elsewhere, and the Spencer syndicate similarly in south Yorkshire and north Derbyshire.

Steel-making was also developed during this period with the aid of skilled German workmen, at first in the sixteenth century by the finery process in a forge, but from the early seventeenth century onwards by the cementation process, in which bar iron was heated, together with charcoal, in closed clay pots in a coal-fired reverberatory furnace. The blister steel thus produced could be used by blacksmiths to make scythes, etc., but for cutlery, scissors, razors and edge-tools it was welded and forged into shear steel. Steel-making was introduced originally in the Weald and Forest of Dean but later developed mainly in the Sheffield and Newcastle upon Tyne areas. Imported Swedish bar iron was mainly used, being of superior quality to English iron.

Charcoal was still required for both smelting and forging iron, except in the final chafery process, where coal came gradually into use. Numerous efforts were made at substituting coal fuel in the primary processes during the seventeenth century, notably by Sturtevant, Rovenson and Dudley, but, despite the early introduction of the reverberatory furnace and vague references to 'charking' coal, none of them seems to have been consistently successful until Abraham Darby's famous achievements from 1709 onwards (see p. 98), based on previous experience with coke-smelting in the copper and lead industries. Therefore, according to Nef, the growth of the iron industry was seriously restricted by the 'timber famine' in the seventeenth century, tending eventually to decline, until coke-smelting was extensively introduced from the mid-eighteenth century onwards; thus the country became increasingly dependent on imports from Sweden and Russia.

Nef's thesis of 'an early industrial revolution' has subsequently received support from other scholars, as shown by Rees's researches into mining and metallurgical developments in Wales during this period, by Gough's survey of the rise of capitalist entrepreneurs in a wide range of industries and by Kenyon's study of the Wealden glass industry. They, too, have stressed the development of industrial capitalism and technological innovations in the coal, metallurgical and many other industries, particularly in new industries and processes in which coal or coke fuel came to be used. They have similarly emphasized the greater requirements of both fixed and commercial capital in deeper mines, bigger buildings, new furnaces and power-operated machinery, as well as in stocks, transport and sales organization.

Though the vast majority of businesses were still individual or family concerns or partnerships, joint-stock organization was evolving, as in the Mines Royal and Mineral and Battery Works companies, as well as in overseas trade, notably with the Muscovy (Russia) and East India companies; developing from the medieval *societas* or partnership and corporate bodies, such as the gilds and regulated trading companies like the Staplers and Adventurers, they provided greater amounts of capital for riskier, more speculative, larger-scale, long-term enterprises. There were even joint-stock booms in the early 1690s and in the famous 'South Sea bubble' of 1718–19, though corporate organization remained generally unusual in industry, except in the mining and smelting of metallic ores and in municipal water-supply.

Capital was also playing a more important role in traditional handicraft trades, in which small-scale workshop or domestic production still predominated. These trades also experienced innovations, such as the 'new draperies', the gig-mill and the stocking-knitting frame in textiles (see pp. 43–50), and, though they were not technologically revolutionized, they were largely brought under mercantile capitalist control in the domestic or putting-out system and increasingly concentrated in particular areas, producing for wider markets. There were even some examples of early 'proto-factory' organization, such as the textile 'manufactories' of Winchcombe and Stumpe in the sixteenth-century woollen industry (see p. 48), the factories of Ambrose Crowley in the late seventeenth and early eighteenth centuries manufacturing nails, etc. at Swalwell and Winlaton in County Durham, and the early button-making factories in Birmingham.

Criticisms of Nef's thesis

Nef's thesis, however, though supported by impressive scholarship, has aroused considerable criticism. His notion of 'an early industrial revolution' has been considered a gross exaggeration by critics such as Coleman, Supple and Clarkson. Even his estimates of increasing coal output appear to have been considerably exaggerated: Langton's findings on the south-west Lancashire coalfield, for example, suggest that between the late sixteenth and late seventeenth centuries production perhaps increased by no more than three or four times, probably less, rather than by fifteen times, though these early statistics are dubious. Moreover, Nef's emphasis on percentage rates of growth is open to the objection that, in the early development of industries starting either from nothing or from very low levels of output, such rates were inevitably high—higher perhaps than in the later Industrial Revolution of the eighteenth and nineteenth centuries—though the absolute increases were far smaller. Indeed, Nef himself has subsequently acknowledged this weakness in his argument. It also appears that the industry was less dynamic technologically than he asserted: evidence recently produced by Hollister-Short shows that in mine drainage generally, before the introduction of steam pumping engines in the early eighteenth century, England lagged considerably behind Germany, where more advanced water-powered rod engines and deeper mines were developed.

Nef also greatly exaggerated the growth and prevalence of large-scale capitalist organization in many industries, particularly by picking out exceptional examples of large works. Even in the coal industry, though some large collieries had developed in Northumberland and Durham, there was a much greater number of small comparatively shallow pits, employing only handfuls of miners. Similarly, the typical iron foundry or forge was a small rural concern, though, as in coal-mining, power-operated machinery driven by water-wheels or horses certainly did require more capital; in iron manufactures, moreover, making nails, cutlery, etc., small-scale workshop or domestic production long remained predominant. Large-scale wholesaling breweries undoubtedly tended to develop, especially in London, with substantial installations of furnaces, boiling coppers, mash-tuns, fermentation vats, pumps and horse-mills, but small brewers and brewing victuallers were still very numerous, especially in the provinces, where home brewing also remained common. London likewise had the biggest soapworks, with similar capital requirements for furnaces, pans, pumps, frames and warehouses, but the typical soapery, particularly in provincial towns, was still very small, with less than half a dozen men and an average output, even in 1785, of only nineteen tons per annum; so, too, was the average chandlery, often combined with soap-making. Similarly, according to Coleman, 'the average paper mill . . . was normally a building not much larger than a corn mill . . [and] probably employed about a dozen people in all'; until the early nineteenth century, rag pulping was the only powered process in paper-making, just as fulling long remained uniquely mechanized in the woollen industry. The average printing office was even smaller: type-setting and press work remained entirely manual until the nineteenth century, little changed since Caxton's day; strictly controlled by the State and Stationers' Company until the lapse of the Licensing Act in 1695, printing was mostly confined to London and the two universities, and printing offices were few in number and generally small, run by a master and one or two journeymen and apprentices. Though coal-fired glass furnaces were larger than their woodland predecessors, glass-making techniques were still handicraft—whether making crown (disc) or broad (cylinder) glass for windows or blowing and moulding bottles, drinking glasses, etc.—and the typical glass-house still employed only a handful of men. In pottery manufacture, rough earthenware was widely produced with simple wheels and kilns, while the developing north Staffordshire potteries were still generally on a small scale. The average limeworks and brickworks was equally small. In shipbuilding, though large dockyards were certainly developing, these were mainly for naval men-of-war, as at Chatham, Woolwich, Deptford, Portsmouth and Plymouth; bigger yards were also required for East Indiamen and ships in the 'sea-coal' trade, but they were greatly outnumbered by diminutive ones, all round the coast and up rivers, producing typically small ships and boats; even in the late 1780s, according to Davis, five out of six merchant ships were of less than 200 tons.

Nef's notion of a 'timber crisis' or 'famine' in this period has also been subjected to powerful criticism, especially in regard to its alleged effects on the iron industry. Flinn and Hammersley, for example, have demonstrated that the timber shortage was nothing like so acute as Nef and later scholars such as Ashton had asserted, pointing out that iron smelting in particular did not consume full-grown trees but only small branches and saplings (cordwood), and that the industry's demands were largely met by growing coppices (a common crop for landowners) or by moving to new woodland areas. Evidence on the numbers of furnaces and forges indicates that the iron industry was not stagnant or declining but continuing to grow in the period up to the Industrial Revolution, though more slowly and shifting in location, so that increasing imports of Swedish and Russian iron became necessary. Another factor restricting the iron industry particularly was the irregularity of water power for operating blast-furnaces and forge hammers, while labour costs were higher and the pressure of population on woodlands was greater than in Sweden. There certainly was a deficiency in the country's timber supplies—timber was becoming relatively more costly, and growing quantities had to be imported—but it seems to have been a *timber* rather than a *fuel* shortage, mainly affecting the building and shipbuilding trades. Nevertheless, rising fuel costs do seem to have had some effect in stimulating efforts to substitute coal or coke for wood and charcoal, as Nef argued, not only in the iron but also in other furnace-using industries.

But even in the relatively new and more capitalistic manufactures, in which such technological changes were most evident, it is clear that 'large-scale industry' had developed to only a limited extent. Many of these industries that were supposedly fostered by patents of monopoly—paper, glass, alum, salt, soap, mining of metallic ores, cloth-finishing, etc.—were not, in fact, very vigorously developed; such projects were generally more notable for their exaggerated pretensions, mismanagement, corruption and eventual failure than for their technological innovations; though they did do something to establish new capitalist industries and processes, this country long remained heavily dependent on foreign imports of glass, paper, iron, copper, brass, etc., despite protective tariffs. Nef's thesis breaks down even more completely, moreover, when one turns to consider the older and still by far the most important and widespread industries—the textile, clothing, leather, victualling and building trades—in which there were no technological changes of any great significance, handicraft manufactures were almost universal and units of production were small.

The woollen industry

The woollen industry had by this time eclipsed all others, especially in overseas markets. England, once a great exporter of raw wool, had in the later Middle Ages developed her own woollen manufactures and become a major exporter of cloth. By the end of the fifteenth century cloth exports probably accounted for some 90 per cent of England's total exports, and the industry's predominance in overseas trade was maintained for the next three centuries; the export of raw wool was prohibited in the early Stuart period, in the interest of home industry and against foreign competitors, especially the Dutch. This growth of the industry had been accompanied, as we have seen, by the decline of the old gild-regulated urban manufactures, as capitalist clothiers acquired more control and developed the domestic or putting-out system, especially in the rural areas of the West Country and East Anglia; migration into the countryside had also been stimulated by the spread of fulling mills. The main feature of this industry, in fact, was its increasingly rural out-working character, in a domestic 'family economy'. Coleman has emphasised this point:

'... although out-working became a feature of various industries, the making of fabrics provides easily the most striking early example ... of the combination of extensive division of labour, the use of the rural worker's household, and commercially organised production for distant markets. The various stages of textile manufacture [carding or combing, spinning and weaving] fitted into the family economy to an unparalleled extent. It was the most labour intensive of all the major industries. Moreover, the making of no other basic requirement of life could be so sub-divided into processes as to provide work for men, women, and children and yet remain, in respect of its central processes, capable of being carried on in the home.'

For these reasons, it was extremely widespread: though certain regions were pre-eminently the 'manufacturing districts', drawing in wool supplies from other areas through wool broggers and staplers, spinning and weaving were to be found in towns and villages all over the country.

The early woollen manufactures were mainly of heavy broadcloth made from fine short-staple carded wool, the cloth being thickened and felted by the fulling process. Exports, expanding rapidly in the first half of the sixteenth century, were mostly of unfinished 'white' or grey cloth (undyed and undressed), mainly to the Low Countries, where the finishing trades were more technically advanced. The finest cloths came from the West Country and Suffolk, which dominated the export trade, but coarser fabrics such as kerseys and dozens were manufactured in Devonshire, Yorkshire and northern counties, where they were usually dyed and finished, while long-staple combed wool was used to make unfulled worsteds in the Norwich area, and peasant manufactures of obscure mixed varieties existed in many localities.

In the second half of the century, however, the old broadcloth industry entered a prolonged period of crisis and stagnation, with the decline of European demand and collapse of the Antwerp market. The situation was worsened by Cockayne's disastrous project in 1614 and the following years, banning exports of white undressed cloth, with the object of developing the dyeing and finishing trades of this country; this was directed against the Dutch finishing trades and the Merchant Adventurers' control of the export trade in unfinished cloth, but it was also part of the early Stuart schemes for exploitation of monopolies. Its failure accentuated the decline in the 'old draperies', which were subsequently hit by the Thirty Years' War in Germany. Later, however, there was some revival in these manufactures, with increasing use of fine Spanish merino wool and improvements in dyeing and finishing, with the aid of Dutch immigrants; for these lighter 'Spanish cloths' or 'medleys', manufactured particularly in Wiltshire, Somerset and Gloucestershire, new markets were found in southern Europe and the Mediterranean, as well as at home.

In other woollen areas, however, the 'old draperies' were mostly superseded by 'new draperies'—worsteds, bays and says, serges, etc.—lighter and cheaper materials, using coarser long-staple wool. Pure worsted 'stuffs', using long combed wools for both warp and weft, were not fulled and showed the weaving pattern; but many of the new draperies were mixtures of carded woollen weft with combed worsted warp, as in Essex bays and says and Devon and Suffolk serges, and they were mostly 'milled' or fulled; others had cotton or silk wefts (for example 'bombazines', early imitations of Indian fabrics). These new manufactures, introduced in the late sixteenth century, may have been partly—or even mainly, as Bowden has argued—responses to changes in the wool supply, with sheep-farming enclosures producing coarser long wools; the declining quality of traditional fine short-staple wool led to growing imports of Spanish merino. But international competition, changing fashions and markets appear to have been more important, with growing demand for cloths that were lighter, brighter and more attractively varied, as well as cheaper; the export difficulties of the old draperies certainly seem to have stimulated efforts to bring in skilled immigrants from Flanders in the 1560s, refugees from Spanish political and religious oppression, who introduced new techniques into Norfolk and Essex, centred mainly in Norwich and Colchester, though the so-called 'new draperies' were similar to older-established worsted manufactures in these and other areas. The new draperies, developing especially in East Anglia and Devonshire, soon began to supersede the old draperies in the export trade. While broadcloth exports to northern Europe were generally declining in the seventeenth century, and the old broadcloth manufactures of the West Country, Suffolk and elsewhere were gradually decaying, the new lighter cheaper manufactures were expanding into warmer south European and Mediterranean markets; together with improvements in the finishing processes and the prohibition of wool export, they enabled English woollen manufactures gradually to supersede the Italians and the Dutch.

These changes, however, involved no technological revolution. Wool was still hand carded or combed, and yarn was still hand spun by ancient distaff ('rock') or spinning wheel; the Saxony wheel (with a flyer device, for automatic winding, and two spindles), introduced from the sixteenth century onwards though not very widely used, was still hand operated, while the distaff was still being used in some areas, as in the Norfolk worsted industry, in the early nineteenth century. Weaving similarly was on hand-looms, and dyeing and shearing also remained manual operations; fulling was the only power-driven process. The gig-mill, with teazling cylinders for raising the nap on cloth for shearing, was generally water-powered, but its use was prohibited by Parliament in 1552 and by royal proclamation in 1633, mainly on account of popular hostility, and its introduction was long delayed. The Dutch swivel-loom or 'engine-loom', introduced into England in the seventeenth century, capable of weaving at the same time a dozen or more ribbons or inkles (tapes, braids and other smallwares), in silk, linen or cotton, also came to be driven by water but was usually hand and treadle operated; it too met with strong opposition.

The woollen industry was, in fact, predominantly a domestic handicraft cottage industry. It was, of course, increasingly capitalist in commercial organization, but the clothiers' capital was mostly not in fixed plant but in stocks of raw materials, yarn and cloth, though many hired out looms and often owned fulling mills, dyeworks and warehouses. Some of the workers still owned their own cards, spinning wheels and looms and were widely scattered in rural areas, though with concentrations in the West Country, East Anglia and the West Riding. Many were still only part-time industrial workers: in areas of poor arable farming, mostly hilly pastoral or wooded areas, and especially where over-population and partible inheritance produced very small holdings, there were strong incentives to take up some subsidiary manufacturing occupation—and for clothiers to put out work where this cheap surplus labour was available—and, as such rural industry developed many cottagers became practically full-time industrial wage earners; in fact it seems probable that industrial development in such areas stimulated population growth and dependence on industry, creating many weavers without land. The industry was by no means, however, entirely rural: urban manufactures still existed, and the trade centred on towns such as Norwich, Ipswich, Sudbury and Colchester in East Anglia, Stroud, Frome, Trowbridge, Salisbury and many other towns in the West Country, Exeter and Tiverton in Devon, Leeds, Halifax and Wakefield in the West Riding, and Shrewsbury for the north Welsh trade. The dyeing and finishing processes and merchants' warehouses were commonly located in the towns.

The domestic or putting-out system was typical of the West Country and East Anglian woollen-manufacturing regions, where large-scale capitalist organization was more developed than in the West Riding. The Yorkshire clothiers were generally of a more primitive type, still mostly independent small masters, often owning some land, buying their own wool or yarn and working it up into cloth in their domestic workshops, on their own spinning wheels and looms, with the aid of their families and perhaps also a few journeymen and apprentices, and marketing their own products in the cloth-halls of Leeds, Halifax, etc.; to the traditional kerseys and dozens, they eventually added new draperies, especially worsteds. Even in the West Riding, however, as Heaton demonstrated many years ago, 'there were clothiers of every gradation, from the smallest independent master, employing only his own family, to the wealthy clothier, employing a large number of people in his house and loom-shop, as well as others who worked for him in their own homes'. In the West Riding worsted industry, as it developed, large capitalist clothiers predominated, like those of East Anglia and the West Country. The small clothiers in the broadcloth industry, moreover, were largely dependent on wool, yarn and cloth merchants, who came increasingly to exercise control over the industry. The differences in industrial organization between Yorkshire and the other two main woollen-manufacturing areas have generally been exaggerated: they were 'a matter of degree rather than of kind'. There were simply more small clothiers in Yorkshire, manufacturing cheaper lower-quality kerseys and dozens, than in the West Country and East Anglia, where production of fine broadcloths and worsteds was generally in the hands of larger clothiers, employing more specialized out-working wage labour. The fullers, dressers and dyers in Yorkshire were also generally small capitalists, with a few journeymen, though these finishing processes were often in the hand of merchants in the towns.

In other woollen-manufacturing areas, on the other hand, the small master clothier or domestic manufacturer was by no means uncommon. In the Witney blanket industry, for example, there were numerous independent master weavers of this type, who usually carried out all processes, except fulling; they formed a chartered company or gild on medieval lines as late as 1711, for regulation of 'the art and mistery of blankett weaving', controlling entry to the trade, number of apprentices, employment of journeymen and dimensions, weights and qualities of cloths, with rules enforced by master, assistants and wardens, right down to the nineteenth century. In Devonshire, capitalist tendencies were more marked, master spinners and master weavers employing men, women and children to card, comb, spin and weave, mainly in rural areas, though many such workers remained independent; the cloth was sold to merchants in Exeter or Tiverton, who then had it fulled and finished, though master dyers were mostly independent. Even in the West Country (Wiltshire, Somerset and Gloucestershire) there were many small independent spinners, weavers, fullers and dyers, as well as small clothiers, though the industry came increasingly into the hands of large mercantile capitalist clothiers. In the Norfolk worsted industry, centred on Norwich, there were master combers who employed journeymen to comb the wool and spinners to convert it into yarn, which they sold to master yarn merchants or weavers; but there were also large capitalists who controlled all processes of manufacture. In the old Suffolk broadcloth industry, too, there were many small as well as large clothiers, though the latter predominated economically. In Norwich and Ipswich, moreover, as in Exeter, Witney, Leeds and other corporate towns, companies or gilds continued throughout the sixteenth, seventeenth and eighteenth centuries, to try to enforce the traditional craft regulations, though with expanding trade, growing numbers of 'illegal' men and 'foreigners', and the spread of rural industry, their efforts proved increasingly unavailing, and capitalist enterprise steadily developed.

Despite these changes in business organization, however, and increasing alteration in products in response to changing markets and fashions, there were no very significant technological developments during this period. Indeed, Coleman has stressed how 'technologically stagnant and conservative' the textile manufactures were 'from roughly the fifteenth to the eighteenth centuries', compared with the later Middle Ages, which had witnessed the introduction of the horizontal frame loom, spinning wheel and fulling mill. Under the domestic system, there was little incentive to technological innovation: growth of population provided a plentiful supply of cheap rural labour (women and children as well as men), there were few fixed-capital requirements, and output and employment could be flexibly varied according to the state of trade.

There were, it is true, a few examples of what Freudenberger has called 'proto-factories', that is factories in which hand workers were brought together for better supervision and control, with subdivision and specialization of labour but without power-driven mechanization, as in the famous woollen 'manu-factories' established by John Winchcombe ('Jack of Newbury') and William Stumpe in the sixteenth century and in the 'loomshops' of later date; but these were exceptional in an industry that long remained on a domestic handicraft basis. On the other hand, it must be emphasized that the domestic system was under thoroughly capitalist control and that an increasing proportion of the workers engaged in it were wage earners, dependent on mercantile capitalist employers. The numbers employed by such concerns, as Ashton has emphasized, 'must often have been far greater than those brought together at a large colliery or ironworks', in some cases several thousands, with correspondingly large requirements of circulating capital and sometimes also of fixed capital, when looms or frames were provided by the employer.

Other textiles and clothing manufactures

Next in importance to woollens in textile manufactures were those of linen, using flax and hemp as raw materials. They, too, were widely dispersed but tended towards concentration in the northern and south-western counties of England—in Lancashire mixed with cotton in fustians—as well as in many parts of Scotland and Ireland. They were mainly part-time peasant handicraft manufactures, with the process of flax preparation, spinning and weaving carried on in cottages, but came increasingly under mercantile control, as in the woollen industry. Throughout this period, however, production was mostly on a small scale for local markets; linen imports were considerable, and it was not until the eighteenth century that the industry expanded substantially, encouraged by tariff protection and bounties (see pp. 90–91).

The lace and silk manufactures were similarly on a small scale. Hand making of lace (pillow, bobbin or bone lace) was a purely domestic manufacture for women and children in southern rural counties such as Buckinghamshire, Bedfordshire and Devon. Silk manufactures, on the other hand, tended to be urban, mainly in London (Spitalfields), with offshoots in Kent and Essex, and with ribbons made in Coventry, mainly under substantial master manufacturers. Raw silk, of course, was entirely imported, from Italy and the Near East, and this exotic industry was unable to compete very effectively with Italian and French manufactures until tariff protection was gradually increased from the late seventeenth century onwards, when the industry was also stimulated by Huguenot immigration. Hand throwing and weaving of silk were mostly in small domestic workshops; it was not until the early eighteenth century that silk-throwing machines were introduced from Italy and installed in water-powered mills (see p. 92).

Cotton was in a similar situation *vis-à-vis* Indian imports. Raw cotton was imported mainly from the eastern Mediterranean, to produce manufactures in imitation of Indian textiles. Developing at first in London and later in Lancashire, they were mainly low-quality mixed fabrics—fustians, with a linen warp and cotton weft—and could not effectively compete with Indian calicoes and muslin until the passing of protective legislation in the early eighteenth century (see p. 79). The infant Lancashire industry was, like other textiles, a cottage handicraft, associated with widespread woollen and linen manufactures, at first with many small independent weavers but increasingly, as markets expanded, organized on the putting-out system in both town and country, under merchants such as the Mosleys and Chethams in Manchester and elsewhere.

All these textile manufactures produced materials for the clothing trades. 'Customer weaving' was widespread in country districts, and much clothing was still home-made, if not home-spun and woven, but the number of tailors, hatters, glovers, etc., continued to grow and all remained hand workers. There was some production of ready-made articles, such as hats and gloves, but most tailoring was still 'bespoke', made to customers' requirements. Mercantile control of domestic workers had long been developing in the towns, but there were still many small independent tailors, catering for local markets, both urban and rural.

Hosiery manufactures, using wool, silk or cotton, were also widespread in rural areas. Hand knitting of stockings was another common by-occupation among peasant smallholders in pastoral districts, particularly in northern areas such as the Yorkshire dales and Lakeland counties but also in Norfolk, the South-West, Wales, etc.—in fact, by the end of the seventeenth century the stocking-knitting industry was very widely dispersed, producing many local specialities, which, Joan Thirsk informs us, were 'as varied in design, colour and decoration, as well as in kind of yarn, as the New Draperies'. This was another 'peasant handicraft that was successfully commercialized', by merchants who marketed the products both at home and overseas.

The invention of the stocking-knitting frame by the Rev. William Lee in 1589 started another branch of the industry, that of framework-knitting. It developed very slowly, however, first of all in London, mainly for silk stockings, and then increasingly in Nottinghamshire, Leicestershire and Derbyshire during the later seventeenth and eighteenth centuries, making woollen and worsted and later cotton as well as silk hosiery; here, in close proximity to raw materials, cheap rural labour was also available. Efforts by the London-based Framework-

Knitters' Company, incorporated in 1657 and 1664, failed to check this expansion and growth of mercantile capitalist control, under the domestic system. By contrast with hand knitting, however, many workers in this branch lived in towns and had less part-time interest in farming, though rural manufacture was widespread in the east midlands. They were also much less independent than hand knitters, or even hand-loom weavers, because the knitting-frame was a fairly large complicated mechanism, involving some substantial capital cost; though some workers acquired their own frames, most were under the control of merchant hosiers and master stockingers who supplied them with rented frames, in addition to raw materials; this apparently became much more common than was the renting of hand-looms in the woollen industry. But the stocking-frame, like the loom, was hand and treadle operated and remained so until the mid-nineteenth century.

Thus, apart from fulling and a few gig-mills, there was no power-driven machinery in textile and clothing manufactures until the eighteenth-century Industrial Revolution. The changes that took place were commercial and organizational rather than technological: despite changes in materials and products, the processes were still mostly manual, carried on in the workers' homes or small workshops.

Leather, wood-working, building and victualling trades

The various leather trades were even more technologically conservative. Tanners, curriers and tawyers continued to prepare hides by traditional hand processes, requiring only small amounts of fixed capital, though there was considerable variation in the size of businesses; there were some wealthy tanners, together with a great many smaller ones, since a relatively large amount of capital was required for stocks of hides in this prolonged process. The tanning of heavy cattle hides involved soaking in lime solution, scraping with a knife to remove hair and fat, 'bating' in an infusion of dog and bird droppings, prolonged immersion in tan-pits containing oak bark and water and finally currying with train-oil or tallow; dressing or tawing of lighter sheep, goat or calf skins with oil or alum were much simpler shorter processes and required less capital.

These trades tended to concentrate in large towns, particularly in London (Bermondsey and Southwark), in proximity to the main meat markets, producing leather for equally traditional shoe-makers, cobblers, cordwainers, glovers, purse-makers and saddlers. Many of these leather workers were small independent craftsmen, but mercantile capitalist control tended to develop, mainly in the light leather crafts, such as glove-making, and especially in London, where the Leathersellers' company predominated. Leather workers also formed important groups—sometimes the most important single groups—in other towns, particularly in the east-midlands pastoral areas, notably Northampton and Leicester, where mercantile capitalism similarly developed, as we have previously seen, but also in many other towns, including Birmingham and Sheffield, more famous for their metals manufactures. The leather trades continued, in fact, to be of widespread importance, including many small tanners, shoe-makers and saddlers in minor towns and villages. Gild or company organization also remained strong, the Bermondsey tanners being incorporated as late as 1703.

Along with leather, wood continued to be extensively used in making a wide range of products, not only domestic utensils and furniture but also such manufacturing equipment as spinning wheels, looms, millwork, etc., as well as in the building trades, so that carpenters, joiners, wheelwrights and millwrights were numerous and widespread. These, together with a medley of others, such as masons, bricklayers, plasterers, tilers, slaters, plumbers and glaziers, all remained manual craftsmen. Larger contractors emerged for bigger building projects, such as London or provincial mansions, but sub-contracting was common, and there was a host of small independent jobbing builders. In timber yards, though water-powered saw-mills were introduced in the seventeenth century, they met with strong popular opposition, and mechanical sawing does not appear to have become common until the late eighteenth and early nineteenth centuries.

In the victualling trades similarly, there were large numbers of small businesses, still run on traditional lines. In corn-milling, water or wind power had been used for centuries, but the innumerable mills scattered throughout the country were small family affairs, employing little wage labour, like the bakeries which they supplied with flour. Small breweries, as we have seen, were equally numerous, together with butchers' and grocers' shops.

In terms of output and employment, all these traditional small-scale mainly handicraft trades, supplying the basic needs of food, drink, clothing, housing, furniture and domestic utensils, vastly exceeded those which formed the basis of Nef's 'early industrial revolution'. At the end of the seventeenth century and long after, most of the country's manufacturing population were still to be found in small and commonly domestic workshops, and commercial capital—in raw materials, finished goods and credit—was far more important than fixed capital, especially in such manufactures, with their simple technology. Though commercial capital dominated many trades, there were still large numbers of small independent craftsmen—weavers, tailors, tanners, shoe-makers, saddlers, coopers, potters, builders, carpenters, smiths, clock-makers, etc.—who produced and sold their own wares. Finally, it must be emphasized that Britain had not become an industrial country, 'a country of "manufactures"', but was still predominantly agricultural and rural. Farming was still the main livelihood, while many industrial workers lived in the countryside, often engaged part-time in agriculture.

Indeed, Coleman, Clarkson and Supple have emphasized that England still had most of the characteristics of a 'pre-industrial', 'under-developed' economy: labour was still much the most important factor of production in most industries, manufacturing techniques were mostly static and there was chronic under-employment and irregularity of labour, resulting from seasonal factors and social customs—these features, rather than surging industrial growth, they consider, were characteristic of the economy.

Significance of Nef's thesis

Nevertheless, despite all criticisms, Nef's work was of great originality and significance in drawing attention to industrial developments *before* the Industrial Revolution, demonstrating that the latter was not a sudden apparition but had deep-rooted origins in preceding centuries. There is no doubt that during the sixteenth and seventeenth centuries this county was becoming more indus-trialized, not only catching up with continental countries but surpassing them in certain fields. The technological progress in coal-mining and use of coal fuel, which Nef so strongly emphasized, was undoubtedly of special importance, particularly the links between coal and the various metallurgical and other furnace industries. Though in quantitative terms—in employment and out-put—these and other 'new' industries were much less important than the tra-ditional manufactures of textiles, leather, etc., from a qualitative technological point of view they were much more significant. Growth of this kind—the intro-duction of novel, more capital-intensive techniques and products, though not yet on a massive scale—was more portentous than expansion or extension of estab-lished manufactures, with comparatively little change in production processes or industrial structure. The famous eighteenth-century innovations in the iron industry and in steam power, and the associated developments in engineering and the growth of factories, were clearly based on these earlier achievements.

It is also evident, however, that increasing industrialization could occur *without* any great change in the technology or scale of industry. Local studies have demonstrated that all the major areas of development in the Industrial Revolu-tion were already industrial to a considerable degree by the early decades of the eighteenth century. Together with the technological innovations overemphasized by Nef, there was widespread development of traditional manufactures, with increasing numbers of rural domestic industries and peasant craftsmen, not only spinners and weavers, but also lace-makers, framework-knitters, nailers, needle-makers, scythe-smiths, etc.—in fact some rural areas had become more industrial than agricultural, what Court termed 'an industrialized countryside', as in the west Midlands—while urban craftsmen were also multiplying, especi-ally in London. Much of the industrialization of the early Industrial Revolution was to be along these lines, with more weavers, more tailors, more miners, more metal-working craftsmen, more carpenters and bricklayers, more shipwrights, more coach-makers and many other manual craftsmen in traditional occupations, though increasingly they were to become a landless urban proletariat. In these manufactures capital was accumulated, an entrepreneurial class was developed, markets were extended and a wage-labour force was created, which provided the basis for the later growth of 'machine industry'.

At the same time, it is clear that by the late seventeenth century British industry was dynamic and changing. Patents of invention provide some indication of increasing technological innovation: in the 1660s only 31 were granted, but in the 1690s there were 102. These developments were remarked on by observant contemporaries, such as John Cary, who declared in his *Essay on the State of England* in 1695 that 'new projections are every day set on foot', with new types of furnaces, 'engines' and mills, new skills and varieties of manufactures, with general emphasis on labour-saving machinery.

This inventiveness was perhaps encouraged by the patent system itself, developing from the Elizabethan and early Stuart patents of monopoly for encouragement of new industries and processes. These tended to degenerate into devices for raising revenue or for lining the pockets of courtiers and 'projectors', but the Statute of Monopolies in 1624, while attacking such abuses, safeguarded the rights of genuine inventors or innovators. It seems probable, however, that profit opportunities, arising from commercial and industrial expansion, provided a much more powerful incentive for entrepreneurial enterprise and technological change.

Nef tended to give a misleading impression, however, that technological innovations during this period were predominantly insular English achievements. This country, still relatively backward at the end of the fifteenth century, drew heavily on the Continent for new or improved techniques and skilled workers, and also for some capital investment, as illustrated by the numerous German, French and Flemish immigrants in the sixteenth century— so important in mining, the metallurgical industries, glass-making, printing, paper-making and the new draperies—followed in the late seventeenth century by another influx of French Huguenot refugees, with a similarly wide range of industrial skills in silk manufacture, glass-making, paper-making, etc. Many of the so-called 'new' developments were, in fact, merely importations from abroad.

It is also clear that Nef exaggerated Britain's industrial lead at the beginning of the eighteenth century, especially by comparison with France, for it appears that this country was still technologically inferior in various manufactures. But there is no doubt that in coal mining and in the use of coal fuel in numerous industrial processes Britain had achieved a leadership of crucial importance in the subsequent Industrial Revolution. There was more emphasis, as Nef observed, in many British manufactures such as textiles, iron, glass, pottery, etc., on production of cheaper utilitarian goods for mass-consumption., rather than on fine-quality luxury articles, a development resulting partly from coal-fuel technology, partly from a freer more market-oriented economy, with growing freedom from gild, municipal and State regulations, and partly from changing social structure, associated with rising real incomes and increased social mobility among substantial sections of the population.

Industrial regulation, laissez-faire and protectionism

All these developments tended inevitably to bring about the disintegration of craft gilds and their industrial regulations. Already in the later Middle Ages, as we have seen (pp. 23–24), the forces of expanding trade and industry were leading to the creation of livery companies, under mercantile capitalist control; as wider national and international markets developed, local gild monopolies steadily disintegrated. Those industries, such as coal-mining, iron-smelting and ship-building, which were never organized in gilds, had become more capitalist in structure; new industries similarly, such as paper-making, sugar-boiling and brass manufacture, also required larger amounts of fixed capital; so, too, did older industries, such as brewing and glass-making, as a result of technological changes. More and more industries, therefore, were developing outside the gild system, on more capitalist lines.

At the same time, in the traditional craft manufactures, mercantile capitalism continued to advance, leading to the general transformation or obsolence of craft gilds and the more widespread development of the domestic or putting-out system. These changes, however, took place very slowly, against strong opposition from small masters and journeymen, from town corporations and from the Tudor and early Stuart governments, which endeavoured to prevent the decline of corporate towns and gilds and to restrict the development of industrial capitalism in these trades. As Unwin and Kramer demonstrated many years ago, new gilds and handicraft companies, such as the felt-makers, pin-makers, clock-makers, framework-knitters, etc., continued to be established throughout the sixteenth and seventeenth centuries, especially under early Stuart 'paternalist' policy, as new trades developed or as specialized crafts sought independence and corporate privileges. At the same time, amalgamations of gilds were frequently formed to provide greater strength, often, apparently, because gild membership was declining and small gilds were tending to collapse. In many cases these developments were motivated by resistance of the handicraft elements to mercantile capitalist control by the trading companies of mercers, grocers, drapers, leathersellers, etc., especially in London; the trading oligarchies of provincial towns similarly fought against encroachments by metropolitan merchants and against mercantile capitalists, such as clothiers in the woollen industry, who were ignoring local gild regulations and employing growing numbers of non-apprenticed workers and 'foreigners' or outsiders, in the suburbs and surrounding rural areas.

The Government backed up these efforts with legislation such as the Acts of 1552, 1555 and 1558, regulating the woollen industry (the so-called 'Weavers' Acts'), whereby clothiers had to be qualified by apprenticeship and could only set up in a town or place where the woollen manufacture had been carried on for more than ten years; no country clothier was to possess more than one loom or to hire out looms to others; and no country weaver was to have more than two looms—thus the urban industry would be maintained and growth of the rural putting-out system would be halted*. The famous Statute of Artificers (1563) was much more comprehensive, with its yearly-service contract for all hired labour, its wages-assessment clauses and apprenticeship regulations, empowering local magistrates to assess wage-rates annually in a wide range of occupations, fixing a seven-year apprenticeship, together with property and income qualifications and restrictions on the number of apprentices for certain crafts, and generally aiming to control the labour supply, particularly with a view to maintaining agricultural employment and the *status quo* in industry. The Government also reinforced gild controls by detailed industrial regulations, such as those in the Acts of 1552 and later years fixing sizes, weights, qualities and methods of manufacturing woollen cloths, enforced by the official aulnagers and searchers; similar restrictions were imposed upon the leather and other manufactures. Trading restrictions were also imposed, as in the series of Acts from the reign of Edward IV onwards, prohibiting or restricting the activity of middlemen in the supply of wool to clothiers and restricting exportation of unfinished cloth, though these regulations were largely ineffective.

There were mixed motives behind this State-interventionist policy. It was partly conservative and reactionary, trying to preserve the established order, maintain traditional employments and prevent social dislocation, but it was also fiscally motivated. The early-Stuart craft companies, for example, were often associated with trading monopolies granted by the Crown to private speculators and were exploited as a source of royal revenue, though there seems also to have been some paternalist concern for the interests of small craftsmen and journeymen; the Crown also derived fiscal profit from licences permitting certain prohibited trading and manufacturing activities—indeed, had all these restrictions been rigorously enforced, they would undoubtedly have stopped the expansion of industry, particularly of the woollen industry. The royally chartered

---

*This restrictive legislation seems to have been motivated by the crisis affecting the cloth export trade in the mid-sixteenth century and was intended to check the growth of the rural woollen industry. But most of the northern, western and eastern clothing districts were exempted from these Acts, either at first or subsequently, and it was in these areas that the later expansion of the industry was to take place.

trading monopolies of the Merchant Adventurers, Eastland, Levant and other companies were similarly restrictive; certainly that is how they were regarded by many manufacturers, by provincial 'outports' and by free-trading 'interlopers'. It may also be doubted whether State 'fostering' of 'infant industries' by patents of monopoly was really beneficial, since such fiscally exploited monopolies likewise blocked private enterprise and competition.

There has been, in fact, considerable debate about the whole of mercantilist policy in the sixteenth and seventeenth centuries. Many scholars regard the 'mercantile system' not as a coherent economic policy for increasing national wealth and power, not as early 'State planning', but rather as a collection of expedients, adopted under pressures of economic circumstances, vested interests and fiscal motives, and all too often degenerating into abuse. On the other hand, it can be argued that they were necessary for government revenue or for national defence, that they were generally protective of the country's trade or that they encouraged industrial growth. There is certainly evidence in this period of a deliberate policy of 'economic nationalism', of 'State control' and 'planned autarky', in pursuit of power and security, as Stone has argued, but the industrial measures adopted were conflicting: on the one hand, for example, there were efforts at developing new industries and trades, but on the other there were restrictive conservative regulations to preserve social stability and public order. Though in some cases stimuli may have been given to industrial enterprises, particularly those of military or naval importance, governments were by no means consistently in favour of innovation. They often looked with disfavour on labour-saving inventions which threatened to cause unemployment, rising poor rates and riots. The workers' hostility was demonstrated in sporadic smashing of gig-mills, saw-mills, ribbon-looms and stocking-frames, long before the better-known outbursts against the textile inventions of Kay and Arkwright in the eighteenth century and the Luddites of the early nineteenth. Town gilds and corporations were also generally opposed to technical inventions threatening their vested interests, and they were able to call in the aid of Government, generally more concerned about public order than economic growth. It was apparently in response to appeals from the organized crafts, for example, that Parliament in 1552 prohibited the use of gig-mills in the woollen industry. In 1623–4 Charles I by proclamation ordered the destruction of an engine lately used in making needles, together with the needles so made. Nine years later he prohibited the casting of brass buckles, in response to complaints from buckle-forging members of the girdlers' company. The gig-mill was again banned in 1633 and the Dutch ribbon-loom in 1638.

In traditional handicrafts, however, technological innovation was very limited during the sixteenth and seventeenth centuries. The forces of *commercial* expansion were mainly responsible for the decline and disintegration of craft gilds and livery companies. The 'free-trade' campaign against monopolies, however, towards the end of Elizabeth's reign and under James I, resulting in the Act against monopolies in 1624 and the subsequent attacks of the Long Parliament, did not interfere with the privileges of gilds and other corporate bodies, which continued to survive far beyond this period, especially in handicraft trades catering for purely local markets, such as the shoemaking, tailoring, victualling and building trades. In London, for example, Kellett has shown that efforts at enforcement of gild membership, apprenticeship and searching were being made throughout the eighteenth century. But where trade was expanding, where industries were developing more strongly in particular areas and producing for wider markets, they came increasingly under the control of mercantile capitalists, who ignored gild ordinances, took on 'illegal' men and extended the domestic or putting-out system. Gilds in these industries, with their apprenticeship regulations, 'searching' procedures and marketing controls, gradually fell into obsolescence. Indeed, even in the small local crafts, the growing forces of free trade, individualism and competition eventually brought about the decline of gild organization. Moreover, the newer industrial towns such as Birmingham and Manchester developed free of gild control, partly because they were unincorporated and partly because of the scattered semi-rural character of the industries in those areas.

At the same time, State regulations fell gradually into disuse, especially after the Civil War, which had resulted partly from opposition by mercantile and manufacturing interests to the Crown's fiscal and economic policies. The system of industrial monopolies was overthrown. Enforcement of the wages and apprenticeship clauses of the Statute of Artificers became increasingly sporadic from the later seventeenth century onwards, long before they were finally repealed in 1813–14, though apprenticeship remained customary in many crafts; from early in the seventeenth century the courts ruled against its legal enforcement in new trades or those not named in the 1563 Act, and it did not apply to large numbers of semi-skilled and unskilled workers, outside the gilds. Manufacturing regulations were also increasingly ignored or abolished.

It may be, however, that British economic historians ever since Unwin have fallen too much under the influence of the liberal *laissez-faire* tradition, and, whilst emphasizing, rightly, the role of individual enterprise and free competition in Britain's later industrialization, have been too inclined to minimize or even to castigate the role of the State in the earlier period. Perhaps Cunningham's view, following the German historical school, was not without some truth, in emphasizing the importance of governmental policy, especially under Elizabeth I. And following Gerschenkron's modern observations on 'economic backwardness' and economic growth, it may be argued that during that period, when England was catching up with more economically advanced countries, the Government did, despite administrative inefficiency and corruption, provide a significant stimulus to the development of new industries and technology, though once industrial growth got under way State intervention was found irksome and there was increasing emphasis on *laissez-faire*. In external relations, moreover, in the extension of empire and overseas trade, in the establishment of naval and mercantile supremacy and in the protectionism of tariffs, bounties and Navigation Acts, the role of the State remained of fundamental importance till the nineteenth-century introduction of Free Trade: in this sphere, in fact, Parliament was even more mercantilist than the Crown. These factors certainly were significant in stimulating growth from the late seventeenth century onwards, as Davis has demonstrated in emphasizing the 'rise of protectionism' and the colonial trades.

PART II

THE INDUSTRIAL REVOLUTION, 1700–1850

3

The Causes
and Characteristics of
Industrialization

The older view of the Industrial Revolution—that it was a sudden cataclysmic transformation, starting around 1760—clearly is no longer tenable. The 'pre-industrial' economy had been gradually becoming more industrialized: the population had been rising, towns had been growing, markets had been expanding, new industries and processes had been introduced, craft gilds had been disintegrating and larger-scale capitalist organization had been spreading. Though serious doubts may be expressed about the alleged agricultural and industrial revolutions of the sixteenth and seventeenth centuries, the light shed by modern scholars on those 'Dark Ages' has revealed, not a static, traditional, still almost medieval economy, but one that was dynamic and changing. Fisher, for example, has shown not only the association between London's phenomenal growth and the expansion of internal and overseas trade but also how the economic balance was already, by 1700, shifting to the north and west, as evidenced by

'... the growth of the textile industries of Devon, Lancashire and the West Riding, of the metallurgical and leather industries of the Severn Valley, and the Black Country, of the potteries of Staffordshire and of coal, glass, and salt production on Tyneside ... [as well as] the rise to commercial importance of Bristol and Liverpool, with their easy access to Ireland, Africa and, above all, America'.

The importance of this overseas expansion, especially of trade with the West Indian and American colonies in the late seventeenth and early eighteenth centuries, has been stressed by Davis, Berrill and other scholars. It certainly stimulated the woollen, metals and other manufactures; in fact as Davis has remarked, 'the process of industrialization in England from the second quarter of the eighteenth century was to an important extent a response to colonial demands' for a widening range of these products, at a time when exports to

European markets were stagnating; at the same time, imports provided raw materials such as textile fibres, dyestuffs, iron and timber for growing British industries. There was also an increasing re-export trade in colonial products such as sugar, tobacco, tea and coffee. By expanding commercial profits as well as markets, colonial trade also appears to have contributed to capital accumulation and industrial investment. But there have been differences of opinion on this point. Pares pointed out many years ago that colonization and colonial trade involved substantial capital exports and 'cannot possibly have done much to build up capital in England and thereby to promote the Industrial Revolution'; moreover, the profits of plantations and the slave trade went mainly into land and stately homes. This view has since been supported by other scholars, but more evidence of links between colonial trade and industrial investment has come to light. While few economic historians other than Marxists would regard the Industrial Revolution as the result of wars, colonial conquests and the slave trade, there is evidence that commercial capital derived from colonial trade did make significant contributions to industrial expansion—through business partnerships and commercial credit, for example, in the growth of manufactures, particularly sugar-refining, tobacco-making, etc., in ports such as London, Bristol, Liverpool and Glasgow, and in provision of capital for the development of other industries.

The main source of industrial investment, however, was ploughed-back profits (see pp. 66–67), and, as Ashton rightly stressed, Britain's main markets were still predominantly in Europe and in utilitarian commodities such as corn, timber and naval stores, textiles, leather and metals manufactures rather than in tropical produce and slaves. By the early eighteenth century about 85 per cent of English domestic exports consisted of manufactured goods, and these overseas sales accounted for nearly a third of total English industrial production.

The importance of overseas trade should not, however, be exaggerated, since it would appear from the evidence produced by A. H. John that industrial expansion in the late seventeenth and early eighteenth centuries was based mainly on rising *internal* demand, resulting from increasing agricultural output (with enclosures, new crops, etc.), cheaper foodstuffs, rising real wages and growing consumption of a widening range of manufactured goods such as clothing, pots and pans, cutlery, furniture and clocks, thus stimulating the textile, iron, coal and other industries. It was reflected in transport improvements, with river navigation schemes and turnpikes, and in growing numbers of merchant middlemen, 'outriders' or commercial travellers and shops. This rising home demand, as Eversley and Perkin have shown, was maintained in the second half of the century, with growing population, real income and consumers' expenditure fired by 'social emulation'.

All these commercial changes can be traced far back into the preceding period.

So, too, can the technological developments associated with the Industrial Revolution. Coal fuel, for example, had already come into widespread use, and the eighteenth-century inventions of Darby, Cort and others, enabling coke to be used in smelting and forging iron, should be regarded not as revolutionary new beginnings but rather as culminations of earlier efforts in this field, following the successful uses of coal or coke fuel in the smelting of copper, lead and tin and in many other industrial processes. Similarly, the power of horses, water and wind had long been used to drive mills of many kinds, and the early Industrial Revolution was based primarily upon these traditional forms of power rather than on the driving force of steam. The first steam-engines of Savery and Newcomen, in the late seventeenth and early eighteenth centuries, followed numerous earlier scientific and technical investigations into atmospheric pressures, the creation of a vacuum and steam condensation, and these engines were invented, like the previous water-powered pumps, for draining mines, which long continued to be their main use. Steam power developed more slowly than generally believed; well into the nineteenth century, long after Watt's improvements, water-wheels were far more numerous than steam-engines in many industrial operations. At the same time, many manufactures remained handicraft processes: down to the mid-nineteenth century, in a wide range of industries, industrialization meant mainly the multiplication of existing small-scale establishments, with manual workers, in order to meet growing demand, and many of them were still in rural areas, though urban concentrations began to develop much more rapidly.

The factory system, however, the concentration of workers in a single building or workplace, usually though not always with power-driven machinery, was certainly not a new phenomenon. We have previously noted numerous examples of mills or 'manufactories' in various industries and of relatively large firms emerging wherever fixed capital requirements grew or where subdivision and specialization of hand labour increased output and reduced costs. Though handicraft production in small workshops still predominated in textiles, clothing, leather, metals manufactures and many other trades, larger-scale factory production had been developing in some industries, especially where coal fuel or water power could be employed, if not to the extent that Nef maintained. Even in textiles, where the factory system was to achieve its most famous triumphs during the Industrial Revolution, there had been earlier fulling mills and gig-mills, while the Dutch 'engine-looms' could also be driven by water-wheels, and the Lombes' water-powered silk-throwing mill of the early eighteenth century was similarly based on much earlier continental innovations. Kay's fly-shuttle, on the other hand, merely improved the hand-loom and was in line with earlier improvements in manually operated machinery such as the Saxony spinning-wheel or the stocking-knitting frame, which fitted into the existing domestic system.

In most industries, as we shall see, there was no sudden dramatic technological transformation. There have been considerable differences of opinion, however, in regard to the timing of the industrial advance. Some historians point to evidence of growth in the late seventeenth and early eighteenth centuries, followed by comparative stagnation or deceleration in the second quarter of the eighteenth century, as a result of declining population growth and low agricultural prices; but others consider that low food prices, by raising real incomes, stimulated a demand for manufactured goods. There is certainly evidence of technological innovation and growth in various industries in the earlier period—such as the introduction of coke-smelting in the copper, lead, tin and iron industries, the invention of the Savery and Newcomen steam-engines for mine drainage, and the first silk-throwing mills—but it is uncertain how far this progress was maintained up to the mid-eighteenth century, before the massive upsurge of the later Industrial Revolution.

That upsurge itself, moreover, has been the subject of considerable historical controversy. Many economic historians have tended to emphasize the evolutionary rather than the revolutionary aspects of industrialization in the eighteenth and early nineteenth centuries. Ashton even toyed with the idea of abandoning the use of the term Industrial Revolution, as being too misleading. Some scholars, however, have reacted against this tendency and have re-emphasized the revolutionary features or at any rate the marked increase in the rate of economic growth, as demonstrated by Hoffmann's index of British industrial production, rising sharply from less than 2 per cent per annum between 1700 and 1780 to between 3 and 4 per cent thereafter*. Rostow, for example, while recognizing the importance of earlier 'preconditions', has located Britain's industrial 'take-off' in the last two decades of the eighteenth century and has linked it with a postulated increase in the proportion of net national income invested from 5 per cent or less to 10 per cent or more, resulting particularly from rapid mechanization and growth of the factory system in the cotton industry, the 'leading sector' in this revolution. Hartwell also regards the Industrial Revolution as a 'massive discontinuity', with unprecedented rates of growth, transforming the whole economy and society, though over a longer period. Whereas Britain in 1750 was still predominantly agricultural and rural, by 1850 it was predominantly industrial and urban: a revolution of unprecedented magnitude had thus occurred.

---

*Other scholars have discerned an earlier acceleration, from the 1740s, though the upward trend from the 1780s was more pronounced. P. Deane and W. A. Cole, *British Economic Growth 1688–1959* (Cambridge, 1964). Their estimates, however, have been criticized by N. F. R. Crafts, 'English Economic Growth in the Eighteenth Century', *Economic History Review*, 2nd series, XXIX (1976), whose revised figures support the evidence of increasing agricultural output and income per head, and hence growing demand for manufactures, in the period before 1740, with a tendency towards stagnation thereafter, as a result of 'Malthusian' population pressures on *per capita* income growth.

Rostow's interpretation, however, has been subjected to considerable criticism. Important changes had been occurring long before the 1780s, and it is difficult to differentiate the 'preconditions' from the revolution itself. It is certainly doubtful whether 'take-off' (a dubious term, anyway) was confined to the last two decades of the eighteenth century; though industrialization had begun much earlier, it had not gone far by 1800—in fact the really massive industrial changes occurred in the nineteenth century. Rostow's theory of a leap in capital formation between the 1780s and early 1800s has been seriously questioned, notably by Deane and Cole, who have argued that there was a more gradual growth of capital investment, which did not reach 10 per cent of national income until the railway boom of the 1840s. But the matter is by no means settled: Feinstein's very recent estimates, though also open to criticism, give support to Rostow's theory; indeed he calculates that, as a proportion of gross domestic product, total investment had risen to as high as 14 per cent by the 1790s. (The researches of Crouzet and Davis, moreover, confirm that there was a similarly marked increase in the rate of growth of British exports, especially of cotton goods and to a lesser extent of iron and steel and other metal manufactures, in the last two decades of the eighteenth century.) In view of the inadequacies of the statistical evidence, however, it seems sensible not to bother too much about differing opinons on the precise periodization of investment but simply to stress the general agreement that a more rapidly increasing rate of capital accumulation was of fundamental importance to industrial growth from the 1780s onwards.

There is also no doubt that the cotton industry did grow prodigiously from that time, and it certainly had important 'linkages' with other sectors of the economy, stimulating developments in engineering, chemicals, transport and overseas trade. But it can be argued that the earlier developments in coal, iron and steam engineering were of more fundamental importance, in providing the basic fuel, power, constructional material and machinery for general industrialization and also greater incentives for improvements in transport, especially for coal. Indeed, many economic historians consider that it is misleading to single out any particular 'leading sector', when developments were taking place on a broad front and were closely interrelated. Nevertheless, some justification for Rostow's thesis is provided by the fact that, even as late as 1870, steam-powered mechanization and the factory system were to be found mainly in textiles, especially cotton, though steam power had also been massively applied in the heavy coal and iron industries (see p. 167).

For all these developments, moreover, increasing quantities of capital were certainly required and were available at lower rates of interest during the eighteenth century, as income rose from land, trade and industry itself and as sources of lending were mobilized more effectively by a growing number of banks and other financial intermediaries such as local attorneys, who arranged mortgage loans and bonds. But investigations into textile and other industries have shown that fixed capital requirements in the early Industrial Revolution were not so great as previously supposed: existing buildings such as corn or fulling mills, old warehouses, barns or even cottages could be utilized; premises or parts of premises—a single room, a floor or a whole mill—could be rented, even including power and machinery; early purpose-built factories were small, and ploughed-back profits were the main source of capital accumulation; considerable increases in productivity could be achieved by concentration, sub-division, specialization and discipline of labour and by improvements in man-agerial and commercial efficiency, with comparatively small increases in fixed capital requirements, as in Boulton's Soho factory, Wedgwood's Etruria or the pin manufactory observed by Adam Smith; 'circulating', commercial or working capital, for stocks of raw materials and goods in various stages of production and marketing, as well as for fuel, rent, interest and wages, long remained more important than fixed capital, and credit arrangements were the basis of industry and trade, debtor and creditor items preponderating in business accounts. Moreover, quality as well as quantity of capital investment was important, particularly in relation to technological progress, in which 'human capital' was more important than physical assets; the development and diffusion of scientific and technological knowledge were of crucial significance (see pp. 71–72), though technological advances were embodied in new capital equipment.

All this research suggests that Ashton—followed by Rostow— placed rather too much emphasis on fixed capital formation and on the role of low interest rates in stimulating investment in the early Industrial Revolution. But there is no doubt that increasingly there was a shift from circulating, or mercantile, to fixed industrial capital, from labour-intensive to capital-intensive methods of pro-duction, with the development of the factory system. Sir John Hicks, in his *Theory of Economic History* (1969), sees this as the 'central' feature of the Industrial Revolution, a view supported by Feinstein's recent estimates, which show that, while circulating capital remained more important than fixed capital until the end of the eighteenth century, it was soon surpassed thereafter by investment in buildings and machinery, leading to rapidly increasing production and pro-ductivity; output per worker and per unit of capital appears to have been growing at well over one per cent per annum by the early decades of the nineteenth century.

This capital accumulation was associated with an increase in the size of businesses and scale of manufacture. But it was achieved by individual entre-preneurs, family firms and partnerships, without much change in business financing. Joint-stock companies remained very rare in industry, not so much because of the 1720 'Bubble Act'—which could be evaded by setting up unincorporated companies under trust deeds—but because the great majority of businesses were initially small and could grow by ploughing back profits, raising loans, bringing in partners or turning to relatives and friends. There were only a few joint-stock industrial concerns in the eighteenth century, such as the Carron Company in the iron industry, the English Linen Company and the Cast Plate Glass Company of St Helens; it was in the field of public utilities, such as canals, waterworks, gasworks and above all railways, that joint-stock organization developed most strongly, and it was not until after the company legislation of the mid-nineteenth century, introducing general limited liability, that it gradually began to spread more widely. There are innumerable examples in the Industrial Revolution of businesses started, as Wadsworth and Mann found in the Lancashire cotton industry, by 'small yeoman capital', by 'small independent men of energy', artisans or small domestic manufacturers, though usually with the aid of loans and commercial credit; some of these men, combining enterprise and personal frugality, built firms of considerable size in their own lifetime.

Banks do not, in general, appear to have provided resources for long-term capital projects, but confined themselves to more liquid short-term trade credit or overdrafts and to the discounting of commercial bills. In view of the initial predominance of circulating capital, however, these functions were of vital importance. Merchants, or merchant manufacturers, also played a very important role not only in expanding markets and commercial credit but also in providing capital for industrial development, often in partnerships, as in the building of early textile factories, demonstrated most notably by Strutt, Dale, Drinkwater and Gott. Merchants of London and Bristol played a similar role in the development of the South Wales iron and coal industries, while those of Liverpool were involved in the coal and salt production of south Lancashire and north Cheshire.

In these various ways capital was generated from within the existing domestic manufacturing, commercial and credit systems. And although the capital of most firms remained fairly modest, larger concerns soon developed, with total assets running into tens of thousands (in a few cases hundreds of thousands) of pounds. Technological advances increasingly required larger quantities of fixed capital investment in iron-founding, copper-smelting, coal-mining, cotton-spinning, engineering, brewing, etc. This, above all, is what constituted the Industrial Revolution: all the circulating capital—raw materials, stocks of finished goods, etc.—in these industries was appendant to it. In the most dynamic industrial sectors such as cotton and iron, fixed capital was increasing much more rapidly than in manufactures generally. The most enterprising and successful firms in these industries were increasing their total capital at as high a rate as 15 to 20 per cent per year, though the general average growth rate was probably about 7 to 8 per cent according to Crouzet; and this investment was intimately related to technological advance, resulting in progressive installation of improved plant and machinery.

Emphasis upon technological revolution and development of the factory system in these industries, however, has tended to obscure the fact that in most other manufactures during this period there were no such revolutionary changes. As we shall see, the growth of steam-powered mechanization took place very gradually, and in the mid-nineteenth century—indeed even in 1870—it was still confined predominantly to textiles, especially cotton, and to the heavy industries of iron and coal mining; in the whole wide range of other industries it had made comparatively little progress. The great majority of these were still small-scale handicrafts, in which most firms employed only a handful of men. As Hobsbawm has rightly observed, among the 1,670 cotton masters who made returns to the Population Census of 1851 (England and Wales), there was

'a considerably greater number ... employing a hundred or more men than ... [among] all the 41,000 [master] tailors, shoemakers, engine- and machine-makers, builders, wheelwrights, tanners, woollen- and worsted-manufacturers, silk-manufacturers, millers, lace-manufacturers and earthenware-manufacturers who reported the size of their establishments'.

The great majority of masters in these and many other trades, such as carpenters, cabinet-makers, hatters, rope-makers, tallow-chandlers, brewers, bakers, prin- ters, smiths, cutlers, nailers, watch-makers and other metal-working trades, employed less than ten men; indeed, out of the total numbers of masters (129,002) who made returns, more than half (66,497) employed five men or less, while a further third (41,732) employed no men or did not state the number employed. The returns of factories and workshops in 1871 showed much the same situation: the average employment figure for all such works, large and small, in the United Kingdom was still under twenty, the relatively small number of big textile, iron and engineering concerns being vastly exceeded by the host of small firms in numerous other industries. Moreover, the workshop returns were very incom- plete and only included employers' workshops, not out-workers, so that the average unit of production must have been a good deal smaller.

It is also evident that the links between land and industry remained closer than once supposed. Many industrial raw materials—wool, hides, timber, malt, tallow, etc.—were still animal or vegetable products. Landowners such as Earl Gower, the Duke of Bridgewater, Lord Dudley, the Earls Fitzwilliam, the Lowther family and many others saw even greater opportunities of increasing rents, profits or royalties in exploiting the mineral resources of their estates (by means of coal mines, ironworks, stone quarries, brickworks and lime-kilns), in encouraging urban housing developments and in the building of docks and harbours and transport improvements; in many cases they were directly involved in such enterprises, providing capital, etc, though more frequently they operated through leases. On the other hand, the landowning aristocracy as a whole engaged in an enormous amount of conspicuous investment and consumption—in expenditure on great houses, luxury goods, gambling and pleasure—which may be regarded as largely non-productive, though it helped to stimulate demand in the building, furniture making and other trades. The amount they invested in industrial enterprises appears to have been relatively small, except in coal and iron, and initiative in development rarely seems to have come from landed proprietors; canal or port builders like the Duke of Bridgewater or the Lowthers do not appear to have been common—landowners apparently provided less than a third of the share capital for canals. Most landed investment naturally went into enclosures and agricultural improvements, and much less into industry, though 'yeoman' capital and enterprise seem to have been common in the origins of many firms, which subsequently expanded from industrial profits. Industrial capital, in fact, came mainly from industry and trade. Moreover, a good deal of industrial and mercantile capital was diverted into the purchase and development of landed estates.

There were other important links, however, between land and industry. Rural demand for ironmongery (nails, horse-shoes and agricultural implements) and other manufactures was a very significant factor in a period when the majority of the population still lived and worked on the land and when agricultural production and incomes were rising in the Agricultural Revolution, which also, of course, enabled the growing manufacturing towns to be fed. At the same time, cheaper foodstuffs provided an increased margin of income for expenditure on other commodities. In the origins of the Industrial Revolution, there was considerable expansion of rural domestic industries, in textiles and metal manufactures, which provided capital, markets, entrepreneurial experience and a labour force for further industrialization. It was from the countryside that labour migrated to the growing industrial-urban areas, and many industrial pioneers came from yeoman stock. The researches of the late Professor Chambers and others, however, have demonstrated the general falsity of the Marxist notion that the peasantry were 'expropriated' and driven into urban factories by enclosures; surplus labour was created mainly by population growth, and workers were attracted into towns by possibilities of employment and higher wages; indeed, industrialization may well have created its own labour force.

Population was now growing much more rapidly, that of England and Wales increasing from about 5½ million in 1700 to 9 million by 1801 and 18 million by 1851; Scotland was added after the Act of Union in 1707, while the population of Ireland, finally brought into political union in 1800, increased even more dramatically. It also appears that incomes generally were rising in the eighteenth and early nineteenth centuries: the estimates of Deane and Cole certainly indicate a substantial growth of national income, while average income per head also seems to have been improving, though the standard of living of the poorest sections of the community may well have declined during the years of prolonged warfare and post-war depression between the early 1790s and about 1820. Thus there was an expanding home market, and also a plentiful labour supply, for industrial development. The movement of goods and people was facilitated by a transport revolution, first with turnpikes and canals and later with railways; indeed almost as much capital investment went into developing the basic infrastructure of industrializing society as into industrial plant and equipment.

The interactions between growth of population and the Industrial Revolution have been extensively, but not very conclusively, debated. Was the population growth exogenously determined by factors such as harvest fluctuations, the declining virulence of certain diseases such as the plague, and medical improvements? Or was it a result of improved food supply, through increases in agricultural production and productivity, brought about by enclosures and advances in agricultural techniques, or were these agricultural improvements themselves responses to population growth? Or did the Industrial Revolution create its own increased labour supply by expanding employment opportunities, breaking down craft apprenticeship restrictions and raising wages, thus stimulating earlier marriages and more children? There is no necessary connection between population growth and industrialization, as demonstrated by Ireland and other non-industrial countries of that period and by predominantly agrarian 'third-world' countries of the present day., The problem is bedevilled by the inadequacies of the statistical evidence, which make it difficult to determine whether population growth in the Industrial Revolution resulted from a falling death rate or a rising birth rate or from both. The death rate certainly seems to have been falling as a result of improvements in food supply, clothing, housing and fuel rather than from medical advances, which, with the significant exception of inoculation and vaccination against smallpox, were of doubtful efficacy and not available to the mass of the population. The effects of population growth are also problematical. A more abundant labour supply might well inhibit labour-saving technological innovation, but population growth, with rising income per head, would tend to encourage it by expanding the market. The latter effect, previously emphasized, seems to have been more potent than the former; in fact, in some industries, such as cotton, there appears to have been a scarcity of labour, especially of skilled labour, leading to mechanical inventions as markets expanded. At the same time, population was increasingly attracted into the industrial towns from the surrounding countryside; technological innovations in certain sectors, though labour-saving, brought about such rapid expansion and created so much additional employment in new industrial occupations, and also in housing, transport and the distributive trades, as well as in the un-revolutionized industries, that there was a growing demand for labour.

The increasing concentration of industry in towns led eventually to the decline of the older forms of dispersed rural manufacture, involving a dramatic redistribution of population geographically and occupationally. The expansion of the new industrial towns was prodigious. Manchester, the great 'cottonopolis', grew from around 15,000 to over 300,000 between 1750 and 1850, and similar rates of increase occurred in Birmingham, Leeds, Liverpool, Sheffield, Glasgow and other towns. At the same time, London's vast growth continued, its population rising to about $2\frac{1}{2}$ million by the mid-nineteenth century. Its industrial expansion, however, has been neglected by comparison with that of the midland and northern towns, though in fact its established predominance in brewing, soap-making, printing, leather-making and many other trades was maintained, while it became the leading centre of engineering in the late eighteenth and early nineteenth centuries, as well as developing iron shipbuilding, chemicals and other industries. In both industry and trade, however, its predominance was no longer so overwhelming.

In these rapidly growing towns there was more social mobility, the remaining gild restrictions gradually disappeared, and wider opportunities were opened for business enterprise and social advancement. The 'Protestant ethic', with its emphasis on individualism and economic achievement, through the virtues of hard work, abstinence and thrift, evidently continued to exercise a significant influence, as shown by the business success of numerous Dissenters, especially Quakers and Unitarians, still excluded from public life and the universities by Anglican intolerance. Developing their own schools and academies, moreover, they made more provision for mathematical, scientific and commercial education. This, however, was part of a general growth of interest in applied science, developing from the earlier 'Scientific Revolution', with the foundation of the Royal Society in 1662 and the widespread establishment of scientific societies in provincial towns, such as the famous Lunar Society of Birmingham and the Literary and Philosophical Society of Manchester, together with the similarly pervasive activities of itinerant lecturers in 'natural philosophy', the establishment of libraries and the widespread dissemination of scientific and mathematical books and journals, down to utilitarian publications for practical millwrights, carpenters, etc. Leading industrialists of the late eighteenth century such as Watt and Boulton of steam-engine fame, Wedgwood the great potter, Smeaton the engineer, Charles Taylor the Manchester calico printer and bleacher, Benjamin Gott the Leeds woollen manufacturer, John Marshall the Leeds flax spinner, and a great many others were profoundly interested and active in applied science and were in close personal contact with scientists such as Black, Priestley, Darwin and Dalton, just as other industrialists continued in the first half of the nineteenth century to associate with Davy, Henry, Faraday and other scientists. Moreover, there is no doubt that applied science played a significant role in the development of the steam engine, in the improvement of water wheels, in the 'chemical revolution' that established the manufactures of acids, alkalis and chlorine bleach, in the development of cast- and wrought-iron building construction and in various other fields.

'Practical science', as advocated by William Fairbairn, the Manchester engineer, in the first half of the nineteenth century, based on rational procedures, industrial experiment and mathematical measurement, had come to be of increasing significance during the Industrial Revolution, so that it is often difficult to distinguish between intelligent empiricism and applied science. The traditional view of these early industrial developments, as entirely achievements of illiterate and innumerate craftsmen, has been largely demolished, though it would be equally wrong to regard the Industrial Revolution simply as a product of the Scientific Revolution. Practical rule-of-thumb craftsmanship still remained of widespread importance, especially in those industries still based on traditional processes; in new industries, too, such as factory spinning and 'machine-making' or mechanical engineering, applied science seems to have been of comparatively minor significance, though such pioneers as Crompton and Maudslay were highly intelligent men, certainly not lacking in practical-scientific abilities.

In many of the industries in which applied science was becoming significant, Britain benefited substantially from continental advances, especially in France. Notable examples were the introduction of chlorine bleaching, originated by the Swedish chemist Scheele and the Frenchman Berthollet, and the synthetic soda process, known by the name of its French inventor Leblanc; French chemists also led the way in dyeing. The development of steam power was based on earlier continental scientific researches and the experimental engines of the Frenchman Papin. In civil engineering, too, a great deal was learnt from the Dutch and the French. In many industries, in fact, even where applied science was less significant, insular British empiricism was by no means solely responsible for improvements. Continental craftsmen and technology continued to be introduced into the glass, pottery, paper and printing industries and also into various metals manufactures. Even in textiles, where British advances are so famous, innovations were introduced from the continent, such as silk-throwing machinery, Jacquard's loom and Heilmann's combing machine. It is true that Britain began rapidly to outpace continental countries from the late eighteenth century onwards, particularly in coal, iron, engineering and textiles and also in overseas trade and shipping, but the insularity of the Industrial Revolution has been greatly exaggerated.

Technological invention in Britain, however, appears to have been encouraged not only by the favourable economic and social factors to which we have referred but also by the patent system. Certainly there was a remarkable increase in the number of patents granted—from 31 in the 1660s to 477 in the 1780s—many of them for important inventions. But those who got patents were not always the original inventors, 'pirating' was widespread, patents were often challenged and quashed and many inventions were not patented. At the same time, patents could be obstacles to further improvements, particularly when, like Watt's steam-engine patent, they were specially prolonged. Nevertheless, the remarkable increase in their number strongly suggests not only that they were regarded as worth the trouble and cost of getting but that they reflect an increasing effort at developing new manufacturing methods. Technological advance, however, did not occur in a series of sudden leaps associated with particularly famous inventions. In most cases, such inventions were only made technically and commercially successful and brought into widespread use after numerous minor improvements spread over many years, as the coke-smelting process, the steam-engine, the power-loom, the wool-combing machine and many other examples demonstrate. Their development was dependent upon the growth and diffusion of the necessary skills in machine-making, etc., and on the gradual creation of a trained labour force to operate new machinery and processes.

A factor of fundamental significance to industrial and commercial enterprise was the development of individual freedom—freedom from the restraints of religious dogma, freedom from the restrictions of manorialism, open-field agriculture, gilds and town corporations, freedom from State intervention, industrial regulation and monopolies, and freedom to exploit market and profit opportunities. Adam Smith provided the gospel for the Industrial Revolution, in denouncing outdated, ineffective and hampering mercantilist controls and in lauding economic freedom, free trade or *laissez-faire*, as the essential basis for increasing the wealth of nations. The whole outlook of the eighteenth century was permeated by a growing economic individualism, and Adam Smith was giving articulate expression to ideas towards which many industrialists, merchants and earlier writers such as North and Davenant had long been feeling their way and which had previously found expression in Parliament. Following the free-trade attacks against monopolies in the seventeenth century, Parliament in the following century voiced its disapproval of industrial regulations established in the Tudor and early Stuart periods. In 1702, for example, in response to petitions from workers in the woollen industry for enforcement of the apprenticeship clauses of the 1563 Statute of Artificers, Parliament declared that 'trade ought to be free and not restrained'. Similarly, in 1757, it abandoned enforcement of the wages-assessment clauses so far as the woollen industry was concerned, and, though Acts were passed in 1769 and 1773 for regulating the wages of London tailors and silk weavers, the general trend was definitely against such intervention and towards freedom of contract, and the wages and apprenticeship clauses of the 1563 Act were finally repealed in 1813–14, after having long previously fallen into widespread disuse.

Manufacturing regulations were also gradually abolished or ceased to be enforced, so that industry became free to develop unhampered by rules regarding sizes, weights and qualities of products, by controls on methods of manufacture and even by bans on certain kinds of machinery. Parliament again voiced rising free-trade opinion in the report of the Select Committee on the 'laws relating to trade and manufacture' in 1751, which recommended that 'a great part ought to be repealed—many as being grown out of use and scarce ever put into execution ...; others entirely local; and others, though perhaps well calculated for the times in which they were made, yet now become prejudicial to trade in its present state; others quite useless'.

Of course there was never complete *laissez-faire*. The State still had an important role in maintaining law and order, protecting rights of property and suppressing 'combinations' of workmen 'in restraint of trade'. And while industrial regulations decayed, other elements of Mercantilism, in the sphere of overseas trade—tariffs, Navigation Laws and the 'Old Colonial System'—were preserved for much longer, because most British manufacturers, shipowners and merchants were still apprehensive of foreign competition. Indeed, tariffs were only raised to really high levels from the late seventeenth century onwards, at first because of revenue requirements in the wars against Louis xiv of France but later from more deliberately protectionist motives. It was not until the second and third quarters of the nineteenth century—not until Britain had fairly clearly established its position as the 'workshop of the world'—that these protective regulations were gradually dismantled. During the eighteenth and early nineteenth centuries the Industrial Revolution took place behind a sheltering wall of tariffs and prohibitions, and the free-trade revolution in commercial policy came later. But it would be wrong to attribute Britain's industrial advance to protectionism, for import duties do not win export markets, and British industries had to overcome foreign tariff barriers. Indeed Imlah has argued that continued protectionism restricted the expansion of British commerce and that free trade was too long delayed, because of deep-rooted protectionist interests, especially the landed interest, which was still politically predominant. But protectionist sentiments persisted also in many sections of British industry and trade: all manufactures did not acquire the cotton industry's competitive superiority, and protectionism was also strong among shipowners and East and West Indian merchants. And whilst cotton manufacturers demanded repeal of the corn laws, in the hope of reciprocal foreign concessions for their yarn and cloth, they remained opposed to free export of machinery right down to the 1840s. The effects of Peel's tariff reforms and repeal of the corn laws in that decade, followed by Gladstone's free-trade budgets in the 1850s and 1860s, were not felt until the second half of the century.

In industrial affairs, on the other hand, in their business operations, British manufacturers hardly needed Adam Smith or Samuel Smiles to point out the virtues of free enterprise and self-help. But the profit motive, though immensely powerful, was not the only driving force behind the Industrial Revolution. McClelland, Hagen, Flinn and other scholars have emphasized the importance of socio-psychological 'drives' or 'achievement motivation', especially among Dissenters, and the importance of 'technological creativity' in inventors, engineers, etc., while many studies have supported Schumpeter's emphasis on entrepreneurial energy and innovation, the drive to succeed in business and to beat competitors, together with the social drive to rise in the world and 'found a family'.

Other scholars, however, taking a more impersonal view, have pointed out that such drives were not new—that a novel type of 'economic man' had not suddenly appeared—but that the men of eighteenth-century Britain were simply responding to a peculiarly favourable conjunction of economic, social and political circumstances, with agricultural surpluses, growing population, expanding trade and empire, rich and favourably located resources of raw materials, political stability and *laissez-faire* policy. But, whilst socio-economic circumstances undoubtedly shape men's attitudes and activities, they are themselves very largely made by men, and the achievements of the Industrial Revolution were the results not of impersonal economic forces but of individual enterprise, of free capitalist enterprise. They were based on triumphs of personal endeavour in establishing and organizing businesses, in inventing and developing new technology, in improving transport and expanding markets, in mobilizing capital, investing, risk-taking and ploughing back profits. No one who has studied the letters and account books of businessmen and technological innovators during the Industrial Revolution can be in any doubt about the enterprise, effort and organizing ability of such men or about the immense problems they faced. Many, in fact, succumbed: bankruptcies were innumerable; the Industrial Revolution was by no means a 'bed of roses' for capitalists. It is customary nowadays to denigrate the Smilesian 'heroic' theory and to explain economic development in impersonal quantitative terms, forgetting that it all rested on individual endeavour. But there is no doubt that such men as Abraham Darby, Richard Arkwright, James Watt, Josiah Wedgwood, Benjamin Gott, Henry Maudslay, George Stephenson and the other pioneers of the Industrial Revolution *were* men of great enterprise and energy, who transformed the life of this country and ultimately of the world. It may well be, as Payne has argued that an unduly 'eulogistic aura' envelops these early pioneers, operating in a 'uniquely favourable economic environment', but nevertheless he recognizes their great achievements, the risks involved in pioneering and the numerous failures.

Socialist writers, however, from Marx and Engels to modern left-wing historians, have generally regarded such enterprise as purely class-exploitative, resulting in social misery for the masses: 'the rich got richer and the poor poorer'. Profit, to most socialists, is still a dirty word, and the Industrial Revolution is still thought of in terms of 'dark satanic mills'. Undoubtedly there is plenty of evidence of exploitation, low wages, unemployment, child labour, bad housing and economic and social oppression during the Industrial Revolution, but 'pre-industrial' conditions had been by no means idyllic for the mass of mankind—all maypoles and roast beef, sturdy yeomen and independent craftsmen—though that is how early social critics were apt to see them, in retrospect. A wage-earning proletariat was no new phenomenon, wages and standards of living had been miserably low, death rates often catastrophically high (famine and pestilence periodically decimating the population), child labour commonplace, hours of work long, manual labour back-breakingly laborious, working conditions bad and working-class houses frequently hovels. Life had, in fact, been 'nasty, brutish and short' for the majority of humanity. The domestic system—also capitalist of course—was marked by comparatively low productivity; working and living were often combined, in insalubrious conditions; long hard monotonous labour was more evident than 'pride of craft'; freedom and lack of supervision in working were counterbalanced by excessively long bouts of toil to get work finished; workers were often heavily in debt to their employers, and truck payment was common; trade depressions, unemployment, deep social distress and riots were endemic, while workers' 'combinations' were severely repressed.

The Industrial Revolution did not, of course, change all these things overnight, but it is very doubtful whether it made conditions worse. In fact there is no doubt that in the long run Marx and Engels were utterly wrong: capitalist enterprise did not lead to the increasing exploitation and immiseration of the masses but to a vast increase in industrial production, national income and wealth, both total and per head, ultimately enabling a population ten times that of 1700 to live in these islands at a standard of living beyond the wildest dreams of early socialist critics; it resulted ultimately in far better working and living conditions, a greatly reduced death rate and far longer average life, together with a vast increase in the quantity and range of consumer goods, while at the same time, through mechanization, it gradually brought about a great lightening of the burden of human labour and reduction of working hours. In the long run, there is no doubt that the Industrial Revolution was a triumph and a blessing for mankind, not a social disaster, as socialists and anti-industrialists have so generally portrayed it.

In the short run, especially during the first half of the nineteenth century, there were certainly serious social problems. The combined effects of the Industrial Revolution and the long French Revolutionary and Napoleonic Wars and post-war depression produced an atmosphere of social revolt. In this half-century, agricultural production—despite enclosures and farming improvements—was barely keeping pace with the rapid growth of population; there were dark years when bad harvests coincided with cyclical trade depression; technological changes were causing unemployment and severe distress among such groups as the hand-loom weavers; and the immense growth of towns was creating problems of housing and sanitation beyond immediate solution by the existing administrative and technical resources. During such unprecedentedly rapid and widespread changes severe social dislocations and distress were inevitable.

In this period, when the basis of British industrialization was being laid, it has been argued that the necessary heavy investment involved 'forced savings' from the working classes, whose incomes and standard of living were held down while profits soared and were ploughed back to provide more fixed capital equipment: the increasing volume of capitalist savings and investment, it has been alleged, inevitably held down the growth of consumption. But there are serious weaknesses in this argument: not only has the theory of increasing 'immiseration' not been proved, but the process and effects of increasing investment have been misinterpreted. The growth in investment took place gradually over a long period, with increasing national production, income and wealth, both total and *per capita* (as shown, for example, by the estimates of Deane and Cole). There is no doubt that profits were the main source of capital growth and that in the most successful firms in the most rapidly expanding industries profits and growth rates were high (see p. 67); but profits came mainly not from squeezing wages, but from commercial enterprise, technological innovation and improvements in managerial efficiency; moreover, investment created more employment and incomes for the growing population and, by reducing costs, led to increased output of consumer goods at lower prices, while wages were generally a good deal higher in industry than in agriculture. Indeed, many economic historians see the Industrial Revolution largely as a response to growing internal demand, resulting from a rise both in population and in the general level of incomes: mass-consumption was a necessary accompaniment of mass-production, and, as Dr McKendrick has emphasized, increased family incomes through the earnings of women and children were an important factor in raising demand. Despite cyclical depressions and structural unemployment, the debate on the standard of living has not produced any clear demonstration that conditions were getting worse: indeed, in material terms at any rate—in average income per head, real wages and consumption of tea, sugar, clothing, soap, etc.—it appears that they were generally getting better, though certain groups, such as displaced hand workers, were worse off, especially in depressed years.

4

The Textiles Revolution

In terms of employment and contribution to national production and overseas trade, textiles remained the most important manufacturing group throughout this period (for employment figures in 1851, see p. 140). The woollen industry continued to maintain its long-established predominance during the eighteenth century, but was being rapidly overhauled by the prodigiously expanding cotton industry in the later decades and was finally surpassed in the early nineteenth century. By 1811, according to the estimates of Deane and Cole, 'more than a half of the output of the manufacturing group of industries was attributable to textiles', which similarly dominated the export trade; textiles then accounted for about 13 per cent of British national income, cotton alone for over 7 per cent. This continued leadership of textiles, based on technological innovation and growth of the factory system, therefore rightly figures in the forefront of the Industrial Revolution.

The cotton industry

The phenomenal rise of the cotton industry has, of course, always fascinated historians, as it did contemporaries. At the beginning of the eighteenth century it was of comparatively recent origin and negligible importance; it was still of no very great significance in about 1770; but by the first decade of the nineteenth century it had become the major British manufacturing industry, as a result of a series of remarkable technological innovations and the rapid development of the factory system, of which this industry has always provided the classic example. Not surprisingly, modern scholars such as Rostow have continued to find in the cotton industry the motive force for Britain's industrial 'take-off' (see pp. 64–65), and, although others may regard developments in coal and iron as of more fundamental significance, the cotton industry's growth was undoubtedly of tremendous importance not only for its own contributions to national manufacturing production and trade but also for its stimulus to other industries such as engineering and chemicals.

It was not, however, in the cotton industry that the first power-driven textile factories were established. Fulling mills, of course, had existed for centuries in the woollen industry, in which gig-mills had also been developed, together with a few striking examples of 'manufactories' employing hand workers (see pp. 24, 45, 48). But it was in the silk industry that the first typically modern textile factories appeared, with the establishment of silk-throwing mills in the early eighteenth century, filled with water-powered machinery and large numbers of workers (see p. 92). This industry, however, never really flourished in Britain and despite heavy protection was unable to beat its continental competitors. The cotton industry, on the other hand, though equally exotic—introduced originally in imitation of Indian calicoes, etc., and also entirely dependent on imported raw materials, at first mostly from the eastern Mediterranean, later from the West Indies and southern United States plantations—and likewise developing under shelter of protection, nevertheless came to dominate the world cotton trade. It was in cotton, not in silk, that the triumph of the factory system was to be most strikingly demonstrated.

The early cotton manufactures of this country were low-quality fustians and checks, mixtures of linen warp and cotton weft, much inferior to Eastern fabrics, imports of which were notably increasing in the late seventeenth century. It was, in fact, to protect the woollen industry against this influx that legislation was passed in 1700, forbidding the import of printed calicoes from India and elsewhere. This, however, led to the import of plain cotton cloth and the development of calico-printing in this country, until another Act was passed in 1721 prohibiting the buying and selling and even the wearing of printed cotton goods. The infant cotton industry, however, was subsequently safeguarded by the 'Manchester Act' of 1736, which permitted the manufacture of fustians, and later on, in 1774, when, as we shall see, the manufacture of pure cotton goods had been developed here, the 1721 prohibition was repealed.

The early cotton industry, like much of the woollen industry, was organized under the domestic system, with merchants in Manchester and other towns putting-out raw cotton to workers in their own homes, for women and children to card and spin and for men to weave, with much the same hand cards, wheels and looms as in woollen manufactures. The finishing processes required more fixed capital equipment in bleachcrofts, dyeworks and printworks, though operations were mostly manual. Many of the workers lived in country areas, some weavers being small farmers, but many were virtually full-time industrial operatives, especially rural cottagers and those living in towns. The tendency towards localization in Lancashire was based more upon this availability of labour and upon the presence of pure water and coal fuel, essential for bleaching, dyeing and printing, than upon the damp climate to which it is usually ascribed; subsequently, with the development of the factory system, Lancashire could also utilize its water and coal for industrial power.

The main incentive to mechanization in the industry seems to have been the growth of demand, at first mainly in the protected home market, with rising population and living standards and a growing taste for light and colourful cotton goods, though there were also large potential markets abroad, which were increasingly exploited in later years. In the early eighteenth century, moreover, there was a technical disequilibrium in the industy, accentuated by the introduction of the Dutch inkle (or swivel or ribbon) loom in the smallwares trade; four to six spinners were required to keep one weaver supplied with yarn, which upset the 'family economy', weavers often having to tramp miles to get supplies. This disequilibrium was increased by John Kay's fly-shuttle (1733), an improvement to the hand-loom, whereby the shuttle could be struck across the loom instead of being passed by hand, thus speeding up the process and also enabling broadcloth to be woven by a single weaver; developed initially for the woollen industry, it was adopted in the cotton industry, though not generally until after about 1760, because of the increasingly serious yarn shortage.

This situation stimulated efforts to improve spinning, resulting in the first roller-spinning machine, invented and developed by Lewis Paul and John Wyatt and patented in 1738. After failure of a small animal-powered factory in Birmingham, a water-mill was set up in Northampton in the early 1740s, followed by one or two elsewhere, but, either through technical difficulties or mismanagement, none of these enterprises proved successful, and it was not until the 1760s that the real breakthrough in mechanical spinning occurred. Meanwhile, however, carding machines of a type also invented by Paul, with toothed cylinders instead of flat hand-cards, began to come into use, turned at first by hand or horse-power and eventually by water-wheel.

During the 1760s James Hargreaves, of Blackburn, developed his spinning jenny, patented in 1770, a simple, mainly wooden, hand-operated machine at first with eight spindles, which fitted into and revived the domestic family economy, by enabling a weaver's family to keep him supplied with yarn. Gradually, however, the number of spindles was increased to over a hundred, and jenny factories were established. As Hargreaves' patent was successfully contested, the jenny came rapidly into use, despite workers' machine-smashing—by 1788 there were estimated to be about 20,000 in England—generally displacing the old hand spinning wheels in the cotton industry. Jenny-spun yarn, however, was rather weak, suitable only for weft, so that linen continued to be used for warp to produce fustians.

More important in the development of the factory system was the power-driven water-frame, utilizing Paul and Wyatt's roller-spinning principle, which was patented by Richard Arkwright of Preston in 1769. Arkwright was almost certainly not the original inventor of this machine—Thomas Highs of Leigh has a better claim, following Paul's earlier pioneering—but he had sufficient technical and even more business ability to develop it and to establish the factory system in the cotton industry. Like Hargreaves, he moved to the Nottingham area, where the hosiery manufacture provided both a market and financial support, which enabled him to build in 1771 his first water-powered mill at Cromford on the River Derwent—probably modelled on Lombe's nearby silk mill—followed by others at Belper and Milford in Derbyshire, then at Chorley, Manchester and elsewhere in Lancashire, Derbyshire, Nottinghamshire, and also in Scotland (the New Lanark mill, later famous for Robert Owen's social experiments), generally in partnership with merchants who were willing to provide capital. He took out patents not only for the water-frame but also for carding and other machinery, but they were eventually quashed in 1785, and the field was then entirely open for development of the factory system. Arkwright himself, however, continued to prosper, being knighted in the following year and leaving a fortune when he died in 1792—the cotton industry's first great tycoon.

As the name water-frame indicates, these early mills were driven by water-wheels and were widely dispersed, mostly in Pennine rural areas, where water power was available. Labour recruitment was a considerable problem, and 'parish apprentices' (pauper children) were often employed, but factory communities gradually developed, factory owners commonly having to provide houses and shops and often also building schools, churches and roads in their localities.

The water-frame enabled all-cotton goods to be manufactured in this country, since the yarn was strong enough for warp, while the finer weft continued to be produced on jennies, so the two machines were complementary; but only calicoes could be made as yet, the yarns not being fine enough for muslins. This, however, was soon achieved with the mule, invented by Samuel Crompton of Bolton, in the late 1770s, combining the principles of the jenny and the water-frame to produce a fine strong yarn. Crompton was unable to patent his machine because of Arkwright's patents, and when these were cancelled the mule was brought very rapidly into use; at first, like the jenny, it was a simple hand-operated domestic machine, but was soon made larger and power-operated, first in horse-mills and then, from 1790 onwards, in water-mills.

By that time, moreover, steam had been applied to the water-frame. At first, both Savery and Newcomen as well as Watt engines were used indirectly to drive mills, by pumping water for water-wheels, as in Arkwright's Manchester mill of the early 1780s, but the introduction of rotative engines enabled steam power to be applied directly to the driving of machinery (see p. 111), and the first such steam-spinning mill was set up at Papplewick in Nottinghamshire in 1785, soon followed by others, especially in Lancashire and Cheshire. With the application of steam to mule-spinning from about 1790, mills shot up in Lancashire towns: there were apparently 52 in the Manchester district by 1802 and 99 by 1830. There was, in fact, a rapid growth and concentration of such mills in these Lancashire–Cheshire urban areas and to a lesser extent in the Glasgow–Paisley district; though water-powered rural mills continued to be built, steam power became predominant in cotton-spinning during the early nineteenth century. These mills were mostly for mule-spinning: by 1811, according to Crompton's census, the number of mule spindles in the cotton trade was 4,209,570, compared with 310,516 water-frame and only 155,880 jenny spindles. Though the latter two figures were underestimates, jennies were certainly tending to disappear, and with them domestic spinning, rapidly overwhelmed by the factory system; water-frame mills, however, continued to turn out coarser warp yarns. Mules were made 'self-acting' or automatic from 1825 onwards by Richard Roberts, the Manchester engineer, though the older type of so-called 'hand mules' (requiring some manual operation) long remained in use. Such mules were built of ever-increasing size, with 600 spindles or more by the early 1830s, and mills also became bigger, some employing over a thousand workers, though the average was much smaller—in 1850 the average number of employees in a spinning mill was 114, in a combined spinning and weaving mill 332—and by that date the total number of cotton spindles in the United Kingdom had risen to 21 million.

This mechanical revolution, however, was for many years confined almost entirely to spinning and the preparatory processes of carding, etc. Although Edmund Cartwright had invented a power-loom in 1785, his early efforts at factory production failed—a large factory which he built in Manchester in the early 1790s was burnt down by hostile hand-loom weavers—and it was many years before power-loom weaving was made a practical success. Meanwhile, recruitment into hand-loom weaving was greatly increased, to cope with the rapidly rising output of machine-spun yarn: by 1820 there were about 240,000 hand-loom weavers, already suffering from declining wages through the influx of hands into the trade. Despite fierce opposition—notably in the machine-smashing riots of 1826—improved power-looms were relentlessly introduced in the second quarter of the century: there were 60,000 in the United Kingdom cotton industry by 1830 and 250,000 by 1850, by which time the number of hand-looms had been reduced to less than 50,000. The hand-loom weavers, in fact, became the classic example of technological unemployment, as they struggled vainly for survival on starvation wages.

In both spinning and weaving, therefore, by the mid-nineteenth century the factory system had triumphed. The number of factory workers (spinning and weaving) in the United Kingdom cotton industry rose rapidly to 331,000 by 1850;

the total number of mills was then 1,932, with a total horse-power of nearly 83,000, of which 71,000 was steam, according to the factory inspectors' returns. The industry had become heavily concentrated in Lancashire: over two-thirds of the factories, factory workers, spindles, power-looms, and steam power were located there in 1850, and most of the remainder were in the neighbouring areas of Cheshire, the West Riding and Derbyshire, with a similar though lesser concentration in Lanark and Renfrew in Scotland. Within Lancashire there was a tendency towards further geographical and technical specialization of spinning in the south (Manchester, Oldham, Bolton, etc.) and weaving in the north (Blackburn, Preston, etc.), though this localization was never clear-cut and well over half the workers were still employed in the larger concerns that combined both processes.

The growth of the factory system was also accompanied by a change-over in the occupational distribution of the sexes. Whereas domestic spinning had been traditionally an employment for women and children, factory mule-spinners were mostly men, though children were employed as piecers, and female labour was common in the preparatory processes. On the other hand, as male hand-loom weavers declined in number, females took over the power-looms in factories. In general, females predominated numerically, comprising over 57 per cent of the total factory labour force in 1850. Factory spinners and weavers, of course, now predominated, but they did not constitute the entire labour force in cotton manufacture, which totalled 470,000 (222,000 males and 248,000 females) in Great Britain in 1851; in addition, there were 31,000 dyers and calico-printers, also increasingly being brought into large works (see p. 84).

The vast growth of the industry was also reflected in the figures of raw cotton consumption, which rose from 1.1 million lb. in 1700 to 6.6 million by 1780, 52 million by 1800 and 588 million lb. by 1850, of which about three-quarters now came from the southern United States, where cotton plantations had been greatly extended; Britain was taking 50 to 60 per cent of the total American crop. Raw cotton had become, in fact, the biggest single import, accounting in 1850 for £21½ million out of total imports of £103 million. At the same time, with ever-decreasing costs of production, export markets had been enormously expanded. The home market could not possibly absorb the rapidly increasing output, the greater part of which came to be exported—about two-thirds of piece goods (cloth) in quantity by the mid-nineteenth century, about half in value, because exports were mostly of cheaper cloth. Whereas in 1700 cottons had accounted for a negligible proportion of total British exports, which were dominated by the woollen trade, they had surpassed woollens by the beginning of the nineteenth century, and by the middle of the century they accounted for over 40 per cent in value of all British exports: £28.3 million out of total United Kingdom domestic exports of £71.4 million in 1850.

This growth in the cotton trade, however, was not based simply on a mechanical revolution in spinning and weaving. The rapidly increasing output of yarn and cloth had to be bleached, dyed and printed, and these processes were more chemical than mechanical. It is true that mechanization was important: in bleachworks, dash-wheels and squeezers for washing and 'mangling' the cloth were driven by water-wheels and later by steam-engines, while in calico-printing hand blocks were gradually replaced by power-driven roller-printing machines, first developed by Taylor and Bell in the 1780s; steam power was also applied to grinding raw materials in dyeworks. But the revolution in bleaching was brought about by the introduction of vitriol (sulphuric acid) in the 'souring' process, by developments in the manufacture of soda (used in 'bucking' or boiling the cloth) and above all by the introduction of chlorine bleaching from the mid-1780s, which gradually eliminated the months-long 'grassing' or 'crofting' process in bleachfields. All these innovations were dependent upon advances in the chemical industry (see pp. 122–3), which also contributed to improvements in dyes and mordants.

These textile-chemical developments, though leading to the emergence of large bleachworks, were essentially capital-saving: capital had no longer to be tied up in bleachfields and goods in process of production. Even in spinning and weaving, as S. D. Chapman has shown, fixed capital formation was not at first so great as Rostow propounded, primarily because of the ease with which existing water-powered mills and other premises could be converted from previous uses. Later, as more and larger purpose-built factories were erected, total fixed capital requirements greatly increased, though unit costs were reduced by developments in mechanical engineering, producing cheaper and more efficient machinery, steam-engines and millwork. Whereas an early horse-powered spinning mill, with primitive machinery, could be established for a few hundred pounds, an Arkwright-type water-mill of the 1780s was generally valued at between £3,000 and £5,000, and the large multi-storied mills being built in the 1790s cost £10,000 to £15,000. Though small firms remained numerous, some very big concerns such as McConnel and Kennedy in Manchester, Ashworths of Turton (Bolton) and Horrocks of Preston were developing in the first half of the nineteenth century, owning several large mills. But most of these began in a very small way. James McConnel and John Kennedy, for example, came to Lancashire from Scotland to be apprenticed to machine-making and subsequently worked as journeymen before going into cotton-spinning in 1791, in partnership with the Sandfords, two well-to-do Manchester fustian warehousemen, who provided most of the initial finance; but the firm rapidly expanded its capital out of profits, from £1,770 in 1795 to £88,375 in 1810. Other Scottish migrants, such as Adam and George Murray and Thomas Houldsworth, who also became large cotton-spinners, began in much the same way; Robert Owen started up in Manchester with only

£100 capital, and other self-made men similarly expanded from small beginnings (see p. 67).

Many of the early cotton mills, however, especially larger ones, were set up with the aid of mercantile capital, provided either by merchant-manufacturers in the putting-out system or by textile and other merchants. Arkwright had been provided with financial backing from Jedediah Strutt of Derby and Samuel Need of Nottingham, two wealthy merchant hosiers, and the Strutts later established their own spinning mills. Other famous examples were Peter Drinkwater in Manchester, Samuel Oldknow at Stockport and Mellor, and David Dale at New Lanark. In fact, as Chapman has shown, investment in the early cotton-spinning mills of the east midlands and Lancashire was characterized by the predominance of mercantile capital. The availability of such capital and of bank credit, together with the expansion and diversification of the market, continued throughout the first half of the nineteenth century to facilitate the entry and survival of small firms, as Gatrell has demonstrated, especially in coarse spinning and power weaving, despite rising capital requirements and growth of large-scale production.

The woollen and worsted industry

All these revolutionary developments in cotton tended to put the woollen industry into the shade. Yet throughout the eighteenth century wool was the major British manufacturing industry, and even after being surpassed by cotton it remained of considerable importance. Moreover, the woollen industry also experienced growth and changes only less remarkable than those in cotton. At the beginning of the eighteenth century, as R. G. Wilson has recently emphasized, its predominance was overwhelming. Though concentrated in the three great manufacturing areas of the West Country, East Anglia and the West Riding, its geographical extent was widespread: 'there was no county which did not include a few score spinners and weavers', and by the 1750s John Smith's contemporary estimate of 800,000 people engaged in it may not have been excessive. Moreover, cloth exports accounted for around 70 per cent of English domestic exports in 1700, and seventy years later the proportion was still well over half. Output meanwhile continued to increase, by about two and a half times in the course of the century, mostly before the 1770s, according to Phyllis Deane's estimates.

This rate of growth has been compared unfavourably with that of the cotton industry, but such comparisons generally overlook the fact that cotton was growing from a very small base, whereas wool was already by far the greatest manufacture in the country. It is true, of course, that by the end of the century cotton was on the point of surpassing wool even in absolute terms, but concentration on cotton has tended to obscure the very substantial growth that took place in wool, especially in Yorkshire. In fact the most striking feature of the eighteenth-century growth is that it was almost entirely in the West Riding, which outstripped its woollen-manufacturing rivals even *before* the Industrial Revolution. Whilst the other main areas of woollen manufacture tended to stagnate or decline during most of the eighteenth century, Yorkshire's output increased by about eight times and must have entirely accounted for the increase in the industry as a whole. Yorkshire expanded its share of the industry's output and export trade from about one-fifth to nearly two-thirds.

Wilson's analysis is confirmed by the evidence of Hoskins in relation to Exeter and of Miss Mann in the West Country. By the end of the eighteenth century, Exeter's once-flourishing export trade in serges was virtually dead and the city's woollen industry 'had ceased to be of any importance'. Miss Mann tells a similar story of stagnation and decline, especially of exports, in the West Country, while the industries of Suffolk and Essex had almost withered away and Norfolk worsteds were also feeling the effects of West Riding competition.

These dramatic changes within the industry are attributable to several factors. Wilson ascribes them mainly to differences in sales organization, the specialist West Riding merchants, operating through the cloth-halls of Leeds, Wakefield, etc., being much more knowledgeable and enterprising than the monopolist London merchants and factors in Blackwell Hall, who dominated the export trade of the other areas; Yorkshire's success was particularly notable in cheap narrow cloths, dozens and kerseys, for which markets were vigorously expanded in the southern European and American markets, though gradually West Riding manufacturers also developed better-quality broad cloths and worsteds. The 'small master' system in Yorkshire also appears to have been more encouraging to industrial enterprise than the more conservative capitalist organization in the West Country and East Anglia. Moreover, the West Riding had the advantages of good water and coal supplies, the former for driving fulling mills and later for scribbling, carding and spinning mills, the latter mainly for the dyeing and finishing processes, before the age of steam. But these geographical advantages were of minor significance before the widespread development of the factory system.

It is well known, of course, that the woollen industry lagged considerably behind cotton in mechanization, for which various reasons have been suggested. This ancient regulated industry is said to have been more traditionally hidebound than the thrusting newcomer, free of corporate and state restrictions. But whilst such conservatism may have had some influence, other factors were probably more important. Wool fibre posed greater technical problems in the application of power-driven machinery. Markets, especially for exports, could not be expanded so rapidly as those for cottons; nor could supplies of raw material. On the other hand, the labour supply seems to have been more plentiful, and there does not appear to have been anything like the same yarn bottleneck as in cotton.

Mechanization therefore developed slowly in the old woollen cloth manufacture. But there was an early and widespread development of the factory system in the preparatory processes of scribbling and carding, especially in Yorkshire, where, as D. T. Jenkins has shown, a large number of such mills were established by 1800. These machines, introduced from the 1770s onwards, mainly in the last two decades of the century, were at first operated by hand, then by horse gins, but increasingly by water-wheels and soon also by steam; the mills were mostly small, many being converted or combined fulling or corn mills; some were 'company mills', owned on a joint-stock basis by groups of small clothiers.

Power-driven mechanization, however, was initially confined to these preparatory processes: spinning and weaving long remained manual. The jenny was coming into use in Yorkshire in the 1770s, though it did not become widespread until the 1780s; mules were introduced much more slowly and did not apparently make much headway before 1830. Both jennies and mules, moreover, were at first worked by hand; so too was the 'slubbing billy', used in preparing carded wool for spinning. All these hand-operated machines fitted into the existing domestic manufacture, though they were sometimes brought together in factories. In Benjamin Gott's famous mill at Bean Ing, Leeds, for example, established in the early 1790s, steam power was applied only to scribbling and carding machines, and to grinding dyewoods, etc., while the slubbers, spinners and weavers in the factory were still hand workers, and many out-workers were also employed. This firm's capital grew prodigiously, from £20,000 in 1792 to £397,000 by 1815, but it was an exceptional example of commercial expansion in an industry still largely unmechanized and in which the small clothier still remained typical; the early mills were mostly set up by 'small men' who had accumulated some capital in the traditional manufactures.

In the West Country, where the cloth trade was comparatively stagnant and where the workers showed more hostility to machinery, there were a few tentative efforts at innovation in the 1770s and 1780s, but it was only from the 1790s that scribbling and carding mills became more common, together with hand billies and jennies; as in Yorkshire, mules were not introduced till the 1830s and 1840s.

During the second quarter of the nineteenth century, however, woollen spinning was increasingly mechanized. By 1850 hundreds of water- and steam-powered mills had been established, mostly in the West Riding. But they were generally small and the total of 1.6 million spindles in the United Kingdom woollen industry was only a small fraction of that in cotton; hand spinning still survived very widely.

In weaving, the progress of the factory system was even slower. In Yorkshire the fly-shuttle was introduced from the 1760s and was common by the 1780s, but it was regarded as an innovation in the West Country in the 1790s and was still causing riots there in the early nineteenth century. Power-loom weaving also made very slow progress. In 1850 there were only about 9,500 power-looms in the whole United Kingdom woollen cloth industry, compared with 250,000 in cotton. Such progress as had been made was mainly in Lancashire and Yorkshire; there were only a few hundred power-looms in the West Country. Hand-loom weaving was still predominant, though weavers were commonly brought together in 'loomshops'.

Mechanization of the finishing processes met with fierce resistance. Gig-mills, for raising the nap, had long been statutorily banned (see p. 45), and, although the ban had been extensively evaded and was finally removed early in the nineteenth century, workers' opposition remained strong. Shearing machines, introduced in the late eighteenth century, were similarly resisted by the hand shearmen or croppers, most notably in the famous Luddite riots of 1811–12, but they came into widespread use in the following years. Water- or steam-powered mills were set up for both these processes.

By 1850, the West Riding had decisively increased its lead over the West Country and other woollen areas. Locational advantages in coal, iron and steam power, combined with greater commercial enterprise, enabled Yorkshire to go further ahead in the factory age. Of 1,497 woollen-spinning and weaving mills in the United Kingdom at that date, Yorkshire had 880, with over half the factory labour force of about 74,000 and around two-thirds or more of the spindles and steam power, though with only about two-fifths of the power-looms (Lancashire having more); Leeds and Huddersfield were the main centres of the finer woollen cloth manufactures, while Dewsbury and Batley specialized in coarser heavier goods, such as blankets.

At the same time, however, power-driven mills were gradually being introduced in the West Country, which still retained its reputation for fine cloth. Moreover, hand weaving, and to a lesser extent hand spinning, was still of widespread importance, and regional concentration in woollen cloth manufacture was not, therefore, so marked as in cotton: of the total of 138,000 people engaged in it at the 1851 Census, 81,000 were in the West Riding, with substantial numbers still in Lancashire, the West Country and Scotland.

Yorkshire triumphed more decisively in the worsted industry, almost totally destroying the once-flourishing manufacture in Norfolk by the mid-nineteenth century. The first worsted-spinning mill in the West Riding was built at Addingham on the River Wharfe in 1787 (following one at Dolphinholme, near Lancaster, in 1784) using water-frames. More such water-powered mills sprang up in the following years, and the first steam mill, with a Boulton and Watt engine, was built in 1793, in Leeds, spinning both worsted and cotton. By 1800 eighteen worsted-spinning mills are known to have been working in Yorkshire. Most of these early mills were water-powered and scattered in rural upland areas, but with the more rapid introduction of steam power in the early nineteenth century, the industry came to be concentrated in factory towns such as Bradford and Halifax. By the 1820s very little worsted yarn was hand spun any more; factory spinning was mostly on modified water-frames or 'throstles', though jennies were used for weft.

Mechanization of the combing process, however, proved more difficult and met with stronger resistance from the male wool-combers. Cartwright had invented a combing machine in the 1780s, but it was not until after the improvements of Heilmann, Donisthorpe, Lister, Holden and Noble in the 1840s and 1850s that this process was finally mechanized successfully. The hand combers, previously crushed in a great strike in 1825, now suffered the same fate as the hand-loom weavers.

As in cotton, weaving also was more slowly mechanized, but in the second quarter of the nineteenth century power-looms made more rapid progress, despite riots in 1825–6; by 1850 there were nearly 33,000 in the worsted industry, and hand-loom weaving was a dying trade. The industry was now heavily concentrated in Yorkshire, which had nearly 31,000 of the power-looms, 746,000 of the 876,000 factory spindles, and 97,000 of the total labour force of 104,000 in Great Britain; the Norfolk trade was almost extinct.

Comparing the woollen and worsted industries with cotton, however, it is clear that Yorkshire had been far surpassed by its great rival across the Pennines (see also p. 93). The slower growth of the factory system in these older industries perhaps accounts for the fact that male employment still considerably exceeded that of females, especially in woollen cloth manufacture, in which there were 87,000 males to 51,000 females, whereas in worsted manufacture the sexes were evenly balanced at 52,000 each; these figures included, of course, many domestic workers, especially hand-loom weavers. In factories, however, well over half the total of 154,000 employed were females, who constituted two-thirds of the 80,000 in worsted factories, though only two-fifths of the 74,000 in woollen mills. The writing was clearly on the wall for skilled men in the traditional handicrafts of combing and weaving.

The expansion of these industries led to increasing imports of raw wool, though native sheep still supplied two-thirds of requirements. By 1850 imports had risen to over 74 million lb., of which more than half now came from Australia, compared with an estimated home clip of about 135 million lb.; about a fifth of imports were re-exported, however, together with some home-grown wool (the long-established ban on raw wool exports having been removed in 1824). Exports of woollen manufactures had been ousted from their ancient predominance by cottons, but they still made a major contribution: in 1850, out of total United Kingdom domestic exports of £71.4 million, they provided £10 million, compared with cotton's £28.3 million. These two industries, in fact, far surpassed all others in the export trade, though the whole group of metals and metal manufactures had now overtaken the woollen industry (see p. 120).

Linen

Linen, as Harte has recently emphasized, was 'the most important manufactured import into pre-industrial England', and among total import values was second only to imported groceries, until overtaken by raw cotton at the end of the eighteenth century. But, as a result initially of purely fiscal requirements during the prolonged wars of the late seventeenth and early eighteenth centuries, import duties were gradually raised to a high level, thus giving protection to the English linen industry and also to those of Ireland and Scotland, which now had free access to the English market and were also encouraged by the Government through the establishment of the Board of Trustees for the Linen and Hempen Manufactures in Ireland (1711) and the Board of Trustees for Manufactures in Scotland (1727). Although imports into England from the Low Countries, Germany and Russia remained substantial, they tended to decline in the second half of the eighteenth century, being displaced by the growing Irish and Scottish manufactures and also by the developing English linen industry, which, like the paper and silk industries, was encouraged by the increasingly high import duties from 1690 onwards. From the 1740s more deliberate State encouragement was given to the industry by export bounties, followed in the second half of the century by similar financial inducements to producers of the raw materials flax and hemp.

Until recently, however, this rising English linen industry has been comparatively neglected by economic historians, though it rivalled the much better known Irish and Scottish manufactures in the eighteenth century, developing from the earlier home-spun peasant products (see p. 48). It appears, in fact, that more linen was produced in England for domestic consumption than was imported from Scotland and Ireland together. With rising population and living standards, it was in increasing demand for table linen, bedding, etc., while the commercial market for sacking, canvas and sailcloth was also expanding; linen warp yarns were also increasingly used, together with cotton weft, in the manufacture of fustians. At the same time, a substantial export trade in linens was developed, which in the 1770s accounted for about 6 per cent of the total value of British exports and ranked second only to woollens. In the period from about 1740 to 1790 English linen production expanded remarkably—it became, in fact, a major textile industry—necessitating growing imports of flax and hemp from north-west Europe and Russia, though there was a considerable increase in home-grown crops. It was a widespread industry, on a domestic basis, located mainly in the north-east, north-west and south-west but scattered also in many other areas. Much of the output continued to be sold in local markets, but larger-scale commercial organization developed in the eighteenth century.

This remarkable growth occurred, as Harte has shown, under the shelter of protection and in response to growing demand, before there was any technological revolution in the industry. Indeed, during the period of technological revolution, from the late eighteenth century onwards, the English linen industry tended ultimately to decline in relative importance. The initial breakthrough in mechanical spinning was made by Kendrew and Porthouse of Darlington in 1787; John Marshall of Leeds, aided by the engineer Matthew Murray, immediately followed with a series of technical improvements and remarkable business expansion—the firm's capital grew from £14,000 in 1794 to £272,000 by 1828—which established that city as the main centre of factory spinning; numerous flax-spinning mills were set up there and elsewhere in Yorkshire, which became 'the great seat of the Linen manufacture in England', according to Warden (1864). But although factories were also established in Lancashire and other northern countries, as well as in Dorset and Somerset, English linen manufactures were faced in the nineteenth century by growing competition not only from cotton but also from the later-mechanized Irish linen industry, located mainly in Ulster, centred on Belfast, and from the Scottish industry, mainly in Forfar and Fife, centred on Dundee. Belfast produced mostly fine linens, while Dundee specialized in coarse goods (sailcloth, sacking, etc.), spun not only from flax, tow and hemp but also (from the 1830s onwards) from jute, imported from Calcutta; other Scottish centres, however, such as Dunfermline, produced fine table linen. By the mid-nineteenth century, Belfast—where John Mulholland set up the first steam mill in 1829, exploiting the 'wet-spinning' process of the Frenchman Philippe de Girard, and James Kay of Preston—was taking the lead in linen manufacture, while its cotton manufacture declined. In 1850 Ireland had 396,000 factory spindles, Scotland 303,000 and England and Wales 265,000.

The preparatory processes of scutching, heckling, drawing and roving had also been mechanized, but power-loom weaving had made very little progress. According to the factory inspectors' returns, there were 965,000 spindles but not 1,200 power-looms in United Kingdom flax factories in 1850, with a total horse-power of about 14,000, of which 11,000 was steam; the number of factory workers was 68,000, but they were probably outnumbered by linen hand-loom weavers. Crofting in bleachfields also remained widespread, because chlorine bleaching proved much more difficult with linen than with cotton. The growth of the linen industry, however, was reflected in the growing United Kingdom exports of piece goods, which nearly quintupled to over 122 million yards between 1815 and 1850, while yarn exports also rapidly increased; the total value of such exports in the latter year was £4.8 million, just under half that of woollen exports.

Silk

It was in the silk industry, as we have previously noted, that the first typical textile mills appeared, with the introduction of silk-throwing machinery from Italy in the early eighteenth century. The famous water-powered silk-throwing mill of the Lombe brothers, built on the River Derwent, near Derby, in 1717–21—but actually preceded by Thomas Cotchett's mill also built there in 1702—was a large five-storied building, filled with machinery, like the later cotton mills. Similar mills were subsequently erected in Derby and elsewhere, particularly Macclesfield, Stockport and other towns in north Cheshire and south Lancashire, producing yarn for the manufacture of hosiery and gloves in the framework-knitting trade, for lace-making and also for weaving into ribbons, scarves and handkerchiefs, as well as for dresses and furnishings. Only the silk-throwing process, however, was at first mechanized—as later with the machine-spinning of cotton yarn—and even in the mid-nineteenth century silk weaving was still predominantly manual; though Dutch 'engine-looms' were introduced in the later eighteenth century, for multiple weaving of ribbons, especially in Coventry, they were still hand and foot operated; so too, were the Jacquard looms, brought in for patterned weaving in the first half of the nineteenth century. Power-loom weaving developed very slowly. By the mid-nineteenth century, however, the hand-loom silk weavers of Spitalfields (London), Coventry, Derby, Leek, Congleton, Macclesfield and Manchester had become almost as depressed as those in the cotton industry, with an excess of low-paid labour, including women and children.

Imports of raw silk, though growing very erratically, had more than doubled between the early 1700s and the early 1800s, when they reached around 1 million lb. They rose much more rapidly in the first half of the nineteenth century towards 7 million lb. by 1850. Exports of silk manufactures had similarly expanded in volume; in value they had reached £1.3 million. At that date, according to the factory inspectors' returns, there were over 1.2 million spindles and about 6,000 power-looms in United Kingdom silk factories, with nearly 4,000 horse-power, three-quarters of it steam; the factory labour force was about 43,000 but was greatly exceeded by hand-loom weavers, total employment in the United Kingdom silk industry in 1851 being nearly 131,000 (about three-fifths females).

Comparing these figures with those for other textiles, we can see that, although silk came a long way behind cotton and wool, it was comparable with linen. Moreover, exports of silk manufactures in 1850 were equal in value to those of coal and exceeded those of machinery and chemicals. But they had a hard struggle against French and Italian competition, especially with the gradual withdrawal of tariff protection between 1824 and 1860.

Comparative mechanization

The comparative progress of mechanization in United Kingdom textiles can be seen from the Factory Inspectors' Returns of 1850, which show very strikingly the enormous lead of the cotton industry.

Textile	Factories	Spindles	Power looms	Horse-power		Number of factory workers
				steam	water	
Cotton	1,932	20,977,017	249,627	71,005	11,550	330,924
Wool	1,497	1,595,278	9,439	13,455	8,689	74,443
Worsted	501	875,830	32,617	9,890	1,625	79,737
Flax (linen)	393	965,031	1,141	10,905	3,387	68,434
Silk	277	1,225,560	6,092	2,858	853	42,544

Hosiery

The hosiery industry, though increasingly concentrated in Nottinghamshire, Leicestershire and Derbyshire, did not alter much in technology or organization until after the 1840s, when steam power began to be applied to framework-knitting, though many hand frames had previously been brought together in workshops. The three branches of the trade—cotton, wool and worsted, and silk, which tended to be localized respectively in those three counties—were engaged in making not only stockings and socks but also gloves, caps, underwear, shirts and knitwear generally. Increasing supplies of cheaper yarn, of course, came from the textile-spinning factories, especially cotton, which merchant hosiers such as Need and Strutt, in partnership with Arkwright, played an important part in establishing. Production was greatly increased as wider markets were opened up both at home and abroad. The labour force of domestic framework-knitters was correspondingly expanded, but these workers, like hand-loom weavers, tended to become a depressed group, with a considerable labour surplus, including women and children, on miserably low wages but charged extortionate frame rents and subject to the truck system, under the control of merchant hosiers, who often subcontracted to middlemen, 'bag hosiers' and master stockingers; the number of small independent frame-owning knitters steadily declined, while some large hosiers acquired hundreds of frames, employing great numbers of workers, scattered over a wide area, though most employers in 1851 had fewer than twenty workpeople. William Felkin estimated in 1844 that there were over 48,000 frames in the whole United Kingdom industry, the vast majority in the three east midlands counties, 'giving employment to upwards of 100,000 workpeople' (including winders, seamers, sewers and others in the finishing trades), mostly domestic and widely dispersed in villages as well as in towns. This estimate, however, was much greater than the 65,000 hosiery workers (35,000 males and 30,000 females) returned in the 1851 Census, but Felkin was probably counting many part-time domestic workers, especially women and children, not returned as such in the Census.

Lace

Hand lace-making continued throughout this period to be a domestic employment for women and children in southern rural counties, but in the later eighteenth century stocking-frame knitters and frame-smiths of London and Nottingham began to modify and adapt their machines for making point-net and warp lace, and in 1808–9 John Heathcoat patented the bobbin-net machine (though, like Arkwright, he was not an entirely original inventor). He established a factory at Loughborough, Leicestershire, but in 1816, after machine-breakers had smashed his frames, he moved to Tiverton in Devon, where he established a water-powered mill and was employing 1,500 workpeople by the early 1820s. Nottinghamshire, however, remained the main centre of the industry, in which factory production—mostly of cotton-lace goods but also of silk—gradually developed, using both water and steam power; further mechanical improvements were introduced, notably by John Leavers, while the Jacquard apparatus was applied, from the mid-1830s, to the manufacture of 'figured' or 'fancy' lace. Hand-operated machines, often rented, long remained in use in homes and workshops, and small independent owners were still numerous, but there was a strong trend towards large-scale production in factories, though sub-letting was common.

This industry provides an example, like cotton-spinning, of male displacing female and child labour through mechanization, which gradually destroyed the hand-made pillow or bone lace of southern rural counties. By the mid-nineteenth century there were around 3,500 frames in the 'machine-wrought' trade, but in addition to the hands directly employed on these there were far greater numbers engaged in mending, embroidering and finishing the net, mostly domestic workers (women and children), making a total employment figure of around 140,000, according to Felkin. In this case, however, there is an even greater discrepancy between Felkin's figure and that of the 1851 Census, showing 64,000 in lace manufacture (less than 10,000 males and 54,000 females).

About half the lace and one-sixth of the hosiery production was exported, and these industries experienced sharp trade fluctuations, as both home and overseas markets were exposed to changes in fashion.

5

The Revolution in Coal and Metals

The Industrial Revolution is still, in most people's minds, associated most closely with the technological changes in the cotton industry and 'the triumph of the factory system'. But these dramatic developments came comparatively late and were dependent for their full realization upon earlier and more fundamental advances that had been made—and continued to be made—in coal, iron, power and engineering, though the prodigious growth of cotton manufactures from the 1780s onwards undoubtedly provided an immense stimulus to these other industries. Nef was, in fact, right in his emphasis upon the importance of the earlier developments in coal-mining and the industrial uses of coal or coke fuel: though they had certainly not transformed industry by the end of the seventeenth century, they had provided the essential basis for the later and more profound changes of the eighteenth and nineteenth centuries, so that W. S. Jevons was able to declare, as an obvious truth by 1860, that 'Coal commands this age'. It had, in fact, by then become the overwhelmingly predominant source of industrial fuel and power.

The coal industry
The coal output figures show how massively, in absolute terms, the increases of the earlier period were now dwarfed. From under 3 million tons in 1700, they rose to 10 million by 1800 and then to over 50 million by 1850. This increased output came from more and bigger pits and more miners; inland coalfields were opened up by the construction of canals and railways, though the Northumberland and Durham coalfield was still producing nearly a quarter of the total British output in the 1850s. Pits had been sunk to nearly 1,000 feet in this coalfield by the early nineteenth century, but the deepest in this period was Apedale pit, near Newcastle-under-Lyme in north Staffordshire, which had been driven below 2,100 feet in the 1830s. Underground workings had also been pushed out hundreds of yards from the pit bottom. By the 1840s the largest collieries in the north-east were employing 500 to 1,000 workers and were producing from

100,000 to 200,000 tons annually; Hetton colliery had nearly 1,300 workers and an annual output of about 235,000 tons in 1843. The total number of coal miners in Great Britain was also growing rapidly, from 118,000 in 1841 to 219,000 (including less than 3,000 females) in 1851.

At the same time, there were still a great many small shallow pits, 'drifts' or 'levels' into hillsides (as in South Wales) with adit drainage, as well as opencast or outcrop workings, employing small handfuls of men. But increasingly more coal was coming from the bigger deeper pits, in which more capital was being invested by landowners and mining partnerships or companies. Increased production was, in fact, made possible mainly by capital investment in improved mining technology. The most important advances were in the utilization of steam power. Steam-engines, or 'fire-engines' as they were first called, were originally developed for draining the tin and copper mines of Devon and Cornwall (see p. 110), first by Thomas Savery in the late 1690s and then by Thomas Newcomen in the early 1700s, but they quickly came into use in coal mines, enabling pits to be sunk to depths previously impossible with horse- or water-powered pumps. Hundreds of the Newcomen or 'atmospheric' engines were at work in coalfields by the end of the eighteenth century. Watt's improved engine (see pp. 110 –11) came gradually into use in the later decades, but its fuel-saving advantages were less significant in coal-mines, and the older engines predominated well into the nineteenth century.

Similarly, horse-gins (or whims) for winding coal long remained common, though Watt's rotative engine, developed in the early 1780s, and later more powerful engines, made it possible to raise coal from increasingly greater depths. By the 1840s metal cages, suspended on iron-wire ropes and running on iron guide-rods, were being introduced in the bigger pits, though coal was still being raised in most areas in free-swinging corves and baskets, and horse-gins were still to be found; the colliers, of course, went down and up in the same way. In some smaller backward pits, coal was still being carried up ladders on the backs of men, women and children.

As pit workings were driven farther outwards, more and more underground transport workers were required. Some were still carrying or dragging coal to the shaft bottom, but in the eighteenth century the primitive tramways or railways were further developed, first into cast-iron plateways, then flanged cast-iron rails were made at the Coalbrookdale ironworks in the late 1760s, and later in the century wrought-iron edge rails were introduced on which corves with flanged wheels could run. Trains of these little trucks could be pulled by pit ponies, which were increasingly introduced, but these could only operate on the main underground ways, and human 'putters' and 'drawers', often women and children—before the Mines Act of 1842—were still required for moving trucks along low passages from the coalface.

As mines became deeper and more extensive, the problem of ventilation was increased, through accumulations of chokedamp and firedamp, the latter frequently causing disastrous explosions. Additional ventilation shafts were sunk, with fires at the bottom of upcast shafts, and air was coursed through the workings by a system of stoppings or partitions; this crude furnace ventilation was still commonly used in the 1840s, though experiments were being made with air pumps and fans. Closely associated with this problem was that of lighting, for candles ignited the gases. Various safety-lamps, enclosing the flame with copper gauze and later also with glass, were invented in about 1815 by the famous chemist Sir Humphry Davy, George Stephenson and George Clanny, but naked candles long continued in use and explosions remained frequent.

The actual 'getting' or hewing of coal was still pick-and-shovel work, though gunpowder came into mining use from the late seventeenth century onwards. The hewers were the aristocrats of the industry, but their occupation was extremely arduous and dangerous, with ever-present threats of accident or death from fire, water or rock-falls. The longwall system of mining, using pit-props, gradually spread from the Midlands area, but the bord-and-pillar system remained widespread, especially in northern coalfields.

The increased coal output went to satisfy ever-growing demands, both old and new. The furnace-using industries, such as glass-making, soap-boiling, sugar-refining, brewing and brick-making, which had adopted coal or coke fuel in Nef's earlier 'industrial revolution', were now expanding much more rapidly. Production of copper, lead and tin, in which coke-fired smelting furnaces had been introduced in the late seventeenth century, was now soaring. More and more coal was also being burnt in domestic hearths, as the population exploded. A new and rapidly growing demand came from the iron industry, with successful utilization of coke fuel in both smelting and forging, finally achieved in the eighteenth century; at the same time, demand continued to rise in those numerous small metals trades, making nails, knives, files, etc., in which coal fuel had long been used. Moreover, the ever-growing numbers of steam-engines, not only in coal-mining itself but also in mining metallic ores and later in ironworks, textile factories and many other industries, greatly increased coal consumption. With the development of steam railways and steamships in the first half of the nineteenth century, demand was raised still further. That half-century also witnessed the birth and growth of the gas industry, burning increasing quantities of coal in its retorts to provide lighting for factories and streets. All these demands stimulated not only transport developments to move coal from collieries to consumers, but also the increasing concentration of industries and towns on the coalfields to reduce transport costs. Coal, not cotton, was 'King' in nineteenth-century Britain.

Most of the coal output went to the home market. Exports were gradually rising, especially in the second quarter of the nineteenth century, to over three million tons by 1850, but this was only about a third of the coastal trade, still mainly from the north-east to London but also from other coastal fields such as those of Cumberland and South Wales.

The iron and steel industry

The industry that became most closely associated with coal was the iron industry. Rising costs of timber and charcoal—even their scarcity in certain areas—had stimulated efforts to substitute coal fuel during the seventeenth century. It is uncertain what measure of success, if any, Sturtevant, Dudley and others achieved; they may possibly have experimented with charked coal, but some coals, classified subsequently as non-coking, contain relatively high proportions of sulphur and other chemical impurities, which damage the iron product, so that results were variable. Abraham Darby, who finally succeeded from 1709 onwards in smelting iron ore to produce pig- or cast-iron in a coke-fired furnace at Coalbrookdale in Shropshire, was perhaps lucky in that the local 'clod' coal was of a good coking type; he had also had previous experience with coke fuel in brass-founding and malting; and he may have used a larger furnace and a stronger blast to improve combustion. It seems, nevertheless, to have taken some years to perfect the process, and until about mid-century, as Hyde has shown, capital and fuel costs remained higher than those for charcoal furnaces. This fact, not Quaker secrecy, accounted for its slow spread beyond Coalbrookdale.

At first this coke-smelted pig-iron was used mainly in producing cast-iron goods, such as pots, kettles, fire-grates, stoves, pipes and also for cannon, steam-engine cylinders and parts of machinery—in fact there was a greatly widening field for cast-iron in the eighteenth century. For some time it was considered inferior to charcoal-smelted pig for making bar- (or wrought-) iron in the forge, as well as being dearer. But, with further cost-reducing developments and rising charcoal prices, it was more rapidly introduced from mid-century onwards, completely revolutionizing the smelting process. Improvements in the blast were particularly important, first of all by the Darbys using a Newcomen engine to pump water for the water-wheel that worked the furnace bellows; then in the 1760s the engineer John Smeaton introduced water-powered cast-iron blowing cylinders at the Carron ironworks; the famous ironmaster John Wilkinson was the first to apply the Watt steam-engine to this operation at his Broseley works in 1776; from then on, and with the introduction of Watt's double-acting engine, coke-smelting rapidly superseded the old charcoal process. By 1806 there were 221 coke furnaces (though not all in blast) and only 11 remaining charcoal ones; total pig-iron production had risen from between 15,000 and 20,000 tons per annum at the beginning of the eighteenth century to about 250,000 tons, most of this increase occurring in the last two decades of the century.

This leap in output was associated with the successful use of coal fuel in the forging process, for conversion of pig- into bar-iron, in which charcoal had still been required. Various patents were taken out, by the Wood brothers, the Cranages and others from the 1760s onwards, using refining and reverberatory furnaces for this purpose, before Henry Cort patented his famous puddling and rolling process in 1783–4. Cort also utilized a reverberatory furnace, similar to those that had long previously been used in smelting other metals; the pig-iron was separated from the coal fuel, and the flames were deflected onto the metal from the roof of the furnace; the molten metal was stirred or puddled with an iron bar through an opening in the front of the furnace—a laborious manual process, carried out in great heat—until practically all the carbon content was burnt out. The spongy ball of iron thus produced was then hammered to expel slag, before being passed through the rolling mill to produce plates or bars.

Cort's process, superseding the previously prolonged refining and hammering in the forge and saving greatly in time as well as fuel costs, was very rapidly adopted (especially as his patent was soon quashed) from the 1790s onwards, so that coal and coke fuel could now be used in all stages of iron production, from smelting the ore to manufacture of finished articles. At the same time, steam power was applied in the forge as well as at the furnace, John Wilkinson again taking the lead, in the 1780s, in using steam-engines instead of water-wheels to work tilt-hammers and rolling mills, though water power continued to be widely used for many years.

Thus the iron industry was freed from what Ashton termed the 'tyranny of wood and water', which had previously dictated its location. Furnaces and forges, especially the former, had been widely scattered in areas where timber (for charcoal) and water (for power) were available, but now the whole industry was based on coal for both fuel and power. Whereas iron ore and pig-iron had often had to be transported long distances to furnaces and forges, which were frequently separated—forges usually being nearer to the iron-manufacturing markets on the coalfields—now all processes could be concentrated on the coalfields, especially where iron ore and coal were mined in the same areas, even from the same shafts. Ironmasters, in fact, began to invest a great deal of capital in coal-mining, and combined coal and iron firms began to develop. Large integrated concerns grew up, such as the Darbys of Coalbrookdale, the Wilkinsons of Bersham, Broseley and Bradley, the Walkers of Rotherham, the Carron Company in Scotland, and the Crawshays, Homfrays and Guests of south Wales, which often had their own iron ore and coal mines, together with blast furnaces and foundries, forges, rolling and slitting mills, producing not only pig- and bar-iron but a wide range of iron goods, including steam-engines, boilers and machinery. Large amounts of capital were invested in such firms—the Coalbrookdale Company had a capital of £166,000 by 1809 and £366,000 by 1851; the

Walkers £299,000 by 1812; the Crawshays £160,000 by 1813 and £238,000 by 1835—and by the second quarter of the nineteenth century the biggest were employing several thousand men, though these dwarfed the average ironworks. Many started in a small way, but technological progress and capital requirements soon raised the threshold of entry into the industry.

The main areas in which these eighteenth-century developments occurred were Shropshire, the Black Country (mainly south Staffordshire) and south Wales, with less important areas in Derbyshire, the West Riding and Tyneside. Further technological advances occurred in the first half of the nineteenth century. Much bigger blast furnaces were built, and in 1828 James B. Neilson of Glasgow patented his hot blast—whereby air, instead of being blasted cold into the furnace, was first passed through heated pipes—which saved greatly in fuel and, by raising the temperature of combustion, permitted raw coal to be used. It resulted in a prodigious increase of Scottish pig-iron output, as the black-band ironstone and coal resources of Lanarkshire were rapidly exploited: by the late 1840s Scotland was producing more than a quarter of total British pig-iron output, which had then reached over two million tons. The hot blast was introduced more slowly into the older areas but was in fairly general use by the 1850s; little interest was shown, however, in other fuel-economizing innovations, such as the utilization of waste heat from furnaces to raise steam in boilers. Heat and by-products continued to be similarly wasted in coking ovens.

The puddling process remained basically unaltered, except for improvements such as Joseph Hall's 'wet-puddling' or 'pig-boiling' process, introduced in the 1830s, using furnace cinder to assist oxidation. In forging, James Nasmyth's famous steam hammer, invented in 1839 (patented in 1842), applied the direct force of steam and soon began to displace the old steam- or water-powered 'helve' or 'tilt' hammers in large ironworks, making possible the production of much more massive forgings, as well as being used for smaller die-stampings.

While coal provided the fuel and power source for the iron and other industries, iron became the basic constructional material for machinery, water-wheels, steam-engines, boilers, machine-tools, cranes and other industrial equipment, as well as for an increasingly wide range of small manufactures in both cast and wrought iron (see pp. 104–7). Iron, in fact, was gradually displacing other metals and wood in many constructional uses, not only in industrial machinery but also in agricultural equipment such as ploughs, harrows and rollers and the new threshing and reaping machines, horse-hoes and seed-drills. Iron pillars and beams came increasingly into use for constructing mills and other large buildings; cast-iron was also used in making water and gas pipes. From the first cast-iron rails at Coalbrookdale in the late 1760s, followed by Murdock's early experiments with steam locomotion and Trevithick's first railway locomotive in 1804, there came the nineteenth-century iron railway age; in the railway 'manias' of the second quarter of the century the demand for iron in building lines, stations, bridges and locomotives enormously increased, so that it became for a time the dominant factor in the industry's expansion. Similarly, from Wilkinson's first iron boat in the 1780s, followed by the early steamboats of Symington, Bell and others and Manby's first iron steamship in 1820, there developed a transport revolution on the seas and oceans, which further stimulated iron and engineering production, though mainly in the second half of the nineteenth century. At the same time, of course, as for coal, the movement of heavy iron goods was greatly facilitated, costs of carriage were reduced and markets were expanded by these revolutionary transport developments, which themselves were based on the revolution in coal, iron and engineering (for the close links between iron and engineering, see pp. 114–8).

The bulk of the increasing iron output went into the home market, which was now largely relieved of dependence on foreign imports. Until Cort's process finally ended dependence on charcoal, imports of bar-iron, mainly from Sweden and Russia, had gradually increased from between 15,000 and 20,000 tons annually at the beginning of the eighteenth century to between 40,000 and 50,000 by the last two decades; by the 1820s the figure had fallen to between 10,000 and 15,000 tons but then rose again to between 30,000 and 40,000 by the 1850s, because high-grade charcoal-smelted iron was still required in steel-making. Imports, however, were now vastly exceeded by exports: in the form of pig- and puddled iron, bars and rails, these had risen rapidly from negligible amounts at the end of the eighteenth century to nearly 800,000 tons by 1850; the development of overseas railways, in which British contractors and engineers played a leading role, gave an immense boost to production from the 1840s onwards, in addition to the home railway demand. Moreover, vastly increasing quantities of iron and steel were also being exported in the form of manufactures, ranging from nails, chains, cutlery and hardware of all kinds to steam-engines, railway locomotives and machinery (see pp. 119–20).

This was, in fact, the Iron Age, the age of cast and wrought iron. The Steel Age was to follow, in the second half of the nineteenth century. Steel, intermediate in carbon content between bar-iron (almost pure iron) and highly carbonized pig-iron, had long been made by the cementation process, in which pieces of wrought-iron and charcoal (carbon) were heated together in closed clay pots in a furnace, to produce blister steel, which was then reheated and hammered into shear steel (see p. 39). This, however, failed to produce steel of uniform quality throughout. In about 1740, therefore, Benjamin Huntsman a Sheffield clock-maker, invented an improved process, heating pieces of blister and shear steel together with charcoal in closed fire-clay crucibles, in a coke-fired furnace at intense heat, to produce molten steel, which was then cast into ingots; these were then forged into bars and slit into rods, for use in steel manufactures. But this process spread very slowly until the late eighteenth century, and steel long continued to be made by the older method, as well as by the Huntsman process. Moreover, by either method steel was produced in much smaller quantities and at much higher cost than cast- or wrought-iron, so that its use was limited to fairly small articles requiring a high degree of hardness, sharpness or tensile strength, such as cutlery, razors, edge-tools, swords, files and clock springs; in the railway age it came increasingly to be used for the springs of locomotives and rolling stock. As we have previously noted, high-grade charcoal-smelted bar-iron, mostly imported from Sweden and Russia, was still required in steel-making. The industry was concentrated particularly in Sheffield, which was also the main centre of cutlery manufacture.

It is somewhat misleading to segregate the primary processes of the iron industry from the closely related manufactures with which they were sometimes combined, but the Census of Great Britain in 1851 showed that there were then 27,000 iron-ore miners and 79,000 in 'iron manufacture', that is in founding and forging, excluding engineers, machine-makers, blacksmiths, nail-makers, cutlers and other metal-working trades. No women were employed in this heavy industry.

Non-ferrous metals

The emphasis upon iron in the Industrial Revolution has generally obscured the fact that by the mid-nineteenth century Britain was producing 'three-quarters of the world's copper and half of the world's lead as well as 60 per cent of the world's tin', according to J. B. Richardson. These metals had an increasingly wide range of uses. Tin was required not only in pewter and bronze but also in the new tinplate industry, in coinage, type metal and solder. Copper was used in making brass as well as bronze, in coinage, in the Birmingham 'toy' and hardware trades, in domestic kettles and pans, in industrial boilers, vats, etc., and in sheathing ships' bottoms. Lead provided shot for firearms, as well as being used more pacifically for roofing and water pipes, in type metal and solder, and also in the paint, glass and pottery manufactures. Non-ferrous metals and their alloys were also important in the new machine age, in making key parts such as journals and bearings or bushes, as well as valves, cocks, pipes, etc., for steam-engines.

Their ores were now mined much more intensively in the mountainous western and northern parts of Britain: in Cornwall and Devon, in the Mendips, in Wales, the Pennines, the Lake District and in various parts of Scotland, mainly in the south-west and west. Many more mines were sunk, to greater depths, and smelting works were established using coke fuel. Other works were also set up, such as brass-making plant, rolling mills, wire-drawing and battery works in the copper and brass industries. Increasing capital investment was required, and there was a strong tendency towards large-scale integrated organization in partnerships, companies and monopolistic combines, employing large numbers of wage-earners. The most outstanding enterprise was that of Thomas Williams, 'the Copper King', in the later eighteenth century, founded on the great Parys and Mona mines in Anglesey, with smelting, brass-making and manufacturing concerns in south Lancashire, south Wales, Flintshire, the Thames valley and Birmingham, with a central office in London and a total capital of £800,000. But there were various other companies, including the English Copper Company, the Bristol Brass Company, the Macclesfield Copper Company and the Cheadle Company, together with combines such as the Associated Smelters in south Wales, and the short-lived Cornish Metal Company in the late eighteenth century. In lead, the Beaumont and London Lead (Quaker) Companies dominated in the northern Pennines, as well as having interests in north Wales, Derbyshire and Scotland. There was, in fact, a marked contrast between these large capitalist companies in the primary processes and the host of small manufacturers who used the ingots, sheets, rods and wire which they produced, as in the Birmingham trades.

Technological developments in the mining and smelting of these metals were of crucial importance in the Industrial Revolution. Coke-smelting in reverberatory furnaces had been pioneered in the non-ferrous metals in the late seventeenth and early eighteenth centuries, and it was in the tin and copper mines of Cornwall and Devon that the Savery and Newcomen steam-pumping engines were originally developed for drainage. Subsequently Boulton and Watt found this area one of the best markets for their engines, because of their fuel-economizing advantages in a non-coal region, and the famous high-pressure Cornish engines, pioneered by Trevithick and Woolf and built at the celebrated Hayle and Perran foundries, made possible pumping and winding from ever-increasing depths; steam power and iron were also applied to stamp-mills, crushing rolls and dressing plant for preparing ores for smelting. But water-wheels, horse-gins, hand capstans and ladders long remained in use, especially in smaller mines; water power was still commonly employed also for driving hammers, rolling mills, etc., though steam power was gradually introduced.

This intensive exploitation and these technological innovations greatly increased production and exports of non-ferrous metals. The most impressive increase was in the output of copper, which rose from between 500 and 600 tons per annum in the early years of the eighteenth century to about 12,000 tons by 1850. The production of white tin rose from less than 1,500 tons annually in 1700 to between 5,000 and 6,000 tons in the 1850s. There are no very reliable statistics of early lead production, but it was perhaps about 25,000 to 30,000 tons in the early 1700s, rising to about 65,000 tons in 1850. Substantial proportions of these metals and their alloys were exported; together with non-ferrous manufactures, they were valued at £2.5 million in 1850.

Copper was not generally smelted in the main areas of production, such as Cornwall, Devon and Anglesey, because it was cheaper to ship the ore to coalfields than the coal to the ore-fields, on account of the tremendously heavy fuel consumption in the successive processes of calcining, smelting, roasting and refining. Swansea became the main centre of copper smelting, but it was also established in other places such as Bristol, Warrington and St Helens. For similar reasons the tinplate industry developed mainly in south Wales and also in the west midlands, after being introduced from Germany in the late seventeenth and early eighteenth centuries; but in this case there were close associations with the iron industry, the plates being produced from rolled bar-iron, which after undergoing a 'pickling' (or cleaning) process was then tinned. Production rose to about 4,000 tons by 1800, of which 2,500 tons were exported; by 1850 it had soared to 37,000 tons (25,000 exported), and Britain dominated the world tinplate trade. There was a rapidly growing home market for it in a wide variety of tinware manufactures, mainly in London and the midlands but also among tinmen or tinkers all over the country.

The numbers employed in mining and smelting these non-ferrous metals had become substantial. The Census of Great Britain in 1851 included over 61,000 engaged in the mining and 'manufacture' of copper, tin and lead, together with 11,000 brass-founders, excluding coppersmiths, tinsmiths, braziers and numerous other metal-working trades.

Small metal manufactures
In the wide range of small metal manufactures, of iron and steel, copper, brass and tinplate—carried on by a multitude of smiths, cutlers, nail-makers, chain-makers, button- and buckle-makers, pin-makers, file-makers, gun-makers, instrument-makers, etc.—there had been comparatively little technological or organizational change by the mid-nineteenth century. In the west midlands metal trades, for example, as Professor Court emphasized, the Industrial Revolution brought about not only the growth of large-scale capitalist undertakings in the primary smelting and forging processes but also 'a vast multiplication of small producers', working on bars, rods and sheets of metal from the rolling and slitting mills. Production for the rapidly growing markets at home and overseas could be expanded simply by increasing the number of such small manufacturing units. Just as the soaring output of factory-spun yarn in the cotton industry led to an enormous increase in the number of hand-loom weavers, so too the rapidly increasing production of iron, copper, etc., supplied a growing army of hand workers in the small metal trades. In nail-making particularly, large numbers were employed, including women and children, and like the hand-loom weavers they eventually became a depressed group on low wages in an overstocked labour market.

There were some tendencies towards mechanization in these trades. Treadle-operated stamps and screw presses with engraved dies were used from the later eighteenth century onwards in the manufacture of buttons, buckles, etc., from rolled sheet metal, and button-making machines were invented before the end of the century, though they were only very slowly introduced. The first nail-making machines similarly were invented in the 1790s, but hand forging of nails survived far into the nineteenth century. Coppersmiths, braziers and tinsmiths were still mostly hand workers in small shops, producing a wide variety of utensils, especially domestic pans, kettles, etc., though bigger concerns had developed from the 'battery works' of the sixteenth century onwards, using power-driven hammers for making larger vessels such as copper vats and cylinders for breweries, distilleries and sugar refineries. (In some industries, however, these were being replaced by iron: the 'coppers' in soap-boiling, for example, came to be made of iron.) The gradual introduction of steam-powered stamps and presses in the nineteenth century greatly widened the range of articles produced. Battery-work, however, had earlier tended to be superseded by casting, using sand moulds and wooden patterns, in numerous brass as well as iron manufactures: brass-founders or braziers became very numerous in Birmingham and other industrial areas.

These industries had long tended towards concentration on the coal-fields—though metal-working trades were numerous in London—since coal could be used without any problems in these final manufacturing processes. In the Birmingham and Black Country areas, in and around Sheffield, in the north-east around Newcastle and in south-west Lancashire around Warrington, there were increasing numbers of such workers. They were mostly organized under the domestic or putting-out system, though there were examples of factory organization such as Ambrose Crowley's works at Swalwell and Winlaton in County Durham, making nails, files, etc., in the late seventeenth and early eighteenth centuries, and the button-making factories of John Taylor and others in Birmingham, including Matthew Boulton's famous Soho factory, built in the early 1760s, which was employing hundreds of workers making buttons, buckles and a wide range of other manufactures before he entered into partnership with James Watt; similarly the pin-making factory noted by Adam Smith and the file-making factory of Peter Stubs of Warrington in the late eighteenth and early nineteenth centuries. But in all these cases workers were brought together in factories not generally to operate power-driven machines, but for subdivision and specialization of handicraft processes, for better control and regularity of output, to stop embezzlement of raw materials and to save time and labour in putting out materials and collecting finished articles.

The great majority of 'manufacturers' in these industries, however, were either small masters, with little capital and few employees, or mercantile capitalists employing larger numbers of domestic out-workers. Putting-out by nail ironmongers, etc., had significant advantages: it required comparatively little fixed plant and overheads, it was flexible in that workers could easily be taken on or stood off according to the state of trade, family labour could be utilized, the scattered labour force could not easily combine and wages were generally low. Production, therefore, was still mostly in small shops or sheds attached to the workers' homes, fitted with simple equipment and hand tools; or, where combined labour was necessary, as in chain-making, small workshops were established by employers. At the same time, however, it was possible, even under the domestic system, for labour to be highly sub-divided and specialized, as in the innumerable metal trades of the west midlands: according to Court, there were 'more than twenty nail-making districts in the Black Country, each making a different kind of nail or spike', while there were hundreds of small specialist firms making gun parts; similar sub-division and specialization existed in the making of watch parts in south-west Lancashire.

Many of these craftsmen still owned their own tools. In some of these trades, in fact, notably the Sheffield cutlery trade and the Birmingham brass and copper trades, there were numerous independent small masters, owning their own workshops, employing a few journeymen and apprentices, buying their raw materials from factors and selling their products to merchants, like the small clothiers in the West Riding woollen industry; indeed, in Sheffield the Hallamshire Cutlers' Company still preserved features of the gild system. These small masters survived in Sheffield right into the twentieth century, though large-scale factories gradually developed in the nineteenth; they often occupied parts of factories, hiring water or steam power for grinding. In Black Country nail-making and chain-making, the domestic system or small workshop remained typical, with little use of mechanical power, though for heavier forging of ploughshares, scythes, spades, etc., water-powered tilt-hammers had long been used in battery-works or plating mills.

By the mid-nineteenth century, with the gradual development of mechanization, some of these trades were in transition to the factory system, and domestic workers such as nail-makers were fighting a losing battle against power-driven machinery, together with the hand-loom weavers. In general, however, the availability of cheap labour, and the possibilities of subdivision and specialization, led to the continuance of traditional handicraft methods. Employers' returns to the 1851 Census demonstrate that in all this wide range of metal manufactures the typical firm and unit of production remained tiny, the great majority employing less than six men and many none.

Total employment, however, in all these metal-working trades was considerably greater than in the primary mining and smelting operations, in which larger-scale production had developed. There were 112,000 blacksmiths, for example, together with a total of about 43,000 whitesmiths, tinmen, coppersmiths, braziers, gunsmiths, locksmiths and anchorsmiths, nearly 29,000 nailers, over 22,000 clock- and instrument-makers, over 14,000 cutlers and file-makers, not counting button-makers, pin- and needle-makers, wire-makers and others: altogether these numerous metal-working craftsmen totalled perhaps a quarter of a million, mostly men, though women and children were employed in some trades such as nail-making.

Industrial motive power

Skilled metal-working craftsmen, such as smiths, instrument-makers and clock-makers, together with millwrights, wheelwrights, carpenters and other traditional manual workers, provided the techniques for the development of power-driven machinery in the textiles, coal, iron and other industries during the Industrial Revolution. In fact, that revolution was initially based on the more widespread application of traditional forms of power, especially water power, the increased importance of which has been inadequately appreciated, because of emphasis on the steam revolution.

We have already seen how widespread water-wheels were before the eighteenth century, in innumerable corn and fulling mills; many were also used for driving drainage pumps and sometimes also winding engines, in coal mines; they were also operating blast-furnace bellows, forge hammers and rolling and slitting mills in the iron industry, and similarly in mining, smelting and working lead, tin, copper and zinc; while many others were employed in brass or battery-works and wire-drawing, in saw-mills and paper-mills, and in pumping water for London and other towns. These uses were continued and multiplied during the Industrial Revolution. Water-wheels powered the early textile mills: Lombe's silk-throwing mill and Arkwright's water-frame mills are famous, but there were hundreds more, in which carding, scribbling, spinning and weaving machines were similarly driven by water power, as well as heckling machines for preparing flax, and dash-wheels and squeezers for washing operations in bleachworks. It is true that by 1839 the Factory Inspectors' Returns of the United Kingdom textile factories, mostly for spinning, revealed 3,051 steam-engines, totalling over 74,000 horse-power, but there were still 2,230 water-wheels, with a total of 28,000 horse-power, in textile mills. And this was the industry in which steam-powered mechanization had won its most impressive triumph.

In other industries and areas, local studies have revealed widespread and varied uses of water power. Water-wheels were commonly employed in the Potteries for grinding flints and mixing clays. It has also been demonstrated that water power was 'the foundation of Sheffield's industries', especially for working tilt-hammers and grinding wheels in the iron and steel trades, making cutlery, files, etc., as well as being used in many other manufactures, and water-wheels remained numerous and important far into the nineteenth century. Similarly in

Birmingham, Pelham has emphasized that 'the Industrial Revolution ... in so far as it was a revolution at all, was based almost entirely on the water mill'; apart from their use in corn-mills, water-wheels were used in this area mainly in blade-mills, in the cutlery and edge-tool trades and in rolling and slitting mills. Boulton and Watt erected only two of their rotative engines in the Birmingham area (outside their own works) in the period up to 1800, and, as in Sheffield, water-powered mills long remained numerous and important. In the South Wales tinplate industry likewise, water-powered plate-rolling mills continued to predominate far into the nineteenth century.

In Cornwall, in addition to the use of water power for draining tin and copper mines, working furnace bellows, etc., Rhys Jenkins discovered 'forges or hammer mills, driven by water-wheels, scattered over the county from one end to the other'. Within a few miles of Kendal, in Westmorland, scores of mills were once used in corn-milling, fulling, iron manufactures, textile mills, paper mills, snuff mills and a wide range of other trades. Similar evidence comes from the mainly rural county of Lincolnshire, where, we are told, water-mills 'must [once] have been numbered in their hundreds', used mainly for corn-milling but also for fulling, paper-making, iron manufacture, furniture-making, grinding bones for manure, etc. In Scotland, too, water power was widely used: a surviving coin token of 1797, for example, records that there were then '46 Water-Mills for Bleaching, Printing, Cotton-Works, Corn, &c. within 4 miles of Perth'.

Many of these water-wheels were no doubt small undershot wheels, with their blades dipping into running water and probably developing less than one horse-power. But even in the later Middle Ages improved types of overshot and breast wheels had been developed, in which water, diverted from a dammed-up stream or river, was channelled through sluices into the 'buckets' which the blades now formed on the wheel, so that power was obtained from force of gravity rather than from impact. The great eighteenth-century engineer John Smeaton carried out a prolonged series of practical-scientific experiments (published in the Royal Society's *Philosophical Transactions* in 1759), in which he clearly demonstrated the superiority of overshot and breast wheels; he also introduced constructional improvements, such as iron axles and gears, and is said to have doubled the efficiency of water-wheels, which he erected in many parts of the country and which were widely copied.

Other engineers, such as John Rennie, also contributed improvements, while more important advances were made by Thomas Hewes and William Fairbairn of Manchester, who built large numbers of wheels of all-iron construction and greatly improved design. Fairbairn has left accounts of his improvements and of the many wheels which he erected in both the United Kingdom and Europe; but Hewes, though only recently rescued from oblivion, was the more original inventor, being especially notable for the 'suspension wheel', in which power was no longer transmitted via the axle but from gearing round the inner circumference of the wheel, which was connected by light wrought-iron rods (rather like those of a bicycle wheel) to the axis, on which the wheel was simply suspended. Hewes, in fact, as the *Manchester Guardian* rightly observed on his death in 1832, revolutionized water-wheel design in the same way that Watt did for the steam-engine. Enormous all-iron wheels—of up to 70 or 80 feet in diameter or of immense breadth, developing as much as 100 or even 200 horsepower—were erected by his firm, by Fairbairn and other engineers, from the late eighteenth century onwards, in various parts of the United Kingdom and abroad, together with millwork and machinery. These huge wheels, in fact, were much more powerful than the early steam-engines, and they continued to be built far into the nineteenth century, though the great majority of wheels were much smaller.

These developments need stressing because they have been so largely overshadowed by the growth of steam power. Horses were also widely used in various industrial operations. They had long worked drainage pumps and winding whims for mines and were commonly employed to drive grinding wheels in potteries and glassworks (flint-mills), in tanneries (bark-mills), in lime-kilns for grinding chalk and in brickworks for mixing clay (pug-mills); they also came to be used frequently to drive carding, scribbling and spinning machinery in early textile horse-mills. There are also references to the industrial applications of wind power—commonly used, for example, in oil-mills or seed-crushing mills and also in land drainage, as in the Lincolnshire and East Anglian fens; occasionally also in paper-mills—but it was in corn-milling that windmills remained most numerous.

Attention has been too much concentrated on the large and generally later steam-powered urban factories in textiles, on the 'dark satanic mills', with their smoking chimneys, in the factory-reform period, and not until fairly recently have detailed researches been made into early factories—and those mainly textile—so that there has been comparative neglect of the extent and importance of other forms of power, of rural as well as urban mills, of small factories, of factories in which premises and power were shared and of non-textile factories. The factory system evolved very gradually, with overlapping development of various forms of power, and the triumph of steam came much later than has been generally supposed. Indeed if the Industrial Revolution is located in the period 1760–1830, as it frequently is, then there are good grounds for regarding it as the Age of Water Power.

The steam-engine had originated in scientific experiments into atmospheric pressure, etc., during the seventeenth century, but early efforts at constructing practical engines, such as those by the Earl of Worcester and the Frenchman

Denys Papin, had proved unsuccessful. It seems very probable, however, that both Thomas Savery and Thomas Newcomen, who built the first 'fire-engines' to be successfully used in industry, were not unacquainted with these earlier experiments. Savery's engine, patented in 1698, was intended for pumping water from the tin and copper mines of Cornwall and Devon. It used both steam and atmospheric pressure: first steam from a coal-fired boiler was condensed in the cylinder, creating a vacuum; atmospheric pressure then forced water up a pipe from the mine into the cylinder; and finally the water was forced from the cylinder by admission of steam, or the water could simply be permitted to run out. In the latter form it came into fairly widespread use not only in mines and waterworks but also for pumping water to drive water-wheels in textile and other mills in the later eighteenth century, and was not, as has often been stated, abandoned as a failure early in the century.

There is no doubt, however, that it was soon eclipsed by Newcomen's engine, invented about 1705, also originally for the Devon and Cornish mines. It used the piston-and-cylinder principle, but its power stroke came only from atmospheric pressure, steam being used simply to create a vacuum by condensation in the cylinder, in which the piston was then forced down by the atmosphere. The piston was connected to one end of a rocking beam, from the other end of which pump-rods were suspended, and when steam was again admitted into the cylinder the weight of these pulled down the beam, thus raising the piston at the other end: so an up-and-down pumping motion was achieved. This 'atmospheric engine' came into widespread use during the eighteenth century not only in the ore mines of Devon, Cornwall and elsewhere but far more numerously in coal mines: Harris has estimated that around two thousand such engines were built during that century, for many industrial purposes. Until the 1780s, however, it was used simply as a pumping engine, with reciprocating motion. It had a voracious fuel consumption on account of the alternate heating and cooling of the cylinder and was only a really economic proposition on or near coalfields or where coal could be carried by water at not too prohibitive a cost.

It was this fuel problem that set James Watt thinking in the 1760s. Watt was a highly skilled instrument-maker, employed in Glasgow University, where he associated closely with Dr Joseph Black, discoverer of the latent heat of steam, and with Dr John Robison and other natural philosophers. After prolonged thought and experiment, he eventually in 1765 hit on the idea of a separate condenser, into which the steam could be exhausted, so that the cylinder could be kept permanently hot, thus cutting fuel consumption by two-thirds to three-quarters. It took him several years, however, with aid from John Roebuck of the Carron ironworks, before he could make a practical industrial engine and he did not take out a patent till 1769. After Roebuck's bankruptcy, he was fortunate in obtaining a new partner, Matthew Boulton, of the Birmingham Soho works, with whose aid and that of the great ironmaster John Wilkinson he was eventually able to achieve success; Wilkinson's improved boring engine was of crucial importance in production of accurate cylinders. Boulton and Watt did not make steam engines themselves until 1795, but obtained a fuel-saving royalty on engines built by local iron-founders and smiths to their specifications; but they supplied special parts such as valves, while nearly all the cylinders were made by Wilkinson, and they also provided skilled engine erectors, since it was a great problem to get the necessary accuracy in construction and fitting of parts before the development of precision engineering (see pp. 114–8).

In addition to introducing the separate condenser, Watt employed the direct action of steam above the piston instead of atmospheric pressure, but his first engines were single-acting, like the Newcomen engines, with working power applied only on the down stroke. And they were still only reciprocating pumping engines, finding their best market in the tin and copper mines of Devon and Cornwall, where their fuel economy was a great attraction; they came much more slowly into use in coal mines, where fuel was cheap and where their higher capital costs and royalty payments were a deterrent. Watt's engine was also used, like those of Savery and Newcomen, to pump water for water-wheels. Its first use other than for pumping water was by John Wilkinson, to work his blast-furnace blowing cylinders (see p. 98).

Protected in 1775 by special Parliamentary extension of his patent to 1800, Watt introduced further improvements in the early 1780s. The most important, patented in 1781, was for rotative action—his famous 'sun-and-planet' geared motion, invented to get round a scandalous patent snatched by a rival who had stolen his idea for using a crank. This, together with further patents for double-action in 1782 and parallel motion in 1784, meant that the driving force of steam, working both ways on the piston, could now be applied to machinery of all kinds without an intermediate water-wheel, though still via the rocking beam.

These inventions heralded the advent of the Steam Age. Though for many years water power still predominated, steam-engines were put to an ever-widening range of industrial uses. In addition to those of Boulton and Watt, Newcomen engines—many adapted to rotative motion, with connecting-rod, crank and fly-wheel—remained in common use, while Watt's patents were pirated by numerous engine-makers, despite legal prosecutions, before the market was finally thrown open in 1800. Researches have shown that in areas such as Cornwall and Lancashire, where steam power was being most rapidly introduced, Boulton and Watt engines probably accounted for no more than a third or a quarter of the total.

John Wilkinson was naturally one of the first to adopt Watt's rotative engines, for driving tilt-hammers and rolling and slitting mills in his ironworks (see p. 99), again demonstrating the importance of the close relationships between iron, coal, steam power and engineering. Other ironmasters followed suit, though water power long remained in use, and, as we have seen, it was not until 1839 that Nasmyth applied steam directly to the forge-hammer. The most important market for Watt engines, in addition to the south-western tin and copper mines, was in Lancashire, where powered mule-spinning was being rapidly developed from the 1790s onwards (see p. 82), and numerous other makers of steam-engines, notably Bateman and Sherratt of Salford, were doing a roaring trade, with a good deal of pirating; steam was being applied not only to carding and spinning but also to calico-printing and calendering machines, to washing and squeezing (mangling) machines in bleachworks and to grinding logwood, fustic, etc., in dyeworks, while the growing demand for coal in these works and as domestic fuel in the rapidly growing towns led to increasing use of mine-drainage and winding engines.

At the end of the eighteenth century, however, the extent of steam-powered mechanization was very limited. Until the 1780s it had been restricted almost entirely to mine-drainage and other pumping operations. In the last two decades, particularly in the 1790s, it had begun to make striking advances in cotton-spinning and to a lesser extent in iron-smelting and forging and also in brewing; a few engines had been introduced into other textile processes and also into flour-milling, pottery manufacture and some other industries (as we shall see in later sections). But steam-engines were vastly outnumbered by water-wheels, while the great majority of manufactures were still handicrafts.

There are no really reliable statistics of total steam power for the ensuing period. By 1800, when Boulton and Watt's patent monopoly expired, they had erected some 500 engines, with a combined horse-power of only about 7,500, out of a total which can hardly have been more than three or four times as great. Harris has conservatively estimated that there were about 1,200 steam-engines of all kinds in use at the end of the century. From then on engine-makers proliferated in all the main industrial towns, but there are no figures of the total number of engines nor of total horse-power for the next half-century. It is only for the textile industry, from the factory inspectors' returns following the 1833 Factory Act, that we have statistics of any reliability (and these have to be used very cautiously because of the problems of comparing nominal with indicated horse-power).

HORSE-POWER USED IN TEXTILE FACTORIES

Year	Cotton		Woollen and worsted		Flax, jute and hemp		Silk	
	Steam	*Water*	*Steam*	*Water*	*Steam*	*Water*	*Steam*	*Water*
1838	46,826	12,977	17,389	10,405	7,412	3,678	2,457	928
1850	71,005	11,550	23,345	10,314	10,905	3,387	2,858	853
1856	88,001	9,131	30,963	9,842	14,387	3,935	4,360	816

Most of the factories were in the cotton industry and were mostly for spinning; power-loom weaving did not develop rapidly until the second quarter of the nineteenth century and then mainly in cotton. The worsted industry, as we have seen, followed fairly closely behind, but the other textiles were comparatively slow in adopting the new mechanical innovations, particularly in weaving; the triumph of the steam-powered factory was by no means complete at mid-century even in textiles, where most such factories had been established.

Outside textiles, however, there is only very scrappy information on steam power in the first half of the nineteenth century. Local statistical estimates for London, Birmingham, Manchester and other Lancashire towns and also for Glasgow show that cotton continued to predominate in the application of power-driven machinery and that, outside the textiles, coal, iron and engineering industries, steam power had spread to only a limited extent, though it was also significant in water-pumping, brewing, saw-milling, corn-milling and other grinding operations. These local figures are confirmed by the first national returns of factories and workshops in 1871, which show that even then the steam power in textile-spinning and weaving factories (475,247 horse-power) was about half the manufacturing total (976,940 horse-power)—more than half if we add the returns for bleaching, dyeing and calico-printing—while the figure for cotton mills alone (300,480 horse-power) was nearly a third of the total. (The mining of coal and metallic ores, however, was not included in the returns of factories and workshops.) It is clear that the steam revolution had so far been mainly in textiles. The only other industries, apart from coal, in which steam power had been introduced on anything like the same scale were the metal manufactures, predominantly iron-smelting, founding, forging and engineering, with a combined horse-power (329,683) between a quarter and a third of the total. Outside these fields, in the whole wide range of other industries—clothing, leather, boot and shoe manufacture, food and drink, building, wood-working, small metal manufactures, glass, pottery, chemicals, paper-making, printing, bookbinding and many other trades—steam power had been introduced to only a comparatively limited extent. At the same time, these statistics demonstrate the overwhelming predominance of steam over water power by this date, though the latter, totalling 55,620 horse-power, was still by no means negligible.

While the quantity of steam power was increasing, the quality of steam technology continued to be improved, in association with iron and engineering. By the early nineteenth century all-iron engines of more elegant design and superior construction were replacing the previously crude and cumbersome types. Watt's prolonged patent appears to have hampered technical progress, though atmospheric engines of the old type continued to be built even after 1800, particularly for coal-mines. Watt had been opposed to high steam pressures because of the danger of explosions, but with improvements in boiler-making and design, such as rolled wrought-iron plates, improved riveting and tubular construction, it became feasible to develop high-pressure engines. Most of these, however, remained condensing beam engines, of which the most notable was the Cornish pumping engine, pioneered by Trevithick and Woolf, though direct-acting types—with piston and connecting-rod acting directly on the crank—were pioneered, mainly for steamboats, by engineers such as Symington, Maudslay and Penn. Most early marine engines, however, were of the beam type, which, in various improved forms, both reciprocating and rotative, developed by Maudslay, Murray and many later engineers, also continued to predominate in industrial operations. Power and efficiency could be greatly increased by 'compounding', that is by using two cylinders, the first high-pressure cylinder exhausting into the second low-pressure one; Woolf was the main pioneer, but compound engines did not become common until the second half of the nineteenth century.

The most striking advance, however, was the development of the high-pressure non-condensing engine by Trevithick (and by Evans in the United States), in which the vacuum was dispensed with and steam was simply exhausted into the atmosphere. After Trevithick's 1802 patent, his engine began to be put to various industrial uses, but its most revolutionary application was in the steam railway locomotive. Murdock and Watt had recognized the possibility of steam locomotion but had not developed it, and it was left to Trevithick to build the first such locomotive to run on iron rails, at Penydaren in south Wales, in 1804. With improvements such as Stephenson's multi-tubular boiler and improved draught from exhausting the steam up the chimney, as in the famous *Rocket* of 1829, Trevithick's original 'puffer' started a transport revolution.

Mechanical engineering

All the developments so far surveyed in the steam revolution were closely interrelated and mutually stimulating. Steam-engines were used to drain mines, which supplied coal for smelting and forging iron, which was used in making not only the steam-engines themselves but also numerous industrial machines, which were driven by steam-engines, fuelled by coal; as steam railways and steamships developed, transport also became closely integrated into this industrial complex, based on coal, iron and engineering.

The development and construction of steam-engines and also of water-wheels, and of all kinds of mills and machinery, depended upon the growth of mechanical engineering. The early mechanical engineers—the term only began to come into industrial use in the second half of the eighteenth century—were recruited from a medley of existing trades, working in wood, iron and other materials. Millwrights had long been building wind- and water-powered mills of all kinds and were accustomed to constructing, installing and repairing not only the prime movers but also the shafting and gearing and often also the machinery which they drove; most of this work was in wood, and carpenters, joiners and wheelwrights could turn their hands to it, as more mills were built. As brass and iron came increasingly into use, smiths of all kinds—blacksmiths, tinsmiths, coppersmiths, etc.—together with brass-founders and iron-founders were called upon for casting or forging machine parts. Clock-makers and instrument-makers were of particular importance—Smeaton and Watt, for example, were both originally instrument-makers—because of their practical-scientific skills with metal-working tools such as lathes, drills, and wheel- or gear-cutting engines, with which they were able to construct what John Kennedy, the Manchester cotton-spinner and machine-maker, called 'their more accurate and scientific mechanism'.

The steam-engine was particularly important in the evolution of engineering, being a more complex industrial machine than any previously in use and requiring more precise methods of construction for pistons, cylinders, valves, condensers, air-pumps, etc., as well as stronger and more efficient boilers. The early engines were rudimentary, with much timber-work and copper boilers, and Newcomen's blacksmith skills no doubt sufficed for their making, but soon iron-founders like the Darbys of Coalbrookdale began to play an important role, in casting cylinders and other parts and in boiler-making; many iron-founders, in fact, later evolved into steam-engine makers and 'machine-makers' or mechanical engineers, and sometimes combined millwrighting with these activities. We have already emphasized the importance of Wilkinson's cylinder-boring engine in the development of Watt's engine. But boring mills were not new: wooden water-pipes, for example, had been bored by water power since the sixteenth century, and similar techniques were applied to the boring of iron; John Smeaton had developed an improved boring engine, though it was less accurate than Wilkinson's. The skilled metal-workers in Boulton's Soho factory, using lathes, etc., were able to make the more delicate steam-engine parts, such as valves, and eventually, in 1795, the Soho Foundry was built for making entire engines. Birmingham, the Black Country and Shropshire therefore became key areas in the evolution of engineering, the work of the Darbys and Wilkinson being carried further by other iron-founders; Rastrick's foundry at Bridgnorth, for example, played a similarly significant role in the early development of Trevithick's high-pressure engine.

London was another important engineering area, which, however, has been comparatively neglected. Here there were considerable numbers of highly skilled metal-workers, clock-makers and instrument-makers, including such famous names as Dollond, Ramsden and Harrison. Their light metal-working tools could be prototypes for heavy industrial machines, and it is not surprising therefore to find such developments occurring in London. Henry Maudslay, for example, towards the end of the eighteenth century, developed the heavy all-iron 'self-acting' lathe, with a slide-rest (a device of much earlier continental origin), and John Clement, another metropolitan engineer, produced further improvements, so that highly accurate turning and screw-cutting were now possible. Maudslay further laid the foundation for precision engineering with his production of true-plane metal surfaces, a measuring machine accurate to one ten-thousandth of an inch, and standard gauges. Moreover, Maudslay collaborated with Joseph Bramah, another outstanding London engineer—the 'father of hydraulic engineering'—in pioneering mass-production with specialized metal-cutting machine-tools for making locks. And shortly afterwards he was similarly involved, together with Sir Samuel Bentham and Marc Isambard Brunel, a French refugee, in the more famous mass-production of standardized pulley-blocks for the Navy. Other outstanding engineers including Rennie, Donkin, Holtzappfel, Penn and many more had their workshops in London, which became the most important centre of engineering in the country by the early nineteenth century, producing machine-tools, steam-engines (including marine-engines) and a wide variety of machinery. Maudslay's works, in fact, became a Mecca for aspiring young engineers and a seed-bed of engineering talent.

With the spread of mechanization and the factory system in Lancashire, there was a prodigious development of engineering in that area, especially in and around Manchester, to produce the jennies, water-frames, mules, power-looms, calico-printing machines, etc., of the rapidly growing cotton industry, and also the water-wheels and steam-engines to drive them. Machine-making firms mushroomed into existence from the 1780s onwards, together with iron-founding, mill-wrighting and steam engine-making concerns, such as Bateman and, Sherratt, Hewes & Co., and Peel, Williams & Co., which were each employing several hundred men by the 1820s. These were followed by more famous engineers, including Richard Roberts, William Fairbairn, James Nasmyth and Joseph Whitworth, but these were only the most outstanding among a large number; by the early 1840s nearly a hundred firms were listed in Manchester and Salford directories under various headings comprising what may be called the engineering group. Numerous engineering concerns, including some large ones, had also sprung up in other towns of Lancashire, which had now become the main engineering area of the country. A high degree of specialization developed in textile machine-making, as well as in the manufacture of machine-tools; some firms even specialized in making machine parts, such as rollers and spindles for spinning machines, though many were still general engineering concerns.

Roberts is most famous for his self-acting mule and other textile machinery, but he was equally outstanding as a machine-tool maker and locomotive engineer and as another pioneer of mass-production methods, for making standardized parts of textile machinery and railway locomotives in the 1820s and 1830s. Nasmyth, equally famous for a particular invention, that of the steam hammer

(1839), proceeded further in these developments, with mass-production of machine-tools and primitive assembly-line manufacture of locomotives, etc. Whitworth, though best-known of all, was not the original pioneer of standardization he is often said to have been, but a great propagandist and practitioner of it, following in Maudslay's footsteps, and becoming the most outstanding machine-tool maker of his day. Fairbairn, on the other hand, was a great general engineer, producing millwork, water-wheels, steam-engines, boilers, bridges, cranes, etc., and becoming also a leading locomotive manufacturer and steamship builder, with works at Millwall on the Thames, as well as in Manchester. These firms were each employing one or two thousand men by the 1850s, with large numbers of power-driven machine-tools.

The production of machine-tools, or machines to make machines, was of fundamental importance in the first half of the nineteenth century. Murray of Leeds and Fox of Derby were among other firms also outstanding in this field. Not only were the existing lathes, drills, boring and gear-cutting engines greatly improved, but new ones such as planing, shaping, slotting and milling machines were invented and developed, so that wrought-iron could be cut and shaped far more rapidly, accurately and cheaply than by the previously laborious hand processes using hammer, chisel and file. It now became possible, with standard gauges and templates, to mass-produce machine parts, fitting together with perfect accuracy—a far cry from Watt's early days. As a Parliamentary Committee on Exportation of Machinery commented in 1841, '[machine] tools have introduced a revolution in machinery, and tool making has become a distinct branch of mechanics, and a very important trade, although twenty years ago it was scarcely known'. Britain had now really entered the Machine Age.

It was in Britain, not in the United States, that this revolution began, though Whitney, North and others did develop mass-production of firearms and light wood-working machinery in the same period. America was far behind Britain in the early production of iron and the development of heavy industrial machine-tools, which formed the basis of standardized mass-production, but the achievements of British engineers in this field have been largely overlooked or under-estimated, most notably by Habakkuk, who has wrongly given most of the credit to the Americans. In the second half of the century, American engineers certainly did take the lead in many fields, but that, as we shall see, is a later story.

Some of the great engineers of the Industrial Revolution, notably Smeaton, Telford, Rennie, the Brunels and the Stephensons, were eminent as both civil and mechanical engineers—in building roads, bridges, canals, railways, docks and harbour-works, as well as mills, engines and machinery. With their civil engineering achievements we are not directly concerned, but, as we have previously emphasized, these were of immense importance in the transport and marketing of industrial raw materials and manufactures—in the transport revolution that was part of the Industrial Revolution—whilst their building gave a tremendous boost to the iron, brick-making and other industries. At the same time, they gave rise to new branches of iron and engineering construction, in locomotive manufacture and shipbuilding. We have already noticed that several of the great mechanical engineers of the early nineteenth century, such as Roberts, Fairbairn, Nasmyth and, of course, the Stephensons, found a rapidly expanding market in the making of railway locomotives. It was not until the second half of the century that the railway companies began to establish their own locomotive workshops, at towns such as Crewe, Swindon, Derby and Horwich, so meanwhile there was a great new engineering field to be developed, both at home and abroad. Some of the above firms, in fact, were already tending by mid-century to specialize in locomotive building.

It is difficult to make a precise estimate of the total number engaged in mechanical engineering, because of the problem of definition. Many iron-founders, for example, were involved in it (see p. 115); so, too, were mill-wrights—there were about 10,000 in the 1851 Census of Great Britain—ranging from traditional craftsmen for water-mills or wind-mills to large engineering concerns such as Fairbairn's. But the distinctive category of 'engine- and machine-makers' included over 48,000, together with about 7,000 'tool-makers' and 'others dealing in tools and machines'; to these we might add 7,500 boiler-makers, while there were more than 14,000 undefined 'mechanics', etc. Obviously these key craftsmen were becoming a sizeable section of the labour force, with an importance, moreover, out of proportion to their number.

The main concentrations of engine and machine makers were in Lancashire and Cheshire (over 14,000), the West Riding (nearly 6,000), and London (over 6,500), with smaller numbers in the west midlands, the north-east, west-central Scotland and scatterings elsewhere. They were clearly very closely associated with the coal, iron, textile and other industries, but in rural areas, too, especially in the eastern counties, iron-founding and engineering firms sprang up—as Booker has shown in Essex—to provide agricultural tools, machinery and prime movers.

The 1851 Census figures also give some indication of the varying sizes of engineering firms. Of the 1,044 engine-, machine- and tool-making employers who made returns, over half (588) had less than 10 men, while another 193 either had no men or did not state the number; but at the other end of the scale 35 had over 100, including 14 with 350 and upwards. There was thus a marked contrast between the large number of small firms and the relatively few big concerns, which in aggregate appear to have employed the greater part of the labour force and were coming to dominate the industry.

Shipbuilding

The building of steamships was another new industry, also developing in close alliance with iron and engineering, which provided the plates for hulls and boilers, together with marine engines (see pp. 113–4). The steamship, in fact, was the complement of the railway locomotive in the transport revolution. But this revolution proceeded more slowly on sea than on land. The early prototypes of Symington, Fulton and Bell in the late eighteenth and early nineteenth centuries were wooden hulled, and it was not until 1820 that the *Aaron Manby* heralded the iron steamship age. The first such ships, moreover, were small paddle-wheelers, with a high coal consumption per ton mile and a limited cargo capacity—even in 1850 the average steamer was only about 140 tons—so they could only compete with sailing ships in river, coastal and cross-channel services to Ireland and Europe. Though they began to make voyages in the Mediterranean, on the Atlantic, to India and to the Far East in the second quarter of the nineteenth century, their coal requirements for such long distances so reduced their cargo space as to make them generally uneconomic; for this reason, steam was often used only as an auxiliary to sails.

Gradually, however, improvements were introduced in iron construction and marine engineering, making possible larger more powerful steamships. By mid-century iron hulls and screw propulsion were rapidly ousting wooden paddle-wheelers, while a few iron-hulled sailing ships were also being built. By that time some sizeable yards had been established for building steamships, such as Laird's on Merseyside, Napier's on Clydeside and Fairbairn's on the Thames, as well marine engineering firms such as Maudslay's and Penn's in London, Fawcett's in Liverpool, and Scott's, Caird's and others on the Clyde.

Despite these achievements, however, the steamship revolution was only just beginning. The total British sailing tonnage of 3.4 million (net) registered tons in 1850—having risen from 1.3 million in 1788—dwarfed the 168,000 tons of steam-shipping, and traditional shipwrights, caulkers, sawyers, sail-makers and rope-makers, in yards great and small all around the coast and up rivers, still greatly outnumbered the new iron shipbuilders, platers, riveters, marine engineers and boiler-makers. The great majority of the 31,000 men employed in ship, boat and barge building in the 1851 Census of Great Britain must have been wood-working craftsmen. Moreover, the typical shipbuilding firm remained small: of the 317 such firms who made returns in 1851 (England and Wales), only thirteen stated that they were employing a hundred men or more, and over half had less than twenty.

Exports of metals and metal manufactures

We have already noted the massive increase in the tonnage of iron exports during the first half of the nineteenth century (see p. 101). Britain also exported substantial amounts of non-ferrous metals, whilst a wide variety of manufactures—ranging from small items such as nails and buttons to large machines, made of iron and steel and non-ferrous metals and alloys—were also exported in growing quantities. At first prohibitions were imposed upon exports of many kinds of machinery and tools, to prevent foreigners from acquiring knowledge of more advanced British technology and thus from competing with our manufactures; but these proved impossible to enforce, whilst they also discriminated against the growing engineering industry, as well as coming into conflict with developing free-trade ideas, so they were relaxed in 1825 and finally abolished in 1843. (There was also a ban on emigration of skilled artisans, equally unenforceable, abolished in 1824.)

Exports of all kinds of machinery were now free to expand; in fact a good deal had been smuggled out previously. But as yet they were not of great significance, compared with exports of pig- and wrought-iron (bars, sheets and rails). In 1850 iron and steel exports were £6.2 million, hardwares and cutlery £2.9 million, machinery £1 million, making a total of £10.1 million, while exports of non-ferrous metals and manufactures totalled £2.5 million, so that the whole metallurgical group of industries contributed £12.6 million out of the £71.4 million total of United Kingdom domestic exports in that year. This was still far below the textiles figure (£44.4 million of piece goods and yarn, with a further £2.5 million of clothing, hats, etc.), but it was rapidly increasing.

6

The Chemical Revolution

The Industrial Revolution is still usually thought of in terms of power-driven machinery, but in fact it was chemical as well as mechanical. Just as mechanical power and engineering were of general importance in their varied industrial applications, so too the developing chemical industry supplied an increasing variety of products to a widening range of manufactures. In textiles, as we have noted, chemical innovations such as vitriol 'sours', synthetic soda and chlorine bleach were as vital as spinning and weaving machines; even earlier, the manufactures of alum and copperas had developed mainly to supply mordants for dyeing (see pp. 34–35). In the eighteenth century, the chemical experimentations of John Wilson, Thomas Henry and Charles Taylor in Manchester made further important contributions to cotton dyeing as well as to bleaching and calico-printing, while manufacturers in other areas, such as Benjamin Gott and John Marshall of Leeds, were equally interested in the applications of chemistry to woollens and linens.

In other industries, too, chemical products were of basic importance, as in the soap, glass, pottery and paper manufactures, with their various requirements of alkalis, salt, glazes, colours and bleaching materials. Chemical processes or products were also involved in the assaying and refining of metals and in the manufacture of metal alloys, in tinplating and other metallurgical processes, in the manufacture of gunpowder and of oils and paints, in brewing, distilling and the manufacture of mineral waters, in tanning and in the production of a wide variety of pharmaceuticals: in fact, as Joseph Parkes emphasized in his five volumes of *Chemical Essays* in 1815, almost all manufactures were in some way 'dependent upon chemistry for their improvement and successful practice'. In these industrial chemical processes above all, one can see innumerable examples of the developing relationships between science and technology, though traditional empirical practices were still widespread.

The heavy chemical industry

Obviously there is no space here to deal with all these ramifications, but we shall briefly examine developments in the production of the most important chemicals—salt, vitriol, soda and chlorine bleach—upon which the heavy chemical industry of the nineteenth century came to be based. Salt, in addition to its importance in preserving and flavouring food, became one of the most important industrial-chemical raw materials, particularly in the manufacture of soda and chlorine bleaching powder. Its production in this country was already well established at North and South Shields, on the Firth of Forth and in other coastal areas, where sea water was evaporated in large iron pans, using coal fuel; salt-boiling was similarly carried on at the Droitwich and Cheshire brine springs, and from the late seventeenth century rock-salt was mined in the latter area. Production in Cheshire expanded enormously during the Industrial Revolution—from 15,000 tons in 1732 to 500,000 tons by 1840—mainly as a result of the rapid growth of the cotton industry, with its increasing demand for chemicals: in fact, the salt–coal–cotton nexus made Merseyside the main industrial-chemical area in the country, though chemical manufactures were also developed elsewhere, as in London, on Tyneside and in the Glasgow area.

Vitriol (sulphuric acid) manufacture was similarly stimulated by the revolution in textiles, coming into use not only as a bleaching sour (instead of buttermilk) but also in the manufacture of chlorine bleaching powder and synthetic soda, as well as in other industrial chemical processes, such as 'pickling' or de-scaling metals. Production was enormously increased with the introduction in the 1740s of the lead-chamber process (in place of Joshua Ward's earlier glass apparatus) by Dr John Roebuck and Samuel Garbett, who established works in Birmingham and at Prestonpans in Scotland; in the second half of the century, vitriol works were set up in other areas, such as London, Lancashire and Yorkshire. In this process, sulphur and nitre (saltpetre) were burned in huge lead-lined chambers or 'houses', to produce sulphur dioxide, which dissolved in water to form sulphuric acid; this was then concentrated by heating and evaporation. Subsequently the process was improved by blowing steam and air into the chambers, which were built of ever-increasing size, while sulphur was produced from pyrites, in place of Sicilian imports.

The natural alkalis, potash and soda, had long been used not only in bleaching but also in soap, glass and other manufactures. They were obtained mainly from vegetable ashes: potash mostly from wood ashes, soda from kelp (burnt seaweed) or barilla (burnt *salsola soda*, a Mediterranean sea-shore plant). Increasing quantities of potash and barilla had to be imported, at rising costs, though a considerable kelp manufacture developed on the western coasts of Scotland and Ireland. Numerous efforts were therefore made to produce synthetic or artificial soda from salt—to convert sodium chloride to sodium carbonate—and several patents were taken out in the 1770s and 1780s, but it was the process patented in 1791 by the French chemist Leblanc which formed the basis of the nineteenth century alkali or soda manufacture; in fact it was a complicated series of processes, beginning with the reaction of salt and sulphuric acid to produce sodium sulphate (salt cake), which was then heated with charcoal and limestone or chalk to form crude soda (black ash), which was then lixiviated with water and crystallized into the final product.

The manufacture was established first of all on Tyneside by William Losh and others in the late eighteenth and early nineteenth centuries, Cooksons of Jarrow eventually becoming the biggest concern; Tennant's of St Rollox, Glasgow, followed, in connection with their production of bleaching powder and sulphuric acid for textiles; and then from the 1820s onwards Muspratt, Gamble and others established large works on Merseyside, at St Helens, Widnes and Runcorn. The 'alkali trade' became strongly localized in these areas—in 1864, of 84 soda makers, 38 were in south Lancashire and north Cheshire and 19 on Tyneside—and production was increasingly concentrated in the biggest firms. As a result of these developments, imports of barilla had practically ceased by mid-century, while the Scottish and Irish kelp industry rapidly declined.

Salt and sulphuric acid, together with manganese and lime, were also the raw materials for production of chlorine bleaching powder. Here again, foreign chemists, the Swede Scheele and the Frenchman Berthollet, made the basic discoveries of the gas chlorine and its bleaching properties in the 1770s and 1780s, but it was in Britain that chlorine bleaching was most rapidly developed, especially in the Lancashire cotton industry (see p. 84). Gaseous chlorine bleaching was highly dangerous and difficult, so bleach liquor was made by absorbing the gas in water, an alkaline solution or lime-water, and eventually, by the end of the century, Macintosh and Tennant developed the manufacture of bleaching powder (calcium hypochlorite). At first most bleaching firms made their own liquid bleach, but bleaching powder was eventually added to the products of chemical works, together with vitriol and other acids, soda, dyestuffs, etc., which could all be produced in a series of integrated processes. Output of bleaching powder soared from the 1820s onwards, while costs were dramatically reduced. Manufacture of all these chemicals was stimulated by the gradual reduction and final abolition in 1825 of the onerous excise duty on salt, which had previously encouraged utilization of the waste residues of bleaching and soap-making for extraction of alkalis.

Since the heavy chemical industry was dependent particularly upon salt as a raw material and coal as fuel, the locational advantages of Merseyside were obvious, especially as it was also in close proximity to much the biggest and most rapidly expanding market for all these chemicals, in the Lancashire cotton industry. Nor is it surprising to find Merseyside becoming the main area of soap and glass manufactures, in which soda was also a basic requirement; moreover, soap was consumed in large quantities in the repeated washing operations in bleachworks. Tyneside was another major chemical area, also with soap and glass, and there were a few large works elsewhere, such as Tennant's at St Rollox, Glasgow, and Chance's at Oldbury, Birmingham, the former associated particularly with textiles and the latter with glass manufacture.

Production of alum was also greatly stimulated by the textiles revolution, being mainly used in dyeing, as well as in leather, paper and other manufactures. In addition to the older works at Whitby and the Isle of Wight, production was developed in Scotland, using aluminous shales discovered at Hurlet near Paisley and Campsie in Stirlingshire, favourably located for coal fuel. It was not until Peter Spence's patent of 1845, however, using sulphuric acid to form aluminium sulphate, that there was any significant change in methods of manufacture from those dating back to the sixteenth century. Establishing works at Pendleton near Manchester, he was soon to become the largest alum producer in the world.

Soap-making

Soap-boiling, with animal fats (tallow) or vegetable oils, soda or potash, and salt as raw materials, and coal as fuel, had originally developed mainly in London, with its large population and meat markets (for tallow), but during the first half of the nineteenth century soap-making expanded prodigiously—alongside the chemical industry—on Merseyside, where some firms such as Crosfields and Gossages combined soap (and candle) manufacture with production of soda and other chemicals and where oils and fats could be conveniently imported through Liverpool; the rapidly growing cotton industry and population of the north-west also provided expanding markets for soap, while an export trade also began to develop. These and other large firms in London and elsewhere tended to acquire an increasing share of the market, installing more and more 'pans', while the number of small local soaperies rapidly declined. In 1785, according to the Excise returns, there were 971 soap-makers in Great Britain, producing altogether just over 17,000 tons of soap, but by 1851 there were only 162, with a total output of 87,000 tons; average output had risen from a mere 19 tons per annum to 537 tons.

Coal-gas lighting and by-products

In all these chemical and allied trades, coal was of fundamental importance as a fuel for furnaces, boilers and steam-engines, but its possibilities as a source of chemicals were only just beginning to be appreciated. Experiments in the late eighteenth century resulted in the development of coal-gas lighting, which was pioneered by William Murdock at Boulton and Watt's Soho factory and was introduced into Manchester cotton mills early in the nineteenth century. Many mills installed their own generating plant, but gas companies were established in almost all towns by the mid-nineteenth century and firms found it cheaper and more convenient to take their gas supply from such companies; the first municipal gasworks was built in Manchester between 1817 and 1820, but the great majority of installations were by private concerns and companies. Gas lighting soon came into widespread use for lighting streets, factories, shops, inns, railway stations and other institutions, but for many years candles and oil lamps continued to be the main form of domestic lighting. Candle-making, mainly from tallow and to a lesser extent from paraffin wax, was often combined with soap-making.

The gas industry was consuming about a million tons of coal annually by the late 1840s and had provided iron-founders and other metal manufacturers with new demands for retorts, gas-holders, mains, pipes, lamp-posts, burners and meters. Linkages with the chemical industry were also gradually developed. At first the tar and ammonia liquor by-products of gasworks were an embarrassing problem, often being dumped in rivers. The manufacture of sal-ammoniac (ammonium chloride) had been developed in the later eighteenth century, for use in dyeing, brazing and tinplating, but, except for distillation of pitch and oils, efforts at extraction and industrial use of coal-tar products were generally not very successful until Charles Macintosh, the Scottish chemist and dyestuffs manufacturer, who was already using gasworks liquor in his Glasgow dyeworks, extracted naphtha and used it in making rubber solutions for water-proofing fabrics, setting up a works in Manchester in the 1820s, which not only produced his famous 'macintoshes' but also played a leading role in the early development of rubber manufacture; he also invented a furnace with tar as fuel, which came into general use in gasworks, with considerable cost saving. In the 1840s Peter Spence also used gasworks ammonia liquor, instead of urine, in the manufacture of alum. It was not until the 1850s, however, that William Perkin extracted the first aniline dye (mauve) from coal-tar, thus starting the synthetic dyestuffs industry. Even then Britain was to lag in exploitation of coal as a source of chemicals; by-products long continued to be wasted at gasworks and in the coke-ovens of the iron and steel industry.

The growing chemical and allied industries had an importance out of all proportion to the relatively small number of people they employed (see p. 140). Only 11,000 were described specifically as being 'engaged in the manufacture of Chemicals' in the Census of Great Britain in 1851, not including bleachers, dyers, soap-makers and others, who produced some of their own chemical requirements. The heavy chemical industry was capital-intensive, with considerable investment in buildings and plant, consuming large quantities of raw materials and coal and with relatively low labour costs; at the same time, the inter-relatedness of the major processes encouraged integration and large-scale production.

Glass

Both glass and pottery manufactures had strong affinities with the chemical industry. Glass-making, for example, required soda as one of its basic raw materials, and so we find James Keir, probably the most scientifically minded glass-maker of the Industrial Revolution, also becoming a manufacturer of soda, soap and other chemical products, at Tipton, Staffordshire; from his Edinburgh University medical studies he developed a profound interest in industrial chemistry, writing a *Dictionary of Chemistry* in 1789, being elected a fellow of the Royal Society and also belonging to the Birmingham Lunar Society and various philosophical societies in London, in which he associated with the leading scientists and scientific industrialists of his day.

Keir, however, was exceptional, and glass-making was still mainly reliant on practical industrial skills. Despite the British lead in the development of coal-fired reverberatory furnaces, Barker has pointed out that this country 'still relied for the greater part on skilled foreign craftsmen [mostly French] to work the molten glass', for making windows, bottles, etc., in the sixteenth and seventeenth centuries. And when new methods of manufacture were later introduced, they were usually of foreign origin. Thus the new mode of manufacturing plate glass—previously blown but now cast and rolled, for mirrors, shop windows, etc.—by the British Cast Plate Glass Company at Ravenhead, St Helens, in the late eighteenth century was initially based on the method used at St Gobain, with management and key workers drawn from the famous French glassworks. Similarly, in the 1830s, the development in this country of the manufacture of sheet glass (called, significantly, 'German sheet glass') by an improved cylinder process—replacing crown glass, mainly for windows—also required techniques and workmen from France (the process having been developed originally in Lorraine as well as in Germany).

But, though the original processes and skills were mostly French, British glass-makers made significant improvements in their large-scale industrial development, especially in improved coal-fired furnaces, in mechanical grinding and polishing and in the application of steam power. By the mid-nineteenth century, such firms as Pilkington's at St Helens, Chance's at Smethwick (Birmingham) and Cookson's on Tyneside, advantageously sited among coal and chemicals, had developed large works to meet the rapidly growing demand for window, plate and bottle glass. In 1851 ten employers had over a hundred workpeople, but most had less than ten. The total labour force was relatively small, only 13,000 being returned in the Census, and these were mainly handicraft workers, for even in 1870 there was only 4,000 horse-power of steam in the industry. Nevertheless, the annual output of 'white glass' (flint, plate, crown, German sheet and broad glass) in England and Wales increased from just over 3,000 tons in 1750 to around 12,000 tons by the early 1840s, while that of common green bottle glass rose much more slowly and erratically from between 9,000 and 10,000 tons to between 15,000 and 20,000 tons. Growth of the industry was restricted by the excise and window duties, together with foreign competition.

Pottery

Pottery also had its great industrial chemist, Josiah Wedgwood, F.R.S., who, like Keir, was deeply interested in both theoretical and applied science and similarly associated with the leaders of science and industry. In such matters as the composition of clays and other minerals, new colours and glazes, and temperature control, applied chemistry obviously offered possibilities of improvement, and Wedgwood not only sought the assistance of professional chemists but set up his own research laboratory; his experimental work on pyrometry was particularly notable. At the same time, he was keenly interested in new styles and decorative techniques, for which he engaged and trained artists and designers, as well as chemists, with results that are still world-famous. He was also outstanding in the development of the factory system in pottery manufacture, with his famous Etruria works, though others such as Turner and Spode were also pioneers. Wedgwood was equally enterprising in commercial techniques for expanding sales of both 'ornamental' and 'useful' wares.

Wedgwood's innovative importance, however, has been exaggerated. As Lorna Wetherill has shown, many improvements had been introduced into the Staffordshire potteries in the preceding century (1660–1760), including the use of coal fuel for ovens and kilns—used not only for firing pottery but also for drying clays and finished wares—together with improved wheels, the application of lathes and moulds, and the introduction of new materials and techniques, such as ball-clay and flint (for making white and cream pottery), salt glazing and biscuit (or double) firing; water-powered flint-grinding mills had also been introduced. These technical innovations, based on practical trial and error, had led to an increase in the scale of manufacture, so that by the mid-eighteenth century some potteries could be considered small factories, with one or two score workpeople; specialization and subdivision of labour were already common, and markets were becoming widespread and highly organized. The industry had clearly passed well beyond the primitive domestic peasant manufacture which it is commonly said to have been before Wedgwood's time; Burslem was already a small pottery town.

Many of the technical developments in this earlier period appear to have been introduced from abroad, especially for finer products in imitation of Dutch Delft-ware or the porcelain of Meissen and Sèvres, just as improvements in glass-making were introduced from the Continent. Salt glazing, for example, as an alternative to lead, is said to have been brought from Delft by the Elers brothers in the late seventeenth century (though there is evidence of its earlier use), and they also apparently introduced lathe turning. Similarly, the Chelsea

Porcelain Works, the principal centre of this manufacture in England until the 1770s, was managed by a French potter and at first imitated Meissen.

Increasingly, however, during the eighteenth century British resources of coal, clays and other materials were successfully exploited, and improvements were introduced in the making of clay bodies, in glazing, colouring and firing, in artistic design and in production of both high-quality and mass-produced wares. There was some application of mechanical power, as water-wheels and steam-engines came to be used for mixing clays, grinding flints and turning lathes. But handicraft skills continued to predominate in throwing and decorating; not until later was power applied to the potter's wheel and also to jiggers and jolleys for shaping wares. Cheaper goods, however, were increasingly produced by pressing and casting, with plaster moulds, and by decorating with printed transfers instead of hand painting; before long, 'flat and hollow-ware pressers' were to outnumber the traditional 'throwers', and the necessity for manual skills was considerably reduced.

Many small potteries still existed, but the tendency was increasingly towards larger-scale factory organization, in which output was increased mainly by subdivision and specialization of labour, according to products and processes. The Census of 1851 revealed thirty-six employers with over a hundred work-people, including seven with over 350, though two-thirds of those who made returns had less than ten; the total number occupied in the industry in Great Britain was 36,000 (26,000 males and 11,000 females). As in glass-making, power-driven mechanization was comparatively limited, only 8,000 horse-power of steam being employed in pottery and other earthenware manufactures even in 1870.

The industry was also becoming more strongly concentrated on the north Staffordshire coalfields, though notable potteries existed in other centres such as London, Bristol, Derby, Worcester, Leeds and Liverpool. As in textiles, small-scale rural manufacture was transformed into urban factory industry, centred on the Five Towns, with their concentration of smoking bottle-kilns. Increasingly however, raw materials were having to be brought in, most notably ball-clay from Devon and Dorset and china-clay from Cornwall; for carriage of these inland and of finished wares out, transport improvements such as turnpikes, the River Weaver Navigation and the Grand Trunk (Trent–Mersey) Canal were vital.

7

The Consumer Goods Trades:
The Extent of
Industrialization

Some of the industries we have already surveyed supplied goods such as coal, cutlery, hardware, soap, glassware and pottery directly to consumers, but the greater part of the output of the textiles, coal, iron and chemical industries went into producing cloth, bars and sheets of iron, and industrial chemicals, or into making machinery, steam-engines and other producers' capital goods. It is on these industries and these kinds of products that most historical attention has been concentrated. Yet the fundamental object of production, as Adam Smith emphasized, is consumption, and the Industrial Revolution was no exception. The consumer goods trades, however, have been comparatively neglected, because, in general, they were not areas of revolutionary technological change. No doubt much of the coal and iron did go into building the capital foundations of the heavy industries themselves, but the vastly increased outputs of cloth, metals, bricks and other products also went into consumer goods—into the clothing, housing, hardware and other requirements of the rapidly growing population, which also stimulated development of the food and drink trades.

The clothing trades
There is a remarkable contrast in this period between the progress of mechanization and the factory system in spinning and weaving and the almost total lack of technological change in the clothing trades which used the rapidly increasing output of textiles. Although growing quantities of yarn and cloth were being exported, the home market was also expanding considerably, with rising population and living standards, but the response to this growing demand in the clothing trades was not technological: there was simply a great increase in the number of tailors, dress-makers, needlewomen, seamstresses, etc., who still plied needle and thread in traditional fashion; it was not until about the mid-nineteenth century that the sewing machine was introduced, and even then it was generally hand or treadle operated and could be used at home.

Many tailors still remained independent small masters, working to customers' orders, but the putting-out system became more widespread, especially in London, where sub-contracting and 'sweating' developed, of the type portrayed in Charles Kingsley's *Alton Locke* and Thomas Hood's 'Song of the Shirt'. Most of the men and women so employed worked in their own homes or in garret workshops; there was a trend towards cheap ready-made clothing or 'slops' for the multitude, even before mechanized mass-production developed, and unskilled or semi-skilled workers were sometimes brought together in larger workshops to specialize on particular parts of such cut-out garments.

Hat-making was also unchanged technologically, with hand 'bowing' of the wool, fur or hair and hand pressing and shaping at the traditional 'kettle' or 'battery'. A number of larger 'manufactories' developed, particularly in London and the Stockport area, south of Manchester, where hatting was becoming localized, but the typical hatting firm remained very small. In hosiery manufacture similarly, hand framework-knitting remained general until the mid-nineteenth century, mostly under the domestic system, controlled by capitalist hosiers (see p. 93, where this industry has been included with textiles, to which it was closely related).

Traditional small-scale production, in fact, remained typical of the clothing trades generally. Of the 10,991 master tailors, for example, who made returns in the 1851 Census (England and Wales), only 434, or 4 per cent, employed ten men or more; the vast majority were working on their own or with only one or two men. But the total number engaged in all the clothing trades was very large, forming, together with boot- and shoe-makers, the second biggest manufacturing group after textiles (see p. 140). It is often forgotten, however, that over 151,000 people (134,000 males and 17,000 females) were in the tailoring trade of Great Britain in 1851, together with over 72,000 seamstresses, 296,000 milliners, straw hat-, bonnet- and cap-makers (all females), 17,000 hatters (13,000 males and 4,000 females), 30,000 glovers (5,000 males and 25,000 females) and 13,000 female stay-makers, as well as many thousands of others occupied in clothing the growing millions.

The leather trades

Leather-making was another manufacture still carried on by traditional methods (see p. 50), but in this trade there was a rather stronger tendency towards large-scale organization, as bigger tanneries developed in the Bermondsey area of London, in Leeds and in other major towns, with rapidly growing populations and large meat and hide markets. In addition to bark mills, steam power came to be introduced for pumping liquors and for splitting and rolling hides. But tanning operations remained predominantly manual, and small tanners and curriers were still very numerous and widely dispersed, greatly outnumbering the larger firms. Two-thirds of the master tanners who made returns to the 1851 Census had only ten men or less, while over four-fifths of the master curriers had five or less. In the whole of Great Britain the total number of tanners, curriers and others in leather-making was about 25,000, almost entirely men.

The various leather-working trades, moreover, were still mostly small-scale handicrafts. Large numbers of shoe-makers, cobblers and saddlers were scattered in towns and villages all over the country—there were more shoe-makers, in fact, than coal-miners, as Clapham pointed out, even in the mid-nineteenth century: 272,000 (241,000 males and 31,000 females) in Great Britain in 1851, together with 93,000 'shoe-makers' wives', who were also involved in the manufacture. Many of these were small masters, themselves working at the trade, like master tailors, but in towns such as Northampton, Leicester, Stafford and the surrounding rural areas, where boot- and shoe-making was becoming increasingly localized, large numbers of workers, including women and children, were employed on the putting-out system or were sometimes brought into workshops and were engaged in the wholesale manufacture of ready-made boots and shoes, with subdivision into specialized processes. As in the clothing trades, however, London was still the most important centre of manufacture, most of it still bespoke, and the processes of cutting and sewing were still everywhere manual, though experiments with riveting and sewing machines were being made. The average firm, moreover, remained very small: of the 17,665 master shoe-makers who made returns in 1851, over three-quarters were either working on their own or had only one or two men, though a handful each employed several hundred, mostly out-workers.

The growth of other industries tended to reduce the relative importance of the leather trades, as leather was displaced by other materials in clothing and utensils, but it continued to be used for a great variety of articles in addition to boots and shoes, including straps, belts, purses, gloves and saddlery. Saddlers and harness-makers, in particular, were still numerous and widespread, in both town and country, as horse-power remained fundamentally important in road and canal transport and in agriculture: there were nearly 19,000 of them in 1851, the vast majority in small workshops, in which master craftsmen were either working on their own or with only one or two men.

Taking all the leather trades together, they still ranked high in terms of total output: indeed, according to contemporary estimates by Colquhoun and McCulloch, they remained second to textiles in the early nineteenth century. But, as with the clothing trades, their importance has been neglected by most economic historians, absorbed in the Industrial Revolution.

Building and wood-working

The immense growth and movement of population during the Industrial

Revolution, particularly the increasing concentration in towns, created an ever-growing need for more houses and furniture, at the same time that industrial demand for factories and warehouses was rapidly increasing. Despite these pressures, however, there was remarkably little technological change in the building trades during this period. Iron framing, with iron columns, beams and roof supports, began to displace wood in mills and other large buildings from the late eighteenth century onwards, and iron structures also came into widespread use in bridges, railway stations, etc. Cement, made by heating certain types of limestone and clay in coal-fired kilns, was also introduced in the same period, originally for use in harbour-works and lighthouses. For the most part, however, buildings were still constructed of traditional materials, by a growing army of bricklayers, stonemasons, slaters, tilers, carpenters, joiners, plumbers, glaziers and painters, together with unskilled labourers, using tools and techniques that had remained unchanged over the centuries. It was still fairly easy to set up in the building trade, usually on a speculative credit basis, and the great majority of firms were small, especially in jobbing work; larger contractors were growing in number to carry out more extensive building operations, but sub-contracting to smaller men was common.

In the wood-working trades, the use of powered saws, now driven by steam as well as water, was extended not only in saw-mills but also in large joiners' shops, into which planing and mortising machines were also being introduced. The great majority of workshops, however, were still small and hand saws, planes, chisels and hammers remained in general use; mass-production methods, pioneered by Bentham, Brunel and Maudslay in their famous block-making machinery (see p. 116), still appear to have been exceptional in the wood-working trades of this country in the mid-nineteenth century; more rapid progress had been made in this field in the United States.

Comparative lack of technological innovation in building was associated with generally small-scale production. Of the 26,360 employers in this medley of trades who made returns to the 1851 Census of England and Wales, only seventy stated that they were employing a hundred men or more, while three-fifths had only one or two or were working on their own. As in the clothing trades, however, this growing multitude of traditional small firms has tended to be overlooked, though scholars such as Parry Lewis have emphasized their significance in the building trade cycle. Altogether they provided employment for an immense number of workers, almost entirely male: 499,000 builders, carpenters, joiners, masons, bricklayers, slaters, plasterers, plumbers, glaziers and painters in Great Britain 1851, to which we can add 35,000 sawyers, 40,000 cabinet-makers and many thousands of other wood-working tradesmen, as well as innumerable labourers.

The increased demand for building materials stimulated the establishment of more brickfields, quarries and lime-kilns. Most of these were still small-scale local affairs, though improvements in transport led to larger workings, as in the north Wales slate quarries. But little mechanical equipment was used: the horse-driven pug-mill, for grinding and mixing clays in brickworks, appears to have been introduced in the late eighteenth century, and steam power came gradually into use, but bricks were still almost entirely hand moulded and stacked before firing in traditional fashion; quarrymen similarly cut and dressed stone and slates by hand. Increased production therefore necessitated growing numbers of such workers: by 1851 the total for stone- and slate-quarrying and lime-burning in Great Britain was 27,000, while brick-makers totalled 30,000.

The output of bricks in England and Wales increased very erratically with trade fluctuations, from around 600 million annually in the late 1780s, to between 1,500 and 2,000 million in the late 1840s. The earlier introduction of coal fuel was, of course, of vital importance to this industry, which provided one of the basic building materials of the Industrial Revolution. Supplies of timber came increasingly from abroad; perhaps as much as a third of shipping tonnage entering British ports from overseas carried timber, which was, in fact, the largest single import by bulk, reaching nearly two million tons in 1846.

Coach-making

The horse-drawn carriage was the equivalent in the eighteenth and nineteenth centuries of the modern motor car, both as a means of conveyance and as a status symbol, ranging from gig to gilded coach. At the same time, in and between the cities and towns, cabs and coaching services plied a growing trade, until the longer-distance traffic was taken over by the railways. Horse-drawn vehicles were therefore built in increasing thousands, yet surprisingly little attention has been given to what was a considerable and thriving coach-making manufacture, especially in the larger cities. Moreover, the body-building techniques and styles of this industry were to be transmitted to the building of early railway 'coaches' or 'carriages' and later to the 'coachwork' of early motor cars. Indeed, the assembly-line method of mass-production, so closely associated with Henry Ford and modern motor-car manufacture, existed in a rudimentary form much earlier in coach-building. Thus we find George Dodd describing in his *Days at the Factories* in 1843 the very extensive works of Messrs Pearce and Countze (formerly Baxters), of Cross Lane, Long Acre, in London, a large building of several storeys, housing several specialized departments engaged in the manufacture of the carriages, bodies, axles, springs and numerous metal and leather parts, and finally painting the finished coach. In the coach-making loft, for example, a room eighty or ninety feet in length, 'work benches are placed round the sides on which the pieces of wood are fashioned and prepared; while the centre contains the carriages in progress'. (See p. 116–7, for James Nasmyth's similar manufacture of machine-tools, steam hammers, locomotives, etc., on the 'straight-line system' in the 1830s and 1840s.)

Similar works existed in other cities, such as the large 'carriage manufactory' of Joseph Cockshoot in Manchester—a firm still existing today, after making the transition to the motor-car trade—shown in an illustrated railway guide of 1861, with an impressive series of three-storey buildings, with a factory chimney at one end and glass-windowed showroom at the other. This was clearly, in fact, a considerable factory, probably producing some of its own castings or forgings, though the great majority of workers in the various departments were manual craftsmen. But there were many less impressive concerns in smaller towns—of the 945 coach-making employers who made returns in the 1851 Census, only about a fifth had more than ten men—as well as numerous village carpenters and wheelwrights making carts and wagons, with the aid of blacksmiths. There were more wheelwrights (30,000), in fact, than coach-makers (17,000) in Great Britain at that date.

Food and drink trades

The feeding, like the clothing and housing, of the rapidly growing population continued to be mainly by traditional methods, and the rising demand was similarly met by an increasing number of producers rather than by any technological revolution. There was a considerable expansion of urban markets for corn, meat, cheese, butter and vegetables, especially in London and the major towns, but shops were becoming much more numerous—mostly small, though some larger metropolitan shops and stores were emerging by the first half of the nineteenth century; bakers, butchers and grocers proliferated.

Most of the country's corn was still ground in windmills and water-mills. A slow revolution began with Boulton and Watt's famous steam-powered Albion Mill at Blackfriars, London, 1784—unfortunately burnt down seven years later—but rural corn-mills, scattered all over the country, continued working throughout the nineteenth century, some even into the twentieth. By the mid-nineteenth century, steam-mills in towns were becoming more numerous, including a few large ones employing up to fifty or even a hundred or more workers, but they were greatly outnumbered by the traditional small ones, as Clapham says, 'run by the miller, his mate and his lad'; most of the 37,000 millers in Great Britain in 1851 were of that kind.

Bakeries remained even smaller and more numerous, rarely employing more than three or four men: the dough was still kneaded by hand and put into timber- or coal-fired ovens on long-handled peels in centuries-old fashion. Home baking also remained common, especially in rural areas and in the north. The earliest use of mechanical equipment was in biscuit-making: by the mid-1860s, for example, Huntley and Palmer's had installed dough-mixing and biscuit-cutting machines and travelling-band ovens in their Reading works, in which over 800 people were employed. But this was an exceptional example of factory organization in a generally small-scale handicraft trade. Of the 5,203 master bakers in England and Wales who made returns in the 1851 Census, only 89 employed more than five men: nine-tenths of them were either working on their own or had only one or two men; but altogether there were 75,000 bakers and confectioners (64,000 males and 11,000 females) in Great Britain. Butchers and grocers provided very similar statistics.

In brewing, on the other hand, large firms such as Whitbreads, Barclay Perkins and Trumans in London and Youngers in Edinburgh were coming to dominate the trade. Their great multi-storied breweries, with tall chimneys and large warehouses, with steam-engines (instead of horse-wheels) to grind malt, work pumps, turn mashing machines and operate elevators, were examples of the factory system no less striking than Manchester cotton mills. Indeed, these large breweries were, in a sense, more highly mechanized, each requiring perhaps less than a hundred workers, while the capital invested in them dwarfed that in most other industrial firms, even before the Industrial Revolution: that of Samuel Whitbread, for example, was £116,000 in 1762 and over £271,000 by 1790; by 1830 the total partnership capital of Truman, Hanbury and Buxton had reached £575,000, that of Barclay Perkins £758,000. Such large breweries, moreover, were characterized not only by mechanical innovations but also by more scientific control of production processes, by means of the thermometer, hydrometer, attemperator (for temperature control) and the beginnings of chemical research, though traditional empirical skills were still of primary importance.

Many small breweries still existed, however, together with a much larger number of 'brewing victuallers' (mostly innkeepers), while home brewing remained widespread, still accounting for about half the total consumption in 1830. The statistics of the 1851 Census show that of the 776 brewers in England and Wales who made returns only about one-seventh had ten men or more, only five more than a hundred: over 18,000 people were occupied in brewing in Great Britain, together with more than 46,000 licensed victuallers and 'beershop-keepers' (and a large number of their wives), most of whom did their own brewing. Because of transport costs, production was confined to local markets, and large-scale brewing could develop only in London and the bigger provincial cities. Burton-on-Trent, the sole example of a specialized brewing town, was initially able to exploit the advantages of its local waters only because of cheap river and canal carriage, mainly for export, and later, from the 1840s, through expansion of the home market by the railways, when such names as Bass, Worthington and Allsopp began to become nationally famous.

In view of the rapid growth of population and towns, however, and the accompanying development of large-scale brewing, it is surprising that the Excise returns show a growth of beer production in England and Wales of less than half between 1700 and 1830, by which time it had reached about $7\frac{1}{3}$ million barrels: consumption per head was declining—from about one to half a barrel per head annually—while that of non-alcoholic beverages, especially tea, was increasing rapidly. It would appear that the tales of increasing industrial drunkenness and moral decline were exaggerated and that the British were being converted from the traditional drink of their forefathers to more insipid brews.

Paper-making, printing and bookbinding
In the paper industry, water power had long been used in processing the raw materials (see pp. 35–36). There were over a hundred water-powered mills by the end of the seventeenth century, widely scattered in rural areas but most numerous in the south-eastern counties. In these early mills, fermenting rags, mostly linen, were pounded to pulp in water by heavy wooden stampers or hammers, driven by water-wheels, as in fulling mills. During the eighteenth century, however, stampers were replaced by wooden rollers, fitted with knives or teeth, which rapidly macerated the rags and dispensed with the lengthy fermentation process; but these 'hollanders', as they were generally called from their country of origin, still continued for a long time to be water-powered. Steam power made very slow progress in paper-mills, which remained mostly small and widely scattered in river valleys; Boulton and Watt erected only one of their engines in a paper-mill before 1800. Moreover, the actual paper-making was still a handicraft process, with vat and wire-mesh mould, forming each sheet separately.

More revolutionary developments occurred towards the end of the century. Chlorine bleaching was introduced for making white paper in the early 1790s, following its application in the cotton industry; as well as saving time and capital, it also made possible the wider use of coloured cotton rags. This chemical revolution was accompanied, as in textiles, by a mechanical revolution, with the invention of the paper-making machine by the Frenchman Nicolas Louis Robert in 1799, subsequently developed in this country by the Fourdrinier brothers and the London engineer, Bryan Donkin; forming a continuous web of paper on a wire-mesh belt, this gradually began to displace the vat and mould of the traditional handicraft, and eventually, with additions of drying and finishing rolls or calenders and cutting machines, the whole sequence of paper-making operations became mechanized. But many years were required to perfect this machinery and it was not until the 1830s that mechanization began to make rapid progress; water-wheels were still widely used, though steam power was now coming in and more mills were being established in northern coalfield areas, especially in Lancashire. With increasing size and output of mills and increasing capital requirements, the industry was gradually becoming more concentrated in the hands of the larger makers, such as John Dickinson in Hertfordshire and

Thomas Crompton in Lancashire, though many small mills still survived. Over half the 214 paper manufacturers in England and Wales who made returns in 1851 had ten men or more, while eleven had over a hundred. Total employment in the industry, however, was not very large—just over 14,000 in Great Britain (not counting stationers)—but with increasing mechanization the total British paper output increased dramatically from around 9,000 tons annually in the early 1780s to between 50,000 and 60,000 by the early 1850s. The number of mills, on the other hand, declined from a peak of 564 in 1821 to 306 in 1860 (England and Wales), as small water-driven rural mills, using the old vat process, were gradually eliminated, though access to abundant supplies of pure water remained important.

The most important market for paper was in the printing industry, though it was also increasingly used for writing and for wrapping and packing. The first paper-mill in England, in fact, had been established soon after Caxton set up the first English printing press in the late fifteenth century, but neither industry had grown very strongly until towards the end of the seventeenth century. The expansion of the printing industry had been limited not only by illiteracy and slow development of commercial demand but also by strict State regulations, exercised mainly through the Stationers' Company, imposing a system of licensing and restrictions on the numbers of printers and presses, which were confined to London and the two universities of Oxford and Cambridge, until extended to York by the Licensing Act of 1662. After the 1688 Revolution and lapse of the Licensing Act, however, the printing industry was free to expand, and presses were soon set up in most provincial towns, in which local newspapers also began to appear. But the 'taxes on knowledge'—imposed on paper, newspapers and advertisements—continued to have a restrictive effect. Throughout this period, therefore, the printing trade in England and Wales continued to be dominated by London, with Edinburgh enjoying a similar predominance in Scotland, and Dublin in Ireland. London was the great centre of book, newspaper, parliamentary and governmental printing, together with the type-founding, book-binding, stationery and publishing trades. Only in London and Dublin were there daily newspapers before the 1850s: all the privincial papers were small weeklies, with local circulations mostly numbered in hundreds rather than in thousands. The average jobbing or general printing office was even smaller, often combined, in fact, with newspaper printing.

Increasing literacy, however, and growing demands for newspapers, books and commercial printing, especially in London, did bring about some technological advances, but these were confined almost entirely to the press department; hand type-setting remained unchanged. Iron and steam were both applied to press work: iron hand presses rapidly began to displace the old-style wooden ones from the end of the eighteenth century, while cylinder machines, printing from flat type-beds, were invented and developed in the same period by William Nicholson and the German Friedrich Koenig; operated either by hand or by steam, they began to be used in larger newspaper and book-printing offices, *The Times* being first 'printed by steam' in November 1814. Larger machines, with more cylinders, were gradually developed and by the mid-century rotary machines, printing from type fixed onto a cylinder—soon to be replaced by curved stereotype plates—were being introduced into London newspaper offices. But in small printing offices—the vast majority—hand presses or single-cylinder flat-bed machines still sufficed. Moreover, there was no revolution in the composing room: all type was still set by hand; early experiments with composing machines in the 1840s proved unsuccessful. Lithographic printing, stereotyping and electrotyping had been invented but were as yet little developed.

The number of printers in the United Kingdom grew from just over 9,000 (London 4,000) in 1831 to nearly 20,000 (London 8,000) by 1851, but these were still mostly employed in a very large number of small offices, each employing less than half a dozen men, in every town of any size, though there were a few large firms in London with up to a hundred or even two hundred men. Bookbinding similarly remained mostly a skilled handicraft though, like book-printing with which it was associated, it was organized on a rather larger scale than general printing and was more concentrated in London. Type-founding, likewise, was still a manual craft, despite early attempts at mechanical casting, and was also concentrated mainly in London, though there were also type-founders in Birmingham, Sheffield, Edinburgh and Glasgow.

Miscellaneous trades

Our survey has demonstrated that the Industrial Revolution had by no means transformed everyone into a cotton-spinner or a coal-miner. The Census returns of the mid-nineteenth century refer, in fact, to hundreds of different trades, the great majority of which were traditional manual crafts, producing food and drink, clothing, housing, furniture and domestic utensils. To those already mentioned we can add others such as sail-making and rope-making, employing nearly 20,000 in 1851, located mainly in ports and along rivers, where long low roperies or rope-walks, with their hand spinning-wheels, were still common. Coopers (another 20,000) continued to cut timber staves and hazel hoops for casks and barrels—essential for storage and transport of beer, wine, tallow, herrings, etc.—as well as vats, tuns, tubs, buckets and other containers. Growing imports of colonial products stimulated various manufactures, chiefly in the main ports: sugar-refining, for example, continued to expand and tobacco manufacture was developing long before the cigarette age; as Alford has shown, W.D. & H.O. Wills had already, from the late eighteenth century onwards, established a prosperous business, with hand sorting, blending, rolling and packing of tobaccos in their

Bristol works, and there were many firms in London, Liverpool, Glasgow and elsewhere. The making of clay and wood pipes, therefore, was correspondingly widespread.

Despite urban industrial concentration, many rural crafts still survived. We have seen that hand-loom weaving, framework-knitting, lace-making and glove-making still existed in rural areas; country millers, blacksmiths, carpenters, wheelwrights, saddlers and cobblers were still very numerous; most of the workers in straw, rushes and willow-cane—as many as 70,000 in 1851—making hats, baskets and thatching were in the countryside, and charcoal burners were still to be found, though in diminishing numbers, in woodland districts.

The extent of the Industrial Revolution by 1850

At the end of the seventeenth century, the British economy had been predominantly agricultural. By the mid-nineteenth century it had become predominantly industrial and commercial. Britain had been transformed from a 'pre-industrial' to an industrial economy: in the sense of industrialization, therefore, it would seem that an industrial revolution had occurred. But in other senses it is evident that this industrial revolution was very limited in extent.

It is very difficult, as we saw in Chapter 1, to differentiate between agriculture and industry, or between industry and trade, in the earlier period, and this difficulty was recognized by Deane and Cole in their statistical estimates of the changing structure of the national product in the eighteenth century. But their estimates, though admittedly very tentative, suggest that between the late seventeenth century and about 1770—that is, even *before* the Industrial Revolution—agriculture's contribution to national income was already well below half, in fact between 40 and 45 per cent, while that of industry (manufactures, mining and building) was 20 to 25 per cent and commerce 12 to 13 per cent, with domestic service, the professions, government service and housing rent accounting for the remainder. There seems to have been little change in this broad distribution over that whole period. By 1851, however, there is no doubt that a considerable transformation had occurred. Agriculture's share had declined to little more than 20 per cent, while that of industry had risen to over 34 per cent and that of trade and transport to nearly 19 per cent—together contributing well over half the national income. This shift in economic balance was also reflected in the percentage distribution of the occupied population, the 1851 Census showing less than 22 per cent in agriculture, forestry and fishing, compared with about 43 per cent in industry, nearly 16 per cent in trade and transport, 13 per cent domestic and personal and nearly 7 per cent public, professional, etc.

These figures, however, whilst indicating the undoubted progress of industrialization, tend to give a misleading impression of 'industrial revolution'. In contrast, it should be noted that in 1851 about half the population was living in what the Census classified as rural areas: clearly, though industrial towns were growing very rapidly, many industrial as well as agricultural workers were still living in the countryside. Moreover, as we have seen from our industrial survey, many—indeed most—industrial workers were still in trades that had not yet been revolutionized. Even in industries where the most striking technological advances had occurred, there were still large numbers of traditional hand workers. In cotton, for example, hand-loom weavers, though a dying race, were still numerous, while in other textiles—wool, linen, silk, lace and hosiery—hand looms and frames still predominated. In the metal industries, similarly, though the primary processes of smelting and forging had been transformed, craftsmen in the wide range of finishing trades, making miscellaneous small manufactures, were still mostly working with traditional hand tools in small workshops. Some of

OCCUPATIONAL GROUPS IN GREAT BRITAIN, 1851
(in thousands)

	Males	Females	Total
Agriculture, horticulture and forestry	1,788	229	2,017
Fishing	36	1	37
Domestic offices and personal services	193	1,135	1,328
Textiles	661	635	1,296
Clothing (including boot- and shoe-making and repairing)	418	491	909
Metal manufacture, machines, implements, vehicles, etc.	536	36	572
Building and construction	496	1	497
Transport (roads, railways, canals, docks, sea, including domestic coachmen and grooms)	433	13	446
Food, drink and tobacco	348	53	401
Mining and quarrying, and workers in their products	383	11	394
Wood, furniture, etc.	152	8	160
Bricks, cement, pottery and glass	75	15	90
Paper, printing, books and stationery	62	16	78
Skins, leather, hair, etc.	55	5	60
Chemicals, oil, soap, etc.	42	4	46
Commercial occupations	91	—	91
Professional occupations and subordinate services	162	103	265
Public administration	64	3	67
Armed forces	63	—	63
All others occupied	445	75	513
Total occupied	6,545	2,832	9,377

Source: B. R. Mitchell and P. Deane, Abstract of British Historical Statistics (1962), p. 60. The figures given in their tables do not, however, add up exactly to the totals.

the biggest industrial groups such as the building, wood-working, clothing, leather and shoe-making, and food and drink trades had been comparatively little changed, while many others such as letterpress printing, pottery manufacture, brick-making, glass-making, soap-making and dyeing, though experiencing technological innovation in certain processes, were for the most part still traditional handicraft trades. In mining, too, though steam-powered drainage and winding engines had been introduced, most of the labour force, engaged in hewing and moving coal or ores, were still manual workers. Similarly in transport, workers on railways and steamships accounted for a very small proportion of the total number employed, who comprised mainly carters, wagoners and coachmen on the roads, boatmen on rivers and canals and seamen on sailing ships. To all these traditional trades, we must add by far the biggest single occupational groups—those in agriculture and domestic service.

It is evident that the typical British worker in the mid-nineteenth century was not a machine-operator in a factory but still a traditional craftsman or labourer or domestic servant. Increasing industrialization had meant, for the most part, not more power-driven mechanization but more and more manual craftsmen and labourers, while the middle classes, increasing in numbers and wealth, were employing a growing army of domestic servants. The great majority of workers in manufacturing industry, moreover, were not employed by great capitalists in large factories but by innumerable small employers in small workshops, as revealed by the Census returns of masters and workmen in 1851. The domestic or putting-out system was still widespread in many industries; many small town tradesmen and rural craftsmen were still catering for local markets; smiths, carpenters, building workers, tailors and shoemakers were still to be found widely dispersed over the country; while many commodities were still home-made. Of course, as we have seen, large-scale mercantile-capitalist organization had long existed in such handicraft trades, with national and international markets, and some of them had become concentrated or localized in certain areas, as shown again by the mid-nineteenth century Census returns: small metals manufactures, for example, in the Birmingham, Black Country and Sheffield areas; hosiery and lace manufactures in the east midlands; shoe-making in Northampton and Leicester; hat-making in the Manchester–Stockport area; glove-making in Worcestershire and Somerset; and straw-plait manufacture in Hertfordshire. But these local specializations had long been developing; they merely became more marked during the Industrial Revolution, encouraged by expanding markets. In such areas, moreover, it became more common for domestic workers to be brought together in 'manufactories', for increased subdivision and specialization and better supervision.

Where power was employed, it was still very often that of a water-wheel. And where steam-engines were used, they were still mostly small: even in the cotton industry, a 60 horse-power engine was regarded as a large one in the 1820s; by the early 1840s a mill engine of from 300 to 400 horse-power was considered remarkable. Steam-engines were still often used, as we have seen, to drive the machinery of several small manufacturers occupying parts of the same building. Many firms started in this small way, with very modest amounts of capital—often only a few hundred pounds—relying on credit and their own enterprise. Some of them had grown very big by the mid-nineteenth century, employing hundreds or even thousands of hands, but the vast majority of firms were still small, with employees numbered only in single or double figures.

Entrepreneurial and managerial problems

The Industrial Revolution has often been portrayed as an almost purely technological phenomenon. Technological developments—mechanical, metallurgical and chemical—were certainly of fundamental importance: without them there could have been no industrial revolution. But technological expertise was not enough to ensure business success, and there are many examples of inventors who failed as entrepreneurs or whose inventions were only developed successfully by men with entrepreneurial, managerial and commercial talents, such as Richard Arkwright or Matthew Boulton, who, though not without technical ability, were primarily businessmen. The Industrial Revolution was, in fact, as much their achievement as that of the inventors, if not more. In that period, indeed, Professor Pollard has traced the 'genesis of modern management'.

Industrial expansion requires entrepreneurial drive, risk-taking, capital accumulation, commercial acumen and managerial skills, particularly the capacity to train and organize labour, as well as technical knowledge. These abilities, which left-wing historians are apt to denigrate as aspects of 'capitalist exploitation', are in fact required in any expanding industrial society, whether capitalist or socialist. Under a socialist regime they have to be stimulated by higher salaries, status differentials and official privileges, but in the Industrial Revolution private profit was the main incentive, in conjunction with various social and psychological drives (see p. 75) that were needed to overcome the unprecedented problems involved.

The tendency among modern economic historians has been to place most emphasis on demand factors, on expanding markets at home and overseas. But these markets were not given; they had to be developed by commercial and industrial enterprise. Studies into the modern relationship between science, technology and economic growth have demonstrated that inventions are not simply responses to market forces, that rising demand may follow rather than precede technological innovation: entrepreneurial energy and capital are required, and risks have to be taken, to develop new products, to put them on the market and to overcome consumer inertia and opposition from those whose position is threatened by innovations, including business competitors as well as workers. These conclusions are supported by evidence from the Industrial Revolution, in which leading innovators such as Boulton, Wedgwood and Manchester cotton manufacturers largely *created* markets for new products by vigorous sales promotion, as well as by technological developments that reduced costs or improved quality. By establishing close links with London and overseas markets, with wholesale houses and the world of fashion, by employment of travellers and agents, by preparation of pattern-books, catalogues and advertising and by an endless stream of handwritten commercial correspondence, they successfully assessed and also shaped consumer tastes and developed markets. At the same time, an equally careful eye had to be kept on supplies, prices and qualities of raw materials.

For all these commercial operations, as well as for their industrial undertakings, increasing amounts of capital and credit were required. Additional fixed capital was generally obtained by ploughing back profits, by raising loans on mortgages or bonds, or by bringing in new partners. Commercial credit and working capital were based on bills of exchange and on arrangements with banks for short-term loans or overdrafts. These increasingly complex trading and financial affairs required development of more sophisticated accounting or book-keeping procedures; more time had to be spent in counting-house or office than in factory, and as businesses grew a hierarchy of managers and foremen had to be created, or various forms of sub-contracting were adopted. Transport arrangements and costs had also to be considered, whether by road or canal, or later by rail, or by shipments to and from overseas; in fact industrialists generally played a leading role in developing new forms of transport, which were essential to expansion of markets; the Duke of Bridgewater's colliery and canal-building activities, Josiah Wedgwood's involvement in the Grand Trunk Canal, and the multifarious interests of Lancashire manufacturers and merchants in both canals and railways are only the best known of innumerable similar associations.

These industrialists, indeed, are often said to have been much more concerned about these commercial matters and about their inanimate machinery than they were about the human beings whom they employed. There certainly was a tendency, encouraged by or reflected in the current political economy, to regard workmen only as 'hands', to treat labour simply as 'a factor of production', and undoubtedly there was a good deal of exploitation. But there has been much exaggeration in judging the Industrial Revolution by modern standards—themselves based on the industrial and social advances of the last two centuries—rather than by comparison with preceding conditions. There was not a pre-industrial 'golden age'. Many of the evils attributed to the Industrial Revolution, such as child labour and low wages were not new, but had long existed in domestic trades and small workshops, as well as in agriculture. In fact, workers were attracted into urban-industrial and factory employment by higher wages than were obtained in agriculture and other rural occupations, while mechanization and the factory system relieved physical labour and eventually made it possible to reduce working hours, at the same time greatly increasing output of consumer goods. Many factory owners provided good conditions for their workers, by contemporary standards, often including houses, shops and schools; some of them supported factory legislation, as did the elder Sir Robert Peel, Robert Owen, the Fieldens of Todmorden, John Wood of Halifax and various others, though the majority certainly opposed State regulation. Evidence given before official enquiries shows that factory conditions had been improving before the first effective Act in 1833 and that they were better than in many domestic trades, workshops and mines.

Child labour and long working hours were traditional in all these industries, and it may be said that factory legislation was a sign, not of social degradation in 'dark satanic mills', but of social improvement and rising moral standards, which became possible when factory machines so raised productivity that relentless toil was no longer the inevitable human lot. The extent of child labour in factories, moreover, has been considerably exaggerated: in 1835, according to the Factory Inspectors' Returns, there were only 29,000 children under thirteen (the vast majority over ten) in cotton factories, out of a total labour force of 219,000, and by 1850 this number had been reduced to 15,000 out of 316,000, by which date they were 'half-timers'. The proportion of young children was no doubt somewhat higher before the 1833 Act, but clearly the cotton industry was not, as often alleged, built on the blood and bones of child workers. (Cobbett, for example, in a famous speech in favour of the ten hours' bill, referred to the '300,000 little girls in Lancashire' on whose exploitation the industry was based.)

The employment of children had been resorted to not only as cheap labour for light ancillary jobs such as piecing but also because of the difficulty of recruiting adults into the early mills. These mills, powered by water, were often in remote rural areas, where labour was not easily available. This problem was relieved by the growth of steam-powered urban factories, but there was still an aversion against what was regarded as the prison- or workhouse-like confinement and discipline of factory employment, compared with the freer and easier conditions in domestic handicrafts. Factory owners were therefore faced with considerable problems not only of recruiting but also of training these workers to operate the new machines, on which labour, though physically lighter, was inevitably more regular, constant and monotonous; hence the higher wages in factories and also the strict discipline, fines and dismissals. The casual nature of the domestic system could not possibly survive in factories, with power-driven machinery: the factory clock and the factory bell became symbols of the new industrial system. (Even Robert Owen, the 'father of socialism', recognized the necessity of disciplined regularity.) At the same time, factories gradually destroyed traditional handicrafts, in both town and country, though they also created additional demands for labour.

Many workers, therefore, went beyond passive resistance to machines and factories, which they saw as depriving them of employment and bread. Machine breaking became endemic, as illustrated by the attacks on the early jenny and water-frame factories, the destruction of Cartwright's Manchester weaving mill, the notorious Luddite smashing of shearing frames, etc., in 1811–12, the power-loom riots of 1826 and numerous other outbreaks. The developing trade unions gradually changed, however, from 'collective bargaining by riot' to more subtle forms of opposition to machinery, with restrictive practices in regard to manning, output and piece-work rates. Labour relations were therefore among the most serious of managerial problems.

One response, of course, was authoritarian repression, with the aid of the common law of conspiracy, the master and servant law and the more notorious Combination Laws; strikes were innumerable, bitter and often prolonged, sometimes verging on social revolt, especially in periods of trade depression and bad harvests, when they were apt to become involved in political radicalism. Another response was to curb trade unions with more labour-saving machinery, as with Roberts' self-acting mule, Fairbairn's boiler-riveting machine, various wool-combing machines and other inventions that were so motivated. But it is misleading to portray industrial relations entirely in terms of industrial warfare and class struggle: many employers maintained good relations with their men; in many trades collective bargaining began to develop, trade unions were openly recognized and legal prosecutions were rare. It has been shown that the Combination Laws were much less generally repressive than was once supposed, and they were repealed in 1824–5. Although trade unions did not finally achieve clear legal status until the 1870s, in many industries efforts were being made long previously to reduced industrial conflict by negotiations or by conciliation and arbitration procedures. With gradually rising real wages, and with social legislation beginning to improve conditions in towns, factories and mines, the revolution that Marx and Engels were predicting did not occur.

Economic growth, however, though seemingly inevitable in the long run and in historical retrospect, was by no means easy or unbroken. The eighteenth-century industrial changes took place in a period of almost endless wars—the wars against Louis xiv of France, the War of the Austrian Succession, the Seven Years War, the American War of Independence and finally the long French Revolutionary and Napoleonic Wars, lasting until 1815. These, as Professor John has shown, were by no means entirely damaging: in fact, up to 1763, they were perhaps beneficial, stimulating the heavy metal industries, coal-mining, ship-building and overseas trade. But the later wars were more dislocating; Ashton showed how widespread these disruptions were in trade and industry. To these were added the effects of harvest failures, commercial instability and credit crises, which produced never-ending problems for manufacturers and merchants and also periodic bankruptcies.

The nineteenth century was relatively free from wars, but economic fluctuations continued, in the more regular pattern of an approximately ten-yearly trade cycle. The post-1815 depression was followed by economic recovery in the early 1820s, reaching a peak and economic crisis in 1825–6; the ensuing slump lasted into the next decade, but the economy was booming again by the mid-1830s; crisis and depression recurred in 1837 and the following years, and the pattern of boom and slump was repeated once more in the middle and later 1840s, centred on the economic crisis of 1846–7. Various causal factors can be discerned: fluctuations in capital investment, whether in factories, mines and railways at home, or in overseas projects; over-optimism and speculation in booms, leading to over-production, falling prices and slump; banking and monetary instability, dislocating note issues, credit and exchange-rates; harvest fluctuations, affecting food prices, the level of consumer demand and the balance of payments; disturbances abroad, especially in the American economy. Businessmen had to keep an ever-watchful eye on the economic barometer; but even apparently sound concerns could go under in sudden commercial squalls. Much of the dislocation and distress associated with economic growth was caused by forces beyond contemporary means of forecasting and control; even in the twentieth century, we have by no means solved these problems. But the slumps were short-term, and the succeeding booms raised output to new heights: growth occurred unevenly, in spurts, but in the long term production was rising remarkably, in an apparently exponential curve. Early Victorian optimism was justified.

PART III

MASS PRODUCTION AND
MASS CONSUMPTION, 1850–1914

8

Growth and Retardation

British economic historians have generally tended to place too much emphasis on the Industrial Revolution of 1750–1850 by comparison with developments in the second half of the nineteenth century. Yet, as Beales very perceptively observed many years ago, 'the England of 1850 resembled more closely that of the eighteenth century than it did the England of 1914'. In 1850, as we have seen, half the population was still living in rural areas, over a fifth of the occupied population was engaged in agriculture and the next biggest occupational group was in domestic service; the great majority of industrial workers were skilled handicraftsmen or labourers, working in small workplaces or at home; only a small minority of the total labour force was in factories; many industries were still unmechanized, and in many of those where machinery had been introduced, it had as yet made only limited progress; only in a few industries such as cotton, coal and iron had steam power been introduced on a large scale; water-wheels were still numerous and widespread; much of the production and trade of the country was still in limited local markets. Truly, much of the England of 1850 was not very strikingly different from that of 1750.

The general interpretation presented in most textbooks, however, is that the Industrial Revolution had taken place by 1850, that the factory system had triumphed and that not long after the mid-nineteenth century signs of retardation appear. By the 1870s the massive application of iron and steam is said to have ended, British industry is alleged to have become stagnant and conservative, growth rates were falling and economic historians have vied with each other in searching for causes of Britain's decline and in masochistic observations on entrepreneurial deficiencies and national decadence. It has even been argued that, in theory at any rate, there is no reason why a country holding industrial leadership, as Britain then was, should not be able to maintain that leadership, since it has the established advantages of the largest capital resources, the most advanced technology, the most resourceful and experienced entrepreneurs and the most skilled labour force. What, then, was *wrong* with Britain that she *failed* to maintain her leadership? That she was tending deplorably to lag has been demonstrated by the declining percentage growth rates in particular industries and in the whole economy: whereas, in the late eighteenth and first half of the nineteenth century, industrial production—according to Hoffman's index or variants of it—had been growing at three to four per cent per annum, it began to fall in the second half of the century and down to 1914, first to two or three per cent and then to one or two per cent, while productivity or output per head declined even more depressingly, to well below one per cent per annum, until it was almost stagnant or even declining in the years before 1914; in overseas trade similarly, the annual rate of growth in the volume of manufactured exports fell from four or five per cent in the third quarter of the century to only about two per cent between the mid-1870s and the early twentieth century. Meanwhile, Britain's industrial competitors, such as the United States and Germany, were now increasing their industrial production at four to five per cent per annum and eventually surpassing us in total output.

AVERAGE ANNUAL PERCENTAGE RATES OF GROWTH, 1870–1913

Country	Total output	Output per man-hour	Industrial production	Industrial productivity	Exports (1880–1913)
United Kingdom	2.2	1.5	2.1	0.6	2.2
United States	4.3	2.3	4.7	1.5	3.2
Germany	2.9	2.1	4.1	2.6	4.3

Source: D. H. Aldcroft (ed.), *The Development of British Industry and Foreign Competition 1875–1914* (1968), p. 13, and references cited therein.

The causes of this sad decline have been numerously catalogued. The 'third generation' was lacking in the energy and enterprise of its forefathers; family firms had become conservative and complacent; the advantages of the industrial pioneer, the 'early starter', had now become disadvantages, with the problems of technical obsolescence and 'interrelatedness'; we clung too long to outdated machinery and failed to innovate; we were 'overcommitted' to the old staple industries and slow in developing new ones; we were lagging in applied science; we were exporting too much capital; we were too absorbed in imperialism; we were too complacent in foreign trade, lacking in competitive drive and adaptability; the benefits of free-trade had turned sour, yet we still persisted in a liberal commercial policy. By 1914 one is almost led to believe that this country had degenerated into a kind of industrial museum.

These views are very largely misleading. In fact there are good grounds for regarding the period 1850–1914 as that in which the Industrial Revolution really occurred, on a massive scale, transforming the whole economy and society much more widely and deeply than the earlier changes had done. On the eve of the First World War, well over four-fifths of the population were living in urban areas; only about 8 per cent of the occupied population were now in agriculture; most manufactures had become mechanized, and the factory system had spread throughout industry; steam power had been enormously increased, to an industrial total of 9,650,000 horse-power by the first Census of Production in 1907, dwarfing that of 1850 and making that of 1800 seem almost insignificant; moreover, the power of gas and oil engines and electric generators was being added to that of steam, while water-wheels, now greatly reduced in number, had become archaic survivals, and windmills were also rapidly disappearing or falling derelict; skilled handicrafts were similarly declining in most trades, machine-minders or operators were multiplying, and many goods were being mass-produced and marketed nationally and internationally, though local trades and markets still survived, as Unwin observed at that time (see p. 13). It is true that

OCCUPATIONAL GROUPS IN GREAT BRITAIN, 1911
(in thousands)

Trade	*Males*	*Females*	*Total*
Metal manufactures, machines, implements, vehicles, etc.	1,795	128	1,923
Transport (roads, railways, canals, docks, sea, including domestic coachmen and grooms)	1,571	38	1,609
Textiles	639	870	1,509
Clothing (including boot- and shoe-makers and repairers)	432	825	1,257
Mining and quarrying and workers in their products	1,202	8	1,210
Building and construction	1,140	5	1,145
Food, drink and tobacco	806	308	1,114
Paper, printing, books and stationery	253	144	397
Wood, furniture, etc.	287	35	322
Chemicals, oils, soap, etc.	155	46	201
Bricks, cement, pottery and glass	145	42	187
Skins, leather, hair, etc.	90	32	122
Agriculture, horticulture and forestry	1,436	117	1,553
Fishing	53	—	53
Domestic offices and personal services	456	2,127	2,583
Commercial occupations	739	157	896
Professional occupations and subordinate services	413	383	796
Public administration	271	50	321
Armed forces	221	—	221
All others occupied	827	98	839
Total occupied	12,927	5,413	18,340

Source: Mitchell and Deane, op. cit., p. 60. The figures given in their tables do not, however, add up exactly to the totals.

domestic servants, mainly female, formed the largest occupational group and that in the building and constructional group, still one of the biggest, manual workers remained predominant; this was also true of mining, into which a huge number of workers had been drawn for hewing and underground transport. But other major industries such as textiles, engineering and shipbuilding were now largely mechanized, while in many other trades such as clothing, boot- and shoe-making, metal manufactures, wood-working, printing, pottery manufacture and glass-making, mechanization had made considerable progress. Similarly in transport, steam railways and steamships were now predominant and the internal combustion engine was beginning to revolutionize road transport. Indeed, in the late nineteenth and early twentieth centuries one can see the beginning of a 'second industrial revolution', based on new sources of power (oil and electricity), on new forms of transport (motor cars, buses and lorries) and on new materials produced by the chemical industry. And though Britain no longer led the way, as she had in the 'first industrial revolution', there is plentiful evidence, as we shall see, of continued British technological innovation and entrepreneurial enterprise in many fields. Whereas excessive emphasis has been placed on the insularity of Britain's early pioneering (see p. 72), there has been, by contrast, an exaggerated emphasis in the other direction in many studies of the later period, stressing Britain's technological stagnation by comparison with foreign innovating enterprise in the 'second industrial revolution'.

A great deal of this distortion springs from excessive concentration on percentage rates of growth and from the unrealistic theoretical notion that somehow Britain ought to have been able to maintain her industrial leadership and that in losing it she was lamentably negligent or deficient. There has been, until recently, a strong tendency among modern post-Keynesian economists to assume that economic factors can be so regulated as to achieve steady and continuous rates of industrial growth, with very little consideration of the scientific-technological or social factors involved: if the purely economic factors such as investment, income and expenditure are correctly manipulated, then apparently endless growth can be envisaged; supply will almost automatically respond to demand; technological solutions will be effortlessly provided. History, however, casts serious doubts on these assumptions, while those economists who have, belatedly, examined the 'non-economic' scientific-technological factors in economic growth have found, to their apparent surprise, that these 'residuals' are much the most important factors of all and that they are not so easily manipulated by economic means as had previously been supposed. It is unrealistic to assume that the British economy could have gone on growing at the same percentage rate of growth as in the early stages of industrialization and that Britain could have indefinitely maintained her industrial leadership. In the early Industrial Revolution, starting from comparatively low absolute levels of output, percentage rates of growth had been inevitably high, but by the later nineteenth century these innovation effects were working themselves out and, unless there was some immense new technological impetus even greater than the coal–iron–cotton–engineering stimulus of the 'first industrial revolution', then percentage rates of growth were bound to fall. This, in fact, is what happened, until the 'second industrial revolution' really got under way in the twentieth century, when, as we shall see, growth rates started to rise again. But it cannot, except with historical hindsight, be sensibly argued that Britain ought to have developed electricity, motor transport, etc., at an earlier date. Such major technological advances do not, in fact, necessarily occur just when required economically but are dependent on scientific-technological as well as economic factors. Moreover, their full potential, when they came, was not immediately evident to contemporaries, and their development inevitably took time.

Expectation of continuously high percentage rates of growth in particular industries is even more unrealistic. It is a well-observed historical fact that the growth pattern of most national industries over the past two centuries has been parabolic. After initially high percentage rates of growth, there is a slowing down, followed in many cases by stagnation and decline. Such retardation was visible in many British industries by the later nineteenth century and may be regarded as historically or empirically, if not theoretically, inevitable. There clearly were limits to the continuance of high growth rates within the available raw material resources, technology and markets. This applied not only to individual industries but to the whole economy: technological developments in the new industries were only in the embryonic stage in the late nineteenth and early twentieth centuries, and it was to take several decades for these industries to reach such a scale that their rapid growth rates could offset the retardation in the old massively established industries. Moreover, it made sound business sense at the time to continue investing and expanding production in the old basic industries such as coal, iron and steel, shipbuilding and textiles: markets continued to expand for their products, and profits continued to be reasonably good (though cyclically fluctuating, of course) right up to 1914. Victorian and Edwardian businessmen in these industries could not possibly have foreseen the catastrophe of the inter-war period.

Moreover, there has been excessive concentration on percentage rates of growth, which, unrelated to absolute quantities and industrial-technological and commercial actualities, over long historical periods can be very misleading. In absolute terms, the increases in production in the period 1850–1914—like the growth in steam power—were far more massive than in the previous hundred years, when percentage growth rates were higher, and these realities in tons of coal, yards of cotton, etc., need emphasizing; very much bigger absolute increases in the output of these industries—which would have been necessary to maintain the percentage rate of growth of the whole economy, in the embryonic stage of the new industries—were beyond the bounds of practical possibility.

INDUSTRIAL OUTPUTS, 1850–1913

Year	Coal (million tons)	Pig-iron (million tons)	Steel (million tons)	Raw cotton consumption (million lb)	Mercantile steamships (thousand tons)
	Great Britain	Great Britain	United Kingdom	United Kingdom	United Kingdom
1850	50	2.0	—	588	15
1875	133	6.4	0.7	1,229	227
1913	287	10.3	7.7	2,178	1,170

Source: Statistical Abstracts; Board of Trade, *British and Foreign Trade and Industry*, Cd.1761 (1903) and Cd.2337 (1904); see also industrial histories listed in the Bibliography.

These figures demonstrate the tremendous industrial achievements of late Victorian and Edwardian Britain, which have been very inadequately appreciated by comparison with the earlier years. It is true that in terms of productivity the achievements were less impressive, but, again, there were limits to further technological gains in those industries, though growth in output per man-hour was substantially higher than in output per head (see p. 150), and we must remember the social gains from reduced working hours in that period.

It is also misleading to compare the percentage growth rates of the comparatively mature British economy, after over a century of industrial revolution, with those of the up-and-coming economies of the United States and Germany, which were now experiencing their industrial revolutions and were at the stage of initially high growth rates through which Britain had previously passed. Moreover, it was inevitable that eventually they would also catch up with and surpass Britain in absolute terms in view of their larger areas, populations and resources: as Clapham put it, 'half a continent [the United States] is likely in the course of time to mine more coal and make more steel than a small island'. Britain could not possibly keep the Industrial Revolution within her own shores and had abandoned the impracticable bans on the emigration of artisans and export of machinery. Indeed, British technology and overseas investment had been of immense importance in the industrial development of other countries. In any case, Britain had no monopoly of science, technology and inventiveness, nor could she prevent foreign countries from erecting tariff barriers to protect their own growing industries or from encouraging their exports by discriminatory pricing policies and subsidies.

Inevitably, therefore, in the later nineteenth century these countries were overhauling and eventually surpassing Britain, so that this country, though still growing remarkably in absolute terms, was declining relatively; her share of world industrial production and trade was falling, while that of her competitors was increasing.

PERCENTAGE DISTRIBUTION OF WORLD
MANUFACTURING PRODUCTION

Year	United Kingdom	United States	Germany
1870	31.8	23.3	13.2
1913	14.0	35.8	15.7

Source: F. Hilgerdt, *Industrialization and Foreign Trade* (League of Nations, 1945).

The United Kingdom maintained its position as the world's leading industrial exporter right up to 1913, but Germany was rapidly catching up. Britain's share of world exports in manufactured goods fell from 41.4 to 29.9 per cent between 1880 and 1913, while Germany's share rose from 19.3 to 26.5 and the American from 2.8 to 12.6 per cent.

The 'inevitability' argument may, no doubt, be pressed too far, as an easy excuse for British failings, as Aldcroft has emphasized, but even he admits—despite his castigation of British entrepreneurial deficiencies—that 'the major cause [of Britain's relative decline] was the emergence of new and powerful industrial nations with an increasing propensity to export'. The really remarkable thing is not that Britain was now being caught up but that this small island should have acquired such an overwhelming industrial predominance and that she held it so long.

Britain's predominance had been well maintained in the third quarter of the nineteenth century, an era of 'Victorian prosperity', and there was further rapid growth in the iron and steel, textiles, coal and shipbuilding industries, in which Britain continued to produce as much as, or more than, the whole of the rest of the world. Railway building at home and overseas continued to provide a stimulus to iron and engineering, at the same time reducing transport costs and widening markets. Business optimism was also inspired by rising prices, following the gold discoveries in California and Australia, while commercial expansion was encouraged by the final adoption of Free Trade. For a time it seemed that the Cobdenite vision of international economic liberalism would be fulfilled, following the Anglo-French commercial treaty of 1860 and other trade agreements, lowering tariff barriers. Britain had become the 'workshop of the world', her exports massively increasing, and progress seemed unbounded: between 1850 and 1873 total United Kingdom domestic exports rose from £71.4 million to £255.2 million (current values).

Professor Church, however, has recently demonstrated that 'the Great Victorian Boom' of 1850–73 has been greatly exaggerated by comparison with the subsequent 'Great Depression', which Beales, Musson and Saul had previously shown to be largely mythical. That third quarter of the century, usually looked back on with euphoria, was not, in fact, a period of constantly rising growth, prices and profits and of unchallenged British industrial supremacy, but was marked by considerable economic instability, as evidenced by the 1857 and 1866 crises and subsequent depressions, as well as by the 'cotton famine' of the early 1860s. There were also fears of growing foreign competition: 'even before the 1860s, weaknesses [in British industry] were being exposed and publicised, heralding the inevitable intensification of competition with the emerging industrial countries'. Industrial growth was cyclically fluctuating and has tended to be exaggerated by the great boom of the early 1870s. 'The difference between the rate of growth in immediately preceding decades and in the comparable time period after 1873 was relatively small, which hardly justifies attributing to 1850–73 a special unity.'

There has been considerable argument, however, as to when the rot set in, when the watershed or climacteric was reached. Some have put it in the 1870s, others in the 1890s, but in terms of percentage rates of growth Hoffmann has discerned retardation much earlier. In particular industries, indeed, he sees it at a ludicrously early date—in copper-mining by the end of the eighteenth century, in cotton by about 1800 or even 'as early as 1785', in coal and shipbuilding by about the mid-nineteenth century—while in the economy as a whole the percentage rate of growth began to level out around 1820 and to decline by the 1860s. In absolute terms, however, it is clear that the really immense growth of coal, cotton and shipbuilding occurred later. There would also seem to be little support for Coppock's view that the 'massive application' of iron and steam ended around 1870, when steam power was to be so greatly extended after that date and when steel production soared even more dramatically. On the other hand, criticisms of British industry and fears of foreign competition were being voiced much earlier. Even before the 1851 Exhibition revealed that Britain did not lead the world in everything, critics were pointing to the superiority of many foreign manufactures and 'schools of art and design' were being set up from the late 1830s onwards to try to remedy such deficiencies. Babbage, since at least as early as 1830, and Playfair and others subsequently, had long been commenting adversely on Britain's comparative weakness in applied science. Much evidence had been presented to parliamentary committees on the exportation of machinery in 1824–5 and 1841, and serious apprehensions had been expressed on the growth of manufactures and machine-making in Europe and the United States. Similarly, after the international exhibitions of 1862 and 1867 in London and Paris, renewed concern was voiced at the growth of foreign competition and at British inadequacies in scientific education and technology.

The situation did not suddenly change around 1870 from Victorian prosperity and optimism to depression and gloom. The so-called Great Depression in the last quarter of the nineteenth century was largely a myth. In terms of production and employment, there was no great trough in that period: even the misleading percentage growth rates do not support the notion, for they had been tending to fall earlier, and they went on falling right down to 1914, though, as we have seen, production increased massively in absolute terms. Nor was there any marked change in average unemployment, which, at around 5 per cent of the skilled labour force, was very little higher than in the preceding or following periods. The main reason for attaching such a misleading label to this quarter-century is that prices were falling—the average fall was about 40 per cent in the period 1873–96—but they had been similarly falling in the period from 1815 to mid-century, generally regarded as one of rapid industrial growth. Moreover, this was an international phenomenon, not peculiar to Britain, and the basic cause seems to have been monetary, related to declining world gold production in the era of the gold standard; although the price trend was reversed from 1896 onwards, with the increasing development of South African gold mines, there was no associated rise in the British industrial growth rate. It appears, however, that falling prices did tend to squeeze profit margins and that there was some slight shift in distribution of national income towards wage earners, which may have accounted for some fall in investment (see p. 162); this situation changed after 1896, with rising prices, and, as we shall see, in the period up to 1914 there is evidence from some industries that more vigorous efforts were being made to remedy technological deficiencies and that Britain, in her turn, was beginning to catch up in fields where she had been tending to lag. But the statistics of industrial production and productivity show a marked decline in percentage growth rates in the early 1900s.

It has been argued, with some validity, that British entrepreneurs and technologists in the late nineteenth and early twentieth centuries might have been more flexible, less attached to the old basic industries and established technology and more enterprising and inventive, especially in the newly developing industries in which they showed up poorly in comparison with those of some other countries. Even allowing for historical hindsight, there does seem to be something in this argument, particularly in regard to applied science. The voluntary educational agencies of earlier years no longer sufficed in an increasingly scientific-technological age, but a State system of education, especially of technical education, was slow in developing: religion combined with the established classical tradition and social rigidities to delay the spread of scientific and technical education in schools and universities, and this lag certainly seems to have contributed to the relatively slow development in Britain of new industries such as organic chemicals, electrical engineering, internal-combustion engines and motor vehicles, as well as new scientific-technical processes in old industries. The persistence of the family firm and a tendency towards 'third generation' debility may also have had some retarding or stagnating effect, though as Saul,

Wilson and others have pointed out, there are many examples both of 'third generation' recovery and of the entry of new firms, with innovating enterprise, in both old and new industries (see p. 163–4).

It would appear, in fact, that in so far as retardation did occur, it was brought about not so much by socio-biological factors, as by forces largely beyond the control of British industrialists. The main factor, it has been strongly argued, was the rapid growth of industries, tariffs and trade competition in foreign countries such as Germany and the United States. Not only were British exports to those markets reduced, but they had to face far stronger rivalry in world markets generally. An outstanding example was the catastrophic effect of American tariffs in the 1890s on the British tinplate and alkali industries, which thereby lost almost entirely their main foreign market, while similar though less dramatic changes were affecting other industries. Even in the home market by the 1890s and early 1900s there was growing alarm at the influx of goods 'made in Germany' and at the 'American invasion'.

Perhaps Britain was mistaken in her adherence to free trade; though it continued to provide the benefits of cheap food and raw materials and was the basis of multilateral world trade, it deprived Britain of retaliatory weapons against tariff barriers, bounties, dumping and other protectionist practices by foreign competitors, as well as sacrificing British agriculture. It may, of course, be doubted whether a return to protectionism in Britain would have greatly affected the changing international trading situation, while it might have tended to bolster up industrial and commercial inefficiency—hence the early protectionist arguments were couched in terms of 'fair trade' and 'reciprocity', which would put Britain on level terms with her rivals while preserving the stimulus of competition—but Britain could hardly continue indefinitely as a free-trade island in an increasingly protectionist world. Nevertheless, free-trade policy was maintained right up to the First World War and beyond.

It can be argued, however, that the success of foreign competitors was attributable not so much to their protectionist policies as to investment in more advanced technology and new industries and to more vigorous commercial enterprise. From around mid-century, if not earlier, as Burn showed many years ago, one can discern the 'genesis of American engineering competition' in all kinds of labour-saving machinery and mass-produced goods, such as machine-tools, wood-working machines, small arms, typewriters and agricultural machinery. Britain's lead in mechanical engineering was being lost in many fields. Perhaps, contrary to some theoretical notions, her early start was now proving a handicap instead of an advantage, in the shape of obsolescent buildings and plant and cluttered industrial sites, which required scrapping and rebuilding, whereas the late starters were more easily able to install the most up-to-date machinery. We were actually assisting in this process: whilst a textile-engineering firm such as Platts of

Oldham was equipping the rest of the world with the latest spinning and weaving machinery, there were mills in Lancashire full of antiquated mules and looms. Perhaps this was due to a conservative attitude, even taking pride in the continued working of old outdated plant. Perhaps too little of profits was now being ploughed back into new investment and too much was going into land, houses and conspicuous consumption, though that kind of expenditure and social metamorphosis was by no means new. Perhaps too much of a *rentier* attitude was developing, and too much capital was being invested abroad, instead of being used to re-equip old industries and develop new ones.

Most studies of the British economy in this period emphasize the continued over-commitment to the old basic industries. In 1907 coal, iron and steel, engineering, shipbuilding and textiles still accounted for nearly half the net industrial output and 70 per cent of all exports (see pp. 243–4). This over-commitment, of course, derived from the period when Britain was the 'workshop of the world' and dominated overseas trade in these products. But it could not last: as Kindleberger has pointed out, 'an exporter with 75 per cent of the world market in a commodity, as the British had at various times in cotton textiles, iron rails, galvanized iron, tinplate, locomotives, ships and coal, can have no expectation of maintaining it'. Inevitably, as other countries began to industrialize rapidly and to compete commercially, Britain's rate of export growth was bound to decline. Many critics have therefore argued that Britain's economy ought to have been more diversified and that capital and labour should have been redeployed, especially into new industries. But decline in the old basic industries was long delayed: right up to 1914, in fact, it was only foreshadowed in their slower percentage growth rates and relative retardation; in absolute terms, as we have seen, growth continued to be very impressive. In such circumstances, it is not surprising that over-commitment continued to be a feature of the British economy; there has been excessive historical castigation of late Victorian and Edwardian businessmen in cotton, iron and steel, coal and shipbuilding, for what was a perfectly rational adherence to these still-expanding and profitable industries. There has been too strong a tendency to regard the pre-1914 British economy in the light of later experience, after the First and Second World Wars, when circumstances had changed considerably: hindsight is easier than foresight.

It is also easy for economists and economic historians to talk about redeployment of resources, but in actual industrial practice there are serious problems. Contraction and redeployment are very difficult and painful processes. Capital is not easily transferred from cotton mills, coal mines and shipyards into new plant in new industries, nor can labour—specialized businessmen, managers and skilled workers—be redeployed very readily, with the necessary occupational and geographical mobility, retraining and rehousing. Only under very severe pressure, as in the period between the First and Second World Wars, is such massive redeployment likely to take place, and even then only with grave difficulties. Between the 1870s and 1914 there was no such severe pressure, despite talk of a Great Depression. Indeed, as Saul has emphasized, 'Britain retained a wide lead in many industrial sectors to 1914 ... [in] cotton textiles and textile machinery, heavy machine-tools, custom-built locomotives, ships and steam engines ... [and] continued investment in them before 1914 was justified by their relative profitability'. Only by historical hindsight can we say that such investment was mistaken, that in view of what was to happen after the war these industries should have been contracted and resources redeployed into new industries. In this period it was easier to meet foreign competition by modifying the existing pattern of production and overseas markets—towards more specialized or finer quality goods, for example, or towards primary producing countries, especially in the Empire—than to undertake major industrial redeployment.

The real problem, in fact, was that of developing new industries alongside the old, while the latter still continued to grow profitably. It appears, however, that there were plenty of savings and capital resources that might have been used for new industrial developments. British overseas investments or capital exports continued to grow prodigiously. According to Imlah's estimates, they rose from a mere £10 million in 1815 to a total of about £250 million by 1850 and then to a staggering £4,000 million by 1913, mainly in railways and foreign or colonial government bonds, and to a lesser extent in industrial enterprises, mines and plantations. Some economic historians and economists have argued that this capital would have been far better invested in British industry, but others have pointed out that there is little or no evidence of a capital shortage in home industry, while foreign investment stimulated the capital-export trades such as iron and engineering and also helped to provide this country with cheap raw materials and foodstuffs from overseas developments, as well as being largely responsible for maintaining a favourable balance of payments through 'invisible' investment income. Though this is true—Britain did have an almost continuous balance of payments surplus between 1850 and 1913, thanks also to shipping earnings—there was what seems, in retrospect, a disturbing increase in the visible trade gap on current account, even allowing for re-exports.

BRITISH OVERSEAS TRADE, 1870–1913
(Current values in £ millions. Volume index, 1880 = 100)

Year	Total imports		Re-exports		Domestic exports	
	Current values	*Volume*	*Current values*	*Volume*	*Curent values*	*Volume*
1850	103.0	28	12.0	24	71.4	32
1875	373.9	85	58.1	87	223.5	84
1913	768.7	220	109.6	183	525.2	239

Source: A. Imlah, *Economic Elements in the Pax Britannica* (Cambridge, Massachusetts, 1958).

These figures show, however, that exports were continuing to increase massively, though at a lower percentage rate, and suggest that criticisms of Britain's lagging export performance have been considerably exaggerated, especially in view of the changing world manufacturing and trading situation. Indeed Sir Arthur Lewis has suggested that Britain was exporting as much as she needed to at that time. But she was to an increasing extent living off her accumulated overseas investments. If these were to be seriously reduced—as they were to be in the First and Second World Wars—then British industry would have to perform much better in export markets to pay for imports but would be handicapped by previously inadequate home investment. Again, however, this is historical hindsight, and it is questionable whether, in the circumstances of the time, there was a seriously inadequate export effort or maldistribution of capital resources.

Marxists, of course, regard the growth of overseas investment as an imperialist escape from the impending 'crisis of capitalism': as British workers were increasingly exploited and 'immiserated', outlets for surplus capital and goods had to be sought in colonial territories, particularly in Asia and Africa, where imperialism was both capitalist and racist. But this theory has little factual foundation. In the first place, there is no evidence of any prolonged capitalist 'crisis' in Britain, though there were, of course, cyclical fluctuations, unemployment and social distress. Secondly, the standard of living of British workers rose substantially between 1850 and 1914, and a growing volume of consumer goods was marketed at home. Thirdly, by far the greater part of British capital exports went, not to Asia and Africa but to Europe, the United States and the colonies of white settlement such as Canada, Australia and New Zealand, or to territories outside the Empire; investments in non-white colonies generally produced a lower rate of return, because of necessary expenditure on the economic infrastructure in undeveloped territories.

Statistical estimates of home and foreign investment do tend to suggest, however, that too much capital was being invested abroad, especially in overseas investment booms such as those of the early 1870s, the late 1880s, and above all between 1905 and 1914, when it greatly exceeded domestic capital formation. British investors were free, of course, to place their capital wherever they wished, and many preferred the relatively safe returns from railway bonds, government stocks and other fixed-interest securities abroad to investment in riskier new industrial ventures at home. It seems unfortunate, from a national point of view, that they did not put more capital into modernizing British industry. That they did not do so, however, would seem to suggest that the capital market institutions (the issuing houses, stock exchange and banks) were deficient in providing channels for industrial investment, or that there was inadequate industrial demand for capital, or that British investors found investment in British industry less inviting than foreign securities, even though these generally produced lower yields. There is no doubt, as Cairncross has demonstrated, that most British industrial investment continued to come from ploughed-back profits, that the stock exchange played a minor role and that British banks were still mainly concerned with provision of short-term commercial credit and were not, like those in Germany, heavily involved in long-term fixed industrial investment. But it seems doubtful whether British industry was thus starved of capital resources or that investment was not forthcoming where industrial prospects seemed favourable. Edelstein has produced evidence of considerable growth and flexibility in the British capital market during this period; it has also been argued that the British economy could not absorb the massive volume of savings generated in Britain. Kennedy, on the other hand, considers that the *rentier* attitude of British investors and their preference for foreign securities reduced the level and raised the cost of domestic capital formation and reinforced the tendency towards over-commitment in the established export industries, which were geared to overseas investment; this attitude he attributes mainly to the 'conservative' 'risk-averse' motives of investors and to the bias of the capital market towards safe well-known securities, both domestic and foreign, whereby new industries were inadequately financed.

These various factors no doubt contributed to the relatively low levels of domestic capital formation in Britain during this period, by comparison with her industrial competitors. Fundamentally, however, the level of domestic investment depended upon the vigour or otherwise of British industrial enterprise and technology. It may be that funds did not flow more copiously into British business on account of limited demand for new capital, because of relative slowness in developing new technology and the tradition of self-finance in family firms. Profits, as a proportion both of industrial income (profits and wages) and of national income were tending to decline in the later nineteenth and early twentieth centuries, according to the estimates of Feinstein and others, and this affected the level of investment. But the level of profits itself depends to a considerable extent on enterprise in exploitation of both technical and marketing opportunities.

NET DOMESTIC CAPITAL FORMATION
AS A PERCENTAGE OF NET DOMESTIC PRODUCT

United Kingdom		Germany		United States	
Years	%	*Years*	%	*Years*	%
1855–74	7.0	1851–70	8.5	1869–80	13.9
1875–94	6.8	1871–90	11.4	1889–1913	12.9
1895–1914	7.7	1891–1913	15.0		

Source: S. Kuznets, 'Long-term Trends in Capital Formation Proportions', *Economic Development and Cultural Change*, IX (1961), p. 10.

Late Victorian and Edwardian businessmen have often been accused not only of technological conservatism and inefficiency but also of weak salesmanship, inadequate regard to the particular requirements of foreign customers, reliance on the agency system instead of developing direct selling and general lack of competitive vigour. But studies by Saul, McCloskey, Sandberg, Harley and others have demonstrated that some of these criticisms of British manufacturing and sales performance in the established industries have been based on inadequate consideration of factor costs and markets: that in the engineering, steel, shipbuilding and cotton industries, for example, British firms pursued rational economic policies in their continued reliance on cheap skilled labour, specialized techniques and products, cheap coal and steam power and that they adjusted reasonably well to the existing market situation. On the other hand, how are we to explain the allegedly slow development of new industries, with potentially greater market opportunities?

To some extent we may be misled by the quantitative measurements of British industrial growth in this period. Hoffmann's and later revised estimates, because of the nature of the available statistical evidence, tend to place too much emphasis on the old basic industries and on the quantity or volume of production, neglecting the rapidly expanding consumer goods and service trades and improvements in the quality of manufactures. In an age of rising living standards—estimates by Prest and Feinstein show national income (both total and per head), real wages and consumers' expenditure all going up substantially during this period—Britain was reaching the stage of mass-production and mass-consumption, and, as Wilson has emphasized, the consumer goods trades, now producing foodstuffs, clothing, footwear, furniture, soap, pharmaceuticals, cigarettes, books and newspapers in factories, were increasing in relative importance, together with the associated wholesale and retail distributive trades, particularly department stores and multiple shops or chain stores. There was a consumer goods revolution with the development of packaged and branded (trade-marked) products, nationally advertised. One has only to mention such names as Lever's, Boot's, Cadbury's, Rowntree's, Marks and Spencer's, Lewis's, Burton's, Lipton's, Wills's and Harmsworth's—all firms founded or rapidly developing in the late nineteenth and early twentieth centuries—to demonstrate that there was no lack of entrepreneurial enterprise and business expansion in these trades. Nor were frugality and investment lacking in this new generation of industrial and commercial pioneers: according to Wilson, 'in the 1890s William Lever [for example] was making £50,000 a year, living modestly on £400 a year and with the remainder creating and purchasing his own ordinary shares'. And Lever, though outstanding, was by no means untypical.

There were also improvements in the quality of manufactures that are difficult to quantify and that do not appear in crude figures of raw cotton consumption, pig-iron output, etc. In the cotton industry, for example, better-quality yarns and improved dyeing and finishing, as Marrison has shown, were enabling British exports to maintain their competitive position, while in the soap trade production of toilet soaps, flakes and powders was being developed, in place of or in addition to household soaps, and such goods were being wrapped and packeted to preserve quality and attract consumers. Moreover, the various production indices take no account of the comparatively rapid growth in non-industrial services, the 'tertiary' sector, including not only the distributive trades but also banking, insurance and the professions, which become of increasing significance in highly developed economies (see p. 151, for the Census figures). A good deal of investment was also going into the social field, into improved sanitation, education and amenities such as hotels, catering and holiday resorts—all features of a higher-income society.

Other evidence also suggests that criticism of technological stagnation in British industry during this period has been greatly exaggerated. Whilst it is true that advances were now more frequently being made abroad—which was inevitable as foreign industrialization gathered pace—many of these were soon introduced here, and at the same time there are numerous examples of continued British inventiveness and innovation, and there was a continuous infusion of new enterprise, in new as well as old industries. In the manufacture of machine-tools, for example, new firms such as Craven's and Herbert's were sustaining Britain's engineering reputation; Humber, Raleigh and Rudge Whitworth led in bicycle manufacture; in the development of internal-combustion engines and motor-car manufacture, the names of Crossley, Ackroyd Stuart, Rolls Royce, Napier, Austin and Morris can be placed alongside those of foreign pioneers; in rubber and tyre manufacture, Dunlop's were similarly pioneering; in chemicals, Brunner Mond, Levinstein, Crosfield's and others were introducing new processes in the manufacture of soda, dyestuffs, soap, oils and fats; in the development of electricity, following the early scientific-technological achievements of Faraday, Wheatstone and others and introduction of the electric telegraph, Swan's name is coupled with Edison's in electric lighting, while Parsons was the inventive genius in steam turbo-electric generation. Nor was innovating enterprise confined to new industries and new firms: Wedgwood's in pottery, Pilkington's in glass, Courtauld's in textiles, Napier's in engineering and Crosfield's in soap and chemicals all confound the theory of 'third generation' atrophy.

The family firm, subject of so much criticism, was clearly still a source of innovation. At the same time, considerable changes were taking place in the structure of British business. Joint-stock company organization was spreading rapidly in the late nineteenth and early twentieth centuries, and, though many limited companies were still really family firms, new sources of capital were thus being tapped, and new professional managerial talent was being introduced—a 'managerial revolution' was, in fact, beginning—and this provided fresh vigour (see pp. 245–55). There was also a continued infusion of foreign enterprise, as illustrated by Mond, Levinstein and Nobel in chemicals, Singer in sewing machines, Daimler and Ford in motor car manufacture, and Westinghouse and General Electric in electrical engineering. Whilst this may perhaps be regarded as indicative of British backwardness, especially in new industries, it also shows that enterprising foreigners regarded Britain as a favourable field for such industrial developments, and in these and other industries such as machine-tools, printing, boot-and-shoe and glass manufactures the American impact provided a particularly strong stimulus to technical innovation.

An argument frequently put forward at the time was that the adoption of new industrial techniques in this country was hindered by the growing strength of trade unions. Certainly British trade unionism was rapidly developing by the late nineteenth century, extending to unskilled and semi-skilled workers, as well as embracing more and more skilled craftsmen, and there is plentiful evidence of opposition to new machinery and manufacturing methods, restrictions on manning and output, demarcation disputes, 'ca'canny' or go-slow practices and general work-spreading to safeguard against unemployment. Unions in Germany and America were much weaker. On the other hand, British employers have been blamed for poor labour relations, in their efforts to keep down wages rather than to reduce unit labour costs through higher productivity at higher wages, though the workers' fear of redundancy generally stood in their way. In America, as Habakkuk has argued, where labour was relatively dear compared with the price of capital, it paid to go in for more capital-intensive production, whereas British industry still relied considerably on relatively cheap skilled labour. In Germany, on the other hand, where wages were lower than in Britain, different explanations of rapid industrial growth have been suggested, such as scientific-technological education and investment banks. Clearly trade-union restrictions by no means account for Britain's relative retardation: they certainly did not prevent considerable labour mobility and changes in occupational structure. Perhaps, indeed, it is futile to search for scapegoats, either among entrepreneurs or trade unions, for what was an inevitability in the developing world economy.

9

Industrial Power, Coal and Metals*

The Industrial Revolution in Britain was based fundamentally on coal and steam power. Although water-wheels were at first of widespread importance for driving machinery of all kinds, they were being rapidly superseded by coal-fired steam-engines by the mid-nineteenth century, while iron and other metals, smelted with coal, were in ever-increasing demand for millwork and industrial machinery, as well as for innumerable hardware manufactures. It was the steam-engine that had made possible the enormously increased output of coal from deeper mines, of iron from power-driven furnaces and forges, of machinery from power-operated machine-tools in engineering works, and of textiles and other products of the factory system. As the Industrial Revolution spread in the later nineteenth century, as furnaces multiplied and manufacturing mechanization was more widely extended, while steam and iron similarly revolutionized transport on sea and land, industries providing the basic power, fuel and materials for this transformation were even more vastly developed.

The growth of industrial motive power

Throughout this period steam continued to be the main driving force of British industry. Water and wind power dwindled into insignificance, and, although gas and oil (internal-combustion) engines and electricity were becoming important from the late nineteenth century onwards, steam-engines still remained dominant in most industries right up to 1914—indeed, in Britain, where possibilities of hydro-electric generation were very limited, the new electrical power was itself dependent mainly on steam-driven generators.

Meanwhile, further developments occurred in steam engineering. The old beam engines were increasingly displaced by direct-acting types (see p. 114, 184), and power was greatly increased by higher pressures and by compounding, first

---

* Metals in this chapter will include only the primary production of iron and steel and non-ferrous metals. Metal manufactures will be dealt with in Chapter 10.

with two (high- and low-pressure) cylinders, followed from the 1870s onwards by triple- and quadruple-expansion, with great improvements in steel boiler and engine construction. Whereas in the 1840s mill engines of 300 to 400 horse-power were considered enormous, by the early twentieth century engines of ten times that power were to be found in large cotton mills, of even higher power in iron and steel works and far more powerful still in great steamships. Not only could they drive more or bigger machines at higher speeds, but they did so with greatly increased efficiency in terms of fuel consumption.

All these engines were of the traditional reciprocating, piston-and-cylinder type, until in 1884 Charles Parsons of Newcastle upon Tyne patented his steam turbine, in which high-pressure steam was used even more efficiently to produce direct high-speed rotary motion (18,000 r.p.m.) by expansion through rings of steel blades fitted round a shaft enclosed in a cylinder, on a principle similar to that of the water turbine. It was in electricity generation, however, that the turbine was to have the most revolutionary effect, in the form of the turbo-dynamo or turbo-alternator, simultaneously patented by Parsons (see p. 193–4); although the turbine was also developed for industrial use, reciprocating engines retained their predominance right up to 1914.

These developments in steam technology and the spread of steam-powered mechanization in this period need emphasis, because economic and engineering historians have devoted their attention mainly to the heroic pioneering of the early Industrial Revolution and have created a very misleading impression that by about 1870 the steam revolution was virtually over. Yet the statistics of steam power for 1870 and 1907 produce a very different impression. The Factory and Workshop Returns for 1870 provide the first reasonably reliable national survey of steam power, demonstrating the overwhelming predominance of textiles and

INDUSTRIAL MOTIVE POWER IN THE UNITED KINGDOM, 1870

Trade		Steam (horse-power)	Water (horse-power)
Textiles		513,335	35,062
Metal manufactures		329,683	7,570
Leather manufactures		2,658	97
Chemical and allied trades		21,400	362
Food and drink trades		22,956	1,185
Building and woodworking trades		17,220	923
Paper manufactures		27,971	8,412
Miscellaneous manufactures		41,717	2,009
	Total	976,940	55,620

Source: Returns of Factories and Workshops, Parliamentary Papers, 1871, LXII. The figures appear to have been of indicated (that is actual rather than nominal) horse-power but are somewhat suspect; they are of engines 'in use', not of capacity.

INDUSTRIAL MOTIVE POWER IN THE UNITED KINGDOM, 1907

Trade	Steam engines			Internal-combustion engines (gas, oil, etc.)	Water power	Other power	Total capacity	Electricity purchased
	Reciprocating	Steam turbines	Total					
	h.p.	h.p.	h.p.	h.p.	h.p.	h.p.	h.p.	1000 B.T.U.s.
Mines and quarries	2,415,841	3,560	2,419,401	23,191	8,295	44,247	2,495,134	3,405
Iron and steel, engineering and shipbuilding trades	2,109,631	69,577	2,179,208	215,252	21,181	21,800	2,437,441	233,879
Other metal trades	55,612	480	56,092	20,110	7,707	—	83,909	3,877
Textile trades	1,873,169	13,665	1,886,834	39,972	51,612	110	1,978,528	20,883
Clothing trades	46,352	1,727	48,079	35,338	972	417	84,806	11,242
Food, drink and tobacco trades	266,299	3,252	269,551	65,891	42,722	2,007	380,171	24,538
Chemical and allied trades	182,456	734	183,190	25,709	4,490	1,381	214,770	39,818
Paper, printing and allied trades	179,762	3,498	183,260	43,192	11,077	44	237,573	31,828
Leather and allied trades	45,613	31	45,644	8,330	870	47	54,891	1,581
Timber trades	113,187	907	114,094	54,293	5,348	78	173,813	7,957
Building and allied trades	347,647	6,257	353,904	74,875	4,042	163	432,984	13,564
Miscellaneous trades	3,900	—	3,900	5,274	178	65	9,417	1,561
Public utility services	1,379,376	427,204	1,806,580	67,630	18,138	312	1,892,840	50,148
Factory owners, power only	99,973	—	99,973	1,120	1,095	10	102,198	175
Total	9,118,818	530,892	9,649,710	680,177	177,907	70,681	10,578,475	444,456

Source: First Census of Production, 1907, Final Report, 1912, Cd. 6320, p. 17. The figures are of engine capacity.

metal manufactures in use of power-driven machinery, though they do not include the coal industry, a major user of steam-engines, comparable with textiles. The limited extent of steam power at that time is further emphasized by the fact that cotton-spinning and weaving factories alone accounted for over 300,000 horse-power and iron blast-furnaces and mills for over 221,000 horse-power.

By the Census of Production in 1907 there had been a great extension of steam-powered mechanization in other industries, as well as an immense deepening of its use in textiles, iron and steel and coal. Steam-engines, both reciprocating and turbine, had also been applied to generating electricity, while gas and oil (internal-combustion) engines provided another new form of industrial power. Including a few additional returns, the total power of all engines was 10,755,009 horse-power. Unfortunately, although firms were instructed to state the capacity of their engines in either nominal or indicated horse-power, no such distinction was made in the Census statistics, so that precise comparisons cannot be made with the earlier figures; but clearly there had been a very great increase in industrial power since 1870, mainly in reciprocating steam-engines, turbines not yet being much used outside electricity generation. Water and wind power of the traditional kind, though understated in these figures, was now of little significance, though new-style hydraulic and pneumatic machines were being increasingly developed. Internal-combustion engines were of growing importance: coal-gas engines, first introduced from the Continent in the 1860s, and then oil engines of the Ackroyd Stuart and Diesel type, developed from the 1890s onwards, were coming into widespread use, especially in small establishments (see p. 188–9). But the main rival to steam power was electricity, which, after successes in telegraphy and lighting, was also introduced for industrial power from the 1880s onwards, with development of the steam-driven dynamo (see pp. 191–6, for the general growth of electrical engineering). It was estimated in the 1907 Census that 'about one-quarter of the total engine capacity ... was used in driving dynamos for the production of electrical energy, and about three-quarters were used directly for driving machinery'. Of that electrical generating capacity, totalling 1,747,672 kilowatts (see p. 170), the greater part was in the power stations of electricity supply undertakings (included in the above table under Public utility services), but many industrial firms had their own generating plant, comprising over a third of total dynamo capacity, though, as the statistics indicate, many purchased electricity. About three-quarters of generating capacity was driven by reciprocating steam engines.

Electricity was generated for lighting and traction, however, as well as for industrial power, which probably accounted for only about two-fifths of total consumption. It is clear, moreover, that the great bulk of industrial machinery was still driven directly by steam-engines. Except in the engineering and

GENERATING CAPACITY IN THE UNITED KINGDOM, 1907

Dynamos belonging to	Kilowatts	Dynamos driven by	Kilowatts
Electricity supply		Reciprocating steam	
Undertakings	1,020,312	engines	1,285,243
Industrial firms	613,984	Steam turbines	350,586
Railways and tramways	113,376	Other engines	111,843
Total	1,747,672	Total	1,747,672

Source: *First Census of Production*, 1907, *Final Report*, p. 16.

ship-building trades, where 40 to 50 per cent of engine capacity was used to generate electricity for power and light, the electrical revolution was making slow progress: in iron and steel, for example, the proportion was little more than 10 per cent, in coal-mining 7 per cent, in the cotton trade 4 per cent, while these and other industries purchased comparatively little electricity from the supply undertakings (see also p. 193–4).

The coal industry

Throughout this period British industry continued to be based primarily on coal for fuel and power. Ever-increasing quantities were consumed in the furnaces and steam-engines of iron and steel works, textile mills and a widening range of other manufactures, in gasworks and coking plant, in railway locomotives and steamships, and also in domestic households. And when electricity began to be developed in the later nineteenth century, the steam-driven generators still depended on coal. Oil fuel and the internal-combustion engine presented no serious challenge to coal and steam power before 1914. Moreover, coal exports soared from little more than 3 million tons in 1850 to about 98 million (including bunker coal) in 1913, when they accounted for over one-tenth in value of Britain's export trade and for more than a third of annual coal output, which had risen from between 50 and 60 million tons to 287 million over the same period.

This huge increase in production was achieved largely by an even greater expansion of the labour force, which Professor Taylor has estimated as rising from around 255,000 in 1851 to 1,107,000 in 1913. Until the early 1880s productivity continued to be increased by further technological advances in steam-powered pumping, winding, ventilation and underground haulage; annual output per man employed (both above and below ground) rose from around 220 tons in 1851 to 326 tons in 1881. But it then fell gradually to 260 tons in 1913. This was partly explicable in terms of diminishing returns, caused by the increasing difficulties of working at greater depths, on thinner seams, and at greater distances between coal-face and pit-bottom. At the same time, working hours were also reduced, while there seems to have been some diminution of physical effort: rising wage-rates were accompanied by increasing absenteeism and labour stoppages.

Although further mechanical improvements were introduced in screening (sorting) and washing of coal at the pit-head, together with more coke-ovens (though mostly of the beehive type, without by-product recovery), there was a lag in underground mechanization: coal-cutting machines were being experimented with from the 1860s onwards, but in 1913 only about 8 per cent of British coal output was cut by machines (pneumatic and electrical), compared with over two-fifths in the United States, while an even smaller proportion was mechanically conveyed.

To some extent this lag was caused by geological difficulties, but mainly by lack of entrepreneurial and managerial enterprise, though trade union hostility was also a factor: as Taylor has said, a 'plentiful supply of relatively cheap labour hardly provided an incentive to technological innovation'. Structural weakness was also evident in the multiplicity of pits of varying sizes; the distribution of landed surface property was often inconducive to efficient underground workings; many pits, especially in the older areas were small, outdated and inefficient, though new ones were continually being sunk, as in south Yorkshire, the east midlands, south Wales and Kent. Although the size of the average mining company and colliery tended to increase, industrial concentration was much more limited than in the Ruhr. In 1913 there were 3,289 collieries in Britain, operated by 1,589 separate undertakings: thus the average colliery employed 340 men and produced 87,000 tons annually. About four-fifths of the total output came from about a quarter of these undertakings, but the survival of many small units, with inadequate capital resources, militated against industrial reorganization and technological innovation.

Nevertheless, the industry continued to expand and to be profitable, because of the ever-growing demand for coal and the rising trend of prices. This favourable economic situation, together with Britain's geographical export advantage in cheap sea transport, may have tended to mask the industry's shortcomings, but it was still competitively efficient: pit-head prices were lower than anywhere else in Europe, despite higher wages. It is true that other countries were catching up: Britain was no longer producing as much coal as the rest of the world—her share of world output had, in fact, fallen to about a quarter, and she had been far surpassed by the United States in both production and productivity—but she still retained the European lead, though just before 1914 Germany reached the same level of output per miner. Moreover, British exports continued to dominate the world coal trade. No doubt the industry's declining productivity and the rise of oil and electricity were disturbing features, but the future seemed secure with continually increasing production and exports. Indeed, abundant supplies of relatively cheap coal and gas for fuel, power and lighting probably induced prodigality in use of this natural resource, delaying adoption of fuel-saving techniques and of electric power in British industry.

Iron and steel

British iron output continued to soar dramatically in the third quarter of the nineteenth century. Annual production of pig-iron rose from two or three million tons in the early 1850s to six or seven million by the early 1870s, while that of puddled iron went up from just over one million to around three million tons. Britain continued to maintain an astonishing predominance over the rest of the world, and exports totalled over three million tons by the early 1870s, mainly of pig- and railway-iron, dominating the international trade.

During this period some of the older iron-producing areas, such as Shropshire and Staffordshire, stagnated or declined, as their iron ore resources were worked out and they had increasingly to 'import' ore or pig-iron from new areas that were now rising rapidly into prominence, most notably the north-eastern Cleveland district, centring on Middlesbrough, which was producing about a third of British pig-iron by 1875; output from the Cumberland and Furness district also increased rapidly, and Barrow rose with it. New orefields were also beginning to be exploited in east midlands counties such as Lincolnshire and North-amptonshire, which were as yet, however, sending most of their output to furnaces in the older areas. At the same time, imports of foreign ore, previously negligible, were beginning to rise sharply by the early 1870s, to nearly a million tons in 1873, mainly from Spain; but as yet they were only a small fraction of home ore output, which had then reached 15 to 16 million tons.

It was in the new areas, especially in the Cleveland district, that the most striking technological progress occurred, as bigger and more efficient furnaces were built, operating at higher blast pressures and temperatures and saving fuel by use of waste gases to heat the blast and raise steam for the blowing engines, etc. In the declining areas, older furnaces remained in use, some still with cold blast and most with gases flaring to waste. Nowhere had much improvement been made on beehive coke-ovens, which similarly wasted heat and chemical by-products; in this field, Britain lagged behind France and Belgium. Puddling still remained mostly a laborious manual process, despite efforts at mechanization, but this was the great age of puddled iron, before it was displaced by steel: demand was insatiable, from railways, shipbuilding, engineering and iron manu-factures generally, so puddling furnaces multiplied, while improvements in rol-ling mills increased the output of sheets, plates, bars, rails, angles, wire, etc.

It was in this period, however, that the 'Steel Age' began, with Henry Bessemer's converter. In his famous paper to the British Association in 1856, Bessemer proposed to produce wrought-iron or steel from pig-iron 'without fuel', by blasting air through the molten metal taken directly from the blast-furnace, thus burning out the carbon and other elements. In practice it proved impossible to determine precisely when conversion to steel had occurred, so the blow had to be completed and then the appropriate amount of carbon could be added, in the form of spiegeleisen or ferro-manganese, which also removed embrittling excess oxygen, as discovered by Robert Mushet and others. It also proved impracticable for some years to convert molten pig-iron straight from the blast-furnace, and remelting of graded pig-iron was generally necessary until later in the century, when metal of more consistent quality could be ensured. But the main drawback of Bessemer's process was that it did not remove damaging phosphorus and sulphur, so that only non-phosphoric or acid ores, such as Cumberland haematite, could be used. Bessemer successfully developed it, however, in Sheffield from the late 1850s onwards, and his steel, produced much more cheaply and in greater quantities than by the old Huntsman or crucible process, gradually began to challenge wrought iron in various constructional uses, as Bessemer's process came to be operated under licence by a growing number of iron and steel works.

The Bessemer process itself, however, soon had to face competition from another steel-making innovation, when the open-hearth process was invented by William Siemens (and improved by Martin in France) in the early 1860s. In this invention, a regenerative gas-furnace was used to remove carbon from pig-iron in an open bath, with additions of scrap or ore, followed by spiegeleisen or ferro-manganese; the process was slower and more controllable, and it produced more reliable steel than Bessemer's, which it therefore began to displace in the later nineteenth century. Siemens established a steelworks at Landore, Swansea, in the late 1860s, which could soon produce a thousand tons a week. In 1875, however, out of a total British steel output of over 700,000 tons, only about one-eighth was open-hearth. This process, moreover, like Bessemer's, was confined to the use of non-phosphoric ores; increasing steel production therefore necessitated growing imports of Spanish and Swedish ores, which rose to over three million tons by the early 1880s.

By that time, however, another technological breakthrough had been made, with the invention of the basic process by Gilchrist Thomas, patented in 1879. By putting a basic or limestone lining, instead of silica (acid) fire-brick, in a Bessemer converter, and also by adding limestone to the pig-iron charge, he was able to remove phosphoric acid by chemical combination, forming basic slag (which came to be used as an agricultural fertilizer). This invention could also be applied to the open-hearth process, but most basic production came from converters until the early twentieth century (see p. 175).

Until 1880, therefore, in steel as in pig- and puddled-iron, Britain continued to maintain its industrial predominance. Despite some evidence of foreign scientific-metallurgical superiority, the main steel-making innovations had been made in this country, which had therefore established a world leadership in steel production. Steel was now clearly the constructional material of the future, coming rapidly into use for railways, shipbuilding, engineering, armaments, etc. The output of puddled iron in Britain fell from its peak of nearly three million tons a year in the early 1870s to an annual average of little more than a million in the first decade of the twentieth century; now used mainly for the rougher work of blacksmiths, chain-makers, etc., it tended to concentrate in the Black country area.

In the late nineteenth and early twentieth centuries, however, other countries, notably the United States and Germany, rapidly caught up with and then far surpassed British pig-iron and steel production. Whereas in 1870 Britain had produced over half the world's pig-iron and not far short of half the steel, by 1913 her share had fallen to about 14 per cent for pig-iron and just over 10 per cent for steel, while the United States was now producing over two-fifths and Germany between a fifth and a quarter of the world's iron and steel.

PRODUCTION OF IRON AND STEEL
(million tons)

Year	Great Britain		Germany		United States		World	
	Pig-iron	Steel	Pig-iron	Steel	Pig-iron	Steel	Pig-iron	Steel
1870	5.96	0.22	1.24	0.13	1.67	0.04	11.84	0.51
1880	7.75	1.29	2.43	0.69	3.84	1.25	18.16	4.18
1890	7.90	3.58	4.03	2.10	9.20	4.28	26.75	12.28
1900	8.96	4.90	7.43	6.36	13.79	10.19	39.81	27.83
1973	10.26	7.66	16.49	17.32	30.97	31.30	77.90	75.15

Sources: Various works on the iron and steel industry listed in the bibliography.

Britain was also being overtaken in iron and steel exports: these rose from 2.71 to 4.93 million tons between 1870 and 1913, but German and American exports soared from almost negligible figures to 6.40 and 2.90 million tons respectively. Moreover, in 1913 iron and steel imports into Britain were 2.23 million tons, nearly half the export figure, compared with only 0.3 million (Germany) and 0.25 million (United States); in fact Britain was now the world's largest importer of iron and steel.

This dramatic loss of leadership has generally been regarded as the most striking manifestation of Britain's relative economic decline. Not surprisingly, the iron and steel industry has been the main hunting ground for explanations of alleged British industrial failure in this period, which historians such as Burn, Burnham and Hoskins, and Orsagh have attributed mainly to entrepreneurial deficiencies. These have been demonstrated particularly by the slowness in developing the Thomas basic process and in exploiting the east midlands ores; foreign competitors, especially the Germans, were quicker to introduce this British-invented process and to utilize their resources of phosphoric ores. At the same time, they developed larger-scale integrated plants, with bigger and more efficient blast furnaces and rolling mills; they were more progressive in mechanization, in utilizing waste heat and gases for driving steam or gas engines or for generating electricity, and in installing by-product-recovery coking plants. These larger foreign concerns were less conservative than British family firms and more advanced in scientific-technological developments; their more rapid progress was also attributable to more vigorous capital investment, aided by closer links with the capital market and particularly with the banks.

UNITED KINGDOM STEEL OUTPUT BY PROCESS
(thousand tons)

Year	Bessemer		Open-hearth		Total
	Acid	Basic	Acid	Basic	
1875	620		88		708
1890	1,613	402	1,463	101	3,579
1900	1,254	491	2,863	293	4,901
1913	1,049	552	3,811	2,252	7,664

Source: Mitchell and Deane, op. cit., p. 136.

These criticisms, however, have been strongly countered in recent years by Sinclair, Temin and McCloskey, who have argued that Britain's relative decline was inevitable, as the United States and Germany developed their larger resources and home markets, protected their industries by high tariffs and also competed strongly with Britain in the rest of the world; the consequently slower rate of growth of the British steel industry therefore tended to result in a lower level of investment, older plant and higher costs. Yet even so, technological progress was apparently better than previously portrayed, and in terms of productivity and costs the British industry compared reasonably well with its competitors. The alleged technological lags can be explained by rational factor-cost, marketing and technical considerations: for example, the advantages of large-scale integration, bigger blast-furnaces and rolling mills, etc., were associated particularly with the Bessemer process, but increasing British concentration on the open-hearth process, which could be conducted economically on a much smaller scale, was dictated mainly by the growing demands and technical requirements of the shipbuilding, engineering and other industries, which found Bessemer steel unreliable (chiefly because of excess nitrogen absorbed in blowing); the main market for large-scale Bessemer production, in rail-making, was declining and increasingly competitive from the 1880s onwards. Moreover, as Harley has pointed out, there were opportunities for the British industry to exploit its greater resources of cheap skilled labour in both open-hearth and rolling-mill operations. It also made economic sense to use high-grade foreign ores—7.4 million tons in 1913—developed with the aid of considerable capital investment by British iron and steel firms and cheaply imported by sea; at the same time, the lag in exploitation of east midlands ores—rising from little more than a million tons in 1870 to $6\frac{1}{2}$ out of a total 16 million tons of home-produced ores in 1913—has been exaggerated; there was a rapid shift to basic open-hearth steel-making after introduction of the Talbot continuous (tilting-furnace) process around 1900, considerably reducing costs. And after all, there was a huge increase in British steel output during this period, despite massive tariff-supported competition from much bigger countries, now rapidly industrializing. Though not without failings, British entrepreneurs in this industry certainly seem to have put up a better performance than has often been alleged: indeed, if we accept McCloskey's view, 'they did very well indeed'.

Moreover, considerable structural changes were going on in this and closely related industries such as engineering and shipbuilding, resulting in larger-scale integrated company organization (see p. 251). These tendencies had, of course, long been present in the older pig- and puddled-iron industry, but now they became much more striking. Not only did many steel-making firms own their iron ore and coal mines, but some integrated forward into manufacturing sheets, tinplate, tubes, wire, etc., and into engineering and shipbuilding, while horizontal amalgamations also occurred, leading to the emergence of large companies combining interests in the Midlands, south Wales and Scotland. Though these mergers and combines were not run on the same scale as in America and Germany—perhaps through entrenched family control—they certainly did a good deal to rationalize and reconstruct the British industry.

Technical improvements were also stimulated by the Iron and Steel Institute established in 1869. Most works now employed metallurgical chemists, and progress was made in the development of steel alloys, by addition of manganese, nickel, chromium, tungsten and other metals; much experimentation was carried out in Sheffield, where the cementation and crucible processes remained in common use for production of special steels, such as stainless steels and high-speed steels for machine-tools. But the British industry lagged in the saving of waste heat, gases and by-products, in mechanical charging and handling, in exploitation of the 'direct process', in development of the electric furnace and in establishment of large highly mechanized rolling mills for standardized mass-production. (Some of these innovations had originated in England, for example the universal, three-high, reversing and continuous rolling mills, but were developed more slowly here than in the United States and Germany.) McCloskey's statistical researches have by no means disposed of such evidence of entrepreneurial, technological and scientific-educational deficiencies. But there is much truth in the argument that technological retardation was the result, rather than the cause, of inevitably slower growth. Britain's extraordinary world predominance could not last, and in the decades before the First World War, as

Payne has concluded, 'the British iron and steel industry assumed ... a relative position more appropriate to its resource base, to the size of its home market and to the share of the export market which it might justifiably expect to supply'.

Tinplate

The growth of the tinplate industry was closely associated with that of iron and steel, which provided the basic rolled sheets. The range of tinware manufactures was extended from the 1840s onwards by the development of steam-powered pressing and stamping machines, and in the late nineteenth century the intro-duction of food-canning and petrol-cans greatly increased demand. Britain's lead in both iron and steel and tin production gave the British tinplate industry a virtual monopoly of world trade, and exports expanded prodigiously, especially to the United States, much the largest overseas market, where it was widely used for roofing as well as for pans, kettles, cans, etc. Tinplate production became increasingly concentrated in south Wales, especially west of Port Talbot, and to a much lesser extent in the west Midlands, which was the main area of manu-facturing consumption. Output rose rapidly from 37,000 tons (exports 25,000) in 1850 to 586,000 tons (exports 448,000) in 1891, but expansion was then checked by the McKinley tariff in the United States, which dealt a crushing blow to the export trade; but output recovered in the early twentieth century to 848,000 tons (exports 481,000) in 1912.

This remarkable increase in production was achieved by increasing the number and size of works and also by more mechanization. Steam gradually displaced water power in the plate-rolling process, and power-driven machinery was also introduced for shearing the plates, dipping them in pickling acid and passing them through tinning pots; costs were also cut by rolling thinner sheets and reducing the tin coating, to produce disposable tin cans, etc. But a con-siderable amount of manual labour, both skilled and unskilled, was still employed in operating this machinery and in handling the plates or sheets, in and between these various processes; by contrast with America, where there was more emphasis on labour-saving, manual skills were relatively plentiful and cheap in the Welsh industry.

Until 1860 most of the tin supplies continued to come from Cornwall, but thereafter increasingly from the expanding mines of Malaya and Australia. In the last quarter of the century puddled iron, which had only recently displaced charcoal iron for making the plates, was itself displaced by steel, especially Siemens open-hearth steel, which was superior to Bessemer steel for this purpose. Tinplate works now generally abandoned forging their own bars and bought supplies from steelworks; the growth of open-hearth steel-making in south Wales further accentuated the predominance of this area in tinplate manufacture, but there was rarely any technical integration, tinplating actually becoming more of a separate trade. In the later nineteenth and early twentieth centuries there was a tendency towards the linking of steel and tinplate interests, especially in larger firms such as Richard Thomas & Co. and Baldwin's, but the great majority of tinplate firms remained small, independent and specialized.

Non-ferrous metals

All mineral-extractive industries operate under the threat of diminishing returns and ultimate exhaustion. Jevons drew attention to our finite coal resources as early as the 1860s, and Britain was having to import increasing quantities of iron ore in the later part of the century, but the approach of Nemesis was most alarmingly evident in the mining of non-ferrous ores. With the long historical growth of tin, copper, lead and zinc mining, this had never previously been envisaged, but from the last quarter of the nineteenth century, with the working out of seams, the increasing costs of deeper mining and the opening up of cheaper foreign sources in South America, Malaya, Australia and Africa, all these industries experienced dramatic decline, despite continuing technological advances in mining and smelting.

'In 1865 Cornwall produced 40 per cent of the world's tin but in ten years it had dropped to less than a quarter and by 1939 to one per cent while today it is negligible' (J. B. Richardson). The annual output of tin ore, around 10,000 tons in the mid-nineteenth century, rising to over 16,000 tons in the early 1870s, fell to about 8,000 tons in 1910–14, and this decline continued in the post-war period. Copper-mining experienced an even worse catastrophe, the output of ore falling from around 300,000 tons in the mid-1850s to about 200,000 in the mid-1860s and then plunging to below 40,000 tons by the mid-1880s. Soon there were hundreds of miles of abandoned drowned underground workings, while many Cornish and other miners emigrated, as the industry expired; the Swansea smelting industry died with it, being nearly extinct by 1914.

Lead-mining experienced a similar but more protracted fate. The output of ore, around 100,000 tons in the early 1850s, began to fall gradually from the early 1870s to about 25,000 tons just before the First World War, though it was to recover temporarily in the inter-war period. The production of zinc-blende, closely associated with lead-mining, followed a similarly declining course. The lead- and zinc-mining areas of the Mendips and Pennines, like the tin and copper mines of the south-west and elsewhere, were gradually to become derelict, as Britain's dependence on imports increased, though British capital and technology were mainly responsible for opening up these overseas supplies. At first ores were imported, to be smelted and refined in this country, but soon these processes were developed abroad and increasing quantities of the metals were imported, especially of copper and lead.

In production of the non-ferrous newcomer aluminium, French chemists led the way from the mid-nineteenth century onwards, developing a process for reduction of aluminium chloride with metallic sodium. The American chemist Castner introduced this process on a large scale at Oldbury, Birmingham, in the 1880s, but it was soon superseded by the Héroult–Hall electrolytic processes (again Franco-American), in which Britain stood at a great disadvantage, having only relatively small resources of the raw material bauxite and little cheap hydro-electric power by comparison with other countries such as Switzerland, Norway and Canada. The British Aluminium Company, founded in 1894, started production in Scotland, but Britain was to remain heavily dependent on foreign imports. Before 1914, however, the manufacture of aluminium pans, etc., was trifling by comparison with those of tinplate and other metalwares.

10

Mechanical and Electrical Engineering, Shipbuilding and Other Metal Manufactures

During this period the engineering, shipbuilding and other metal manufactures, together with the primary processes of iron and steel making, overtook and greatly surpassed textiles in their contribution to British industrial output (see p. 242). Fundamentally, in fact, they were of greater importance, being the foundation of power-driven mechanization in all industries and transport. They formed a very heterogeneous though closely interrelated group of trades, as illustrated by the following table from the 1907 Census of Production. Moreover, this list does not include non-ferrous metals and manufactures, separately categorized, with a gross output of £93.5 million (£11.9 million net) and employing over 114,000.

Many of these trades had themselves become great power users—notably iron and steel, engineering, shipbuilding and railway workshops, which were also the biggest employers of labour—but some less important trades, such as cutlery, blacksmithing, needle-making, lock-making and small arms manufacture, obviously were still not very highly mechanized. Small-scale light metal manufactures of the latter kind, together with the making of chains, nails and other hardware, were differentiated from the primary metallurgical processes of smelting, rolling, etc., though these supplied them with their raw materials, whereas the heavier manufactures of tinplate or tubes, though also specialized, tended to be more closely related to primary production; some iron-founding and forging firms had also integrated forward into the making of steam-engines, boilers and machinery, and these developments continued in this period as closer associations or amalgamations were formed between iron and steel, engineering and shipbuilding firms (see p. 251).

The engineering group, much the most important in this list in terms of net output and employment, was itself composed of many varied and increasingly

IRON AND STEEL, ENGINEERING, SHIPBUILDING, ETC., 1907

Trade	Gross output	Net output	Persons employed excluding out-workers	Engine power
	(£ million)	(£ million)	(thousands)	t h o u s a n d
Iron and steel (smelting, rolling and founding)	105.3	30.0	261.7	1,383.6
Tinplate	9.2	2.0	20.7	68.8
Wrought iron and steel tube	6.6	2.2	20.2	23.0
Wire	6.6	2.1	18.3	31.0
Anchor, chain, nail, bolt, screw and rivet trades	5.6	2.3	28.0	23.0
Galvanized sheet, hardware, hollow-ware, tinned and japanned goods and bedstead trades	16.0	6.5	74.8	27.3
Engineering (including electrical engineering)	103.0	50.5	461.7	331.3
Shipbuilding and marine engineering (private firms)	42.6	18.5	188.3	114.5
Cycle and motor	11.6	5.9	54.0	15.4
Cutlery	2.0	1.1	14.8	5.2
Tool and implement	3.7	2.1	23.7	19.2
Blacksmithing	2.5	1.5	20.9	4.1
Needle, pin, fish-hook and button	1.6	0.8	13.3	3.3
Lock and safe	1.0	0.6	7.9	2.3
Small arms	0.7	0.5	4.9	2.6
Heating, lighting, ventilating and sanitary engineering	2.9	1.6	14.3	3.5
Railway carriage and wagon	9.8	3.6	28.9	30.4
Total (private firms)	330.7	131.8	1,256.3	2,088.6
Railways (construction, repair and maintenance of permanent way, rolling stock, plant, etc.)	34.7	17.1	241.8	273.3
Royal and naval ordnance factories	3.4	1.5	15.6	13.6
Government shipyards, etc.	6.5	2.5	25.6	62.0
Total (railways and government departments)	44.6	21.1	283.1	348.9

Source: First Census of Production, 1907, Final Report, p. 93. The columned figures, expressed to the first decimal point, do not in every case add up precisely to the totals.

specialized trades*. Some of these, such as the manufacture of steam-engines, textile machinery, railway locomotives and machine-tools had already become well established in the earlier Industrial Revolution, and they continued to develop in the period up to 1914, but new branches were now growing, with extending mechanization and introduction of new forms of power and transport. Specialization developed in the making of machines for wood-working, small arms manufacture, watch- and clock-making, sewing, boot- and shoe-making, printing, harvesting, grain-milling and other increasingly mechanized processes, while the development of hydraulic power, the internal-combustion engine and electricity gave rise to new branches of engineering, of which motor manufacturing and electrical engineering were especially important.

In these developments, particularly in the new industries, there is no doubt that Britain lost much of her earlier predominance. As Burn showed many years ago, the genesis of American engineering competition was clearly evident by the third quarter of the nineteenth century, especially in new branches of light engineering, with the development of standardized mass-production in wood-working and in the manufacture of small arms, sewing machines, watches, typewriters and agricultural machinery, with new machine-tools such as milling and grinding machines and turret lathes, later utilizing high-speed steels. Even in steam engineering the United States challenged with the high-pressure Corliss engine, and later in the century Britain tended to lag behind France, Germany and the United States in development of the internal-combustion engine, motor manufacture and electrical power and engineering. In the older basic industries, too, of coal, iron and steel, and cotton, mechanization was more rapidly extended in America, with coal-cutting machines, three-high rolling mills, ring-spinning machines and automatic looms, for example, and the story is similar in the leather and boot and shoe manufactures, in hosiery and lace, in printing, glass-making and other trades, in which more automatic machinery was being developed mainly in the United States.

Such catalogues of lost leadership have often been produced in damning indictments of British mechanical engineering in this period. But, as we have already seen in the coal, iron and steel industries and as we shall similarly see in others, these criticisms have been greatly exaggerated. Undoubtedly they contain some truth, but as a number of scholars, both British and American, have more recently demonstrated—notably Saul in several penetrating studies of the engineering industry—a broader more balanced assessment leads to conclusions more favourable to British industry. In the first place, it was inevitable that as

---

*We are concerned here with mechanical not civil engineering, though the two were closely associated. The major developments in civil engineering—the building of roads, canals, railways, docks, water and sanitary installations—resulted from the growth of mechanized industry and transport and were facilitated by the development of power-driven pile-drivers, cranes, pumps, etc.

other countries developed industrially they would begin to challenge and even surpass Britain in various areas of mechanical engineering; nor was it deplorable that British firms should adopt such advances from abroad. Secondly, factor costs and markets were different, comparing Britain and the United States: it made economic sense for British firms to utilize their greater resources of relatively cheap skilled labour rather than go in for the same degree of mechanization as in the United States, where not only was skilled labour in relatively short supply but there was a larger more homogeneous internal demand, more suited to mass-production than Britain's varied home and overseas markets. It must also be emphasized that, despite the growth of foreign industry and competition, Britain retained her leadership in several important branches of engineering, while achieving reasonable progress in others, often by adoption of foreign techniques, enabling her to catch up where she had been lagging.

The older branches of engineering: engine- and machine-making in the steam age
As the 1907 Census of Production demonstrates, the older branches of engineering continued to predominate in Britain into the early twentieth century, though by then new branches were rapidly developing. And they were still remarkable for their growth and technological progress.

THE UNITED KINGDOM ENGINEERING OUTPUT, 1907

Main branches	*Gross output (£ million)*
Textile machinery	13.1
Steam engines (excluding railway locomotives and agricultural engines)	6.9
Railway locomotives (Private builders 4.5) (Railway companies 7.9)	12.4
Railway carriages and wagons (Private builders 7.6) (Railway companies 8.2)	15.8
Agricultural steam engines and machinery	2.4
Machine-tools	2.9
Mining machinery	1.3
Hydraulic prime movers and machinery	1.4
Other machinery	11.7
Internal-combustion engines (except motor vehicles)	2.1
Cycles, motor cycles and parts	5.7
Motor vehicles and parts	5.2
Electrical engineering	14.1

Source: First Census of Production, 1907, Final Report, Section III, (Marine engineering was separately classified with shipbuilding, see pp. 196–9.)

In textile engineering, Britain maintained an immense international pre-dominance right up to 1914: Platts of Oldham alone, with 12,000 workers, had an output equal to that of the whole American textile machinery industry. Other old-established firms such as Asa Lees (Oldham) and Dobson & Barlow (Bolton) also continued to flourish, while relative newcomers such as Hetheringtons and Brooks & Doxey (Manchester), Howard & Bullough (Accrington) and Tweedale & Smalley (Rochdale) also built up great reputations; these firms were each employing 3,000 to 6,000 men by 1913. West Riding textile engineering firms established similarly outstanding international reputations, especially in worsted machinery. British pre-eminence was particularly marked in spinning machines, including not only improved mules but also the new ring-frames, a high pro-portion of which went overseas, as the home cotton industry was relatively slow in their adoption (see pp. 203–4). Although British machine-makers were less pro-gressive in the manufacture of automatic looms, Northrops being developed here with American capital in the early twentieth century, exports of textile machinery in 1913 were three times higher than those of Germany, the nearest competitor.

In steam-engine manufacture also, Britain remained ahead, with high-pressure compound (double-, triple- and quadruple-expansion) engines, together with high-speed direct drives, in the development of which British engineers such as Elder, Brotherhood, Willans and Bellis played leading roles, while Parsons pioneered the steam turbine from the 1880s onwards. In the associated boiler-making, crucial to increasing steam pressures, Adamsons and Galloways (Manchester) and Babcock & Wilcox (Glasgow) also became world-renowned. These technological advances brought about a revolution not only in industrial and marine engines but also in electricity generation (see pp. 166–7, 193–4, 196–7). Meanwhile, agricultural engineering firms in the eastern coun-ties—Ransomes (Ipswich), Hornsbys (Grantham), Rustons (Lincoln), Clayton & Shuttleworth (Lincoln), Marshalls (Gainsborough) and others, all large firms employing thousands of men—making portable steam engines and boilers, steam tractors and excavators, as well as threshers, etc., added to British dominance of world trade in steam-engineering products.

Another major and closely related branch of engineering in which Britain had acquired an early lead was the manufacture of railway locomotives, carriages and wagons. Some of the pioneering locomotive-makers, such as Stephensons, the Vulcan Foundry, Sharp Stewart (formerly Sharp Roberts), Kitsons and Nas-myth Wilson, continued into the twentieth century, while new ones, notably Beyer Peacock, Neilson and Dubs, rose into prominence—Manchester, Leeds, Newcastle and Glasgow (particularly) becoming the main locations. (In 1903, Neilson, Dubs and Sharp Stewart, three of the largest firms, combined into the North British Locomotive Company in Glasgow.) But these firms found the home market shrinking as the major railway companies set up their own engineering works, which soon developed to great size; Swindon, in fact, with 14,000 employees, was the biggest in the country in 1914, and many thousands were also employed at Crewe, Stratford, Derby, Doncaster, Horwich, Wolverton and elsewhere.

The manufacture of railway carriages and wagons, as the above table indicates, was of even greater size, though less spectacular, than that of locomotives. It tended to become specialized, the railway companies having separate departments at Swindon, Wolverton, etc., while private manufacturing was located mainly in the Birmingham area and to a lesser extent in Manchester, Gloucester and various other towns; most of the major private firms merged in 1902 into the massive Metropolitan Amalgamated Carriage & Wagon Company, centred on Birmingham. Private builders of both locomotives and rolling stock were driven increasingly into overseas trade, where there was growing competition from German and American manufacturers. Export to Europe and North America dwindled, but important markets were retained in the Empire (especially India), South America and elsewhere.

Considerable advances were also made in hydraulic engineering, in which the early pioneering of Bramah and other British engineers was followed most famously by William Armstrong at Elswick, Newcastle upon Tyne, as well as by Tangyes of Birmingham and other British firms, which built an increasing range of hydraulic machines, including cranes, lifts, jacks, capstans, swing and draw-bridges, lock-gates and pumps, as well as hydraulically powered tools for flanging, riveting, punching, drilling, bending and shearing, especially for shipyards. In the development of pneumatic and electrical tools, however, the United States took the lead, though by the early twentieth century, as we shall see, British engineering and shipbuilding firms were quickly adopting the new forms of power.

All the developments in traditional heavy engineering, closely associated with those in shipbuilding and marine engineering (see pp. 196–9), were dependent upon continued advances in the iron and steel industries and in the making of machine-tools. In the latter field, as in others, Britain no longer led the world, but, as Saul says, she still maintained 'a machine-tool industry of the highest calibre'. It was in the lighter branches of engineering, already mentioned, and in the new industries such as motor manufacture and electrical engineering that the Americans went ahead with standardized mass-production, using new machine-tools such as milling and grinding machines, turret lathes and twist-drills. Moreover, though Mushet, Hadfield and other Sheffield steel-makers had made many experiments with special steel alloys, the Americans took the lead in the late nineteenth-century development of high-speed steels, such as chromium–tungsten steels, for machine-tools. British machine-tool and heavy engineering firms, however, not only made increasing use of the traditional lathes, planers, etc., but also gradually adopted the new machine-tools—some of which, in fact, had originally been pioneered in this country. The earlier developments in standardized, interchangeable mass-production by Maudslay, Roberts, Whitworth and others were carried into widespread practice in the second half of the nineteenth century, and though some of the older machine-tool firms died out or turned to other activities—Maudslay, Field & Co., for example, went increasingly into marine engineering, Whitworth into armaments and steel, Sharp Stewart and Nasmyth Wilson into locomotive manufacture—they were succeeded by other progressive firms, such as those of Muir, Hulse, Cravens, Smith & Coventry and Richards, who carried on the Whitworth tradition in Manchester, while Smith, Beacock & Tannett, Buckton, and Greenwood & Batley followed Murray in Leeds, and several notable firms sprang up in other West Riding towns; Archdale, Herbert and Ward led a remarkable growth in the making of machine-tools in the Birmingham–Coventry area in the later nineteenth century, while Shanks and Langs, of Johnstone, maintained the Scottish reputation. As we shall see, the development of the cycle, motor and electrical industries gave a great boost to this vital sector of British industry.

Nevertheless, there does appear to have been some stagnation in British tool-making in the later nineteenth century, associated with the relative slowness in development of the new lighter branches of engineering. This no doubt mainly accounts for the industry's relatively poor export performance in this field and also in a broad range of miscellaneous engineering production by comparison with Germany and the United States, though in the other traditional heavy engineering sectors the British performance was much more creditable.

ENGINEERING EXPORTS, 1913
(£ million)

Branch	United Kingdom	United States	Germany
Prime movers and boilers	7.0	1.9	5.5
Textile machinery	8.3	0.3	2.8
Locomotives (rail and road)	3.4	1.2	3.9
Agricultural machinery	3.0	6.7	2.5
Machine-tools	1.0	2.9	4.0
Sewing machines	2.4	2.4	2.8
Miscellaneous	9.7	14.2	15.7

Source: Saul, 'The Engineering Industry', in Aldcroft, op cit., p. 227. The table excludes cars, cycles, firearms and railway carriages and wagons. The miscellaneous section is probably largely made up of cranes, pumps, and mining, hydraulic, sugar, grain-milling, paper-making and wood-working machinery.

New branches of engineering: from sewing machines and cycles to motor cars

That Britain lagged behind the United States in the development of harvesting machinery is not surprising, in view of the immense American home market, suited to large-scale mechanization. The same is true of wood-working machinery, though British firms soon began to make up the leeway, as Robinsons of Rochdale victoriously demonstrated at international exhibitions from 1862 onwards. The most famous triumph of 'the American system of manufactures' was in the mass-production of small arms (revolvers and rifles); though the methods were quickly adopted by the Government factory at Enfield in the 1850s, as well as by Whitworth, the Birmingham Small Arms Company and others, the Birmingham gun-makers long continued with their traditional craft techniques, having to cater for smaller more specialized markets, especially for sporting guns. In the manufacture of sewing machines similarly, it was the American Singer factory, established in Glasgow in 1867 and making its own machine-tools, that came to dominate technologically and commercially, largely accounting for the favourable export situation in this sector in 1913; though English manufacturers such as Bradbury (Oldham) and Jones (Guide Bridge) adopted similar mass-production methods, they were on a comparatively small scale, as a market for mass-produced ready-made clothing developed slowly in late nineteenth-century Britain (see pp. 228–31). In the production of typewriters and cash registers American manufacturers likewise predominated. They also led the way, as we shall see, in the mechanization of other manufactures such as printing, glass-making and boot- and shoe-making, though many of their techniques were soon adopted in Britain, either by progressive British firms or by American branch companies.

In many of these manufactures, no doubt, more varied market requirements and cheaper skilled labour accounted for the slower development of mechanized mass-production in Britain. In some cases, however, craft conservatism appears to have been the main cause of relative technological stagnation, as in British watch- and clock-making, centred in Coventry and Prescot. Internationally dominant in the eighteenth and early nineteenth centuries, when its techniques and tools had played an important role in the evolution of British engineering, it was, as Church has shown, almost destroyed in the second half of the nineteenth century by American and Swiss mechanized mass-production. This manufacture, together with those of small arms and sewing machines, made vital contributions to the development of precision machine-tools and standardized production in the United States, while British light engineering generally lagged behind.

This lag, however, as Musson and Saul have shown, has tended to be exaggerated. Standardized mass-production had been developing in Britain during the first half of the nineteenth century, in the manufacture of textile and other machinery, steam-engines, railway locomotives and machine-tools (see pp. 114–8), and in the late nineteenth and early twentieth centuries it came to be adopted in the newly developing industries. The most notable example was in bicycle manufacture, which sprang up from the late 1860s onwards, mainly in Coventry and Birmingham, where it was able to draw on established techniques in the making of watches and clocks, sewing machines, small arms and other light metal trades (see pp. 199–201). In Nottingham, another area of cycle manufacture, light engineering had similarly developed for the making of lace and hosiery machines. With standardization of the rear-chain-driven 'safety model' in the 1880s, with wheels of equal size and diamond frame, and with the introduction of the Dunlop pneumatic tyre, this manufacture mushroomed on mass-production lines, using not only imported American milling and grinding machines but also those of new local machine-tool firms such as Herbert's and Ward's; new specialized manufactures were also developed for light weldless steel tubing and ball bearings, as well as for rubber tyres and tubes, lamps and other components or accessories. Scores of firms entered this new industry, but as mass-production developed, with its greater technological, organizational and capital requirements, a few larger firms came to predominate, such as the Coventry Machinists (originally makers of sewing machines, later the Swift Cycle Company) and Rudge Whitworth in the Birmingham–Coventry area and Humber and Raleigh in Nottingham, each employing over a thousand men by the 1890s and turning out scores of thousands of cycles annually. The total output of the industry in 1907 was 623,800 cycles. As Saul and Harrison have shown, this new highly competitive British industry achieved a striking international superiority: 'in 1913 Britain exported 150,000 cycles, Germany 89,000 and the rest of the world hardly any at all'. The industry popularized mass-production techniques and, as Saul has pointed out, 'proved a jumping-off ground for some of the most important motor car manufacturers ... many making motor cycles too' (see p. 189–90).

In the initial development of internal-combustion engines and motor vehicles, however, Britain lagged behind France, Germany and the United States. And this, of course, was a development of far more revolutionary importance. Just as in the first industrial revolution the steam engine played the central role in the mechanization of industry and transport, displacing water, wind and horse power, now from the late nineteenth century onwards it was itself challenged by new forms of power, the internal-combustion engine and electricity, that were to be of similarly central importance in the 'second industrial revolution'. In neither of these developments did Britain predominate as in the age of steam. But there were some important British achievements, and rapid progress was being made by the early twentieth century.

The first gas-engines of industrial significance were developed on the Continent, by Lenoir, Hugon and Otto in the 1860s, using coal- or producer-gas, and it was Otto's improved four-stroke 'silent engine' of 1876 that achieved the real breakthrough. But British firms were quick to grasp their possibilities—Crossleys of Manchester most notably in manufacturing and developing the Otto engine—and after the Otto patents ran out many other firms entered this field; small engines of this type, attached to local coal-gas supplies, came quickly into use, especially in lighter industries such as the Birmingham metal trades.

Oil engines offered even wider scope, and British engineering firms were pioneers in their development, first Priestmans of Hull and then Ackroyd Stuart in collaboration with Ruston & Hornsbys of Lincoln, makers of agricultural steam engines and machinery. Stuart's engine, in fact, was a truer prototype of the modern oil engine than that later developed by Diesel in Germany. Hornsbys and other makers of oil engines, such as Crossleys, turned out many thousands of such engines in the 1890s and early 1900s, mainly for light industrial or agricultural use and for electricity generation.

In the development of the heavy oil engine, however, for both industrial and marine engineering purposes, Diesel and associated German engineering firms were much more progressive and found a more responsive market than in Britain, where steam and cheap coal were dominant. A few British firms such as Mirrlees of Glasgow (and later of Stockport) took up Diesel engine manufacture, and successive Diesel Engine Companies were established, but progress was comparatively slow. Germany was similarly more enterprising with heavy gas engines, especially in the steel industry, utilizing blast-furnace and coke-oven gases, widely wasted in British works.

It was in Germany, too, that Daimler and Benz pioneered the development of motor manufacture, with the light petrol engine, from the late 1880s onwards, and this manufacture was initially taken up much more quickly in France than in Britain, where the first motor company—significantly the Daimler Company—was not established until 1896. At first most cars, engines and parts were imported, particularly from France, and many of the early British car firms were merely assemblers. Nevertheless, the industry soon began to grow rapidly—59 firms had been established by 1900, 393 by 1914, though the majority were small and ephemeral, only 113 still existing by the latter date. Imports, which had been eight times greater than exports in 1904, were less than double in 1913 and included an increasing proportion of parts, as assembling developed in Britain. At the same time, a growing number of specialized firms sprang up, making components such as engines, chassis, bodies, wheels, tyres, brakes, radiators, carburettors, batteries, lamps, etc., though the larger manufacturers prided themselves on making most of their own cars. An immense stimulus was given to the iron and steel, engineering, rubber, electrical and other trades, encouraging large-scale standardized production to a much wider extent than the cycle industry.

From that industry, however, emerged many of the best-known car manu-facturers: Swift, Singer, Rover, Riley, Humber, Star, Sunbeam, Belsize and Alldays & Onions all began that way, together with two firms from French backgrounds, Clément–Talbot and Darracq, while Morris and the Dennis brothers started with cycle shops. Some made motor cycles, gross output of which increased sharply from £139,000 in 1907 to £1,631,000 in 1912, when about 38,000 were produced, while the number exported shot up from 800 to nearly 21,000 by 1914. Other manufacturers came from diverse origins, though usually with engineering experience. Saul has listed the names and output of the most important firms in 1913, as shown in the following table.

OUTPUT OF MOTOR VEHICLES, 1913

Albion	554	Lanchester	200
Argyll	622	Maudslay	50
Armstrong Whitworth	80	Morris	300
Arroll Johnston	1,150	Napier	743
Austin	1,500	Riley	15
Belsize	1,000	Rolls	650
Clément–Talbot	500	Rover	1,600
Crossley	650	Singer	1,350
Daimler	1,000	Standard	750
Dennis	500	Star	1,000
Ford	6,139	Sunbeam	1,700
Hillman	63	Swift	850
Humber	2,500	Vauxhall	388
Iris	50	Wolseley	3,000
Jowett	12		

Source: Saul, 'The Motor Industry in Britain to 1914'; *Business History*, V (1962–3), p. 25. Saul emphasizes that the figures embrace cars of very different sizes.

The total output, which had been less than 10,000 complete vehicles in 1907, rose to 34,000 by 1913, when it had reached about three-quarters of the French production; of this output, nearly a quarter was exported, valued at £2.4 million in 1913 (excluding chassis and parts from all these figures). Over 100,000 people were employed in the industry and the biggest firms had grown to considerable size: Daimler had 5,000 workers, Wolseley 4,000 and Humber and Sunbeam about 2,500 to 3,000, comparable with the largest engineering concerns; the Dunlop tyre works also employed 4,000 men. Firms such as Leylands, Crossleys and Maudslays were developing the manufacture of motor buses and lorries, starting another revolution in commercial transport.

The industry was located mainly in the west Midlands (Birmingham, Coventry and Wolverhampton), where links with the cycle and other metal trades were particularly important, especially for pressing and stamping bodies and parts (see pp. 199–201), but some firms set up elsewhere, including Rolls Royce (first Manchester, then Derby), Morris (Oxford), Vauxhall (Luton), Ford (Manchester) and Argyll and Arroll Johnston in Scotland.

Clearly the industry was expanding very vigorously after a late start. By 1907 it already accounted for a significant part of all engineering output (see p. 183), and it grew more rapidly than other branches thereafter. It seems to have had little difficulty in raising capital, which was readily subscribed for ordinary and preference shares and debentures. Nor were new men, enterprise and technical ability lacking. But Saul has criticized the adherence to traditional engineering production methods: although the industry was well equipped with machine-tools, these were used mostly for high-quality precision engineering rather than for cheaper mass-production—the same conservatism as had been earlier exhibited in watch- and clock-making and in other branches of light engineering. The American motor industry, on the other hand, benefiting from previous advances in such fields, dwarfed that of Britain (and France) by 1914, with an output of 485,000 cars. Whereas Ford and other American manufacturers had vigorously developed assembly-line production, its possibilities were only just beginning to be explored in the British industry. Significantly, Ford's branch works in Manchester, assembling over 6,000 'Model Ts' from American-made parts in 1913, had the biggest output in Britain. Though the American industry had a bigger domestic market, British manufacturers did not sufficiently exploit their own opportunities at home and abroad, by going in for cheap standardized production—mainly, it appears, because of a traditional craft engineering approach and a narrow commercial outlook—though they were doing well, in both output and quality, with expensive and medium-priced cars.

There was a similar lag in development of the British aircraft industry, which was only in its infancy before the First World War. There were a dozen makers of air-frames, working mainly with wood, fabric and wires, but aero-engines were only slowly developed, mainly by makers of car engines. In this field the French led the way: significantly, it was Blériot who first flew the Channel in July 1909.

Electrical supply and engineering

In the 'second industrial revolution', electricity was to be of even wider importance than the internal-combustion engine, for which it provided the vital spark. Scientists in many countries had investigated electrical phenomena in the late eighteenth and early nineteenth centuries, and, following the development of electrical cells or batteries, which provided steady current, the basic principles of electrochemistry and electromagnetism had been discovered. These discoveries, to which British scientists such as Davy, Henry and Faraday made distinguished contributions, were to have revolutionary industrial applications, first in telegraphic communications, then in electroplating, leading eventually to electrolytic and electrothermal production and refining of metals (see p. 220), and, of even more profound and widespread importance, in electric lighting and power, with development of the dynamo (generator) and electric motor.

The electric telegraph was first developed in this country by Cooke and Wheatstone from the 1830s onwards, revolutionizing communications as wires and cables were spread across land and under sea. It also provided the first example of nationalization, when the telegraph companies were taken over by the Post Office in 1868. It was followed, from the late 1870s, by the telephone, pioneered by Bell and Edison in America. After various companies had merged into a monopolistic National Telephone Company, the Post Office again took over, first trunk lines under an Act of 1892 and then local exchanges at the end of 1911; but telephones spread slowly in Britain—there were only 360,000 in 1911. The Post Office was also interested in Marconi's development of wireless or radio telegraphy from 1896 onwards, but this made little progress before the First World War, except on ships.

Electrical manufactures thus began with batteries, telegraph and telephone apparatus, wires and cables, which were well developed in this country by the end of the nineteenth century. To these demands were now added those of electric light and power. Though carbon arc lighting had been introduced earlier in the century, it was not until improved dynamos were developed by Gramme, Siemens and others, from the 1870s onwards, that it became economic, compared with gas or oil lamps, for lighting streets and public places. In the late 1870s, moreover, Swan and Edison, in England and America respectively, invented their electric 'glow lamps'—incandescent carbon filaments in vacuated glass bulbs—which made possible electric lighting of homes, factories, etc. The earliest electricity generating plants in Britain were for this purpose, but progress was slow: gas companies were well established, providing lighting that was not only cheaper but also greatly improved by the incandescent mantle in the 1880s. Moreover, paraffin lamps were also becoming popular, in place of candles, especially in rural areas. It was only gradually, therefore, as costs were reduced, that electric lighting was more widely adopted. The efficiency and life of electric lamps were later greatly increased by the development of metal (mainly tungsten) filaments in the early 1900s. Their production became one of the most lucrative branches of electrical manufacturing, controlled by national and international cartels.

The first application of electric power was in transport. From the 1880s onwards the old horse and steam trams in towns were gradually displaced, and electrified tramways were rapidly extended in the early twentieth century, to a total of some 2,500 miles by 1914, largely municipalized, though the British Electric Traction Company and other concerns had participated in this urban transport revolution. The London underground was also electrified, as well as the Brighton line and one or two suburban railways.

The introduction of electric power in industry, however, was a slow process. This is hardly surprising in view of the massive development that had already taken place in steam power, the increasing efficiency of steam technology and the cheapness of coal. Except where relatively low-cost hydro-electric generation was possible, the production of electric power itself depended on steam-engines to drive the dynamos, and until central generating stations were built each works had to have its own plant. From the early 1880s, a growing number of such stations were established, either by companies or by municipalities, but these were mainly for lighting and tramways, and, though there was a gradual increase in industrial purchases from electricity supply undertakings, many firms continued to have their own generating plant, comprising over a third of total dynamo capacity in 1907 (see pp. 169–70).

UNITED KINGDOM GENERATING CAPACITY, 1907
(kilowatts)

Trade	Driven by reciprocating steam engines	Driven by steam turbines	Driven by other power	Total
Mines and quarries	109,224	2,585	2,791	114,600
Iron and steel, engineering and shipbuilding	258,608	37,507	50,558	346,673
Other metal manufactures	7,903	402	6,677	14,982
Textiles	73,153	4,969	4,164	82,286
Clothing	5,759	1,089	3,203	10,051
Food, drink and tobacco	25,039	1,569	4,467	31,075
Chemical and allied	19,836	336	8,703	28,875
Paper, printing and allied	17,712	2,621	6,358	26,691
Leather, canvas and india-rubber	5,989	4	467	6,460
Timber	8,332	297	1,689	10,318
Clay, stone, building and contracting	12,490	3,962	3,220	19,672
Miscellaneous	1,129	—	484	1,613
Public utility services	738,572	295,245	18,988	1,052,805
Factory owners (power only)	1,497	—	74	1,571
Total	1,285,243	350,586	111,843	1,747,672

Source: First Census of Production, 1907, *Final Report,* p. 18.

Of that total, reciprocating (piston-and-cylinder) engines accounted for about three-quarters. In early generating plants, these engines were of the traditional low-speed type, with belt or rope drives to dynamos, but soon high-speed direct-coupled engines such as those of Willans, were introduced, with compound or triple-expansion cylinders in larger power stations. In 1884, moreover, Charles Parsons patented his steam turbine, which, in the form of the turbo-dynamo or turbo-alternator, was admirably adapted for large-scale electricity generation. In the numerous small local plants, however, reciprocating engines long continued to predominate, and in 1907 steam turbines accounted for only a fifth of total generating capacity (see pp. 166–70).

By that time about a quarter of the total United Kingdom horse-power of 10.8 million (predominantly steam-engines, reciprocating and turbine, but also including internal-combustion engines, water power, etc.) was used for driving generators, the other three-quarters, of course, being used for driving machinery directly. The distribution of dynamo capacity among different industries provides an indication of the varying extent to which they had adopted electricity (see p. 193 and also pp. 169–70).

These figures demonstrate that electricity supply undertakings (included in public utility services) accounted for nearly two-thirds of dynamo capacity and that, outside the iron and steel, engineering and shipbuilding trades, investment in electrical generating plant had been comparatively limited. The iron and steel, engineering and shipbuilding trades also accounted for over half the industrial purchases from electricity supply undertakings (see p. 168). Moreover, the 1907 Census of Production shows that much the greater part—over three-quarters—of the electricity sold by electricity supply undertakings was for lighting and traction, and a good deal of the electricity generated by industrial firms was similarly used. Clearly, although electric motors were being gradually introduced to drive many kinds of machinery, the steam-engine still held overwhelming supremacy in British industry.

This was not, as often alleged, simply conservatism, though undoubtedly the long-established steam and gas technologies and the large amounts of capital invested in such plant tended to retard electrical development in this country. As Clapham pointed out, 'British factories had their steam engines, belts and shafting in good running order. . . . Coal was cheap.' So British industrialists were quite rational in not tearing everything out and going in for electrification, which was for many years relatively costly and unreliable: faced by the medley of electrical equipment, voltages and frequencies, by the conflicts between the D.C. and A.C. systems and between private and municipal undertakings, by the slow development of efficient electric motors and by the capital costs involved, they were understandably cautious.

On the other hand, British electrical invention and enterprise were not lacking. It is true that many developments were made in America, Germany and elsewhere, but early British pioneers such as Faraday, Cooke and Wheatstone were followed in the later nineteenth and early twentieth centuries by Swan,

Crompton, Thomson (Kelvin), Hopkinson, Parsons, Ferranti, Merz and others, combining great scientific and technical talent. In electrical engineering, it is true, foreign technology, enterprise and investment were of great importance: the American Edison, Brush, British Thomson-Houston (American G.E.C.) and Westinghouse companies, for example; the German Siemens & Halske and A.E.G., the Swiss Oerlikon and Brown–Boveri—all of these either founded branch factories here or imported electrical equipment. But there were also some enterprising British firms such as those of Swan, Crompton, Parsons, Mather & Platt, Dick Kerr & Co., and the British G.E.C., as well as several very successful cable-making firms (British Insulated Wire, Callender's and Glover's). The industry was developing not only in the old heavy engineering centres, such as Manchester, Newcastle and Glasgow, but also in new centres, such as Rugby and Stafford. None of the British firms, however, compared in size with the American and German giants, and the British electrical industry in general was relatively small: by 1913 its total output was little more than a third of the German, its exports barely half.

No doubt the tangle of restrictive legislation such as the Electric Lighting Acts of the 1880s hampered developments, encouraging municipal parochialism, though the effects have been exaggerated. Small-scale local generation and the lag in establishment of large central power stations and long-distance distribution have also been criticized, but there were considerable technical problems to be overcome, such as the development of turbo-alternators, transformers and high-voltage A.C. transmission, so that a 'national grid' did not become feasible till the inter-war years (see pp. 353–5). Consequently, there remained a plethora of local electricity supply undertakings, run by 327 municipalities and 230 companies in 1914, with generating capacities of 705,000 kilowatts and 430,000 kilowatts respectively, as well as numerous private plants. (The situation was much the same, however, in the gas industry.)

There was a similar multiplicity of suppliers of electrical equipment such as generators, transformers, motors, batteries, switches, lamps (bulbs), cables and meters, though the larger integrated companies, British and foreign, tended increasingly to predominate and combine in manufacturers' associations. By 1914 a widening variety of electrical consumer goods were coming into the market—ovens, radiators (fires), irons, kettles and vacuum cleaners—but these were as yet in their infancy, and there was strong competition from gas in cooking and heating as well as in lighting.

The 1907 Census of Production showed, as Clapham ruefully observed, that electrical engineering accounted for 'only about 14 per cent of the whole national engineering output by value' (see figures on p. 183). But this was perhaps a matter for congratulation rather than concern, bearing in mind the vast range of established engineering production; electrical engineering output (£14.1 million) exceeded that of industrial steam engines and boilers (£11 million). A considerable proportion of this output, moreover, was exported: at that date electrical exports (£3.5 million) were more than double the imports (£1.7 million), and by 1913 they had risen to £7.7 million, compared with imports of £2.9 million—hardly a discreditable performance. (The 1913 export figure of £5.4 million in Mitchell and Deane, op. cit. (see p. 244) refers only to 'electrical goods and apparatus' and does not include £2.3 million of 'electrical machinery', such as generators, motors, etc.) This growth owed much to the entry of foreign firms, which, though generally regarded as indicative of British weakness, provided a stimulating technological infusion and accelerated the process of electrification.

Capital investment in electrical plant and machinery averaged over 10 per cent of the United Kingdom fixed-capital formation in the early twentieth century, and the industry was also becoming a sizeable employer of labour. According to the 1911 Population Census, about 109,000 were occupied in the electrical supply and manufactures of England and Wales.

Shipbuilding

While the internal-combustion engine and electricity were beginning to revolutionize transport and industry on land—though not yet very seriously challenging steam power and railways—there was a steamship revolution on the high seas, based on advances in the established iron and steel and engineering industries, which now became increasingly associated with shipbuilding. The massive triumph of iron and steam over wood and sail did not, in fact, occur until after 1870, and in this revolution British shipbuilding and marine engineering acquired a massive international predominance, which was maintained right up to 1914.

During the third quarter of the nineteenth century, sailing ships—greatly improved in design and construction and increasingly built of iron—continued to maintain their predominance over steamships in long-distance bulk trades with the Americas, Asia and Australasia. In such trades, steamships, with their low-pressure single-cylinder engines and heavy coal requirements, limiting cargo space, could not compete with sail, though increasingly successful with passengers, mail and low-bulk cargoes, especially on shorter-distance routes; steam, therefore, was often combined with sail, just as wooden planks were put on iron frames in 'composite' ships.

In the mid-1850s the higher-pressure compound (double-cylinder) marine engine was developed by John Elder on Clydeside, while the opening of the Suez Canal in 1869 also reduced sail's advantage in the Eastern trades. But it was not until the development of triple- and quadruple-expansion engines in the 1880s and 1890s that sailing tonnage dramatically decreased.

Though total sailing tonnage gradually declined from around 1870, the building of new sailing ships (now mainly of iron, later of steel) was maintained, though fluctuating, until the 1890s—indeed, it reached its highest United Kingdom peak of 287,000 tons in 1892—but from then onwards there was a rapid decline in both total tonnage and building of sailing ships, the latter falling to only 30,000 tons by 1913.

UNITED KINGDOM MERCANTILE
SHIPPING TONNAGE
(million net tons)

Year	Sailing ships	Steamships
1850	3.4	0.2
1865	4.9	0.9
1875	4.2	1.9
1885	3.4	4.0
1895	2.9	6.1
1913	0.8	11.3

Source: Statistical Abstracts.

Meanwhile, steamship building increased rapidly, surpassing sail in 1870, with an output of 268,000 tons (net), and then continuing to rise strongly, though also with massive cyclical fluctuations, to a peak of nearly 1.2 million in 1913. Long before that date paddle-wheelers had become archaic survivals—twin screws were introduced in the 1880s—while iron, having largely displaced wood in steamship building by the 1850s, was itself rapidly superseded by steel from the mid-1880s onwards.

The advances in shipbuilding and marine engineering were closely related to those in iron and steel and engineering generally, which not only resulted in stronger and cheaper frames, plates, engines, boilers, etc., but also enabled shipyard costs to be reduced by steam-powered lathes, drills, hammers, plate-bending, shearing, punching, drilling and riveting machines; by the late nineteenth and early twentieth centuries, these were coming to be driven by hydraulic, pneumatic or electric power. The ships thus built were bigger and faster, with much greater cargo capacity and lower operating costs than earlier steamers; liners of 10,000 to 15,000 tons were on the Atlantic before the end of the century, and though the average steamer built in 1913 was only about 1,300 net tons, this was a great increase from the mid-nineteenth century (see p. 119); and this figure, of course, included numerous small coasters and cross-channel boats.

The vast majority of these ships were driven by reciprocating steam engines, but more revolutionary developments were by that time under way. In the late 1890s Charles Parsons, whose turbo-generators were already being used for lighting ships, developed the marine turbine engine, which was soon adopted for new liners and warships. At the same time, oil fuel began to be used instead of coal for firing boilers, though less than 3 per cent of the world's sea-going tonnage burnt oil in 1913. The future challenge to steam and coal was also foreshadowed by the development of the internal-combustion engine for marine propulsion, but the first large motor-ships, with heavy-oil Diesel engines, were only just being built on the eve of the First World War. On sea as on land, steam still reigned supreme.

Some of the latest technological developments appear to have been more quickly adopted in Germany, America and elsewhere, but the United Kingdom continued to retain a commanding predominance in shipbuilding, still producing more than three-fifths of world mercantile tonnage in 1910–14, over five times the output of Germany, her nearest rival. Not merely was the British shipping fleet built almost entirely in home yards, but a considerable proportion, varying from a fifth to a third of production, together with as much if not more old shipping, was sold abroad: Britain was, in fact, the world's shipbuilder. At the same time, she also built far more warships than any other country—about a third of world output—in both Admiralty dockyards and those of the great shipbuilding companies, closely linked with steel and armaments (see p. 251).

This extraordinary predominance was based on massive British shipping and naval supremacy, associated with her industrial, commercial and imperial pre-eminence. Britain, the centre of a world-wide empire, the greatest free-trade market, drawing on the whole globe for foodstuffs and raw materials and still also the largest exporter of manufactures, was the hub of world sea-borne trade: in the period before 1914 about 40 per cent of that trade was with the United Kingdom, and over half of it was carried in British ships. Her merchant shipping fleet of 11.7 million tons in 1911 was a third of the world total, dwarfing the 3 million tons of Germany, her main rival.

Thus British shipyards had huge home and overseas markets, which enabled great shipbuilding companies to develop and to introduce large-scale, often standardized, production of specialized types of vessels, with similar specialization among marine engineering firms and suppliers of other components. The geographical location of British coal and iron in close proximity to the sea also favoured the growth of large shipyards on the Tyne, Wear and Tees, on Clydeside and Merseyside and at Barrow; smaller vessels were still built on the Thames, Humber and lesser rivers, but many of the older yards declined or died out. Belfast, on the other hand, where some of the biggest shipyards were located, had to import its coal, iron and steel; other yards also became less dependent on local supplies, often obtaining cheaper imported steel plates, etc., dumped in this country from abroad. Nevertheless, British shipyards consumed a high pro-portion of domestic steel output—nearly a third just before the First World War, while the Clyde yards took two-thirds of the output of Scottish steelworks—and steel production was closely geared to the technical requirements of British shipbuilders (see p. 175), who were thus generally able to get supplies more cheaply than any of their foreign competitors.

The major shipyards were also favourably located at or near the great ports, in close association with shipowning firms. More important perhaps than these locational advantages, however, was the established strength of the industry, with its large supplies of skilled labour and experienced management. Many foreign shipyards, lacking such skilled labour, were over-capitalized with mechanical equipment, while the productivity of British shipyard workers, making fuller use of often less technically advanced machinery, remained substantially higher, and British shipbuilding costs were substantially lower, than those of other countries.

There is little evidence, in fact, of 'relative stagnation' or 'retardation' in this industry during this period. It continued to grow massively, to build better and cheaper ships than its competitors and to maintain an astonishing international predominance right up to 1914. The rise of the great shipbuilding firms—Napier's, Elder's (Fairfield), Thomson's (later John Brown's) and Denny's on Clydeside; Palmer's and Swan Hunter's on Tyneside; Doxford's on the Wear; Cammell Laird's at Birkenhead; Vickers at Barrow; Harland & Wolff's and Workman Clark's at Belfast, to mention only a few leading names—forms a story of remarkable business enterprise. Hindsight, of course, and the plight of Clydeside and Tyneside in the inter-war years, lend support to the 'over-commitment' theory, but right up to 1914 these areas continued to experience remarkable growth and prosperity, based upon a high degree of industrial localization and specialization.

Shipbuilding had certainly become one of the major industries of the country, contributing (together with marine engineering) about £51 million gross (about £22 million net), or nearly 3 per cent of total industrial output in 1907; exports of new ships and boats were valued at £10 million, while imports were negligible. Total employment in this industry was then 217,000; but it provided employment for many more, since shipbuilding had become, as L. Jones says, 'essentially an assembling industry', with numerous components of machinery and equipment supplied by sub-contractors outside the industry proper. External economies of this kind in the great shipbuilding areas contributed considerably to the British predominance.

Other metal manufactures

In the early twentieth century, despite the growth of large-scale highly mechanized heavy engineering and shipbuilding industries, there were still numerous light metal manufactures in which power-driven factory production had developed much more slowly (see p. 181). In the Birmingham and Black Country trades, for example, producing a plethora of smallwares in iron, brass, copper and precious metals—hardware and hollow-ware of all kinds, buttons, small arms, tinplate, japanned, enamelled and galvanized wares, gold and silver jewellery and electroplate, household fittings, lamps, edge-tools, agricultural implements and saddlers' ironmongery, nails and screws, nuts and bolts, steel pens, pins and needles, anchors and chains, locks and keys, wire and tubes, axles and springs, bedsteads, fenders and fire-irons—handicraft skills, small factories, workshops and domestic production long survived. In the primary and heavier processes, power-driven machinery was already being employed at the beginning of this period, for rolling, drawing, hammering, punching, shearing and grinding metals, and steam was ousting water power; but in the more numerous and varied lighter manufactures, though stamps, presses and lathes were common, these were mostly hand or treadle-operated and many processes were entirely manual: according to Allen, 'there had been no "industrial revolution" in Birmingham and District'.

Even in some of the lighter trades, however, such as the making of pins and needles, nails and screws, mechanized mass-production was making progress, and in the later nineteenth century it gradually destroyed the old handicrafts. In 1830, for example, there were perhaps 50,000 hand nail-makers, but by 1914 their number had dwindled to probably no more than a thousand. At the same time, power-driven presses and stamps were also increasingly introduced into other manufactures, so that larger-scale factory organization became more general. Nevertheless, small-scale handicraft production—based on intensively specialized skills in highly sub-divided but closely co-ordinated trades—continued to exist alongside the large factories. In many factories, moreover, manual processes, or manually operated machinery, long remained common, while many factory owners also employed out-workers. Factory space and steam power were often sub-let to small masters in separate workshops, while gas and oil engines and electric motors were suited to small producers. Even in 1927, as Allen observed, 'the transition to the factory in those [small metal] trades has been very slow and is still far from complete'.

Nevertheless, a great transformation occurred in the Birmingham and Black Country trades during this period, especially from the late 1880s onwards, in connection with the new cycle, motor, engineering and electrical industries, which greatly stimulated mechanized mass-production of standardized parts. While some of the older trades, making nails, buttons and guns, went into decline, many of the other hardware trades, together with the new industries, were revolutionized by the widespread adoption of power-driven machinery—presses, stamps and machine-tools of all kinds—with the new internal-combustion and electric prime movers, as well as steam and hydraulic power. At the same time, gas- and oil-fired furnaces began to supersede the coke- or coal-fired types. In fact there was a metallurgical-engineering revolution in the trades of this area. The tendency was increasingly towards more automatic standardized factory production with machines tended by semi-skilled labour, including growing numbers of females. Larger, more integrated concerns developed, many under joint-stock company organization, employing hundreds or thousands of workers, though small factories were still numerous; in some trades, such as the nail, gun, chain and jewellery trades, workshops and domestic out-work still survived, but in general they were declining. There was also a tendency towards migration away from the old congested industrial centres into suburban or country areas, to the south, east and north of Birmingham, where rates and labour costs were lower; coal's dominating locational influence was being reduced and industrial decentralization was beginning.

In the cutlery, file, saw and edge-tool trades of Sheffield, there was an even more prolonged survival of traditional craft techniques and forms of industrial organization. Cementation and crucible (Huntsman) steels continued to be used for high-quality articles, though Bessemer and open-hearth products became increasingly competitive. In 1913 Lloyd emphasized that 'manual skill ... still remains one of the most characteristic features of the cutlery trades', though power-driven hammers, stamps and presses were being increasingly introduced, while steam had largely displaced water power for grinding-wheels from the mid-nineteenth century onwards. Relics of gild organization survived in the Hallamshire Cutlers' Company, though its powers of trade regulation had disappeared except for control of trade-marks; 'little masters' were still common, together with the domestic or out-work system, under which, it was stated in 1913, 'much of the cutlery and file manufacture of Sheffield is still carried on'. Despite a gradual increase in the number of factories—including many tenement factories—there were some 2,800 separate establishments in the industry, averaging only three adult male workers each, in striking contrast to the large-scale steel and engineering works of the Sheffield area. The prolonged survival of small-scale production was attributed not only to craft conservatism and cheap labour but also to 'the immense variety of type and design' demanded by customers, which 'makes standardization difficult'. In the United States, however, with higher labour costs, standardized factory production had been much further developed. Not surprisingly, in view of the relatively slow technological progress in the British hardware and cutlery trades, exports of their products less than doubled between 1850 and 1914 (see p. 244).

11

Textiles

Textile manufactures continued up to the First World War to be one of Britain's major industries, but in employment, mechanical power and output they lost their long-established predominance (see pp. 151, 168, 242–3, for detailed figures). In employment, with a total of 1,509,000 in 1911, they were now the second largest manufacturing group, below iron and steel, engineering and other metal manufactures, while slightly greater numbers were also employed in transport and in agriculture. In mechanical power also, they were no longer the leading sector, having fallen to third place. And although in 1907 they contributed nearly one-fifth of the United Kingdom gross industrial output, they were now second to the metals group, while in net terms they were also below mines and quarries. But they still retained their predominance in exports, though it was less overwhelming, declining from over three-fifths to about a third of total United Kingdom domestic export values between 1850 and 1913.

The relative importance of the different textile manufactures can be judged from the returns of the 1907 Census of Production (see p. 203).

Cotton

Among these textile manufactures, cotton was still 'king'. Though the industry's percentage rate of growth was inevitably declining, after the rapid development of steam-powered mechanization in the period before 1850, it continued to grow remarkably in absolute terms. According to the Factory Inspectors' Returns (which differed somewhat from those in the 1907 Census of Production), the labour force in spinning and weaving factories increased from 331,000 in 1850 to 577,000 (about three-fifths of them females) in 1907, while production and trade rose much more, as indicated by the figures of raw cotton consumption and exports.

Mechanization was carried further, not only with more mules, spindles and power-looms but with larger, faster-running and more efficient machines, driven by

TEXTILE MANUFACTURES, 1907

Textile	Gross output (£ million)	Net output (£ million)	Number employed (thousands)	Engine power (thousand h.p.)
Cotton	174.6	45.0	572.1	1,239.2
Woollen and worsted	75.9	18.6	264.0	325.2
Jute, hemp and linen	32.1	9.5	154.5	168.1
Silk	5.2	1.8	32.2	18.9
Lace	10.7	3.6	36.8	10.3
Hosiery	9.1	3.1	51.2	7.8
Rope, twine and net	4.0	1.1	14.3	15.3
Bleaching, dyeing, printing, etc.	17.9	10.5	103.8	190.3
Others	4.0	1.2	24.1	12.6
Total	333.6	94.4	1,253.0	1,987.8

Source: First Census of Production, 1907, *Final Report,* p. 285. The figures for cotton, wool, etc. are for the main branches of spinning and weaving. Separate figures are provided for bleaching, dyeing, etc. in *all* textiles. The columned figures, expressed to the first decimal point, do not in every case add up precisely to the totals.

more powerful and economical steam-engines: the total power employed in spinning and weaving factories, which had risen to 309,000 horse-power (only just over 8,000 water power) by 1870, soared to 1,239,000 horse-power (almost all steam) in 1907. Fixed capital therefore grew more rapidly than the number of workers, and productivity increased, especially in the first half of this period. Nevertheless, small and middling firms still abounded, alongside the large concerns.

Cotton-spinning had already been brought into factories before the mid-nineteenth century, but mechanization was further developed with longer mules, carrying more and faster-rotating spindles, and with self-actors, which were now more generally adopted, though the so-called hand-mule held its own for a long time, especially in fine spinning, where more operative skill was required. Ring-spinning, a development from the early water-frame or throstle, was also introduced but made much slower progress here than in the United States, where it

GROWTH OF THE UNITED KINGDOM COTTON INDUSTRY, 1850–1913

Year	Raw cotton consumption (million lb.)	Exports of piece goods (million sq. yd.)	Year	Spindles (millions)	Power-looms (thousands)
1850	588	1,358	1850	21.0	250
1875	1,229	3,562	1874	41.9	463
1913	2,178	7,075	1912	55.7	786

Source: Mitchell and Deane, op. cit.; R. Robson, *The Cotton Industry in Britain* (1957).

was dominant by the early twentieth century; in Britain there were still 45.2 million mule spindles in 1913 but only 10.4 million ring spindles.

Power-loom weaving rapidly completed its conquest of hand-loom weaving in the cotton industry after 1850, as it was developed to manufacture the finest patterned goods. The number of hand-loom weavers shrank from the surviving 50,000 of the late 1840s to an insignificant few thousand by the early 1860s. Power-loom shuttle speeds were considerably increased, while mechanical efficiency was improved, so that the average Lancashire female weaver was able to manage four looms. But very little progress was made with automatic looms of the Northrop and other types, in which the cop or bobbin in the shuttle, or the shuttle itself, was automatically changed, so that large numbers of these machines could be supervised by a single operative. Again there was a striking contrast with the United States, where these looms were much more rapidly introduced; there were less than 10,000 in Britain in 1914.

These technological lags have frequently been cited as evidence of British conservative backwardness. G. T. Jones argued that productivity (per spindle, per loom and per operative) tended to stagnate between the 1880s and 1914 and that there was little if any improvement in technical efficiency and costs over that period. Though the industry was still growing massively in numbers of mills, spindles and looms and though mills continued to increase in size, investment was mostly in the same kind of machinery, without much further technological innovation. But, as Sandberg has pointed out, criticisms of Lancashire's performance have been exaggerated: the industry was, in fact, still improving its productive efficiency and expanding its exports; it was rationally adapted to factor costs and markets, with increasing emphasis on finer yarns and higher-quality fabrics, in production of which it still retained a comparative advantage with skilled mule-spinning and traditional looms; ring-spinning and automatic looms were better suited to the less skilled labour and production of plain coarser goods in other countries. With the growth of cotton manufactures and tariffs in Europe and the United States, British exports to those areas fell off, but markets were greatly expanded elsewhere, and, as Marrison has shown in the South American trade, British products more than held their own, especially with improvements in finishing. On the eve of the First World War, the British cotton industry was still dominant internationally, with well over a third of world spindles and a similar proportion of power-looms; production of piece goods (8,050 million linear yards in 1912) was a quarter of the world total in quantity, and more in value; Lancashire's dominance of world exports was even more striking, accounting for about three-fifths in quantity. Between 1850 and 1913 United Kingdom cotton exports had risen from £28.3 to £127.2 million (mainly of piece goods, with yarns accounting for only about one-eighth of the total), and though their share of domestic export values had declined from two-fifths to a quarter, they still far surpassed all others, while imports were relatively negligible.

The industry was in a highly vulnerable position, however, exporting over four-fifths of its production, especially to India (which took about two-fifths of United Kingdom cotton exports before 1914), as well as to the Near and Far East and South America. By this time, not only was European competition increasing, but India and Japan were developing their own industries more rapidly. With historical hindsight, therefore, knowing what was to happen after the First World War, it is not surprising that criticisms have been made of the pre-war British cotton industry, though these sometimes involve the contradiction of castigating Lancashire entrepreneurs both for the declining percentage rate of growth and for over-commitment to cotton. In fact, in a period when a declining growth rate was inevitable, the industry was still able to maintain profits, increase production and expand exports; new firms were being established and new larger mills were built right up to 1914. No one could foresee the catastrophe of the inter-war years: there was some apprehension about the growth of foreign competition, but even such a well-informed contemporary as S. J. Chapman, writing in 1905, saw no cause for immediate concern, though he thought there might be a gradual retardation of the industry's rate of growth. No doubt there is some evidence of conservative complacency—of outdated mills and machinery, while Lancashire textile-engineering firms were equipping foreign competitors with the latest plant (see pp. 158–9)—but the industry in general was still vigorous and expansive.

It was now highly concentrated in Lancashire and north Cheshire, which had about 90 per cent of the labour force by 1911, while the Scottish industry declined almost into insignificance in face of competition. At the same time, a high degree of process specialization and localization developed. Combined spinning and weaving mills gradually declined and the two processes came increasingly to be conducted in different districts, the former in the south Lancashire towns around Manchester, the latter in the north Lancashire area, though complete geo-graphical segregation never occurred. There was further specialization in spin-ning, according to coarser and finer yarns, with lower counts in the Oldham district, for example, and finer yarns in the Bolton area, while in weaving specialization was more intricate, varying according to types of cloth between different towns and mills. Manchester ceased to be a cotton-manufacturing town and became the great commercial capital of the whole region: spinning and weaving mills had mostly disappeared from the inner city by the 1880s, being replaced by or converted into warehouses and offices; the city's merchant-converters or finishers played a key role in determining what patterns, qualities and quantities of goods should be produced, and the Royal Exchange was the central United Kingdom market for cotton yarns and cloth. Liverpool's Exchange, of course, performed a similar function for raw cotton, which continued to be by far the most important raw material import, averaging about £73 million per annum in 1910–13, over a tenth of total United Kingdom imports.

In the finishing processes of bleaching, dyeing, printing, calendering, etc., there was similar specialization, though some firms combined two or three of these operations. Traditional grassing or crofting had long disappeared with the continued chemical revolution, which also increasingly affected dyeing, especially with the introduction of synthetic dyes (see p. 219); at the same time, hand-block printers accompanied hand-loom weavers into the industrial limbo, as cylinder-printing machines were developed capable of producing the most complex coloured patterns. Developments in these processes, especially for finer-quality goods, were important to maintenance of Lancashire's superiority; specialized firms tended to be concentrated on the Pennine slopes, for soft water supplies. Of the gross output of about £18 million attributed to these processes for all United Kingdom textiles in 1907 (see p. 203), cotton's contribution was about £14 million.

Woollen and worsted manufactures

Before the mid-nineteenth century, mechanized factory production had made considerably slower progress in woollen and worsted manufactures than in cotton (see pp. 85–89). During the third quarter of the century, however, with more rapid introduction of power-driven machinery (see table below), these manufactures probably grew even faster than cotton. In these decades, traditional hand combing, spinning and weaving were almost destroyed, though 37,000 hand-looms still survived in the United Kingdom in 1871, mostly weaving wool, especially in the 'fancy' trades and in the upland villages of Yorkshire, Wales and Scotland. At the same time, the industry was further concentrated into urban steam-powered factories on the West Riding coalfields. The ancient worsted trade of Norfolk virtually disappeared, while the woollen cloth manufacture of the West Country became almost insignificant by comparison with that of Yorkshire, which continued not only to mechanize but also to diversify its products, particularly with mixed 'stuffs', embodying cotton and silk yarns, together with alpaca, mohair and other new materials, as well as using recovered rag wool, 'shoddy' and 'mungo', in cheaper woollen manufactures, originally introduced in the 1830s but now more rapidly developed; at the same time, growing quantities of raw wool were imported, especially from Australia, imports exceeding the home clip by the 1860s. By such cost-reducing innovations, the industry not only catered for a growing home market, with rising population and incomes, but also rapidly expanded exports; whereas in the first half of the century these had formed a declining proportion of total output, this trend was now reversed, and by the boom of the early 1870s they perhaps accounted for not far short of half:

between 1853–4 and 1870–4 average annual exports of woollen and worsted tissues rose from 143.6 million linear yards to 324 million, while yarn exports rose from 14.8 to 37.7 million lb.

Expansion of production and trade was accompanied by changing industrial organization. In woollen mills, vertical integration tended to develop, combining all processes from scribbling wool to finishing cloth, though specialized spinning, weaving and dyeing firms were still numerous; but in worsted manufactures, with their more varied yarns, fabrics and markets, these processes, and also the preparatory combing process, tended to be horizontally separated, though many combined firms existed; worsted mills, moreover, were generally much bigger than woollen mills. The traditional small West Riding clothiers and the associated cloth-halls were declining, with the development of larger-scale factory and mercantile organization and more direct trading relationships, though small firms and mills still abounded.

THE UNITED KINGDOM WOOL-TEXTILE INDUSTRY, 1850–1904

Year	Spindles (thousands)			Power-looms			Numbers employed in factories (thousands)		
	Woollen	Worsted	Total	Woollen	Worsted	Total	Males	Females	Total
1850	1,595	876	2,471	9,439	32,617	42,056	72	82	154
1861	2,183	1,289	3,472	21,770	43,048	64,818	81	92	173
1878	3,684	2,097	5,781	57,738	87,393	145,131	116	154	270
1890	3,448	2,403	5,851	62,880	67,391	130,271	132	170	302
1904	2,901	2,938	5,839	51,789	52,725	104,514	109	153	262

Sources: Deane and Cole, op. cit., p. 200; Mitchell and Deane, op. cit., p. 199.

This rapid growth in the third quarter of the century, however, contrasts with retardation—even decline in some respects—between the late 1870s and 1914 (see table above). This resulted mainly from the development of foreign tariff-protected industries, which not only created greater difficulties for British exports but also led to increasing competition in the open home market. Decline was most marked in the number of power-looms, particularly for worsteds, but this contrasted with a continued, though slower, rise in spindles. The former figures reflect the decline in exports of woollen and worsted fabrics from an annual average of 324 million yards in 1870–4 to 153.9 million in 1900–04, in which both manufactures shared; in the following years, however, while worsteds continued to decline, woollen exports recovered strongly, surpassing worsteds, so that the combined total rose to 174.3 million yards in 1909–13, though this was still far below that of the 1870s boom. (Measurement in linear yards, however, takes no account of increasing widths of fabric and so exaggerates the decline.) The recovery of woollens was based mainly on increased use of rag wool in cheaper varieties of cloth, but the previously successful mixed worsted stuffs tended to go out of fashion in competition with finer all-wool French goods, imports of which rose to four-fifths of worsted fabric exports; woollens, on the other hand, suffered comparatively little from imports and were beating foreign competition in markets outside Europe and the United States, especially in the Empire. Moreover, exports of yarns and tops (overwhelmingly worsted) continued to rise remarkably, to a combined annual average of 103.7 million lb in 1909–13, being in growing demand for foreign manufactures, especially in Germany, so that worsted-spinning firms prospered by comparison with those in weaving and finishing. Total export values of wool-textile goods, therefore, experienced fluctuating fortunes in this period: after having risen from £10.7 million annually in 1850–4 to £31.5 million in 1870–4, they declined—in a general deflationary period, of course—to around £20 million at the turn of the century, but then rose strongly to £30.6 million in 1909–13, probably around a third of total output. As a proportion of United Kingdom exports, however, they had now sunk to less than 7 per cent, having fallen much further behind cotton, while being overtaken by coal, iron and steel and machinery (see p. 244).

Tariffs and foreign competition certainly reduced the industry's rate of growth, but it continued to expand. The home market was buoyant, with rising population and living standards and growth of ready-made clothing factories, especially in Leeds; the industry was also doing well in hosiery and other knitwear (see pp. 213–4, 228–31). Output therefore rose substantially, as indicated by estimates of the average annual consumption of raw wool, which, after rising from 241 to 435.5 million lb between 1850–4 and 1870–4, continued to increase to 845.9 million lb (over four-fifths of it now imported) in 1909–13. The total power employed, which had risen to 116,000 horse-power (nine-tenths steam) by 1870, increased to 325,000 horse-power by 1907. The continued growth of production, despite the declining numbers of spindles, looms and employees, was, in fact, made possible by further technological improvements, raising productivity, though these were achieved mainly by increasing the size, efficiency and operating speed of existing types of machinery rather than by introducing new techniques; factories also became bigger, though small firms remained very numerous. The number of woollen (including shoddy) factories had risen from nearly 1,500 in 1850 to nearly 2,000 by 1870, fluctuating around that figure until about 1890, but then declining to just over 1,500 by 1904; worsted mills, on the other hand, increased steadily from about 500 to nearly 850 over this whole period. Overall, there were not many more mills in the early 1900s than in the mid-nineteenth century, but the average mill was a good deal bigger.

Process specialization also developed further, especially in worsted manufacture, though it was not at all clear-cut, and further localization occurred.

Leeds remained the chief centre of the finer woollen trade; Dewsbury and Batley specialized in heavy woollens (heavy cloths, blankets, carpets, etc., including the shoddy trade); Bradford, Halifax and Keighley were still the main worsted centres, and there were many complex local specialities; but both woollens and worsteds were manufactured in Leeds and Huddersfield, and local specialization was nowhere complete.

This high degree of specialization, similar to that in the cotton industry, reflected the fact that the West Riding was still the world's largest producer and exporter of wool textiles. At the same time, the West Country still manufactured its superfine broadcloths, Kidderminster its carpets, Witney its blankets, Leicester its hosiery yarns and the Scottish border counties their tweeds, though these and other scattered areas of production were of relatively minor importance compared with the West Riding. In 1901, for example, out of about 260,000 employed in the whole United Kingdom woollen and worsted industries, about 187,000 were in the West Riding, with a further 12,000 in the neighbouring areas of Lancashire. As Clapham pointed out in 1907, Yorkshire had 'almost a monopoly' of the worsted industry; but in woollens it had 'only a little over half of the spindles and just under three-fifths of the looms in the kingdom', while in quality the best woollen cloths were still West of England or Scottish.

Flax, jute and hemp manufactures
In the flax, jute and hemp manufactures, as in other textiles, the conquest of handicraft by mechanized factory production was completed in the second half of the nineteenth century. Steam-powered spinning mills were already dominant by 1850, and power-looms rapidly eliminated hand-loom weaving from then onwards.

MECHANIZATION IN THE UNITED KINGDOM FLAX, JUTE AND HEMP MANUFACTURES, 1850–1905

Year	Spindles (thousands)	Power-looms (thousands)	Horse-power (thousand h.p.)
1850	965	4	14
1871	1,697	40	57
1905	1,400	68	168

Source: Mitchell and Deane, op. cit., p. 203, based on Factory Inspectors' Returns.

These figures indicate that the dynamic phase of development was in the third quarter of the century. As Gill pointed out in his work on the Irish linen industry in 1925, the industry had already, by the 1860s, been 'transformed to an organization and methods similar to those of the present day', steam-powered urban factories having largely destroyed the old scattered rural domestic manufactures. From the 1870s onwards, though growth continued, it was at a much slower rate; indeed, there was an overall reduction in the number of spindles.

According to the inspectors' returns, the numbers employed in United Kingdom flax, jute and hemp factories increased from 68,000 in 1850 to 151,000 in 1907. Nearly three-quarters of the labour force were women, who predominated in both spinning and weaving; out-workers had virtually disappeared by the early twentieth century. The 1907 Census of Production figure for total employment in factories and workshops was slightly higher, 154,496, of whom 12,439 were in England, 69,608 in Scotland and 72,449 in Ireland.

These aggregate figures, however, do not reveal the growth and decline in particular sectors, as local specialization and concentration developed. While Lancashire concentrated on cotton and Yorkshire on wool and worsted, flax and related manufactures declined markedly in these and other English counties—Marshalls, the great Leeds firm, was wound up in 1886—while Ulster, and particularly Belfast, forged ahead in linens and Dundee became the main centre of jute manufactures. In the years just before the First World War, it was estimated that there were about 935,000 spindles and about 36,000 power-looms in the Irish linen industry, compared with less than 50,000 spindles and between 4,000 and 5,000 power-looms in England, and 160,000 spindles and 17,000 power-looms in Scotland. In both England and Scotland the linen industry had gradually declined from the 1860s onwards, under competition from cotton and also from Irish linen manufactures, which were increasingly concentrated in large Belfast mills. As in the Lancashire cotton industry, spinning and weaving tended to be specialized in separate mills.

A similar concentration took place in jute manufactures, which grew prodigiously in Dundee during this period. Indeed, according to the 1907 Census of Production, the output of jute and hemp manufactures greatly exceeded that of linens in weight, though, being coarser goods (sacking, canvas, etc.), they were much less in value. Of the total number employed in Scottish flax, linen and hemp manufactures, over half were concentrated in Dundee, which was now diversifying into coarse cloths, linoleum backings, carpets and matting.

Employment in the manufacture of sailcloth and ropes declined with the eclipse of sailing ships by steam and with the displacement of the old-style rope-walks by mechanization. Just over 14,000 were employed in the rope, twine and net trades in 1907, mainly in English steam-powered factories.

Most of the raw materials, as well as some yarns, for these manufactures—flax, hemp, and jute, all produced from fibrous plants grown in various parts of the world—had to be imported, but well over half the piece goods manufactured were exported, together with a much smaller proportion of yarns. United Kingdom manufactured exports of all these goods totalled £16.1 million in 1913, compared with manufactured imports of £9.8 million. Belfast and Dundee were only just holding their own, and the period of rapid growth was obviously over. This was particularly evident for linens, exports of which had tended to stagnate from the 1870s onwards and compared very unfavourably with those of other textiles, especially cotton. Exports of piece goods, which had soared to 122 million yards by 1850 and then to around 250 million in the 'Cotton Famine' of the mid-1860s, fell to between 150 and 200 million yards annually in the period up to 1913. Including yarns, total linen exports had barely doubled, from £4.8 to £9.5 million, between 1850 and 1913.

Silk and rayon

The silk industry had always found difficulty in meeting foreign competition but was now to experience the trauma of Free-Trade, following the Anglo-French or Cobden treaty of 1860, which finally abolished all duties on imported silk goods. There was only a brief preceding period of mechanization and expansion. Silk-throwing, of course, had long been a factory process and the number of spindles only increased from 1.2 to 1.3 million between 1850 and 1861, before decline set in. There was a sharp increase, however, in the number of power-looms, from 6,000 in 1850 to 15,000 by 1867, many of them in 'cottage factories', hiring steam power; exports of silk manufactures also rose from £1.3 to £4.1 million by 1872. From then onwards, however, the industry steadily declined. Hand-loom weavers long struggled to maintain an existence, especially in finer-quality patterned goods, and there were still nearly 2,000 hand-looms in 1907, but these were only a remnant of the scores of thousands that had once existed; even power-looms had declined in number to about 7,300, though this figure was probably incomplete. The number of people employed in the industry had fallen from nearly 131,000 in 1851 to just over 32,000 (over two-thirds females) by 1907. And while exports had declined to £2.2 million by 1913, foreign imports had risen from £3.5 to £14.7 million between 1854 and 1913.

The silk industry also suffered from the competition of cotton, especially with the development of 'mercerizing' (giving a silk-like lustre), and was increasingly superseded in lace, hosiery and other manufactures; alpaca and mohair were also introduced as substitutes in mixed goods, with cotton and worsted; changing fashions, as well as the lower relative costs of these other materials, also contributed to silk's decline. But, as the trade figures indicate, foreign competition was the main factor. The 1907 Census of Production revealed that, although 70 per cent of silk broadstuffs were exported, net imports were about five times as great as home production, while the value of ribbons manufactured in the United Kingdom was only about one-twentieth of the net imports. By this time the silk manufactures of Spitalfields, Derby, Coventry, Manchester and other centres had mostly died out, and they survived only with difficulty in Macclesfield, Leek and elsewhere. Among textiles generally, silk had declined almost into insignificance (see p. 203).

Against this generally depressing background, however, some remarkable examples of enterprise stand out, notably the development of silk-waste spinning by Samuel C. Lister (of earlier wool-combing fame), who combined this with manufactures of velvets, plushes and silk sewing thread at his giant Manningham Mills, Bradford, and the crêpe-manufacturing business of Samuel Courtauld & Co., nucleus of what was to become a far greater industrial empire, originally centred on Bocking and Braintree in Essex. While silk-throwing declined, silk-waste spinning grew, mainly in Yorkshire, Lancashire and Cheshire, so that by 1907 production of spun silk was four times that of thrown, and exports greatly exceeded imports; Britain had, in fact, taken the lead in this field. Far more portentous for the future, however, was the development of the first semi-synthetic fibre, 'artificial silk', 'viscose' or 'rayon' as it is now called, pioneered in this country. The links between chemistry and textiles had become increasingly close with developments in bleaching, dyeing and printing, especially with artificial or synthetic dyes, to colour natural fibres; now the very fibre itself was to be a chemical product (see pp. 222–3). Chemical experiments on cellulose (obtained from wood-pulp, etc.) led first to Cross's patent of 1883 for electric-lamp filaments and then in 1892 to Cross and Bevan's patent for viscose, which was developed, in collaboration with Stearn and Topham, first for electric-bulb filaments and then as a spun textile yarn. In 1904 the long-established silk-manufacturing firm of Courtaulds acquired a factory, appropriately at Coventry, where they started commercial production of this artificial silk, and their United Kingdom yarn output soared to 3.8 million lb by 1914, while their American subsidiary produced 2.4 million lb.

Hosiery and lace

The second half of the nineteenth century witnessed a technological revolution in the hosiery trade, which was transformed from the traditional hand knitting-frames of the domestic system to steam-powered circular and rotary frames in factories. After early experiments in the 1840s, progress was at first slow: by 1870 there were 129 hosiery factories in the United Kingdom, but they employed only 9,692 persons. Small-scale sub-letting was common, while many of the factories were really workshops containing hand-frames; the abundance of cheap domestic labour, the frame-renting system, and the independence of out-workers were obstacles to change. But with further mechanical improvements, such as Cotton's patent of 1864, in the manufacture of high-quality fashioned goods, larger-scale factory production spread more rapidly: twenty years later 24,838 persons were employed in 257 factories, and by 1901 the factory population reached 38,549.

Mechanized factory production brought about considerable changes in the structure of the labour force. In 1867 Felkin estimated that there were 150,000 hosiery workers, of whom about 50,000 were hand-frame knitters, predominantly men, and about 100,000 winders, menders, seamers and others in the finishing trades, mostly women and children. By the early 1890s, however, the number of hand-frame knitters had dwindled to about 5,000, and though out-workers were still numerous, employment was greatly reduced, with the increased productivity of factory machinery. In 1907 the industry had a total labour force of 51,213 (38,196 females) in factories and workshops, with a further 5,803 out-workers. It was located mainly in the east midlands, with smaller centres such as Hawick in south-eastern Scotland. The factories, however, were not concentrated in the two main cities of Nottingham and Leicester but were increasingly dispersed in the traditional hand-frame knitting villages and small towns of the surrounding areas, where the wives and daughters of miners and other male workers provided a supply of relatively cheap non-unionized labour; Nottingham and Leicester tended to become commercial rather than manufacturing centres. About three-quarters of all hosiery workers were now females, while male hand-frame knitters, like hand-loom weavers, were fast disappearing and not generally going into factories. Women and girls, in fact, were increasingly substituted for men on more automatic power frames, while those previously employed as out-workers in the finishing processes were also being brought into factories on power-driven sewing machines. At the same time, however, as male employment declined and the old hand-frame knitters were eliminated, factory production brought great improvements over the previous domestic system, ending the exploitation of frame-renting, truck and child labour and providing better working conditions, lighter labour, higher wages and reduced working hours. The belated industrial revolution in this trade was, as Wells says, 'on the whole of immense benefit to the hosiery worker'.

These changes occurred in an increasingly competitive situation. Many new firms challenged the old-established hosiery manufacturers, often renting factory space and power and getting machinery on credit, though the older firms, with their commercial experience, were generally more successful in surviving the technological revolution. At the same time, foreign competition became fiercer: British silk hosiery manufactures dwindled almost completely away under French competition, while exports of cotton hosiery also declined considerably, as German firms captured foreign markets; by the early 1900s cotton hosiery imports greatly exceeded exports. Woollen hosiery exports, on the other hand, rose very substantially, far surpassing imports. In 1913 total hosiery exports were valued at £2.7 million (nearly £2 million woollen), while imports were £3.5 million (about £3 million cotton). There was, in fact, a marked shift in the British industry towards woollen manufactures (stockings, socks, underwear, jumpers, etc.); all-wool products constituted about 55 per cent, all-cotton only a fifth, of total hosiery output in 1907, the remainder being of mixed yarns; Leicester, rather than Nottingham, was becoming the main centre of the industry.

A similar revolution occurred in the lace industry of that area. Although the number of lace factories, with power-driven bobbin-net machines, had gradually increased after Heathcoat's invention in the early nineteenth century, the typical unit of production in the Nottingham trade in 1840 was still the small workshop, with hand-operated machines, often housed in long-windowed attics. From then on, however, steam-powered factory production developed rapidly; by the early 1860s hand-operated machines were almost extinct, though many small independent producers survived by renting factory space and power, under the 'stall' system, especially in the fancy trade. Following Deverill's successful application of the jacquard principle to the leavers bobbin-net machine in 1841, there was an ever-multiplying variety of patterns, suited to small-scale production; it was in the plain-net trade that larger factories developed.

The number of lace factories rose from 29 or 30 in 1836 to 224 by 1870, with a labour force of 8,370; by 1890 there were 403 factories, with 16,930 employees, concentrated mainly in the Nottingham area. The dressing and other finishing processes were also brought into employers' workshops and warehouses. The total United Kingdom labour force of the industry, in both factories and workshops, in 1907 was 36,840, of whom 20,459 were females (employed especially in the finishing processes), together with 5,171 out-workers, mostly female. Little now remained of the once-widespread lace-making in southern rural counties.

Expanding factory production was associated with a rapidly increasing demand for lace, as rising living standards were reflected in women's dress and window curtains in the late Victorian era. Overseas markets also expanded rapidly, and exports of cotton lace soared from around £0.5 million annually in the mid-1850s to £4.9 million in 1907, though tending to decline in the following years; there was growing competition, especially from Swiss and German machine-embroidered lace, and the trade in silk lace—as in silk hosiery—gradually dwindled, but total imports were not much more than half the value of exports in 1913; about two-thirds of total lace production was, in fact, exported. In a trade so swayed by fashion, mercantile capital played a key role, with specialized merchant-converters or finishers acting as intermediaries between machine holders or manufacturers and home and overseas markets. Nottingham, in fact, with its 'Lace Market', became the industry's commercial centre, like Manchester in the cotton trade, with manufacturing carried on in surrounding areas such as Long Eaton.

The technological revolution in the east midlands lace and hosiery manufactures did not, however, produce a factory system on the same scale as in cotton. In 1890, for example, the average employment figure in lace factories was only 42, in hosiery 97; nor were they great users of power (see p. 203). In these competitive fashion trades, small factories and workshops were able to survive in the machine age. There are signs, however, that these British industries, having led in early mechanization, were tending to lag technically by the late nineteenth and early twentieth centuries, as evidenced by the German dominance in cotton hosiery, the American lead in developing more automatic machinery and the British slowness in adopting lace-embroidery machines. Many of the new machines were now imported, and though, by re-equipping with these, the British hosiery and lace industries were able to maintain their efficiency reasonably well in the face of foreign competition and tariffs, there is evidence here, as in other manufactures, of weakness in British machine-making (see pp. 182, 187).

12

Chemicals and Allied Industries

In terms of employment, the chemical and allied trades were not among the major British industries of the nineteenth century. Although the number employed in these trades increased from 46,000 to 201,000 between 1851 and 1911, they still formed only 1.1 per cent of the total occupied population or 2.1 per cent of the industrial labour force. Nor were they great users of mechanical power (see pp. 167–8): the chemical revolution involved matter-transforming reactions in furnaces, boilers, vats and stills rather than steam-powered mechanization. In terms of output, however, being capital rather than labour-intensive, they were of more significance, contributing 3 per cent net industrial output in 1907. Their products, moreover, were extremely varied, supplying the requirements of many other industries, as well as consumer goods trades: they included not only alkalis, acids, bleaching powder, dyestuffs, coal-tar products and many other heavy chemicals, but also drugs, medicines, perfumery, oils and tallow, soap and candles, fertilizers, glue, disinfectants, paints, colours, varnishes, explosives, ammunition, fireworks and matches. Almost all industries, in fact, depended to some extent upon these chemical trades, which were of as pervasive importance in supplying essential materials as were the engineering and metal-manufacturing trades in providing machinery and other industrial hardware. At the same time, many industries came to depend increasingly upon knowledge of chemical reactions, as in dyeing and calico printing, brewing, tanning, metal refining and the manufactures of glass, pottery, paper and rubber.

It is impossible, in this brief space, to deal with developments in all these multifarious trades. Attention will therefore be concentrated firstly on the heavy inorganic chemical industry—the 'alkali trade', as it was called, producing soda ash (sodium carbonate) by the Leblanc process, together with saltcake (sodium sulphate) and caustic soda, and the closely associated and increasingly integrated manufactures of sulphuric and other acids, bleaching powder and related products (see pp. 122–4). Centred mainly on Merseyside and Tyneside, near to resources of salt, limestone and coal and with markets in the textiles, soap, glass and other northern manufactures, this remained the predominant sector of the industry throughout the nineteenth century. Various improvements were introduced, such as Gossage towers for recovery of previously wasted and damaging hydrochloric acid gas in the Leblanc process; this could be used in bleaching powder production, which was thus firmly integrated into the alkali trade, especially following the Weldon and Deacon processes in the 1860s for oxygenizing this product to produce chlorine. A similar problem, that of recovering the sulphur content of alkali waste (calcium sulphide), was eventually solved by Chance's process in the late 1880s. Chemical-engineering advances were also made, such as Glover towers in the lead-chamber (sulphuric acid) process and mechanically operated furnaces in Leblanc soda production. Output expanded remarkably: that of sulphuric acid, for example, rose from around 10,000 tons annually in the early 1820s to about a million tons by 1900; soda, from about 70,000 tons at mid-century to nearly 270,000 tons by 1880; bleaching powder, from about 10,000 to more than 130,000 tons over the same period. British chemical exports, moreover, rose even more rapidly, mainly to Europe and the United States, especially to the latter, which were taking well over half the British exports of soda and bleaching powder by the 1870s. Chemical exports as a whole rose from an almost negligible figure at mid-century to nearly 4 per cent of total export values in 1880, by which time over half the total chemical output was being shipped abroad.

Technologically and commercially, in fact, Britain continued to dominate the world chemical industry and trade until the last decades of the century. In 1878, for example, this country accounted for 46.2 per cent of world production of sulphuric acid, compared with the United States' 13.8 per cent and Germany's 8.6 per cent. By 1913, however, these relative positions had dramatically altered, the United Kingdom having fallen to third place, with 11 per cent of all chemical production, behind the United States with 34 per cent and Germany with 24 per cent. The United Kingdom still produced about half the world's soda ash in the early twentieth century, but this provides another example of over-commitment, resulting from her early start. Moreover, the British industry was now lagging technologically, still clinging to the Leblanc process, while in Germany and other European countries and in the United States the Belgian Solvay or ammonia-soda process, introduced in the 1860s, had been much more rapidly developed. (This involved the reaction, in Solvay towers, between carbon dioxide, obtained from limestone, and concentrated brine saturated with ammonia, to produce sodium bicarbonate, which was then calcined to the carbonate soda ash.)

This lag has frequently been emphasized as another instance of British scientific-technological backwardness and entrepreneurial conservatism, and there is undoubtedly some substance in this criticism, but there are other points to be considered. The Leblanc manufacture had been developed far more exten-sively in Britain than in other countries, and it continued, as we have seen, to be technically improved; though the Solvay process could produce cheaper soda ash, it wasted the chlorine recovered in the older process, which was also better adapted to produce caustic soda. It was not until those latter products came to be produced electrolyticaly from brine, from the late 1880s onwards (see p. 220), that the Leblanc process was doomed. In view of the large quantities of capital previously invested, it is therefore understandable why the Leblanc manu-facturers combined defensively in the United Alkali Company of 1890 (see p. 249), seeking output and pricing agreements and alternative overseas markets rather than going in for wholesale scrapping.

It must also be emphasized that British chemical firms were now operating in a much less favourable economic environment. With the rapid growth of powerful tariff-protected chemical industies in Germany, the United States and elsewhere, the British industry's heavy dependence on exports made it very vulnerable, a situation similar to that of the iron and steel and tinplate industries (and later of the cotton, coal and shipbuilding industries). British alkali exports to the United States, for example, so important in expansion of the industry up to 1890, had virtually disappeared by the end of the century, as a result of the McKinley and Dingley tariffs and the rapid growth of American Solvay production. America and Germany, with relatively little commitment to old processes, were in a better position to invest in such new developments. Under these circumstances, as Saul has pointed out, Britain 'held her own reasonably well' in chemical exports, which, as a result of developing new markets outside Europe and the United States, especially in the Empire, rose from £8 million in 1880 to £24 million in 1913, though declining from 29.4 to 21.9 per cent of the world chemicals trade.

British chemicals production continued to grow substantially, though less rapidly than that of her rising competitors. Output of sulphuric acid increased by over 80 per cent between 1878 and 1913, soda ash production doubled in the twenty years after 1875, while the United Kingdom chemicals output as a whole rose by 48 per cent between 1900 and 1913. At the same time, the pattern of production was gradually adjusted to changing technology, though the problems of obsolescence were far greater than in other countries. United Alkali, for example, were rapidly running down production of Leblanc soda ash by the early twentieth century, while still striving to retain their markets for other alkali products. Undoubtedly the Solvay process was cheaper, and higher profits could have been made by scrapping and conversion. There was the remarkable example of Brunner Mond & Co., who, under licence from Solvay, established an ammonia-soda plant at Winnington, Cheshire (headquarters of the modern I.C.I. Alkali Division), in the early 1870s and increased their output of soda products to well over 700,000 tons by 1913, with annual profits of 15 to 20 per cent or more, compared with the United Alkali Company's 3 per cent average; the latter did go into ammonia-soda production at Widnes and Fleetwood, but failed to develop it on a large scale. Several other firms also established ammonia-soda plants in the Cheshire and north-eastern salt regions, but were eventually taken over by Brunner Mond & Co., who dominated Solvay production in Britain before the First World War.

Ludwig Mond was a German–Jewish immigrant, with the advantages of a scientific technical education in German universities, but who recognized the British chemical industrial potential. Superiority in applied science was undoubtedly a major factor in Germany's remarkable progress in chemical manufactures. In addition to rapid exploitation of the Solvay process, Germany also led the way in developing the contact process for production of sulphuric acid, in place of the old-established lead-chamber process. By 1914 Germany was apparently producing about 25 per cent of its sulphuric acid by the new process, compared with 14 per cent in America and 11 per cent in Britain. But this process was economical only in producing the most highly concentrated acid, for which the market was then limited, and Britain's lag in this case, according to Lindert and Trace, 'apparently cost her nothing before 1914'. Significantly, however, the main demand for concentrated acid was in the manufacture of synthetic coal-tar dyestuffs, in which Germany had established an overwhelming predominance. In this and other branches of developing organic chemistry Britain lagged much more seriously. After Perkin's production of the first synthetic aniline dye in 1856, followed by synthetic alizarine in 1869, gradually displacing natural vegetable dyes, it might have been expected that Britain—with her immense advantages in production of the basic materials, coal-tar, sulphuric acid, etc., together with a huge domestic market in the textile trades—would have become the leader in the synthetic dyestuffs industry. But in fact Germany, increasingly powerful in chemical science and technology, had by 1914 developed an industry twenty to thirty times the size of that in Britain, which was then importing almost nine-tenths of her synthetic dyestuffs requirements from Germany, to which she was exporting a considerable proportion of her coal-tar products. Perhaps from a free-trade economic point of view, as Hardie has argued, there was nothing wrong in this exchange, but from a scientific-technological angle it has generally been regarded as 'the most conspicuous example of Britain's failure to keep pace in organic chemicals', as Richardson has emphasized. Significantly, two of the most outstanding figures in this branch of British chemicals manufacture, after Perkin, were the German–Jewish immigrant Ivan Levinstein, who established works at Blackley, Manchester, in 1864 (later he was also involved in two ammonia-soda companies, eventually taken over by Brunner Mond), and Charles Dreyfus from Alsace, who founded the Clayton Aniline Company in Manchester in 1876, with Swiss financial backing (it was acquired by the Swiss dye firm Ciba in 1911);

German university-trained and employing German chemists in his works, Levinstein was particularly critical of British entrepreneurial conservatism and deficiencies in applied science, whilst also becoming a strong tariff reformer. There were some native British firms, such as Read Holliday & Sons of Huddersfield that were successful in this field, but none could compare with the German dyestuffs giants.

Britain could not, of course, realistically be expected to maintain leadership in all branches of the chemical industry, but her relative lag in these new organic developments was disturbing. Another example was provided in electro-chemicals. Following the pioneering laboratory discoveries of the British chemists Davy and Faraday in the early nineteenth century, it was not until the last two decades of the century, with the development of electric-dynamo generation, that major industrial applications were made, though electroplating had been developed earlier. An important breakthrough was in the electrolysis of brine to produce caustic soda and chlorine, but in this Britain lagged far behind the United States and Germany, which swung over rapidly to the new process. Significantly, again, the leading firm in this country was the Castner–Kellner Alkali Company, formed in 1895, with backing from the Solvay Company, to develop the mercury-cathode cell invented by the American Castner (with works at Oldbury, Birmingham, for the manufacture of aluminium, see p. 179) and by the German Kellner. Electrolytic processes were also introduced for the manufacture of aluminium and copper refining, but in these as well as in new electro-thermal processes (electric furnaces) for production of metals or metallic compounds, such as phosphorus and calcium carbide, as well as steel, Britain did not play a leading role. This, however, was not simply a result of scientific-technological backwardness, but largely because these electro-metallurgical processes could be most advantageously developed in countries with abundant resources of relatively cheap hydro-electric power.

The strength of foreign competition was reflected in growing imports of chemicals, which rose more than twice as fast as exports between 1880 and 1913, so that, although Britain remained a net exporter of chemicals, the surplus on this trade was diminishing. Germany was a strongly growing competitor in both the home and overseas markets. Britain's export performance, however, should not be underrated. While Germany dominated in dyestuffs and many fine chemicals, British exports of heavy inorganic chemicals were still considerably greater than Germany's in 1913; in exports of fertilizers, particularly ammonium sulphate (more than twice the value of imported dyestuffs in 1913), she held a clear superiority, and her export performance in coal-tar products, paints, drugs and medicines, soaps and explosives was also very creditable. Overall, however, Germany's chemical exports were nearly twice the value of Britain's.

In both explosives and soaps, Britain was again indebted to foreign scientific-technical expertise and enterprise. The early development of nitro-cellulose (guncotton) explosives in this country, from the 1850s onwards, was based on the original researches of the Swiss chemist Schönbein, while the famous Swedish chemical entrepreneur Alfred Nobel was the leading figure in the later manufacture of nitro-glycerine explosives such as dynamite, blasting gelatine (gelignite) and the 'smokeless powder' ballistite, followed by other explosives such as cordite, lyddite and trinitrotoluene (TNT); these products of chemical research, closely related to those in dyestuffs, were used for blasting and as military propellants, displacing gunpowder. Nobel's factory established at Ardeer on the Ayrshire coast in 1871 became the largest of its type in the world, and the companies which he formed dominated this branch of the British chemical industry in the period up to the First World War.

In soap manufacture, there was plenty of vigorous British enterprise. National soap output rose from about 90,000 tons per annum in the early 1850s to about 260,000 tons in 1891 and then to 366,000 tons by 1912; exporting about a quarter of this output, British firms still held the leadership in world trade. William Lever (later Lord Leverhulme) was, of course, outstanding for his organizational, commercial and advertising flair, establishing his famous Port Sunlight works in 1889, gradually taking over other firms and establishing a large business empire before 1914. But in scientific-technological developments the old-established Merseyside firm of Crosfields of Warrington was more progressive, assisted by German chemists and developing German processes. The hydrogenation or fat-hardening process, of crucial importance for both soap and margarine manufacture, was based on the German Normann's patent of 1903; 'Persil' (sodium perborate) soap-powder was similarly based on a patent of the Germans Giessler and Bauer obtained in that same year; and in the development of these and other processes, not only in soap-making but also in oil-making and the manufacture of chemicals such as glycerine, caustic soda and sodium silicate, the firm owed a great deal to German chemists whom they recruited, notably Markel, though in the years just before the First World War these were being replaced by some able British chemists. Crosfields thus became the largest United Kingdom producer of silicate, and the second largest of caustic soda, as well as of soap. (German chemists were similarly employed by some brewing firms, as Sigsworth has pointed out, as well as in more purely chemical manufactures.)

Crosfields had close links with Brunner Mond & Co., by whom they were eventually taken over in 1911, but were transferred to Lever Brothers in 1919. There was a strong tendency towards large-scale business organization in the chemical and allied trades in the late nineteenth and early twentieth centuries, (see pp. 249–50), resulting in numerous amalgamations and agreements on markets, production and prices, at both national and international levels. The progress of chemical research was creating innumerable technological, industrial and business interrelationships, which, in the struggle for wider markets, led to the growth of the first great multinational enterprises, international commercial rivalries and eventually division of world markets. The domestic rivalries between United Alkali and Brunner Mond and between Brunner Mond, Lever Brothers and Crosfields were small-scale by comparison with the international involvements of the Solvay Company, the Nobel companies, the huge American and German trusts and cartels and their smaller British counterparts. Under these pressures, British family firms were gradually being forced into larger-scale company organization, amalgamation and combination.

Clearly, however, the traditionally gloomy impression of the British chemical industry in the later years of this period, created by the obsolescent Leblanc soda' industry and the eclipse of British synthetic dyestuffs, is somewhat misleading. Though British weakness in scientific-technical education is indicated by the frequent reliance on German and other foreign chemists, their recruitment is indicative of growing entrepreneurial awareness of their value. Moreover, there are many examples of scientific-technical skill and business enterprise in other sectors of the chemicals industry during this period.

In alum manufacture, Peter Spence, having established works in Manchester in the mid-nineteenth century, at the heart of the principal market for this dye-fixing mordant (see p. 124), became the largest alum producer in the world by the 1880s; with factories also at Birmingham and Goole, he had a near monopoly of the United Kingdom manufacture.

Production of sodium cyanide, used especially in gold-extraction, electroplating and other metal industries, was developed in this country mainly by the Cassel and Castner–Kellner Companies from the 1880s onwards, and by the eve of the First World War Britain was producing about half the world output. Albright & Wilson of Oldbury, Birmingham, were similarly outstanding in the development of phosporus manufacture, chiefly for the match industry, in which Bryant & May likewise predominated.

British chemists and entrepreneurs also played leading roles in the development of semi-synthetic materials, or chemically modified forms of natural materials, such as rubber-tree sap and wood cellulose, forerunners of fully synthetic modern plastics. The early rubber industry was based on the inventions of Macintosh and Hancock, the former producing water-proofed fabrics from the 1820s (see p. 125), the latter developing his mastication and sulphur-vulcanization processes from the 1830s onwards. In the later nineteenth century, with the introduction of bicycles and motor-cars, the demand for rubber was enormously increased and Dunlop pioneered the development of pneumatic-tyre manufacture from the late 1880s onwards.

Meanwhile, Alexander Parkes of Birmingham, after developing an improved rubber-vulcanizing process, went on in the 1850s and 1860s to exploit the possibilities of nitro-cellulose, first for guncotton explosive and then for the production of what eventually became known by its American name as celluloid. These possibilities were further exploited in new fields such as the manufacture of electric-lamp filaments, developed from the early 1880s by Swan and Stearn, followed by the invention of viscose in 1892 by the chemists Cross and Bevan, who were subsequently associated with Stearn, Topham, Beer and others in its development as a textile fibre, leading to Courtaulds' artificial silk or rayon manufacture from 1904 onwards (see p. 212). Britain shared with Germany the lead in rayon production in 1913.

In the early 1900s, moreover, James Swinburne, who had been associated with Swan, played a leading role in developing production of the first wholly synthetic new materials, made from phenol–formaldehyde resins, patented by the American Baekeland in 1906–7 and hence known as bakelite; starting the modern plastics industry, these materials could be moulded into electrical insulators, gramophone records, etc., or could be used as lacquers.

In pharmaceuticals, the enterprise of Jesse Boot of Nottingham paralleled that of Lever in the soap and allied trades. Starting similarly in a small retail business, he began to expand sales of his packaged and branded goods by commercial advertising, then launched Boots Pure Drug Company in 1883, went into drugs manufacture and established multiple retailing outlets in towns all over the country, subsequently developing these into more general stores. Thus he became the country's leading retailer and manufacturer of pharmaceutical goods. In this same period, Thomas Beecham of St Helens similarly made his name a household word by manufacturing and selling his pills, from which the modern Beecham Group has grown. But these men, like Lever, were primarily commercial entrepreneurs, not industrial chemists. And in the development of synthetic pharmaceuticals—dependent upon advances in organic chemistry, like the dyestuffs industry—Britain lagged far behind Germany. It was, in fact, in the new science-based organic and electro-chemical manufactures that British deficiencies were most strongly evident.

Coal-gas, coal-tar products and oil

The coal-gas industry was already well established by 1850, and by the early twentieth century there were about a thousand gas undertakings in Great Britain, a mixture of municipal and company enterprises, consuming altogether about 15 million tons of coal annually. Their prime function was still gas lighting, greatly improved by introduction of the incandescent mantle in the 1880s, while gas cooking and heating were also developed from then on. Gas also came to be used in industrial furnaces, as well as in the new internal-combustion engines (see pp. 188–9). At the same time, gasworks developed a growing trade in by-product coke, tar and ammonia liquor. From the 1880s onwards, moreover, the coking plants of some iron and steel works, and also collieries, began to be equipped with by-product recovery ovens, utilizing the gas for heating or power and selling off the tar and liquor, though primitive and wasteful beehive ovens remained in widespread use (see pp. 171, 172, 175).

The coal-tar and ammonia liquor by-products of gasworks and coking plants became increasingly important as raw materials for the chemical industry. The ammonia was used mainly in production of ammonium sulphate fertilizer, for which there was a rapidly growing market both at home and abroad. The tar, once a waste problem, then crudely distilled to produce naphtha and creosote, now became an increasingly valuable source of organic chemicals or hydro-carbons, such as benzene, toluene, naphthalene, phenol and anthracene, fractioned out in tar distilleries—from the 1870s benzene was also recovered by extraction from coal-gas—while the residual pitch was used as a wood preservative, etc., as well as on roads. These chemicals were themselves bases for the manufacture of synthetic dyes (aniline, alizarine, etc.), explosives, solvents, drugs, perfumes, disinfectants and the first plastics. But in this exploitation of coal-tar products, as we have seen, the British chemical industry lagged behind that of Germany, to which, in fact, large quantities of these materials were exported (see p. 219).

Until the First World War and indeed long after, coal remained the basic source of heavy organic chemicals. The development of petrochemicals—the exploitation of petroleum as a raw material for such hydrocarbon products—was as yet only distantly foreshadowed. The early development of the shale-oil industry in Scotland before 1870, and the subsequent imports of oil from the United States, were stimulated mainly by the growing demand for paraffin (kerosene) in oil-lamps and for lubricants. Then from the late nineteenth century onwards the introduction of the internal-combustion engine gave a tremendous boost to exploitation of oil resources in various parts of the world. The United States took the lead and the Anglo-American Oil Company, set up in 1888 by the Standard Oil Company (New Jersey) as its United Kingdom distributing subsidiary, at first acquired a virtual monopoly of the sale of petroleum products in this country. But with the opening of new supply sources in Russia, the Near and Far East and Mexico, British interests were soon established in oil-wells, refineries, tankers and distributing depots: the Shell, Russian Petroleum, Anglo-Persian, Burmah, and Anglo-Mexican companies appeared on the scene between the late 1890s and 1914. But petrol, like paraffin, was imported in bulk, and the development of oil-refining and petrochemical manufactures in this country lay far in the future.

Glass and pottery manufactures

In terms of employment, the glass and pottery manufactures were among the small industries—in 1911 glass employed 31,000, pottery 70,000, in England and Wales—but their products were in widespread demand. There was a rapidly growing market for glass in this period, initially encouraged by abolition of the excise duty in 1845 and window duty in 1851 and then sustained by the growth of population, house and factory building and rising living standards, with consequently rising demands for sheet and plate glass (for windows, mirrors, etc.), bottle glass (for beer and mineral-water bottles, jam-jars, etc.) and flint or crystal glass (for wine-glasses, table-ware, vases, etc.). But the British glass industry had always been heavily dependent on foreign skills, and even though coal-fired furnaces and steam-powered grinding and polishing machinery had been developed in this country, foreign competition remained severe. With the gradual removal of protective tariffs in the 1840s and 1850s, under free-trade policy, there was a flood of foreign (especially Belgian) imports, which by the 1870s were probably not far short of home production, and this situation persisted right up to 1914. And while imports soared, exports tended to stagnate; foreign tariffs, especially the McKinley and Dingley tariffs in the United States in the 1890s, seriously restricted overseas markets. In the first Census of Production in 1907, when the gross British output of glass was valued at nearly £5 million, glass imports were three-fifths of that figure and more than twice the exports.

The greatest difficulties were experienced in the flint-glass trade, in which cheaper skilled labour gave a competitive advantage to foreign producers, despite the introduction of moulds for mass-production. The other branches of the industry, however, put up stronger resistance by means of technological innovation and larger-scale organization. Siemens' regenerative gas-fired furnace was applied in the 1860s, his tank-furnace (in place of pots) in the 1870s, making possible continuous working; new tunnel lehrs were also introduced in place of the old annealing kilns, for continuous cooling of glass sheets; further advances were made in machine rolling, grinding and polishing of plate glass; and in the early twentieth century the drawn-cylinder process was developed for mechanical production of sheet glass, using compressed air instead of hand blowing. By that time, moreover, electricity had already begun to displace steam power in glassworks.

In the face of foreign competition and the growing capital requirements of advancing technology, many firms failed or were taken over by more progressive concerns, so that the glass industry was tending to be dominated by a few large firms, such as Chance's of Birmingham, Hartley's of Sunderland (though they went out of business in 1894) and Pilkington's of St Helens. This was particularly evident in sheet and plate-glass manufacture, in which Pilkington's, with a capital of £1,400,000 and a labour force of about 3,000 by the end of the century, were increasingly predominant as a result of enterprising investment, technological innovation, commercial drive and favourable location in the Merseyside coal-chemicals area. Few, if any, of the numerous smaller firms in other branches of the industry, however, were as progressive.

Several of the new inventions in this period came from abroad, especially from the United States. Although patents for bottle-making machines, for example, were taken out by British inventors in the second half of the nineteenth century, the real revolution in this branch of the industry came with the American Owens machinery in the early twentieth century; the drawn-cylinder process was similarly of American origin. But Pilkington's, in particular, were very quick to take out manufacturing licences, as well as to make improvements themselves, and in the years before the First World War the British industry was holding its own, with rising exports, except in flint- and optical glass, where foreign skills and applied science were still predominant.

Pottery, like glass, was in growing demand, with rising population and living standards, so that an immense variety of manufactures—not only table-ware but also ornaments, all kinds of domestic fittings, sanitary ware, tiles, drainpipes, electrical insulators, etc.—were produced, ranging from cheap earthenware to fine bone-china and porcelain, with new designs, decorations, colours and glazes. To meet this expansion in both home and export markets, the industry was increasingly mechanized. Water- or steam-powered mills for grinding flints, etc., were already general, and in the second half of the nineteenth century the laborious operations of blunging or mixing clay and wedging or kneading it, preparatory to throwing, were gradually displaced by mechanical blungers and pug-mills. Potters' wheels became power-driven; mechanical jiggers and jolleys, with moulds and profiles, reduced the need for manual skills in shaping pots; plaster-casting also tended to displace hollow-ware pressing, while paper-transfer prints, mechanically reproduced from copperplate or lithographic presses, were increasingly used for mass-production instead of hand decoration. By the early twentieth century, moreover, experiments were being made with new types of gas-, oil- or electric-fired tunnel kilns, through which the wares could be moved mechanically, thus making possible continuous working, instead of intermittent firing in the old-fashioned bottle-ovens.

It was only gradually, however, that the pottery industry moved into the machine age. Manual skills had by no means been eliminated, while bottle-kilns were long to remain the predominant feature of the Potteries landscape; with continued industrial expansion, therefore, there was no really serious labour redundancy. Despite the growth of factory production by large firms such as Wedgwoods, Copelands, Mintons, etc.—already, by 1870, the average pottery employed about 84 workers—there were still a great many small ones, not only in north Staffordshire, where the industry was increasingly concentrated, but also in various other towns. Nevertheless, mechanization tended inevitably towards large-scale mass-production and the dilution of craft skills. Nearly half those employed in the trade before the First World War were women and girls, though the development of factory legislation and elementary education brought about the decline of child labour.

Though some scholars, such as Clapham, have referred to the industry of this period as being 'technically old-fashioned', there is, in fact, plentiful evidence of continued technological innovation, commercial enterprise, and changing industrial organization, alongside survivals of traditional techniques and small firms. Many old firms were still progressive, while new ones rose into prominence. The industry remained in the van technologically—William Boulton of Burslem, for instance, was the most outstanding figure in the development of ceramic engineering during this period—and it also retained a strong position in world markets, though there was still much imitation of foreign styles, ancient and modern; the Ceramic Society, founded in 1900 in north Staffordshire, acted as a medium for technological improvement, and there was some, though inadequate, attention to technical education in local schools of art and design. The strength of exports is evident from the fact that in 1907, out of the industry's gross output of nearly £8 million, over a third was exported, while imports were valued at only about one-ninth of British production.

The continued expansion of the pottery industry increased the demand for ball- and china-clay from Dorset, Devon and Cornwall, where quarrying was further extended and coastal shipments continued to grow, to some extent compensating for the decline of copper mining in that area.

13

The Consumer Goods Revolution

In the mid-nineteenth century, despite revolutionary changes in the basic industries producing textiles, metals and coal, the British people were still clothed, fed and housed in mainly traditional fashion by tradesmen whose techniques had changed comparatively little over the centuries, working for the most part in small units with simple manual equipment. This was very largely true, not only of the clothing, leather, boot and shoe, food and drink, building and printing trades, with which we shall be concerned in this chapter, but also of the cutlery and other domestic hardware trades, as well as hosiery, knitwear and lace manufactures, dealt with in previous chapters. By 1914, however, though large numbers of such manual craftsmen still existed, the Industrial Revolution had extended, or was extending, into these consumer trades, stimulated by continually rising population and real incomes, and was bringing about a considerable transformation with mechanized factory production.

The clothing trades
The clothing trades lagged considerably behind textile spinning and weaving in technological and organizational development. The factory system, with power-driven machinery, did not appear in these trades until the 1850s and it only spread slowly thereafter. Though Howe, Singer and other sewing machines were then introduced from America, they were at first mostly hand- or treadle-operated and fitted into the existing small workshop and domestic putting-out system. The wholesale manufacture of ready-made clothing had already begun to develop (see p. 130), with subdivision and specialization of hand labour, under mercantile-capitalist control, though with extensive sub-contracting, and this system was greatly extended with machine production in the later nineteenth century, in London, Leeds, Manchester and other centres of clothing manufactures.

For better-quality clothes, however, bespoke (made-to-order) tailoring by small firms, with hand sewing, remained customary, while even in the production of 'cheap and nasty' goods small workshops and domestic out-work manufactures continued to flourish, especially in London, where they were stimulated by efforts to escape from the restrictions of factory and workshop legislation and where the 'sweating' system became notorious, employing the cheap labour of Jewish immigrants, women and children. It was in the northern towns, at the sources of supply of woollen, cotton and other fabrics and catering for the rapidly growing urban-industrial populations, that the factory system developed most strongly, utilizing power-driven machinery not only for sewing but also for cutting-out, with band-knives working through layers of cloth, and for other processes such as button-holing, pressing, etc. Rising incomes stimulated production not only of better-quality wholesale ready-made goods but also of factory-manufactured made-to-measure (wholesale bespoke) clothing; both types were increasingly being sold direct to the public through multiple shops, along lines developed by firms such as Hepworths and Burtons of Leeds, though most wholesale manufacturers still supplied retailers with ready-made clothes.

In the hatting trade similarly, factory production developed mainly in the north, especially in Stockport and Denton, where machinery was introduced to mass-produce cloth hats and caps, while the market for traditional hard top-hats declined. Numerous small milliners' shops, however, still existed, often out-working, while straw-hat making survived, though declining, as a domestic handicraft in the Bedford–Buckingham–Hertford area, centred mainly on Luton.

Even in the Leeds and Manchester clothing trades, small workshop and domestic production still flourished, especially among the immigrant Jewish community, greatly increased by an East European influx in the late nineteenth and early twentieth centuries. Most of the new machines could be used in the workshop or the home, while sub-contracting and subdivision of manufacture enabled cheap unskilled labour to be employed; out-work also survived on the fringes of factory production, for finishing machine-made goods.

The clothing trades, therefore, were characterized by two contrary tendencies during this period: one centripetal, concentrating production in factories; the other centrifugal, scattering manufactures among numerous small workshops and domestic out-workers. This latter tendency is well illustrated by the occupational tables of the Population Census of England and Wales, 1911, which show that out of the total of over 591,000 tailors and dress-makers, for example, about a third were working at home, the majority of whom (especially female dress-makers) were still 'working on [their] own account' (see table on p. 230).

A similar situation existed in other sections of the clothing trades. Not surprisingly, in view of this widespread small-scale production, these trades were not great power users: the total power in the United Kingdom clothing, handkerchief and millinery trades, according to the 1907 Census of Production, was below 18,000 horse-power.

Larger-scale mechanized manufacture of clothing, however, was now rapidly developing, bringing considerable changes in the composition of the labour force. As in the textiles, hosiery and lace trades, there was a marked tendency for women and girls to displace men, though even in the mid-nineteenth century they had formed over half the number working in the clothing trades (see p. 140). The 1907 Census of Production showed that nearly four-fifths of those employed in the factories and workshops of these trades were females. With expanding trade and production, however, there was no reduction in total employment: in fact, the number of clothing workers in Britain gradually grew to a total of over 1¼ million in 1911 (including the boot and shoe trades), when they were still one of the largest industrial groups, comprising nearly 7 per cent of the whole occupied population (see p. 151; see also p. 242 for their contribution to industrial output).

EMPLOYMENT IN TAILORING AND DRESSMAKING,
ENGLAND AND WALES, 1911

	Employers	Working for employers	Working on own account	Others or no statement
Working in factories				
Tailors	15,797	207,403	14,794	11,473
Dress-makers	12,459	185,545	113,991	30,060
Total	28,256	392,948	128,785	41,533
Working at home				
Tailors	6,946	25,237	11,802	3,870
Dress-makers	9,028	16,096	103,726	17,160
Total	15,974	41,333	115,528	21,030

These trades, however, have been comparatively neglected by economic historians, since the change-over to mechanized factory production came after the traditionally accepted period of the Industrial Revolution and took place very gradually; hence they were among those trades referred to by Unwin in the early twentieth century as illustrating the prolonged survival of primitive forms of industrial organization (see p. 13). In Unwin's Manchester, however, and across the Pennines in Leeds, the clothing trades were well into the age of mass-production, the former specializing mainly in cotton shirts, dresses, blouses and underwear, the latter in cloth outerwear (trousers, suits and coats). Glasgow, where Singers built their British factory (see p. 187), became another centre of the clothing industry, and there were lesser centres in Colchester, Norwich, Bristol and elsewhere; but London was still the most important, with nearly a quarter of the total labour force. Independent master tailors and dress-makers were still catering for the better-off, and out-working was still common, while at the lower income levels a good deal of clothing was still home-made and there was still a second-hand market, but rising living standards for the masses were bringing about a belated revolution in these trades and machine-made goods were not only catering for more working-class consumers but were also beginning to challenge traditional hand tailoring and dress-making, as products were improved in style and quality and the market gradually extended up the social scale. Clothing exports also increased substantially in the late nineteenth and early twentieth centuries.

The leather trades

The leather trades, comprising the making of leather from hides and skins, together with the manufactures of boots and shoes, gloves, saddlery, etc., experienced a similarly delayed technological revolution in this period. Their long-established relative importance among British manufactures declined in the second half of the nineteenth century, with the rapid growth of other great staple industries, but they were still of considerable significance. (Church has estimated their gross output at over £40 million in 1907.) There was an ever-growing demand for boots and shoes, with rising population and living standards, while that for saddlery and harness also continued to increase with the number of horses in agriculture and transport, until the early twentieth century; leather also continued to be used for gloves, purses, travelling bags and cases. The total number employed in the leather trades therefore more than doubled between 1850 and 1914.

In the mid-nineteenth century the ancient processes of tanning, currying and dressing hides and skins, to produce various kinds of heavy and light leathers, remained substantially unchanged from earlier centuries, despite some increase in the size of firms and some use of mechanical power. In the period up to 1914, however, more significant changes occurred. There was a marked decline in the number of small country tanneries as the industry tended increasingly to be concentrated into fewer and bigger works, especially on Merseyside and in Yorkshire (particularly in Leeds), where over half the labour force was employed in 1911. London declined in importance as a tanning centre but maintained its leadership in currying and dressing light leathers for the fancy trades. Increasing mechanization occurred in pumping operations, in grinding barks, etc., in splitting and rolling hides and in their general handling (see pp. 167–8 for figures of motive power), while more varied and potent vegetable tanning agents were introduced and applied chemistry led to more revolutionary developments such as mineral (chrome) tanning from the late nineteenth century onwards. In both mechanization and applied science, however, the British industry lagged behind its rivals in America and Germany, and leather imports grew rapidly to an annual average of £10.7 million in 1910–14, greatly exceeding exports averaging only £3 million. Ever-growing quantities of hides were also imported, as home supplies became increasingly inadequate; hence the tendency towards location of tanneries in or near ports.

The British lag in mechanical and chemical developments in tanning, especially by comparison with the United States, appears to have been associated with the survival of traditional small family firms, as well as with weakness in applied science, though differences in costs of materials and in markets and tariffs were also important. As Church has shown, larger and more up-to-date British plants were certainly developing, and the number of tanning and currying firms fell by half between 1871 and 1911, but there were still nearly a thousand at the latter date, when the average tannery employed only 25 to 30 people, while currying and dressing were conducted on a smaller scale.

In leather manufactures, however, the challenge of foreign competition was met more successfully during this period. In the boot- and shoe-making trades, there was a mechanical revolution similar to that in the clothing trades. Sewing machines for stitching or 'closing' uppers and also for 'making' or fastening uppers and soles together, as well as machines for cutting-out, riveting and other operations—mostly of American origin, like the Howe, Thomas and Blake–McKay sewing machines introduced from the 1850s onwards—led to the gradual development of the factory system, though domestic putting-out and small workshops long survived, as in the clothing trades. Handicraft production still continued, especially for better-quality bespoke shoes, and also for army and navy contracts with conservative specifications, but the previous trend towards wholesale ready-made manufacture was now strongly reinforced by technological innovation. Despite initially strong trade-union opposition, large factories eventually developed, employing hundreds of workers on power-driven machinery, and some well-known modern firms emerged, such as Stead and Simpson, Clarks, Manfields, Norvic, K-Shoes, Saxone, Timpsons, Dicks, and Freeman, Hardy & Willis, though small-scale factory production remained common, often in specialized lines, while small cobblers (mostly repairers) and clog-makers were still numerous.

The trend towards large-scale mass-production, however, only became really strong from the 1890s onwards, under pressure of American competition. The early machines, as in the clothing trades, were hand- or treadle-operated and could be used in homes or workshops; the out-working system avoided fixed-capital costs and could utilize cheap labour, especially women and children, free from factory legislation. But 'the American invasion' of home and overseas markets in the 1890s and early 1900s stimulated much more rapid mechanization, so that by 1914 the factory system was predominant, with numerous specialized machines for different processes and intensive subdivision of labour.

The Population Census of 1911, however, revealed a situation somewhat similar to that in the clothing trades, with a large number of small employers and independent craftsmen, as well as a good deal of surviving domestic production. In England and Wales there were 10,338 employers, with a total labour force of 153,402, about a quarter of them female, while, in addition, 31,782 were 'working on [their] own account'; of the latter category, 24,359 were 'working at home', together with 4,789 of the employers and 15,829 employees. But these figures include the considerable number of small shoe-makers and cobblers; domestic out-workers comprised only about a tenth of all employees, the great majority of whom were now in factories.

In this trade, however, the technological revolution did not follow the same pattern as in the clothing trades by displacing skilled male labour with cheaper female machinists. In fact, the proportion of male adult workers tended to rise with factory organization, while wages were improved with increasing mechanization and productivity, so that the trade unions came to favour concentration of the industry into factories.

This was also accompanied by a changing geographical distribution of the industry. Northampton remained a major centre, but London and Stafford tended to decline in importance with the rise of other centres such as Leicester, Norwich, Street (Somerset), Bristol, Leeds and Kendal; there was a more marked regional concentration in Northamptonshire and Leicestershire, where about 40 per cent of the labour force was located in 1911.

As a result of active innovation, especially in these areas, the industry held off the challenge of foreign competition and in the years before the First World War exports greatly exceeded imports—£4.2 as against £0.9 million in 1913—though most of the machinery was supplied by an American-controlled engineering concern, the British United Shoe Machinery Company, established in 1899, with headquarters in Leicester. As in the clothing trades, mechanization was accompanied by improvements in the style and quality of wholesale ready-made products and by developments in marketing; in addition to supplying growing numbers of specialist boot and shoe retailers, several of the larger manufacturers themselves went into multiple-shop retailing in order to extend their trade.

In other leather manufactures, changes were less striking. Saddlery and harness-making were still mostly small-scale and ubiquitous, though there was a marked concentration in the west midlands. Employment in this trade continued to grow gradually until the early twentieth century; in 1911 the total of over 24,000 in England and Wales was still rather higher than in 1871, including over 3,000 employers and about the same number working on their own. Glove-making was much more localized, especially in the south-western counties (with over half the labour-force) and to a lesser extent in the midlands; it was still largely a rural out-working, mainly female occupation, but numbers were declining—from 23,000 in 1871 to 11,000 in 1911—as in other rural crafts such as pillow-lace, straw-plaiting and hat-making in the southern counties. On the other hand, however, there was a growing demand for fancy leather goods, travelling bags and accessories for the cycle and motor trades.

The food and drink trades

These trades continued, of course, to be one of the major occupational groups (see p. 151), growing with population and rising living standards, but they still provided striking contrasts between developing factory production and traditional small-scale units. Throughout the nineteenth century rural windmills and water-mills continued to grind a good deal of the country's corn, despite the gradual growth of steam power; the early steam-mills, moreover, still used circular grinding stones. In the later nineteenth century, however, a revolutionary change occurred with the introduction of steel roller-grinders, which led to the rapid establishment of big steam-powered mills, also equipped with centrifugal dressers and other machinery. These mills, established by large firms such as Spiller's and Rank's, were mostly sited in the major ports or on main rivers, into which a growing volume of imported corn was now flowing—Britain was importing four-fifths of her wheat supplies just before the First World War—and so the small rural mills began to fall rapidly into disuse. In 1911, however, there were still nearly 3,000 employers in the milling trade of England and Wales, with an average labour force of only seven men.

The bakeries supplied by these flour-mills, moreover, long continued to be mostly small concerns, in which hand-kneaded dough was baked in small wood- or coal-fired ovens in traditional fashion. The workshop returns of 1870 revealed an average employment figure of three to four, and in the early 1890s the average London bakery still had only five or six men. The metropolitan multiple-shop Aerated Bread Company, started in the early 1860s, was an augury of the future, but failed to establish itself in the provinces, where the working master-baker was still the common figure and home-baking remained widespread, though declining. In biscuit-making, however, large-scale factory production developed earlier, as in Huntley & Palmer's works at Reading in the 1860s (see pp. 134–5), and in the later nineteenth century technological changes began to spread in bread baking and larger firms grew up, with machines for mixing and sifting flour and for kneading and rolling dough, together with gas-fired and steam-tube ovens; such firms not only distributed their own bread but also sold to retail shops. It is not clear from the 1911 Census tables how accurate was the distinction between 'bread, biscuit, cake, etc. makers' and 'bakers, confectioners (dealers)', but in the former category the average employment figure of about thirty was obviously influenced by the growth of larger firms, while in the latter category there were still tens of thousands of very small shops, run by people working on their own or with no more than three or four employees, like the similarly numerous butchers and grocers.

Brewing had already developed on a large scale, using steam-powered machinery, during the eighteenth and early nineteenth centuries, and this trend continued, leading in the late nineteenth century to the growing dominance of large brewing companies, many of national repute (see p. 249), in London and other major cities, particularly Burton-on-Trent, with rings of tied public-houses. A large number of smaller private mostly local breweries still existed—at the 1911 Census the average labour force of the 1,556 brewery employers in England and Wales was only sixteen—but there was a striking decline in the number of petty brewing victuallers and beer-sellers (mostly publicans), under competition from increasingly large-scale production and distribution. A great many were taken over by the big brewery companies, fighting for licensed retail outlets, while the rapidly developing market in brewery shares also facilitated mergers between firms, large and small, frequently on a local or regional basis. The number of breweries was thus reduced from over 11,000 in 1880 to only about 4,000 in 1914.

These developments were accompanied by the spread of Burton pale ales, followed from the late nineteenth century onwards by light sparkling bottled beers, at the expense of local heavy draught varieties; the introduction of machines for making bottles and glasses (see p. 226) encouraged this trend. But though breweries increased in size and output, their production processes were not greatly revolutionized, though, following the researches into fermentation by Pasteur and other scientists, the role of chemists, laboratories, microscopes and chemical analysis in brewing operations gradually became more important. Many breweries were reconstructed on the 'tower principle', and there were further improvements in mechanization, temperature control and cleanliness, but these appear to have been empirical rather than scientific developments.

Food-processing industries also developed during this period, notably the canning or tinning of meat and fruit, though such products were largely imported from America, Australia and elsewhere. This provided a considerable stimulus to the south Wales tinplate trade (see p. 177), and mechanization was also developed in the canning process itself. Factory production of jam, marmalade, etc., was similarly established, using bottling machinery. Cadburys, Rowntrees, Frys and other manufacturers were at the same time developing large-scale production of cocoa, chocolate and related products: Cadburys were employing about 6,000 people in their Bournville factory in 1914. Crosse & Blackwell (preserved foods), Bovril (meat extracts) and Colmans (mustard) were also among the largest British joint-stock companies by the early twentieth century, while Lever Brothers were producing margarine as well as soap (see pp. 249–50). For these and other consumer goods, machinery was developed not only for the production processes but also for packing and wrapping, as well as for manufacture of bottles and jars (see pp. 226, 239–40); though many foodstuffs were still sold loose, the modern mass-production packaging revolution had begun, closely related to that in mass advertising and selling of branded goods. The preservation of foodstuffs, especially meat and fish, also began to be transformed by the development of ice-making and refrigeration plant for cold-storage warehouses and ships.

In all these fields, progress was remarkable from the last quarter of the nineteenth century onwards, as living standards rose and Britain entered the age of mass-consumption. This was evident not only in foodstuffs but also in other consumer goods such as soap and cigarettes, in which mechanized mass-production and packaging were similarly developed, by firms such as Levers and Crosfields (soap and soap-powders), and by Wills, Players and other tobacco-manufacturing firms, eventually combined into the Imperial Tobacco Company.

Building, wood-working and allied trades

Throughout this period, building continued to be not only one of the most important industries in terms of employment and output (see pp. 151, 242–3) but also one of the most traditional, with relatively little change in technology. It expanded considerably with the continued growth of population and industry, though subject to investment cycles, linked with movements in interest rates, building costs and rents. Residential building was almost entirely private; there was very little council-house building before the First World War.

Materials and techniques remained generally traditional, especially in house-building. In factories, warehouses and other large buildings, iron-frame construction, introduced in the late eighteenth century, now came into widespread use, with steel displacing iron in the later nineteenth century, in association with other new materials such as cement, concrete and artificial stone: ferro-(reinforced) concrete and steel frames were combined in larger modern structures. For the most part, however, building materials and handicraft methods were unchanged. Brick was tending increasingly to displace stone, so that brick-layers increased in number while stonemasons declined, but carpenters and joiners, slaters and tilers, plasterers, plumbers, glaziers and painters continued to multiply, together with semi-skilled and unskilled labourers, though these appear to have constituted only 25 to 30 per cent of the total number employed in an industry still dominated by craft skills.

By the late nineteenth and early twentieth centuries, the building and constructional trades accounted for 8 to 11 per cent of the total occupied male population of England and Wales, reaching 1,126,000 in 1901, though declining to 946,000 in 1911; as in mining, this labour force was almost entirely male. The industry was, of course, very widely dispersed, according to population, and used local materials as far as possible, to save transport costs. In the great cities, where bigger buildings and more houses were required, large-scale general contractors were becoming more numerous, some directly employing hundreds of men, but sub-contracting to smaller specialized firms remained usual, while in more widespread building, jobbing and repair work large firms were vastly out-numbered by small local ones, mostly employing less than ten men: in all the building trades of England and Wales in 1911, there were nearly 60,000 employ-ers, with an average labour force of just over twelve, while, in addition, over 49,000 were 'working on [their] own account'. Credit was fairly easily available, enterprising workmen could set up for themselves and speculative building was common. This small-scale local character of the industry, together with con-sumer adherence to traditional materials and techniques, largely accounted for its lack of labour-saving technology.

The employment figures cited above relate mainly to the building trades proper—those involved in the erection and repair of houses and other build-ings—but to these we can add the large numbers in closely related trades, especially the building supply trades. Stone quarries in many hilly regions and slate quarries in north Wales and Lakeland were developed on a larger scale, though still generally labour-intensive, while clay, sand, gravel and chalk pits multiplied, together with lime-kilns: nearly 82,000 were employed in producing these building materials in England and Wales in 1911. Larger works were established for the mechanized mass-production of bricks, tiles, cement and concrete, notably in Lancashire and Bedfordshire (bricks) and the Thames–Medway valley (where the Associated Portland Cement Manu-facturers' combine was formed in 1900, with a capital of £7 million): 62,000 were employed in these trades in 1911. By the time of the 1907 Census of Production, the output of bricks (4,800 million) had increased by two to three times since the mid-nineteenth century (see p. 133). Brick-making machines, with mechanical moulding or wire-cutting, together with continuous kilns, were developed during this period, reducing costs of production, while markets were also expanded by the railways. But small-scale manufacture of hand-made bricks, with old-fashioned kilns and clamps, still survived for local markets, though larger firms developed, such as the London Brick Company, producing the cheaper Fletton (Peterborough) bricks from the late nineteenth century onwards. In that same period, the introduction of the tube-mill and rotary kiln in cement-making led to a similar growth of large-scale production. The rise of large sheet-glass manu-facturing firms such as Pilkingtons was likewise stimulated by growth of the building industry.

Timber was also required in ever-growing quantities and the manufacture of doors, window-frames, flooring, rafters, etc., was increasingly mechanized, with power-driven saws, planes, mortising and tenoning machines, on which semi-skilled labour could be employed; hand sawyers, like hand moulders of bricks, were declining, despite occasionally violent trade-union opposition to machinery. Large numbers of carpenters and joiners, however, were included in the 1911 building trades figures, to which we can add not only sawyers and wood-cutting machinists (over 40,000) but also those in the closely related furniture-making trades: 51,000 cabinet-makers, 22,000 french polishers and nearly 26,000 upholsterers. The great majority of firms in such trades were small, including thousands of craftsmen working on their own account, alongside large saw-mills and mass-production furniture-making (the furniture-manufacturing firms of Maple's and Waring & Gillow's, for example, were among the largest companies in the country by the early twentieth century). At the same time, there were growing demands on other industries for putty and paint, earthenware pipes and sanitary ware, lead piping and roofing, iron screws, nails, locks and other metal fittings, while building also gave employment to the ancillary services of water, gas and electricity. Indirectly, therefore, as well as directly, the building trades accounted for a very substantial part of total industrial employment and output.

We may also include, along with the sawyers, carpenters and joiners of the wood-working trades, various other traditional craftsmen who remained fairly numerous in this period. In 1911 there were nearly 24,000 wheelwrights, making carts and wagons, and over 24,000 coach and carriage makers in England and Wales, catering for the still important horse-drawn transport; though they were being surpassed by railway coach and wagon makers (nearly 38,000 of them, in a relatively small number of large works, see p. 185), and by makers of motor-car chassis and bodies (see pp. 189–90), there was some transfer of skills and terminology to the new 'coach-making' manufactures. Other wood-workers, numbering altogether tens of thousands, included coopers, wood turners and makers of chairs, boxes, packing-cases, tobacco-pipes, brushes and baskets. They were mostly traditional small-scale craftsmen, but some machinery had been introduced, such as box-making machines from America, which, together with similar machinery for mass-producing paper and cardboard bags, cartons and boxes, and also metal tins, formed part of the modern packaging revolution.

Printing and allied trades

The spread of education and literacy, the growing demand for newspapers, periodicals and books, the needs of business and the growth of advertising, all combined to speed technological revolution in the printing industry. The final abolition of the 'taxes on knowledge'—on newspapers, advertisements and paper—between 1853 and 1861, and the Education Act of 1870 were land-marks in these developments. Daily newspapers, for example, mushroomed up from the mid-1850s onwards, so that all main provincial towns came to have a morning or evening paper, while circulations soared to tens or even hundreds of thousands, and from the end of the century dailies for the millions were appearing. There was a similar expansion in book publishing and general printing, while commercial packaging also increased demands on the paper trade. Employment in the printing and allied trades therefore quintupled between 1850 and 1914, despite increasing mechanization. In both employment and net output, in fact, these trades ranked well above the chemical and allied trades (see pp. 151, 243).

The technological revolution was most striking in large newspaper offices. The early flat-bed cylinder-printing machines, such as those first used for printing *The Times* in 1814, had been developed by mid-century into giant multi-cylinder presses, but these sheet-fed machines were superseded from the 1860s onwards by reel-fed rotaries, with cylindrical stereotype plates, in which continuous reels of paper were mechanically fed, printed, cut and folded. Such machines also came to be used for printing long runs of magazines and periodicals, while in smaller newspaper offices and in book and general printing improved flat-bed cylinder-printing machines were introduced, together with small power-driven platen machines. It is significant, however, that, although British engineering firms shared in these developments, some of the leading makers, such as Hoe, Miehle and Goss, were American.

Typesetting also began to be mechanized in this period, first with Hattersley composing machines from the 1860s onwards and then with linotypes and monotypes—again from America—in the late nineteenth and early twentieth centuries. But in 1914 machine operators were still a small minority, compared with hand compositors, though the mechanical revolution had made rapid progress in newspaper printing, and hand type-founding was virtually dead with the development of casting machinery.

New developments had also occurred in other printing processes, such as stereotyping, electrotyping, lithography and, latterly, photogravure. Machines had also been introduced to revolutionize the craft of bookbinding. From the late nineteenth century onwards, moreover, new multiple-process machines were developed for mass-producing paper bags, cardboard boxes, cartons, wrappers and packets of all kinds, in which printing was only one process.

The increasing scale of mechanized production led to the growth of larger firms, some employing hundreds of workers. Many of the big London printing houses established branches in the provinces, where land, buildings and labour were cheaper, while large newspaper combines began to develop, controlling newspapers in many towns. But though these bigger firms were tending increasingly to predominate, small printing offices still abounded, especially in the general or jobbing line; in fact most of the 7,500 or so firms in the printing trade of Great Britain in 1911 employed only a handful of men, and there were still hundreds of printers 'working on [their] own account'.

The rapid growth of the printing industry, of course, greatly stimulated paper-making, for which there were also expanding markets in stationery, wallpaper and all kinds of wrapping and packing. Output of paper soared from about 100,000 tons in 1860 to about 900,000 tons by 1907. Though some small water-mills and vat production still survived, for high-quality papers, the industry was increasingly concentrated in fewer and larger steam-powered mills, with bigger and faster-running machines, the total number of mills declining from 306 in 1860 to 221 by 1900; it also tended to become more concentrated geographically, especially in the north-west, chiefly in south-east Lancashire, with access to coal, soft water and chemicals, though Kent remained an important area of production, near to the London market, and mills were still widely scattered elsewhere. The rapid expansion of the industry created an acute shortage of rags, leading to exploitation of new raw materials such as straw, esparto and, above all, wood pulp, for which the paper industry became increasingly dependent on imports from Scandinavia and North America.

14

Changes in Industrial Structure
and Organization

Having traced the main developments in particular industries, we may now look more broadly at changes in the general structure and organization of British industry during this period. While industry continued to increase in relative importance within the whole economy, structural changes were also occurring within the industrial sector itself, as industries grew at varying rates in terms of employment, output and exports. At the same time, there were important changes in the size and organization of industrial firms.

Structural changes

Looking at the changing distribution of the labour force (see pp. 140, 151), the most notable feature was the continued relative decline of agriculture, compared with other sectors. By the end of this period nearly half the occupied population was in industry, but the shift towards industrial employment during the second half of the nineteenth century was much less striking than in the first; trade, transport and public, professional and other services grew in importance, while the proportion employed in domestic and personal services remained high. These occupational changes were reflected in the distribution of gross national income or product, to which the industrial sector contributed about 43 per cent by 1907, according to Deane and Cole.

PERCENTAGE DISTRIBUTION OF THE BRITISH
LABOUR FORCE, 1801–1911

Year	Agriculture, foresty, fishing	Industry	Trade and transport	Domestic and personal	Public, professional, and other
1801	35.9	29.7	11.2	11.5	11.8
1851	21.7	42.9	15.8	13.0	6.7
1911	8.3	46.4	21.5	13.9	9.9

Source: Deane and Cole, op. cit., p. 142.

PERCENTAGE SHARES OF MAJOR INDUSTRIES
IN TOTAL EMPLOYMENT

Trade	1851	1911
Textiles	13.8	8.2
Clothing	9.7	6.9
Metals, machines, implements vehicles, etc.	6.1	10.5
Mining and quarrying	4.2	6.6
Building and contracting	5.3	6.2
Food, drink and tobacco	4.3	6.1
Wood, furniture, etc.	1.7	1.8

Source: Calculated from the Census of Population figures in Mitchell and Deane, op. cit., p. 60. See pp. 140, 151 for actual figures in these and other industries.

UNITED KINGDOM INDUSTRIAL OUTPUT, 1907
(£ million)

Trade	Gross output	Net output
Mines and quarries	148	120
Iron and steel, engineering and shipbuilding	375	153
Metal trades other than iron and steel	93	12
Textiles	334	94
Clothing (including boots and shoes)	108	48
Food, drink and tobacco	287	90
Chemical and allied	75	22
Paper, printing, stationery and allied	61	34
Leather, canvas and india-rubber	35	9
Timber	46	21
Clay, stone, building and contracting	117	60
Miscellaneous	8	4
Public utility services	77	46
Total	1,765	712

Source: First Census of Production, 1907, Final Report, P.P., 1912, Cd. 6320, p. 21. Gross output is the selling value, net output the value added, after deducting cost of raw materials, etc. The columned figures do not add up precisely to the totals because of rounding to the nearest million.

Within the industrial sector, the basic industries of the Industrial Revolution remained overwhelmingly predominant, but there were some significant structural changes, with the relative decline of textiles and clothing manufactures and the growing importance of the coal-mining, metals, engineering, shipbuilding and other industries, such as the food and drink, building and wood-working trades. Textiles, though still a major industry, were now growing more slowly and had lost their ancient predominance, having been surpassed by the varied metals industries, while the number of coal miners had also rapidly increased. Employment had also risen notably in the chemical and allied trades, paper and printing, bricks, cement, pottery and glass and public utilities (gas, water and electricity supply), as well as in the new industries of electrical engineering and cycle and motor manufactures, but their numbers and output were still relatively small.

The structure of industrial output was revealed in the first Census of Production in 1907. The gross output of electrical engineering (£14.1 million) and the cycle and motor manufactures (£11.6 million), included in the above figures for iron and steel, engineering and shipbuilding, was as yet of relatively minor importance. The Census of Production, in fact, like that of Population, showed the continuing predominance of the old basic industries: textiles, coal, iron and steel (including engineering and shipbuilding, but excluding the new manufactures) employed nearly a quarter of the total occupied population, produced nearly half the net industrial output and provided 70 per cent of total domestic exports, according to Kahn.

In 1907 about a third of British industrial output was exported, but some industries such as building, food and drink catered mainly for the home market, while the basic industries were more heavily dependent on the export trade. This was most strikingly demonstrated by cotton, which exported 84 per cent (by value) of its output, while the woollen industry exported 57 per cent, iron and steel, engineering and shipbuilding 39 per cent (about 60 per cent of steam-engines and machinery) and coal 31 per cent (including bunker coal), according to Kahn's estimates for 1907.

The new industries, by contrast, were still of relatively minor importance and were much less dependent on exports. Including in this category electrical supply and manufactures, automobiles and cycles, aircraft, silk and rayon, hosiery, chemical and allied trades and scientific instruments, they altogether accounted for only 5.2 per cent of industrial employment, 6.5 per cent of industrial output and 7.4 per cent of United Kingdom exports, less than a quarter of their output being exported.

In exports, however, as in industrial production, there had been some notable structural changes. Textiles, though overtaken in net output by the iron and steel, engineering and shipbuilding group and also by coal-mining, still retained a commanding lead in overseas trade—mainly by virtue of cotton exports, especially to India—but their share of total domestic exports had declined from nearly two-thirds to about one-third. Exports of clothing, on the other hand, had raised their share, but the most remarkable increases were in coal, iron and steel, machinery and metal manufactures generally, together with chemicals and ships, while newcomers such as road vehicles (cycles, cars, etc.) and electrical goods were appearing on the scene, though not yet of very great weight.

UNITED KINGDOM DOMESTIC EXPORTS, 1913
(Current values in £ million)

Trade	1850	1913
Coal	1.3	53.7
Iron and steel	6.2	55.4
Hardwares and cutlery	2.9	5.0
Machinery	1.0	37.0
Non-ferrous metals and manufactures	2.5	12.0
Cotton goods	28.3	127.2
Wool goods	10.0	31.8
Linen goods	4.8	9.5
Silk goods	1.3	2.2
Hats, haberdashery, apparel, etc.	2.5	13.3
Leather manufactures	0.4	6.4
Chemicals	1.0	22.0
New ships and boats	—	11.0
Road vehicles, etc.	—	5.4
Electrical goods	—	5.4
Total domestic exports	71.4	525.2

Source: Mitchell and Deane, op. cit., pp. 282–4, 302–6. The figures for particular industries do not add up to the totals, because some items have been omitted.

In exports, as in employment and output, the old basic industries still held overwhelming predominance. And Britain retained her position as the world's leading exporter of manufactures right up to 1913, though increasingly assailed by growing tariff-protected foreign industries and trading competition. Inevitably, with the rapid growth of the United States, Germany and other industrial countries, Britain's shares of world manufacturing production and exports were considerably reduced between 1870 and 1913 (see p. 155). Because of her early industrial predominance and heavy commitments in manufactured exports, Britain was in a specially vulnerable position. Under such circumstances, as Saul has emphasized, she did not do too badly. She still dominated world trade in textiles, ships and railway material, textile machinery, electric cables, boilers and bicycles and was at least equal to her rivals in prime movers and sewing machines; in exports of capital goods generally, Britain still had a slender lead over Germany in 1913, with nearly a third of the world total, though her share had fallen from nearly two-thirds in 1880. Unfortunately, however, it was in the relatively declining sectors of world trade—in textiles, railway equipment and ships, for example—that Britain best retained her predominance, whilst she tended to lag in the expanding trades, such as machine-tools, structural steel, chemicals, motor vehicle and electrical goods; in chemicals and electrical machinery, for example, Germany's exports were twice those of Britain in 1913. In overseas trade particularly, there is evidence of over-commitment and slowness in structural adjustment (but see pp. 152–65 for a discussion of the problems involved).

Another notable feature of Britain's industrial situation was the marked increase in her dependence on overseas supplies of raw materials, seven-eighths of which (excluding coal) were imported (together with half her food) by 1913. She had always, of course, imported raw cotton and silk, together with other textile fibres such as flax and hemp, but she was now also dependent on imports for most of her raw wool, while growing quantities of jute were also being brought in. She was similarly becoming more and more dependent on imported timber, hides, tallow, vegetable oils and various chemical raw materials, such as sulphur, nitrates and phosphates. Equally striking was the growth in imports of ores and metals. Iron-ore imports might have been reduced by more vigorous exploitation of her own east Midlands resources (see pp. 174–6), but foreign supplies could be brought in cheaply by sea. Her copper, tin and lead mines, on the other hand, were becoming exhausted and could not compete with cheap and abundant foreign supplies. The new oil and petroleum fuels, of course, had to be entirely imported, in days long before the discovery of North Sea oil. This growing dependence on raw materials further increased the necessity for scientific-technological versatility to maintain Britain's manufactured exports, so as to pay for these requirements and also for the growing quantities of food and manufactures now being imported. Before the First World War, however, with Britain still retaining her world trading leadership and increasing her 'invisible' income from overseas investments, shipping, finance and insurance services, there was as yet no balance of payments problem.

Changes in industrial organization

Our survey of British industry in this period has demonstrated that, although large-scale factory production had developed extensively during these years, small firms still abounded, especially in certain trades such as building and clothing where the average employment figure was low and many people were still working on their own account or were domestic out-workers. Small-scale manufacture was still common also among boot- and shoe-makers and cobblers, cabinet-makers, bakers, smiths, cutlers, watch-makers, saddlers, printers and many other trades listed in the Census returns and accounting for a not inconsiderable proportion of total employment.

Nevertheless, mechanized mass-production was spreading throughout manufacturing industry, leading to larger-scale factory organization and the growth of 'big business'. The Factory and Workshop Returns for 1913 show a total of 148,000 workshops as against 113,000 factories, but the total factory population (4,489,000) was about seven times that in workshops (638,000); while the average workshop had only 4 or 5 workpeople, the average factory had about 40. Moreover, the concentration in large units was much greater than these figures indicate, since all power-using establishments were classed as factories and many small concerns, employing only a little power—small steam-engines or, increasingly from the late nineteenth century onwards, small gas or oil engines or electric motors—were included in that category, thus inflating the number of factories. But the greater part of the factory population was concentrated in a comparatively small number of large works. In London, for example, in the late 1890s, there were 8,500 factories, but 56 per cent of the factory workers were in 750 of them, according to Clapham. And we have previously seen how, in other areas and in many industries, larger-scale production was coming to predominate. On the other hand, the factory and workshop statistics, and those of the 1907 Census of Production, did not include 'men's workshops', in which no young persons or women were employed, nor the large number of people—estimated at 600,000 in the 1907 Census—'working on their own account'. But the output of all these and others not included in the 1907 figures, totalling 1 to 1¼ million persons—engaged almost entirely in small businesses, 'chiefly in the clothing, boot-and-shoe, laundry and building trades'—was considered to be no more than 7 per cent of total industrial output. Increasingly, in a widening range of industries, production was being concentrated in large establishments employing many hundreds or even thousands of workers.

The trend towards larger-scale business organization would be more clearly evident if statistics were available of the numbers and sizes of business units or firms, as distinct from the units of production (factories and workshops). The classification of employers and employed in the Population Census provides only a very crude indication of expansion. In 1901, for example, there were about 223,000 industrial employers and nearly 7,200,000 employees in Great Britain, so that the average employment figure was about 32—substantially increased since the third quarter of the nineteenth century (see p. 68)—but the figure for employers cannot be simply equated with the number of firms, since a firm, especially a large one, may well have several persons in the employer category as either partners or major shareholders; the growth of joint-stock corporate organization made the notion of individual employers increasingly unrealistic. Moreover, although the vast majority of small firms had only one establishment, there was an increasing tendency for larger businesses to set up or acquire control over a number of such units. This was by no means a new development: during the early Industrial Revolution, for example, large cotton firms emerged owning several mills, most commonly for a single process, whether spinning, weaving or printing (horizontal specialization), but sometimes combining these successive processes (vertical integration), while in the iron industry leading ironmasters owned foundries, forges and rolling mills, as well as mines for ore and coal, usually in the same locality, but sometimes in different areas. These tendencies became much stronger and more widespread, however, in the later nineteenth and early twentieth centuries. Businesses grew larger not only by increasing the number and size of their works but also by taking over or merging with other firms in the same industry and sometimes extending their interests into other related industries. Closely associated with these developments was the growth of industrial combines, varying from loose agreements on prices, etc. to complete amalgamations. Advancing technology required greater resources for plant and machinery, research and development, while increased capital investment and technological interrelatedness called for the economies of large-scale production and distribution. Integration, amalgamation and combination would help to achieve these through control over a wider range of manufacturing and commercial operations; output and prices might also be regulated through oligopolistic or monopolistic arrangements, reducing competition and increasing profits.

These developments were stimulated and facilitated by the growth of joint-stock limited companies. In the early Industrial Revolution, as we have seen, the vast majority of firms were owned by individuals, families or partnerships, who increased their capital by ploughing back profits and private borrowing. Though canals and railways required larger-scale joint-stock organization, industry and trade long continued to manage without it, though unincorporated companies were not uncommon. Eventually, however, in 1825, the restrictive Bubble Act—with its distrust of speculative company promotions, dating back to the South Sea Bubble of 1718–19—was repealed; in 1844 the registration of joint-stock companies was facilitated and regulated by the Companies Act of that year; in 1855–6 further legislation permitted the general extension of limited liability, protecting shareholders from the possibility of unlimited losses in bankruptcies; and the Companies Act of 1862 finally consolidated all this legislation.

The response from British industry, however, was at first slow and hesitant: the tradition of the independent family firm was deeply rooted, and there was a not unjustifiable distrust of company speculation and mismanagement. There were many abortive 'bubble' or boom promotions, while half the companies actually formed failed within ten years. Nevertheless, the number of limited companies was approaching 10,000 by 1885, with total paid-up capital of nearly £500 million (excluding railway companies). From then onwards there was a striking increase, limited companies rapidly spreading into nearly all industries and trades, so that by 1914 they totalled about 65,000, with paid-up capital of about £2,500 million.

They were stimulated not only by the technological and economic pressures towards larger-scale production and distribution but also by the legal and financial advantages of corporate status, limited liability and access to greater capital resources, which were now more strongly publicized by a wider more active share market, by financial advertising and by the promotional activities of finance or investment companies, while the risks of share flotations were reduced by the spread of underwriting.

To a considerable extent, however, these changes were legal and nominal, with little alteration of business ownership and control. Most companies were not new concerns but simply conversions of existing private family firms and partnerships. Until the Companies Act of 1907 there was no legal distinction between public and private companies—all were legally public—but in reality an increasing number were private, in that they had a very small number of shareholders (the minimum legal requirement was seven, but 'dummies' could be created), and they made no public issue of shares, transfer of which might also be restricted, to maintain close control. When new capital was raised by public subscription, this was often preference or debenture (loan) capital, while the controlling ordinary shares were retained by the existing owners of the business. The Act of 1907 gave legal recognition to this situation, and by 1914 three-quarters (about 50,000) of all registered companies were private. For the most part they were small and medium-sized firms, but they included some of the biggest in the country. Such companies were still able to meet their capital requirements from their own resources and from bank loans, without recourse to the market; in fact the stock exchanges still played a minor role in financing British industry. Even in the larger public companies, control was generally kept in the same hands, while ploughed-back profits continued to be the main source of capital accumulation.

Nevertheless, the growth of joint-stock organization was closely associated with a remarkable expansion in the scale of business operations, as large companies developed not only by expanding their own operations but also, increasingly, by taking over, amalgamating or combining with other firms. The joint-stock principle facilitated, through transfer of shares, the merging of private family firms or companies into larger corporate concerns. This growth of 'big business' from the late nineteenth century onwards occurred more slowly in Britain than in the United States and Germany, where huge combines (trusts and cartels) developed; family firms and partnerships were more strongly entrenched in this country, together with belief in free-trade and competition. But even in Britain, with falling prices and growing trade rivalry, both domestic and international, from the 1870s onwards, business attitudes were changing, and there was growing awareness of the possible advantages of mergers and combines. Not that perfect competition had ever existed, except as an economic concept: before and during the Industrial Revolution, manufacturers had frequently formed associations with the aims of regulating output, prices and wages in their particular industries. But these efforts had not generally been very effective or long-lived. In the late nineteenth century, however, economic cicumstances and the growth of joint-stock organization favoured a more widespread and powerful movement towards large-scale companies, combines and associations.

Some firms, of course, grew big by their own expansion, as earlier in the Industrial Revolution, though now being able to tap wider sources of capital. But the biggest were generally products of amalgamations. These frequently occurred piecemeal, as individual firms in the same or related industries gradually came together; but many resulted from wider associations or combines, which now often took the form of company mergers. Such developments were very widespread and were not confined to manufacturing industries—they were similarly notable in railways, shipping, banking and retailing—but in the industrial field they tended to be concentrated in certain trades, especially where capital-intensive methods had been introduced. Among these brewing was perhaps most outstanding, with a remarkable conversion to limited companies from the 1880s onwards. Before and during the Industrial Revolution brewing firms had already provided some of the most striking examples of capital accumulation (see p. 135), and in 1905 they accounted for seventeen out of the fifty largest British companies (as listed by Payne, with capitals ranging from £2 million to £17 million), including such famous names as Watney & Co., Guinness, Allsopp's, Whitbread's, Bass & Co., Barclay Perkins, Cannon Brewery, Charrington's, Ind Coope, Truman & Co., Mann & Co., Walker's, Courage's, Threlfall's and Wilson's, to which we can add the Distillers' Company (1877) in the whisky trade. As we have seen, there was growing competition among breweries to acquire tied public-houses, which, together with increasingly mechanized brewing operations, required greater quantities of capital, so that smaller breweries tended to be taken over or squeezed out (see p. 235).

Large-scale capital-intensive production had also developed at an early date in the chemical and allied trades, in which falling prices and growing competition led to the creation of the Salt Union (64 firms, 1888) and the United Alkali Company (48 firms, 1890), both defensive combines, the latter trying vainly to bolster up the Leblanc soda trade (see p. 218). At the same time, the more technologically and commercially progressive firm of Brunner Mond & Company, exploiting the Solvay ammonia-soda process, was rapidly expanding and beginning to take over the other concerns, while Nobels were becoming similarly dominant in the explosives field (see pp. 218–9, 221). In the soap and margarine trades, now increasingly based on chemical processes, Lever Brothers were likewise growing prodigiously and coming into rivalry with Brunner Mond's, who in 1911 took over the large soap-making and chemical firms of Crosfield's and Gossage's (but transferred them to Lever's in 1919). In other chemically allied trades, large firms were similarly developing, such as Boot's (pharmaceuticals), Pilkington's (glass), Dunlop's (rubber tyres) and Reckitt's (starch), all with millions of capital, while the British Oil and Cake Mills (17 firms, 1899) was another large combine.

Lever's and Boot's were associated particularly with the consumer goods revolution of this period, in which, of course, the great breweries also participated. While Lever was extending his empire from soaps to oils, fats, margarine and many other things, Boot expanded from pharmaceuticals into general goods and multiple-shop retailing, in which the larger manufacturers of boots and shoes and clothing followed a similar, though narrower, path (see pp. 221, 223, 229, 233). On the food-processing side, Lever's large-scale production was paralleled by Spiller's and Rank's (flour-milling), Huntley & Palmer's (biscuits), Crosse & Blackwell's (preserved foods), Bovril's (meat extracts) and Colman's (starch and mustard): these firms figured among the largest British companies of the early twentieth century, mostly developing from family businesses and still under private control, like the breweries. But there were two notable combines in the consumer goods field. The Imperial Tobacco Company (13 firms, 1901) was, in fact, the largest company in Britain, with a capital of £17.5 million in 1905; formed defensively against the American Tobacco Company of James B. Duke, it soon included most of the leading British tobacco firms (Wills, Player, Ogden, Churchman, etc.), of which Wills, of Bristol, particularly, had already grown prodigiously with the rise of cigarette manufacture. The other combine was that of the Wallpaper Manufacturers (1899).

In textiles the emphasis was predominantly on horizontal mergers of firms specializing in particular processes, as demonstrated by the Fine Cotton Spinners' and Doublers' Association (31 firms), the Calico Printers' Association (46 firms), the Bleachers' Association (53 firms), the Bradford Dyers' Association (22 firms), the British Cotton and Wool Dyers' Association (46 firms) and the Yorkshire Wool Combers' Association (38 firms), all founded in 1898–1900 and embracing large numbers of firms. These all figured among the largest companies of 1905, but the list also included some notable mergers centred on a single dominant firm. The most outstanding, with a capital of £11.2 million in 1905, larger than that of any of the textile combines, was the sewing-thread firm of J. & P. Coats Ltd. of Paisley, who established a powerful amalgamation (5 firms) in 1895–6, which became of international stature and which the combines of the English Sewing-Cotton Company (11 firms, 1897) and the Linen Thread Company (6 firms, 1898) could not match. Other large textile companies included Horrocks of Preston (cotton), Lister's of Bradford (silk), and Courtaulds of Essex and also of Coventry (silk and artificial silk or rayon). In the coarse-spinning and weaving sections of the cotton industry, however, and in the woollen, worsted and other textile trades, with large numbers of small mostly private firms, competition remained very active.

In the iron industry, large firms that had emerged earlier in the Industrial Revolution continued to grow during this period, while new giants arose, generally as limited companies. Some of these, such as the Ebbw Vale Company in south Wales and Bolckow, Vaughan & Co. and Dorman, Long & Co. in the north-east, were strongly localized and grew largely by their own expansion, though sometimes absorbing neighbouring iron and coal firms and acquiring ore mines in Spain or Scandinavia; their activities, moreover, were confined predominantly to the primary processes of iron and steel production, though vertically integrated from coal and ore mines, blast furnaces, etc., to steel-rolling mills. But the developing interrelationships between iron and steel, engineering, shipbuilding and armaments during this period led to the creation of broader business complexes, through numerous amalgamations, spreading horizontally as well as vertically and embracing an increasingly wide range of heavy industrial operations in different parts of the country. The most outstanding examples were those formed by Armstrong Whitworth, Vickers, John Brown & Co. and Cammell Laird in the late 1890s and early 1900s. In the first case, we see two great engineering concerns, one on Tyneside, the other in Manchester, having previously integrated backward, into iron and steel and forward into armaments and shipbuilding, now amalgamating and further extending these interests; while the other three cases show Sheffield steel firms integrating forward, through amalgamations, into engineering, shipbuilding and armaments at Barrow, on Clydeside, Merseyside and elsewhere, as well as backward into coal, iron-ore and blast furnaces. Only in a few cases, such as Palmer's Shipbuilding and Iron Company on Tyneside, was such massive vertical integration achieved by local self-development on a very favourable site.

Similar vertically and horizontally integrated combines, linking firms and processes in different areas, also emerged in other branches of iron and steel manufactures. Particularly notable was that of Guest, Keen & Nettlefolds (1902), combining iron and steel firms in south Wales (Guest's, the Dowlais Company, and subsequently Crawshay's) with nut-and-bolt and screw-manufacturing firms in the west Midlands. Baldwin's, Thomas's and Lysaght's provide further examples at this same time, combining iron and steel, tinplate and galvanized-sheet-making concerns in England and Wales, while Stewarts & Lloyds (1902) formed an amalgamation of tube-making firms in Scotland and the Midlands. Not surprisingly, these various companies figured prominently among the biggest of the day, though the British iron and steel industry has been criticized for the limited scale of its amalgamations, by comparison with the giant United States Steel Corporation and the German cartels.

In coal-mining, however, such developments were much rarer. There were some great aristocratic colliery enterprises, notably those of Lord Londonderry in the north-east, and several large companies were established such as the Powell Duffryn Company in Wales, Henry Briggs & Co. in Yorkshire, Andrew Knowles & Co. in Lancashire and Sir James Joicey & Co. in Durham, while the Cambrian Combine of D. A. Thomas (Lord Rhondda) in the early twentieth century was a more ambitious enterprise; but the number of separate colliery undertakings remained very large, many still in private hands, and though the companies had a big share of total production, no general combination was feasible.

In many other industries, such as the building and clothing trades and small metals manufactures, in which there were large numbers of small firms, there was little evidence of combination beyond loose local associations. In the building supply trades, however, where larger-scale mechanized production had developed, there were some notable examples of company organization, such as the combine of Associated Portland Cement Manufacturers (27 firms, with a capital of £7 million) and the much smaller Bedford Lime, Cement and Brick Company, both formed in 1900, while several associations were formed in the early twentieth century to control output and prices of cast-iron goods supplied mainly to the building trades.

Company organization had also developed widely, alongside local authority undertakings, in gas, water and electricity supplies, but mostly on a small-scale local basis (see pp. 125, 193, 195, 223). On the other hand, some of the biggest industrial companies had international interests—Lever's, Coats, Courtauld's, Brunner Mond's, Nobel's, Armstrong Whitworth's and Imperial Tobacco, for example, together with the new oil companies such as Shell, Anglo-Persian and Anglo-Mexican. Such British companies aimed either to secure control over sources of raw materials (iron-ore mines, palm-oil plantations, etc.) or to establish themselves more securely in overseas markets through manufacturing and distributing subsidiaries.

By 1914, then, though small firms were still much the most numerous, an ever-growing proportion of British industry was becoming concentrated into larger joint-stock companies and combines. But the effects of these organizational changes should not be exaggerated. As we have seen, the great majority of companies were private and mostly small concerns—the average paid-up capital of all companies in 1914 was less than £40,000—and they were little different in ownership and management from the family firms and partnerships from which the majority had originated. The same was broadly true even of the large companies, formed by mergers or combines: there was generally little loss of identity by the constituent firms, the same families usually staying in control, often carrying on in much the same way, with a surprising degree of independence, and it took many years to create efficient unified organizations, centrally organized and controlled; indeed, there was a long-lasting belief that some

internal competition should be maintained as a spur to effort. The large combines, such as those in textiles, were particularly ramshackle affairs, with
unwieldy directorates and loose organization. Though American ideas of
'scientific management' were gradually being introduced, with emphasis on
systematic organization of large-scale manufacture, under centralized
professional-managerial control, with planned flow of production and strict cost
accounting, the 'managerial revolution' was a very slow process. It took time to
devise the appropriate administrative and financial techniques for management
of the large new companies, for rationalization of production in their numerous
plants, for co-ordinated research and development and for unified sales organization and policy.

On the other hand, a contrary kind of criticism has often been made: that the
growth of joint-stock organization led to the divorce of ownership and management, creating a new 'managerial class' who could run company affairs with
little effective control by the widely diffused shareholding ownership. Another
criticism is that in such companies there was a greater gulf between capital and
labour, that the formerly close relationships between employers and employed
were disappearing and that companies were becoming 'conscienceless corporations', concerned mainly with profit-making. There is certainly some truth in
such views: larger businesses were inevitably more bureaucratic, with more
departmentalization and hierarchical management; the distance between shop
floor and office or board-room undoubtedly increased. At the same time, however, these larger businesses generally provided higher wages, better working
conditions and more social amenities for their workers than small private firms.
Moreover, there was not generally a divorce of ownership and management: in
fact, as just emphasised, the major shareholders and directors were much the
same as in the family firms or companies before incorporation or amalgamation.
Undoubtedly the new limited companies, particularly the bigger ones, considerably broadened the field for industrial investment, creating numerous
shareholders—perhaps, 1,200,000 in all United Kingdom companies by
1914—but this was less than 3 per cent of the total population, while there was a
great deal of overlapping share-ownership in different companies; the main
blocks of controlling ordinary shares were concentrated in a much smaller
number of hands, mostly those of the previously owning families. Nevertheless,
there was more opportunity for introduction of new managerial blood, particularly where special technical or other skills were required—the recruitment
and training of managers began to receive more attention—though the transition
to the professional managerial age was very gradual.

There have been similar differences of opinion concerning the effects of these
changes in industrial organization upon commercial competition, prices and
profits, and upon society in general. Socialist critics, of course, as well as

individualist free-traders, see the whole movement as a trend to 'monopoly capitalism', exploiting both workers and consumers. In regard to the monopolistic tendencies, however, it must be pointed out that other critics have stressed that industrial organization was not carried *far enough* in this period, by comparison with America and Germany, so that British industry did not reap the full benefits of large-scale production and distribution, because of the traditions of independent family firms, free trade and competition. Several of the combines comprised the greater part of total production, but in no case was there complete monopoly, and in most cases nowhere near it; Hannah has shown, in fact, that only in a few industries—such as textile finishing, sewing cotton, salt, soda ash, boot and shoe machinery, seed-crushing, cigarettes and cement—did the three' largest firms control 70 per cent or more of output. Nor has research into their activities produced much evidence that they kept prices or profits unduly high. In fact, most large mergers of this period were ineffectively managed and tended to suffer from *dis*economies of scale: they neither achieved monopoly prices and profits nor the cost-reducing advantages of large-scale organization. Except in iron and steel, engineering and shipbuilding, most were horizontally organized, not vertically integrated, and they tended to be loose conglomerates. Because of these managerial problems, in fact, there were few multi-firm mergers after the turn of the century.

In most industries, there was a preference for trade associations or cartels, in which certain collective advantages could be achieved without member firms sacrificing their autonomy. Such associations had long existed but now they proliferated in every trade, varying in scope from small local sectional associations to national organizations for whole industries or branches of industry, some even extending into the international sphere. They also differed in the degree to which they sought to control their respective trades, some simply recommending minimum prices, others regulating discounts and rebates as well as prices and also fixing output quotas, with pooling arrangements. But none had any legal binding—indeed, being 'in restraint of trade', they were contrary to common law—and participating firms remained independent; agreements were fragile and often infringed; in most trades the multiplicity of firms and the forces of competition prevented any very effective control. This was particularly true of international trade agreements between such associations: under free trade, the British market was open to increasingly strong foreign competition, so that no purely domestic combination could be effective, but in very few trades was it possible to achieve any lasting international regulation of markets and prices. Even in predominantly domestic trades, such as brewing, competition remained strong, despite the growth of large companies.

Nevertheless, the trend was increasingly towards a more oligopolistic if not monopolistic structure of industry. Competition itself was bringing this about by eliminating small inefficient firms. At the same time, there was a growing desire among industrialists to suppress or control competition by means of mergers and combines. This was largely motivated, no doubt, by the aim of maintaining prices and profits, but it also aimed at increasing industrial efficiency and reducing costs by larger-scale production in bigger business units, vertically and/or horizontally integrated, though progress in this direction was slow.

In fact, there is little general evidence that the growth of 'big business' or 'monopoly capitalism' was exploiting workers or consumers. On the contrary, there is clear evidence of substantial rises in the general standard of living during this period, with falling prices in the last quarter of the nineteenth century and only modest rises thereafter, together with an enormously increased output of consumer goods, resulting from larger-scale mechanized production. At the same time wages were gradually increased and working conditions were improved; after the general introduction of factory and workshop legislation in the 1860s and 1870s, the main difficulties were with small back-street firms and out-working domestic trades, while larger firms were generally more enlightened employers of labour. By 1914 the eight-hour working day had become fairly general, and many of the bigger firms gave an annual week's holiday, as well as providing various social amenities. With growing national wealth, moreover, created by industrial and commercial enterprise, the country was now able to afford universal education, old-age pensions, and unemployment and sickness insurance: the welfare state originated in this period. Larger-scale capitalist organization was clearly not 'grinding the faces of the poor', though, as the surveys of Booth and Rowntree showed, poverty had by no means been eliminated.

PART IV

DECLINE AND GROWTH, 1914–39

15

The General Outlines of
Economic Change

The Effects of the First World War
The First World War (1914–18) is generally regarded as a great watershed in the
economic life of this country, but viewed in the long-term its effects were either
transitory or accelerative of deep changes that had begun much earlier. In the
years after the war, contrasts were often drawn between the stable growth of
pre-war Britain, with her great industries still expanding and prosperous, still
supreme in world trade, and the post-war decline, depression and unemployment. And it seemed reasonable to attribute this dramatic reversal to the
dislocation caused by the war. In the pre-war years, with the exception of copper,
tin and lead mining and silk manufacture, Britain's staple industries had continued to grow; though growth was at a reduced percentage rate, in absolute
terms it remained impressive, and Britain was still the world's leading industrial
exporter; the numbers employed in those industries, as well as in new ones, had
risen steadily, while there had been no increase in the percentage unemployed.
During the inter-war years, however, catastrophic decline occurred in some of the
old industries such as coal, shipbuilding and textiles, especially in their exports;
Britain lost her leadership in world trade, unemployment soared to unprecedented heights and the regions of Britain's former industrial supremacy now
became 'special areas' of chronic depression.

But the *post hoc* argument is open to objections. Long before 1914 there had
been signs of retardation in British industry. The declining percentage rate of
growth of total industrial output had been accompanied by an even slower
growth of productivity; in the coal industry, in fact, output per man was seriously
declining, and in the cotton industry it was tending to stagnate. Britain had been
surpassed in industrial production by the United States and Germany, which
were not only presenting an increasingly serious challenge to British exports,
but even invading the home market. In applied science and technology and
in the development of new industries such as motor manufacturing, electrical

engineering and synthetic dyestuffs, Britain had been relatively slow. As a result of early supremacy in the Industrial Revolution, this country was heavily over-committed to the old basic industries and serious structural changes were ulti-mately inevitable.

Thus the writing had long been on the wall, though not clearly visible to contemporaries, and the decline of those industries in the inter-war years was the eventual outcome. No doubt, as we shall see, it was hastened by the war, but it would be wrong to regard the war simply as the harbinger of economic doom. In fact the period 1918–39 witnessed a remarkable upturn in British economic growth, for the decline of old industries was accompanied by rapid growth of new industries, as well as some older ones, notably building, so that Britain's relative economic performance improved substantially, though this 'second industrial revolution', as we have seen, had also originated long before the First World War. In many ways, therefore, the contrast between stable growth and prosperity in the pre-1914 period and decline and depression in the post-war years is false: though the inter-war problems of the old industries and depressed areas, with their chronic unemployment, were certainly far worse than ever before, total production and productivity were now growing much more satisfactorily, as a result of diversification, structural change, rationalization and increased efficiency in British industry generally.

Nevertheless, throughout the 1920s and even later it was common to ascribe Britain's economic ills to the war and to see salvation in a return to pre-1914 'normality'. The war had certainly caused serious dislocations. Though 'business as usual' became the early wartime slogan, this notion gradually had to be abandoned, and the whole economy had to be organized for 'total war'. The free market economy was brought increasingly under Government control, especially under Lloyd George's War Cabinet from the end of 1916. New ministries for munitions, labour, food and shipping were established; the railways, munition factories, coal-mines, flour-mills and Irish distilleries were directly taken over, and extensive control was also exercised over other industries by requisition of output or licensing; control was similarly exercised over the purchasing and distribution of raw materials, consumer goods and foodstuffs (though food ration-ing was not introduced till 1918); agriculture and food production were also regulated; overseas trade and shipping were controlled; prices were extensively regulated in the later years of the war; restrictions were imposed on the raising and expenditure of capital, including works building; capital exports and over-seas investments were likewise brought under control. It was only very gradually that Government took over direction of the war economy, but by 1917–18 such controls were all-pervasive. Labour had to be controlled as well as capital: conscription and a system of reserved occupations for essential war production were eventually introduced, while agreements with the trade unions permitted wartime dilution of the labour force with unskilled workers, including large numbers of women, and compulsory arbitration was introduced for settlement of disputes. Financing of the war effort required heavy increases in direct and indirect taxation, including an excess profits duty and also heavy Government borrowing, both at home and abroad (especially from the United States), resulting in a massively increased national debt, while a large slice of foreign investments had to be sold, mainly to obtain dollars. Increased monetary supply, stimulated by Government borrowing, by *de facto* departure from the gold standard (not formalized, however, till 1919) and by issues of wartime paper currency, led to inflation, which was also fuelled by shortages of raw materials and consumer goods, by wartime profiteering and by pressure of rising wages in the later years of the war.

Thus industries were faced with immense problems of adjustment to wartime conditions. At the same time, war requirements greatly stimulated some of them, such as armaments, iron and steel, engineering, shipbuilding, chemicals and manufactures of motor vehicles and aircraft. In certain cases, where there had been heavy reliance on German imports, such as synthetic dyestuffs, scientific instruments, ball-bearings and magnetos, vigorous efforts had to be made to develop British production. The McKenna duties of 1915, imposed mostly at $33\frac{1}{3}$ per cent on luxury imports, including motor cars and cycles, watches and clocks, musical instruments and films, in order to save foreign exchange and shipping space, had the incidental effect of encouraging these manufactures in Britain, and became openly protective in the post-war period (see pp. 266–7). But in many other industries, especially consumer goods trades, such as textiles and clothing, food and drink, building, furniture, glass, pottery, paper and printing, production was reduced by diversion of manpower and resources into the armed forces and war industries, by shortages of raw materials, by restrictions on shipping and disruption of foreign trade. Even in essential industries such as coal-mining and mercantile shipbuilding, output fell during the war because of such difficulties. Much capital depreciation also occurred, as industrial equipment was run down and could not be replaced. On the other hand, considerable efforts were made to economize on labour and materials, to increase productive efficiency, to develop applied science (for example through the Department of Scientific and Industrial Research established in 1916) and to rationalize industrial organization by amalgamations and collaboration in industry-wide arrangements with Government departments and trade unions; the tendency towards trade associations and 'trusts' was thereby strongly increased, though not with entirely laudable consequences.

War, however, is essentially wasteful and destructive. About three-quarters of a million men from the United Kingdom were killed and over twice as many wounded; resources were poured into non-productive armaments and munitions;

total industrial output (according to Lomax's index) fell by 18 to 19 per cent between 1913 and 1918 and did not recover to the former level until 1920, so that six or seven years' annual growth were lost. Overseas trade was also seriously affected. Nearly eight million gross tons of British merchant shipping were sunk, and, though much of this was replaced during the war (and all of it very soon afterwards), trade suffered badly from these losses, as well as from Government restrictions and a general decline in world trading activity, with a serious weakening of Britain's position in export markets not only in Europe but also in the Americas, India and the Far East, where the United States and Japan were able to step in; the volume of British exports in 1918 was thus over 60 per cent below the level of 1913.

The wartime difficulties of export industries such as cotton, which suffered from both curtailed production and loss of overseas markets, thus foreshadowed the problems to be faced in the post-war years. At the same time, some of the industries, such as iron and steel and shipbuilding, that had expanded to meet wartime requirements, were also to find themselves with reduced export markets and considerable surplus capacity. Others, however, including the machine-tool, motor, aircraft, electrical, radio and chemical manufactures, in which technical progress had been stimulated by the war, were well placed to seize post-war growth opportunities. But this changing industrial pattern had been foreshadowed in pre-war trends, which were only accelerated by the war. There was nothing 'normal' about the pre-war situation, in which Britain manufactured more cotton goods, built more ships and exported more coal than all the rest of the world, and drastic changes in industrial structure could not have been much longer delayed: the clock could certainly not be turned back to that situation, though there was a prolonged post-war delusion that it could.

Growth in the inter-war economy
Undoubtedly many distortions and restrictions had been forced on the economy under wartime pressure, so when peace came there was an overwhelming desire in the business community to make a bonfire of Government controls and get back to a free market economy. This was, in fact, largely achieved in the boom conditions of the immediate post-war years. Things could never be quite the same as before 1914—the experience of Government intervention in industry and trade was to have lasting effects, protectionist tendencies had been strengthened, the membership and power of trade unions had been greatly increased and there was a political shift towards the Labour party and socialism, with obvious socio-economic implications—but the workings of a free-enterprise capitalist economy were generally restored. Moreover, the incompetence of minority Labour governments in 1924 and 1929–31, and the failure of the general strike of 1926, were not encouraging to anti-capitalist developments, despite the serious

economic and social problems of the inter-war years. Those problems were to bring about major shifts in economic policy, especially from the early 1930s onwards, when the great depression resulted in abandonment of free-trade and increasing governmental intervention in trade and industry (see pp. 266–9), but it was mainly under pressure from market forces that the structure and technology of British industry were changed in this period.

This industrial reorganization was facilitated by the weakness of trade unions resulting from the strike failures of the early 1920s, the General Strike fiasco and the heavy unemployment of the inter-war years. The unemployment, however, was not, as left-wing critics often suggest, deliberately contrived by capitalists to oppress the working masses, but was forced upon this country by world-wide commercial and technological changes. Nor was it evidence of 'the failure of capitalism'. In fact British capitalism was remarkably successful in making the necessary and inevitable changes in industry and trade, in raising the rate of growth of production and productivity and thus substantially improving average income and consumption, whilst also vigorously tackling the housing problem and making improved provision for the less fortunate through unemployment and sickness insurance, public assistance and old-age pensions. There is no doubt that, despite emotive folk recollections and left-wing distortions, acccelerated economic growth in inter-war Britain was clearly improving the quality of life for the great majority of the population (see p. 272). A substantial minority—especially those out of work in depressed areas— certainly suffered distress on a more widespread scale than before the war, but even those 'on the dole' were better off than the pre-war unemployed. The average level of unemployment was undoubtedly much higher—over 10 per cent even in the best years, rising to nearly 23 per cent in the slump of the early 1930s—but it is misleading to declare that this percentage 'could have been added to the output of the economy' simply by 'eliminating' unemployment, more or less 'at a stroke'.* How, in fact, under the prevailing circumstances, could it have been 'eliminated', and would economic growth have been proportionately increased? It may more realistically be argued that, under the pressures of post-war dislocation, increasing foreign competition, recurrent world slumps, trade restrictions and technological changes, heavy unemployment was an inevitable accompaniment of profound structural readjustments in the British economy and more rapid industrial growth, without which there would have been far more social distress.

Popular recollections of this period are heavily coloured not only by the decline and heavy unemployment in the old basic industries but also by the severe slumps

---

* S. Glynn and J. Oxborrow, *Interwar Britain: A Social and Economic History* (1976), p. 32. These authors, however, do seek to balance overall economic growth and prosperity against depression and unemployment.

of the early 1920s and early 1930s. These, however, must be balanced against the vigorous upswings that followed, resulting over the period as a whole in a remarkable rise in the level of industrial output. On average, in fact, total industrial production was rising at 3.1 per cent per annum, compared with only 1.6 per cent in 1900–13, so that by 1937–8 it was about two-thirds higher than in 1913 or 1920, according to Lomax. The increase in industrial productivity was even more striking: whereas output per man had been almost stagnant in the pre-war period, it was now rising at 2 to 3 per cent per annum, despite reduced working hours; output per man-hour was rising even more sharply. Britain's performance therefore now compared much more favourably with that of other European countries and that of the United States, especially in the 1930s; over the period as a whole, British industrial production was growing at about the general average rate.

This reversal of pre-war trends was caused primarily by the 'second industrial revolution', which was now massively under way, so that decline or stagnation in many of the old industries was more than counterbalanced, as we shall see, by rapid growth of the new industries, together with the building, consumer goods and distributive trades; even in the older industries, productivity was being increased by mechanization and rationalization, though at the cost of increasing unemployment. Britain's relative industrial decline, which had been very marked between 1870 and 1913 and accentuated by the war, was thus checked in the inter-war period. Between 1926–9 and 1936–8 world manufacturing production increased by over a third, but Britain approximately retained her proportion, despite industrial growth in other countries.

PERCENTAGE DISTRIBUTION OF WORLD
MANUFACTURING PRODUCTION

Year	United Kingdom	United States	Germany	France	Russia	Japan
1870	31.8	23.3	13.2	10.3	3.7	—
1913	14.0	35.8	15.7	6.4	5.5	1.2
1926–9	9.4	42.2	11.6	6.6	4.3	2.5
1936–8	9.2	32.2	10.7	6.5	18.5	3.5

Source: League of Nations, *Industrialization and Foreign Trade*, 1945.

In exports of manufactured goods, however, Britain was more hard pressed. While world industrial production was rising, world trade in manufactures fell. Compared with 1913 (=100), it had gradually recovered to a slightly higher volume during the 1920s (annual average 1926–9 = 104.3), but then collapsed in the ensuing slump (1931–5 = 75.5), and was still well below the pre-war level in the late 1930s (1936–8 = 92.1). The slump led to a general increase in protectionism (tariffs, import quotas, exchange controls, etc.), and there was fiercer competition for a dwindling amount of international trade. Although Britain managed to maintain her position as the world's largest industrial exporter for most of this period, her share of world trade in manufactures, which had gradually declined to about 30 per cent by 1913 and was sharply reduced by the war, continued to fall in the inter-war years. She was overtaken by Germany in the 1930s, while American competition remained strong, and Japan was presenting a growing challenge.

PERCENTAGE DISTRIBUTION OF WORLD
MANUFACTURED EXPORTS

Year	United Kingdom	United States	Germany	France	Belgium	Japan
1880	41.4	2.8	19.3	22.2	5.0	—
1913	29.9	12.6	26.5	12.9	4.9	2.4
1929	23.6	20.7	21.0	11.2	5.5	3.9
1937	22.4	19.6	22.4	6.4	5.9	7.2

Sources: Saul, op. cit., p. 12; H. Tyszynski, 'World Trade in Manufactured Commodities, 1899–1950', *The Manchester School*, Vol. 19 (1951), p. 286.

This growth of foreign manufacturing production, protection and competition and the associated decline of world trade were mainly responsible for the difficulties of Britain's export industries, especially of the old staple trades, in the inter-war years. Although Britain did fairly well in maintaining her share of world trade, the actual volume of British domestic exports fell catastrophically, while imports rose; in 1938 exports were still less than 60 per cent of the pre-war volume. In values, inflated by the war, the decline during the inter-war years was even more dramatic, because of falling prices.

BRITISH OVERSEAS TRADE, 1913–38

	Volume Indices (1938 = 100)			Current values (£ millions)		
	1913	1920	1938	1913	1920	1938
Total imports	87	77	100	769	1,933	919
Re-exports	165	148	100	110	223	61
Domestic exports	173	123	100	525	1,334	471

Source: Mitchell and Deane, op. cit., pp. 284, 329.

The only comforting feature in Britain's trade situation was the substantial improvement in the terms of trade, the prices of imports generally falling more than those of exports, so that Britain was acquiring raw materials and foodstuffs on increasingly favourable terms, which helped to reduce costs of production and the cost of living. On the other hand, the relative impoverishment of primary producing countries contributed to the reduction of export markets for manufactured goods.

Overall, there was a marked decline in the importance of overseas trade in Britain's economic life. As a proportion of net national income, domestic exports fell from nearly 24 per cent in 1913 to barely 10 per cent in 1938, net imports from about 30 to 18 per cent. But, while the old export trades declined, there was a rapid growth in output of goods and services for the home market, which accounted for the substantial overall growth in industrial production. Some industries, such as building, food and drink, printing, etc., were naturally sheltered from foreign competition, while there was also rapid expansion in such domestic industries as electricity supply, road transport and the distributive trades, as well as in numerous professional, catering, entertainment and other services. Moreover, home industries were now increasingly protected against foreign imports.

The decline of free-trade and laissez-faire

With growing international rivalry and increasing emphasis on the home market, it is not surprising that the inter-war period witnessed the abandonment of free-trade, which had been the basis of British commercial policy since the mid-nineteenth century. Even before the war, with the growth of foreign industry and competition, there had been movements for 'fair trade' and tariffs, and the wartime McKenna duties provided the thin end of the wedge for protection in special cases (see p. 261). These were not abolished after the war (except temporarily by the Labour Government in 1924–5), so that such industries as motor manufacturing were able to develop under the shelter of a substantially protective tariff. Moreover, the products of certain 'key' industries such as synthetic dyestuffs, drugs, optical glass, scientific instruments, wireless valves and magnetos, for which Britain had been heavily dependent on foreign imports before the war, were also given special protection. By the Dyestuffs Act of 1920, importation was prohibited, except under licence, for a period of ten years, and by the Safeguarding of Industries Act, 1921, the other key industries were protected by 33⅓ per cent duties. Consequently, by the late 1920s, the British dyestuffs industry was able to supply the bulk of domestic consumption and to develop an export trade (see p. 339), while the other industries were similarly stimulated.

The 1921 Act also authorized imposition of duties on imports at artificially low prices resulting from foreign currency depreciation, and a few commodities, such as fabric gloves, glassware, hollow-ware and gas mantles, imported from Germany, were subsequently dealt with in this way. In 1925, moreover, this principle was extended to provide protection for industries suffering from exceptional competition attributable to subsidies, bounties or other artificial advantages or to inferior conditions of employment abroad. Several more manufactures, including pottery, cutlery, lace, buttons and a few others, were thereby able to secure some protection, though larger industries such as wool and iron and steel were unsuccessful in their applications. Duties imposed in 1925 on silk, artificial silk (rayon) and hops also had a protective effect.

During this same period Government subsidies were introduced to encourage particular industries, such as house-building, coal, civil aviation and beet sugar, together with general schemes for guaranteeing business loans and export credits, while further encouragement was provided by the derating provisions of the Local Government Act of 1929, intended mainly to relieve the heavy industries and agriculture. Some small support was also given to industry through the Department of Scientific and Industrial Research.

These various forms of State intervention were breaches in the policy of free-trade and *laissez-faire*. So, too, were the schemes of amalgamation forced on the railways in 1921 and on civil aviation (Imperial Airways) in 1924, together with the public corporations established for electricity supply (the Central Electricity Board) and wireless broadcasting (the British Broadcasting Corporation) in 1926, followed by the London Passenger Transport Board in 1933. (There were pre-war precedents, however, such as the Mersey Docks and Harbour Board, 1857, and the Port of London Authority, 1908.) Though these may be regarded as public utilities, the Government was also looking into the state of other industries, especially those suffering from trade depression, such as coal-mining and cotton. The coal mines, like the railways, were returned to private ownership after the war but continued to cause public concern, as shown by the Royal Commissions of 1919 and 1925 and the Mining Industry Acts of 1926 and 1930, which sought to bring about colliery amalgamations (see pp. 299–300). Much more widespread concern was expressed by the Balfour Committee on Trade and Industry in the late 1920s, with its criticisms of British scientific-technological backwardness (see p. 271).

Interventions by Government in this decade, however, could be justified by the special circumstances of particular industries, without seriously affronting the general principles of free trade and *laissez-faire*. Moreover, in 1925, with the return to the gold standard, another pillar of pre-war policy was restored, though at the cost of deflation and increased difficulties for British exports, through overvaluation of the pound. After the brief post-war boom of 1919–20, followed by the slump of the early 1920s, industry and trade had gradually recovered to mildly booming conditions in 1927–9. Things really did seem to be getting back to 'normal', despite the difficulties of the old export trades and over a million unemployed.

By the end of 1929, however, the great world depression had begun, heralded by the collapse of the speculative boom in the New York stock market in September, followed by rapid decline of international prices, trade and industrial production. Under these circumstances, Britain was finally forced to abandon free-trade completely and revert to a policy of neo-mercantilist protection and imperial preference. Governments throughout the world were endeavouring to insulate their national economies from the effects of depression, which was thus exacerbated by international trading restrictions: Britain's exports, shipping earnings and income from overseas investments were seriously reduced, and the consequently adverse balance of payments, together with unemployment approaching three million, caused a financial, commercial and political crisis in the autumn of 1931. This resulted, first, in abandonment of the gold standard in September, allowing sterling to depreciate, thus encouraging exports, and then, following collapse of the Labour Government and return of a 'National' (over-whelmingly Conservative) Government in October, an emergency Act was passed to restrict imports; this was replaced by the Import Duties Act of 1932, which laid the basis of subsequent British commercial policy. A general 10 per cent *ad valorem* tariff was imposed on all imports other than food and certain raw materials, and additional duties could be levied on the recommendation of an Import Duties Advisory Committee, established by the Act. In fact, those on most manufactures were raised to 20 per cent, while higher rates were imposed on some luxury imports and on certain goods, notably iron and steel, for which home producers were considered to need special protection. Quantitative import restrictions (quotas) could also be imposed.

In 1932, moreover, at the Ottawa Conference, a system of Imperial preference was agreed on between the Dominions—extended in the following year to the Crown Colonies—whereby reciprocal tariff concessions were made, in the hope of encouraging freer trade between the complementary economies of the Empire, with exchange of British manufactures for Empire foodstuffs and raw materials. Furthermore, by use of tariffs and quotas, Britain was able to secure concessions from various foreign countries in a series of bilateral trade agreements.

This new protectionist policy may have made some contribution to Britain's economic recovery from 1933 onwards, especially by safeguarding the home market for British industries and to a lesser extent by encouraging imperial trade, but as other countries were pursuing similar policies the result was damaging to international trade as a whole, and the volume of British exports not only remained far below the level of 1913 but failed to regain that of the 1920s (see p. 265). By the eve of the Second World War, therefore, doubts were being felt about such a restrictionist policy and attempts were made to reduce tariff barriers, as in the Anglo-American treaty of 1938, but protectionism still generally prevailed. In the financial sphere, too, departure from the gold standard involved more State intervention, with a 'managed' currency and exchange controls.

There was a similar development of interventionist policy in industry, especi-ally in the depressed and declining trades, mainly in order to encourage or compel their structural reorganization or 'rationalization', involving not only financial and technical reconstruction but also scrapping of outdated or redundant plant and machinery, control of output and prices and reduction of internal competition, under a central controlling body for each industry. We shall look more closely at such schemes in the following chapters, but reference may be made here to the Acts for reorganizing the coal industry in 1930 and 1938 and for the cotton industry in 1936 and 1939. Such reorganization was often tied to Government help, as with tariff protection for the iron and steel industry and subsidies to the shipping and beet-sugar industries. Schemes for voluntary removal of surplus capacity were also encouraged by tax allowances under the Finance Act of 1935. At the same time, assistance towards regional industrial redevelopment was provided by the Special Areas Acts of 1934–7 (see p. 287).

Nor was Government intervention confined to manufacturing industry. Agriculture was similarly assisted and regulated: imports were restricted by tariffs and quotas; home producers were encouraged by subsidies or deficiency payments; and boards were established to control output, marketing and prices of agricultural products under Acts of 1931, 1933 and later. Licensing controls and regulation of competition were likewise features of the Road and Rail Traffic Acts of 1930 and 1933. Competition was also regulated in the shipping industry, in connection with Government subsidies.

Thus traditional free-trade *laissez-faire* policy was everywhere being abandoned in favour of neo-mercantilist regulation and support of national trade and industry. It is doubtful, however, whether Government intervention did much to increase industrial growth. It failed, as we have seen, to revive the traditional export trades, and, while protecting the home market, it contributed to international trading restrictions. In industry, it was concerned largely with organizing decline in the old staple trades, but, whilst this may perhaps have helped to get rid of inefficient firms and surplus capacity, the forces of competition were already bringing this about anyway, and comparatively little was done to encourage industrial redeployment. Structural change was being achieved largely without Government intervention, by the growth of new industries and new industrial areas, and in these developments—the fruits of individual and corporate enterprise, investment, science and technology—we can see the main sources of increasing production and productivity. Together with the housebuilding boom, they brought about Britain's economic recovery; the older heavy industries did not pick up vigorously until the rearmament programme of the later 1930s.

Scientific-technological progress, investment and industrial growth
Investment and scientific-technological innovation provided the springs of economic growth in this period, especially in the newer industries, such as

electric, motor and aircraft engineering, chemicals, rubber, oil, rayon, radio and films. To quote Pollard, 'Whilst the rate of technical progress is difficult to measure, it seems safe to say that in the inter-war years the consumer was offered more new products, and the industrialist more new machinery and materials, than at any comparable period in history.' The contrast with the pre-war period should not be over-drawn: most of the 'new' industries had originated before 1914 but had not reached such a scale as to have had much effect on overall growth rates. Now, however, the industrial balance was shifting decisively. In the pre-war period, capital and labour resources were still being poured into the old basic industries, which had continued to grow massively in absolute terms, though without much technical change—investment was mostly in much the same kinds of machinery—so there was little increase in productivity. But during the inter-war years retardation in those industries turned to stagnation and decline, especially in the traditional export trades, so that plant had to be scrapped and labour forces reduced, though productivity was increased through rationalization and technological advances. At the same time, capital and labour were now being increasingly attracted into the newer industries, for which there were far better prospects of expanding markets and of increasing production and productivity by scientific-technological developments. Under pressure of economic circumstances, Britain's industrial structure and technology were thus being radically changed, so that the overall growth rate recovered to the level of the 'first industrial revolution'.

This renewed growth was associated with changes in both the general level and character of capital investment. Feinstein's recent estimates show that gross domestic fixed-capital formation, which, in real terms, had risen substantially to the early years of the twentieth century but had then fallen markedly up to 1914 and was halved in the First World War, now recovered vigorously to a level in the late 1930s well over twice as high as pre-war. As a proportion of gross national product, moreover, the rise was also significant, from an annual average of 8 per cent between 1870 and 1913 (only 6 to 7 per cent in the immediate pre-war years) to 10 per cent in 1920–38. Capital per worker increased by over a quarter between 1913 and 1938. Even more important was the shift of investment from the old into new manufacturing industries and also into electricity, gas and water supply, building and construction, transport and communications (especially road transport), the distributive trades, social and public services. A great deal of this investment was in new technology, in new forms of industrial power, machinery and transport, with high growth rates. At the same time, there was a reduction in the level of overseas investment—in fact, during the 1930s there was a net inflow of capital, which was now being attracted into British industry instead of abroad, a remarkable change from pre-war (see pp. 160–2).

Recent studies into the relationship between capital investment and technical progress have tended to stress what is termed the 'residual', that is the factors left over after quantitative assessment of the contributions to growth by physical inputs of capital and labour. These include increases in the productivity of capital and labour resulting from scientific-technological advances, educational and training improvements, and better business organization, for example economies of scale, improved plant lay-out, and general 'rationalization' of the kind previously referred to. The effects of these are difficult, if not impossible, to measure directly and to distinguish from capital investment, since new technology is usually embodied in new capital equipment, but they are obviously important. In the period of retardation before the First World War, increases in production had been achieved very largely by increases in the quantity, without much change in the quality, of capital and labour inputs. But during the inter-war years the residual factors became much more important, associated with the structural changes in British industry—particularly the growth of new industries—and with the scientific-technological advances, inventions and innovations of the 'second industrial revolution'.

Such developments were by no means new—indeed they had contributed significantly, as we have seen, to the 'first industrial revolution'—but in the late nineteenth and early twentieth centuries there does appear to have been a scientific-technological lag, which contributed to Britain's industrial retardation and her relatively weak performance, especially in the new industries, by comparison with the United States and Germany. In the inter-war period, however, these deficiencies were being remedied, though criticisms continued to be made, as by the Balfour Committee in its final report: 'Before British industries, taken as a whole, can hope to reap from scientific research the full advantage which it appears to yield to some of their most formidable trade rivals, nothing less than a revolution is needed in their general outlook on science, and in the case of some industries at least, this change of attitude is bound to be slow and difficult, in view of their old and deep rooted industrial traditions.' But such a revolution was now under way. Lord Aberconway, for example, while recognizing Britain's previous lag, pointed out in 1927 that even in the older basic industries there had been a change of attitude, 'and scientific research is now regarded with respect by even the most conservative of our industrial leaders'.

There was a considerable growth of scientific and technical education in grammar and technical schools, colleges and universities, together with a growing popular interest in the new technical marvels of the age. In addition to developing such education, the Government also sponsored applied research—through the Department of Scientific and Industrial Research and through grants in aid of numerous new research associations for particular industries. An increasing number of firms, especially the larger ones, also set up their own research laboratories and invested considerable sums in 'research and development': though individual genius and enterprise still remained important, as Jewkes and others have emphasized, there was a marked tendency towards large-scale organized research, while the scientific-technical complexities and costs of such research and of developing and marketing its products contributed to the increasing dominance of large industrial firms. Such firms, moreover, were in the forefront in applying the principles of 'scientific management', mainly introduced from America, with emphasis on increasing managerial efficiency, staff selection and training, cost accounting, improved plant lay-out, time-and-motion study and generally raising the productivity of capital and labour through better organization and control. Such advances in research and development and in managerial expertise should not be exaggerated, but they were undoubtedly considerable by comparison with pre-war.

Rising living standards
It was as a result of increasing productivity and of improvement in the terms of trade (especially cheaper food imports, see p. 265) that average real income per head and average real earnings rose by about a third between 1913 and 1938, according to Feinstein; if account is also taken of reduced working hours and paid holidays, the total gain for wage earners was substantially higher. This made possible greater consumer expenditure not only on food, clothing and housing but also on household goods, such as furniture and electrical appliances, on luxuries, such as alcoholic drinks, tobacco, cosmetics and hairdressing, and on entertainment and recreation, including the new radio, gramophone and cinema, as well as football, motoring, cycling and dance-halls. There was consequently a remarkable increase in the manufactures, distributive trades and services catering for such consumer demands (see p. 274). Those who remained in full-time employment—the great majority of the population—were thus much better off, while there were also substantial improvements in the social services, including unemployment benefits and pensions. Poverty, caused by unemployment, illness, old age, low earnings and large families, still existed, and statistical averages hide the considerable variations between different sections of the community and between different industries, occupations and regions, but the evidence of general betterment is indisputable. Over-emphasis on depression and unemployment has created a very misleading impression of this period. At the same time, however, as we are about to see, growth and prosperity for most of the working population was accompanied by distressing, though inevitable, decline and depression for people in those industries and areas which had formerly led the world in the 'first industrial revolution'.

16

Structural Changes in the
Second Industrial Revolution

Under the impact of war, scientific-technological innovations, growth of foreign manufacturing competition and depression of world trade, the structure of British industry was considerably altered between 1914 and 1939. Old basic industries, on which Britain's former world predominance had been based, went into decline, while new industries and processes were now more rapidly developed. There was a striking contrast between depression and growth in different industries and areas, with plant closures and massive redundancies on the one hand, and new factories and increasing demands for labour on the other. Despite immense problems of redeploying capital and labour, however, the necessary industrial restructuring was largely achieved, though only at the price of unprecedentedly heavy unemployment.

The changing pattern of employment and output
The population of the United Kingdom grew from 43.7 to 47.5 million between 1920 and 1938, but its age structure changed significantly, as a result of a declining birth rate on the one hand and an increasing average lifespan on the other. The number of children, aged up to 14 years, actually fell, from 12.3 to 10.4 million, while the number of people aged 15 and upwards rose from 31.4 to 37.1 million, including an increase in the number of old people, aged 65 and over, from 2.6 to 4.1 million. Some of the latter had no doubt retired, but the size of the potential work-force was clearly increasing, both absolutely and in proportion to total population. During these years, however, total employment failed to expand sufficiently to absorb the growing number of adults on the labour market: from a total of 20.3 million in 1920, it sank below 18 million in 1922 and did not recover to the 1920 level until 1936, then rising to 21.4 million in 1938, according to Feinstein's figures.

This decline and stagnation in total employment accounts, in broad statistical terms, for the persistently heavy unemployment during this period, even during years of rapid industrial growth. But these aggregates disguise very sharply contrasting trends in different sectors of the economy. The table below shows that the numbers employed in agriculture, forestry and fishing and also in mining and quarrying were declining very sharply, while the total in manufacturing industries fell to a much lesser extent, though within the broad manufacturing group, as we shall see, there were striking contrasts between decline and growth. Similarly in transport and communications, there was only a slight increase, because expansion in road transport and postal and telegraphic services was almost balanced by decline in railways, tramways, shipping and docks. These figures contrast remarkably with the large increases in building and contracting, gas, electricity and water supply, the distributive trades (wholesaling and retailing) and other services, such as insurance, banking and finance, local government, professional and miscellaneous (the latter covering a wide range, including hotels and catering, laundries and dry cleaning, domestic service, hairdressing, entertainment and sport). This growth of the 'tertiary' sector was not new (see pp. 163–4), but it was strongly accelerated in the inter-war period.

EMPLOYMENT AND OUTPUT IN THE UNITED KINGDOM, 1920–38

Industry	Employment (thousands)		Output (1913 = 100)	
	1920	1938	1920	1938
Agriculture and forestry	1,661	1,221	71.5	85.7
Fishing	80	51		
Mining and quarrying	1,325	904	80.9	85.2
Manufacturing	7,208	6,970	99.7	157.4
Building and contracting	927	1,266	101.1	262.5
Gas, electricity and water	185	291	126.3	301.8
Transport and communications	1,641	1,692	95.1	137.6
Distributive trades	2,352	3,090	92.7	116.5
Insurance, banking and finance	369	475	92.0	108.4
National government				
Civilian	257	245	155.3	133.9
Armed Forces	760	432		
Local government	380	556		
Professional services	845	1,115	106.1	130.2
Miscellaneous services	2,307	3,110	64.1	74.6
Total	20,297	21,418	Gross domestic product 93.7	127.1

Source: Based on Feinstein, op. cit., Tables 8, 51, 53, 59.

In the whole industrial sector—including mining and quarrying, all manufactures, building and contracting, gas, electricity and water supply—there was a slight fall in employment, from about 9.6 to 9.4 million between 1920 and 1938, but the index of industrial production, according to Feinstein's estimates, rose from 97.9 to 158.7 (1913 = 100), as a result of technological innovation and increasing productivity, which was rising at an annual average rate of nearly 3 per cent. In agriculture, forestry and fishing, despite a reduction of nearly half a million in the number employed, to about 1.3 million in 1938, the production index rose appreciably, from 71.5 to 85.7 (though still well below the 1913 level), with productivity rising at about the same rate as in industry. In transport and communications, with little overall change in the number employed, the output rose somewhat more slowly, though still substantially, from 95.1 to 137.6, productivity increasing at about 2 per cent per annum, mainly owing to the rapid growth of road transport. In the distributive trades and services, however, although there was a large increase in the total number employed, from about 7.3 to 9 million, the output index rose only from 93.8 to 110.1, and productivity was actually declining. Moreover, the relatively poor performance of transport, distribution and services occurred despite a somewhat higher level of capital investment in those sectors than in industry and agriculture. In 1920, for example, Feinstein's figures show that gross fixed-capital formation in the former sectors was £217 million, compared with £203 million in the latter, while in 1938 the figures were £234 and £189 million respectively at current prices.

Thus though industrial production increased by nearly two-thirds in this period, the gross domestic product grew by not much more than a third, the index rising from 93.7 to 127.1. This poses the question as to whether too much capital and labour resources were going into 'non-productive' sectors of the economy, or into those sectors in which production was growing comparatively slowly and productivity was stagnant or declining. It must be pointed out, however, that increased industrial production was closely related to the growth of transport and distribution and of banking, insurance, finance and other professional services, such as law, accountancy and education. Moreover, with rising real incomes, as we have previously noted, there was a great increase in the distributive trades and services, to meet growing consumer demands not only for basic necessities but also for luxuries, catering, entertainment, sport, holidays, etc., especially in the areas of industrial expansion. But in these generally labour-intensive trades and services there were, as yet, comparatively limited possibilities of improving productivity. (Only since the Second World War, with developments such as self-service shops, supermarkets and business computers, have there been revolutionary changes in these fields.) This was perhaps fortunate, for without the growing employment opportunities in the non-industrial sectors, the unemployment problem would have been far worse even than it was during this period.

INDUSTRIAL EMPLOYMENT IN THE UNITED KINGDOM, 1920–38
(thousands)

	1920	1921	1929	1932	1938
Mining and quarrying	1,325	1,210	1,055	902	904
Building and contracting	927	888	1,011	930	1,266
Gas, electricity and water	185	185	224	242	291
Food, drink and tobacco	619	590	664	662	767
Chemicals and allied trades	253	220	240	219	274
Iron and steel	541	279	358	247	357
Electrical goods	188	186	210	220	337
Mechanical engineering and shipbuilding	1,313	861	738	499	882
Vehicles	353	301	479	439	623
Other metal industries	515	364	468	402	532
Textiles	1,331	1,053	1,304	1,094	1,007
Clothing	896	764	811	779	814
Bricks, pottery, glass, cement, etc.	209	170	256	227	298
Timber, furniture, etc.	323	287	301	277	322
Paper, printing and publishing	393	355	440	444	492
Leather and other manufactures	274	235	253	235	265
Total	9,645	7,948	8,812	7,818	9,431

Source: Based on Feinstein, op. cit., Table 59.

Against this broad background, we may now consider the changing pattern of employment and output within the industrial sector. We have already noted marked contrasts between decline in industries such as coal-mining and rapid growth in building and contracting, electricity, gas and water supply. Within manufacturing industry also, there were similarly contrasting trends: some older industries, such as cotton and shipbuilding, experienced serious contraction in both employment and output; in others, such as iron and steel and engineering, output was slowly expanded, but employment was considerably reduced; while in newer industries such as electrical engineering and motor manufacture, both production and employment rose substantially. It is noticeable, however, that output in the growth industries expanded more rapidly than employment, as a result of capital investment, technological advances, economies of scale, etc., while in the declining industries these factors added to the effects of structural changes in reducing the numbers employed: consequently there was a slight fall in total industrial employment, contrasting with the increase of nearly two-thirds in total industrial production. Moreover, average growth rates over the whole period produce a misleading impression, which needs to be modified by figures for the slumps of the early 1920s and early 1930s: these had traumatic effects in the older basic industries, but in the dynamic newer industries and in the consumer goods trades (food, clothing, etc.) they hardly checked the growth of output and there was comparatively little reduction in employment.

INDUSTRIAL PRODUCTION IN THE UNITED KINGDOM, 1913–38
(1924 = 100)

	1913	1920	1921	1929	1932	1938
Mining and quarrying	106.3	86.1	61.1	99.1	80.6	90.7
Building and contracting	64.0	66.2	91.7	142.2	117.0	171.8
Building materials	—	87.2	84.4	127.9	110.7	168.5
Gas, electricity and water	70.6	90.5	82.8	131.0	140.4	216.3
Chemicals	90.0	101.3	72.9	112.2	109.1	141.0
Iron and steel	105.5	97.1	45.4	104.3	74.7	118.3
Non-ferrous metals	78.3	74.5	45.6	117.8	85.8	174.6
Mechanical engineering	103.0	95.4	62.7	120.9	77.4	130.2
Shipbuilding	156.5	154.9	125.0	109.9	11.3	96.4
Electrical engineering	64.6	94.0	80.4	120.2	126.1	215.5
Vehicles	43.3	70.7	62.7	133.4	106.4	224.7
Metal goods, n.e.s.	—	115.1	71.4	124.1	109.0	180.5
Precision instruments	—	98.2	89.0	129.0	110.9	158.3
Textiles	121.7	107.8	71.6	96.0	95.8	111.3
Clothing	116.8	80.4	86.0	114.1	112.8	129.5
Leather	89.3	75.7	63.5	94.3	103.1	110.0
Food	78.4	89.3	85.7	117.9	131.2	168.3
Drink	127.2	117.3	103.5	99.9	79.1	112.7
Tobacco	69.9	106.9	97.9	130.2	118.7	159.3
Timber	85.9	71.9	66.8	142.6	120.9	178.7
Paper and printing	74.6	89.9	53.3	116.7	122.2	141.7
Total industrial production	90.5	90.3	73.5	115.8	103.2	146.4

Sources: Based on K. S. Lomax, 'Production and Productivity Movements in the United Kingdom since 1900', *Journal of the Royal Statistical Society*, Vol. 122, Part 2 (1959), pp. 192–3. Similar estimates are given in Feinstein, op. cit., Tables 51, 52.

These figures of employment and output show a considerable change in the overall structure of British industry in the inter-war period. The old basic industries, which had dominated industrial output before the war, experienced relative, in some cases absolute, decline, while the newer industries played an increasingly important role. But the relative importance of the latter has tended to be exaggerated, while the older industries have been too readily written off. It is true that the newer industries (electrical, chemical, motor manufacturing, rayon and others) increased their share of net industrial output from 6.5 per cent in 1907 to 19 per cent by 1935 (according to Kahn's estimates, based on the Censuses of

Industrial Production), but these figures also show that much the greater part of industrial output still came from the older industries. Similarly, looking at the employment figures, even if we regard the whole of the gas, electricity and water supply and the chemicals and allied trades as new industries (though some of them were quite old), together with electrical engineering and motor manufacture, they accounted for only about 19 per cent of industrial employment in 1938. Thus, although some of these industries had trebled, quadrupled or quintupled their output since 1913, total industrial production had increased by less than two-thirds.

Moreover, some of the old industries contributed very considerably to that growth, notably building and contracting, which increased their output by

ANNUAL PERCENTAGE RATES OF GROWTH OF OUTPUT AND PRODUCTIVITY, 1920–38.

Old industries			New industries		
Industry	Output	Output per man	Industry	Output	Output per man
Building and contracting	5.4	3.6	Vehicles	6.6	3.6
Timber and furniture	5.2	5.0	Electricity, gas, water	5.0	2.5
Non-ferrous metals	4.8	3.6	Electrical engineering	4.7	1.1
Building materials	3.7	1.6	Precision instruments	2.7	3.0
Food	3.6	2.1	Chemicals	1.9	1.5
Clothing	2.7	2.9			
Paper and printing	2.6	1.3			
Metal goods, n.e.s.	2.5	2.1			
Tobacco	2.2	1.7			
Leather	2.1	2.3			
Mechanical engineering	1.7	3.7			
Iron and steel	1.1	3.5			
Textiles	0.2	1.6			
Mining and quarrying	0.2	2.5			
Drink	−0.2	−1.0			
Shipbuilding	−2.7	1.9	All industry	2.8	2.9

Source: Based on D. H. Aldcroft, *The Inter-War Economy: Britain, 1919–1939*, (1970), p. 121, and statistical sources quoted therein.

between two and three times over that period and were employing over 13 per cent of the total industrial labour force by 1938. Production of building materials, timber, furniture and metal manufactures correspondingly increased. The output of foodstuffs and tobacco doubled (though that of drink declined) and that of clothing and leather grew appreciably, while the paper and printing trades expanded rapidly. It is true that production was growing much more slowly in iron and steel and mechanical engineering, while it was stagnant in coal-mining and textiles (well below the 1913 figure) and declining in shipbuilding, but these industries were still of great size and importance at the end of this period. Moreover, they were now raising their productivity at rates that compared very favourably with those in the newer industries, as they too introduced new machinery and rationalized their production, at the same time drastically cutting their labour forces; technical progress was clearly not incompatible with declining demand and output, as less efficient firms and plant were eliminated, and there was a similar labour shake-out.

On the basis of these statistics, it is somewhat misleading to assert, as Aldcroft does, that 'the division between the new and old industrial sectors comes out clearly', and that 'it is equally clear that the large staple industries acted as a drag on overall growth'. In fact, Aldcroft recognizes, at the same time, that in terms of both output and productivity some of the older industries were at the top of the table, while others, notably iron and steel and mechanical engineering, though increasing their output at a relatively slow rate, were among the most successful in raising their productivity, while the performance of some new industries such as electrical engineering and chemicals was relatively poor in the latter respect. Moreover, if there was over-commitment in the old staple industries before 1914, then it is illogical to imply that they ought to have increased their output more rapidly in the inter-war period: indeed, in view of the international trading situation, the traditional export industries might have been expected to contract more rapidly, and perhaps there was still over-commitment in 1939. As it was, most of the older industries succeeded in maintaining or increasing their output between the wars, while cutting down on labour and increasing productivity, thus releasing workers for employment elsewhere. They also made vital contributions to the general growth of the economy, including the new industries: iron and steel, non-ferrous metals and engineering products were required, for example, together with glass, leather, etc., in motor manufacturing, while the boom in house-building stimulated output not only of building materials but also of gas, electricity and water, and household appliances, which also required metals. At the same time, the food, clothing, leather, furniture and other manufactures catered for the rising living standards of those employed in both old and new industries. Undoubtedly, however, the new industries did introduce more dynamic growth elements into the economy: not only did they boost industrial production and employment by their own rapid growth, but they also stimulated the older industries with new forms of power and transport, new materials and new markets for their products.

PERCENTAGE DISTRIBUTION OF GROSS NATIONAL PRODUCT,
1907 AND 1935

	1907 Great Britain	1935 Great Britain and Northern Ireland
Agriculture, forestry, fishing	6.0	3.9
Mines and quarries	6.0	3.1
Textiles and clothing	8.0	5.6
Engineering, vehicles and metal manufactures	8.2	9.4
Food, drink and tobacco	4.3	5.1
Paper and printing	1.6	2.6
Chemicals	1.1	2.1
Miscellaneous manufactures	2.5	3.5
Gas, electricity, water	1.6	2.5
Building and contracting	3.7	4.1
Commerce	18.0	19.6
Transport	9.5	10.7
Government and defence	3.0	4.7
Domestic service	3.8	3.4
Rents of dwellings	7.4	6.5
All other income (including income from abroad)	15.3	13.2
Gross national product	100.0	100.0

Source: Deane and Cole, op. cit., Tables 40, 41, 79 (pp. 175, 178, 299).

Comparison of the Censuses of Production in 1907 and 1935 certainly reveals marked declines in the contributions to the gross national product of agriculture, mining and textiles, contrasting with the increases in other industrial sectors and in trade and transport, but the overall changes in the industrial structure were less dramatic than might have been expected, under the impact of the 'second industrial revolution' and depression of the old staples. As Richardson has emphasized, however, that revolution was only really getting under way in the inter-war years; structural changes were inevitably difficult and prolonged and have continued into the period after the Second World War. The general improvement in productivity, resulting from renewed technological innovation and investment, was particularly encouraging; although by the late 1930s physical output per worker in manufacturing industry was still less than half that in the United States, with their rich resources, huge home market and larger-scale more capital-intensive production, it was approximately the same as in Germany, according to Rostas.

The changing pattern of exports

The main cause of depression in the old staple industries during the inter-war years was the decline of exports. With the growth of industrial production and protection in foreign countries, world trade in manufactures was declining, while competition was increasing (see pp. 264–5). British exports suffered not only from the growing trade rivalry of Germany, the United States and Japan but also from import substitution in less developed industrializing countries—the most outstanding example was Indian cotton manufactures (see p. 319)—while markets in primary producing countries were also reduced by the slump in prices of raw materials and foodstuffs and thus in their purchasing power. Coal exports, moreover, were affected not only by growing foreign production and competition, but also by the development of oil, gas and electricity as alternative forms of fuel and power. Exports of steam-powered machinery, railway locomotives and ships declined for the same reason, though locomotive builders suffered also from the growth of road transport, while shipbuilding was hit by the slump in world trade.

These changes in the volume and structure of international trade had particularly serious effects on Britain, because of her previous predominance and heavy commitments in what were now declining sectors. Inevitably, the volume of her exports declined: in the slumps of 1921 and 1931–3 they were only about half the pre-war level and were still less than 60 per cent in 1938. Her share of world trade in manufactures also declined, from 29.9 per cent in 1913 to 23.6 in 1929 and 22.4 in 1938, according to Tyszynski. After heavy trading losses during the war, Britain failed to recover her position in the 1920s, and, though the relative decline was slowed in the 1930s, Germany and Japan increased their shares, which is suggestive of British competitive weakness, though Britain's manufactured exports were still about level with Germany's in the late 1930s, constituting between a quarter and fifth of the world total (see p. 265).

Britain's exports were hampered in the later 1920s by the over-valuation of sterling but were assisted in the 1930s by devaluation, the Ottawa agreement in imperial trade and trade bargaining with other countries (see pp. 267–8). Increasing efforts were also made not only to improve the competitive efficiency of the old export industries, in many of which, as we have seen, costs were reduced by increased productivity, but also to develop exports from the new industries and thus to restructure British overseas trade to meet changing world demands. The new industries, however, concentrated mainly on the home market, and, though they also expanded their exports, the increases were comparatively modest and did not compensate for decline in the old staples; indeed, the latter still provided the major part of British exports at the end of this period. Nevertheless, while textiles, especially cotton, were losing their ancient predominance, and while exports of coal, iron and steel and ships were also declining, those of machinery had been substantially increased, together with motor vehicles and electrical manufactures, though chemicals stagnated. The structure of British exports was thus gradually being adjusted to the changing pattern of world trade, but not far or fast enough to prevent overall decline. Tariff protection may, indeed, have delayed reorganization by bolstering up the older declining industries; it may also have encouraged the new industries to concentrate mainly on the home market and on exports to the Empire.

MAIN BRITISH EXPORTS, 1913–38

Trade	Current values (£ millions)		Percentage of total domestic exports	
	1913	1938	1913	1938
Cotton yarn and piece goods	127.2	49.7	24.2	10.5
Woollen	31.8	23.6	6.1	5.0
Linen	9.5	6.3	1.8	1.3
Hats, haberdashery, apparel, etc.	13.3	7.7	2.5	1.6
Coal	53.7	40.7	10.2	8.6
Iron and steel	55.4	42.9	10.5	9.1
Non-ferrous metal manufactures	12.0	12.3	2.3	2.6
Machinery	37.0	60.7	7.0	12.9
Ships and boats (new)	11.0	8.5	2.1	1.8
Road vehicles and aircraft	5.4	24.7	1.0	5.2
Electrical goods	5.4	13.4	1.0	2.8
Chemicals	22.0	22.1	4.2	4.7

Source: Calculated from figures in Mitchell and Deane, op cit., pp. 284, 305–6.

There has been considerable debate, however, about Britain's export performance in this period. It is true that the new industries exported a much smaller proportion of their output than the old staples, generally between 10 and 20 per cent, in some cases less; by 1937 they still accounted for only 17.6 per cent of total domestic exports (compared with 7.4 per cent in 1907), and over half their exports, in some products a higher proportion, went to the Empire (Kahn). Statistical evidence has also been produced (by Tyszynski and Maizels, for example) showing not only Britain's slowness in restructuring her export trade but her competitive weakness in most of the expanding as well as declining sectors. On the other hand, it has been pointed out that, because of previous overcommitment, Britain had immense problems of readjustment, that the fall in her share of world exports was caused mainly by the inevitable decline of the old staples, that the new industries naturally concentrated in the first place on supplying rapidly growing domestic demands, thus providing a stabilizing factor within the British economy in a period of declining world trade, but that, despite growing foreign industrial production and protection, Britain was now successfully developing new exports—for which Empire countries provided the best markets in this period—and thus, as Richardson says, she 'did not lag behind the shifts in the structure of world trade to any great extent', especially in the 1930s. There is certainly much truth in the view that the so-called failure of British exports has been exaggerated, that it is unrealistic to argue as if this country could possibly have retained her former export predominance, and that in the difficult inter-war years her industries and exports were being substantially restructured. But it is also significant that Britain lagged well behind Germany in most manufactured exports, not only in iron and steel, machinery and metal manufactures generally, electrical goods and chemicals, but also in a wide range of other products; only in textiles, motor vehicles, drink and tobacco did she have a substantial lead over her main rival.

Regional redistribution and the problem of unemployment

We have already seen that considerable changes occurred during the inter-war years in the occupational distribution of employment, as numbers engaged in the depressed industries declined, while those in growing industries, trades and services increased, though with little overall increase in employment until the late 1930s (see pp. 273–7). This occupational redistribution of the working population also involved a substantial regional redistribution, for the expanding trades were not generally located in the older industrial areas. The coal, iron and steel, shipbuilding, engineering and textile industries of the 'first industrial revolution' had become established predominantly in the northern English counties, south Wales and west-central Scotland, so that these areas now experienced exceptional depression and unemployment. The newer industries, on the other hand, such as motor manufacturing, electrical engineering, many light industries and consumer goods trades, developed most strongly in the midlands and south-east, especially in the Greater London area, where employment rapidly expanded and unemployment was comparatively low.

Of course, industries had previously existed in the midlands and London areas, but compared with the strongly localized heavy industries of the north and west they were lighter and more varied, including small metal manufactures, hosiery, boot- and shoe-making, brewing, printing, furniture-making, clothing and generally more consumer-oriented trades, of the kind that were to expand rapidly in the inter-war years, as production turned increasingly to the home market. Such industries, of course, were not confined to the midlands and south-east, nor did the newer industries develop only in those areas—there was some industrial diversification and increased employment even in the north and west, which were by no means uniformly depressed—but this broad contrast between the old and new industrial regions of Britain is clearly apparent in the statistics of production and employment. In the short interval between the Census of Production of 1924 and that of 1935 there was a remarkable shift in the distribution of industrial output. The share of the northern English industrial regions, together with those of Wales and Scotland, declined from 55.4 to 43.7, while that of Greater London and the rest of England (mainly the midlands and south) rose from 44.6 to 57.3.

PERCENTAGE DISTRIBUTION OF
NET INDUSTRIAL OUTPUT, 1924–35

Region	1924	1935
Lancashire and Cheshire	20.8	15.5
West Riding	12.6	10.1
Northumberland and Durham	5.9	4.3
Greater London	17.1	24.8
Midlands, South, etc.	27.5	32.5
Wales	5.9	3.9
Scotland	10.2	9.9

Source: Political and Economic Planning (P.E.P.), *Report on the Location of Industry in Great Britain (1939), p. 44.*

There was a related shift in the working population. Whereas in June 1923 the four southern divisions of the Ministry of Labour (London, south-east, south-west and midlands) had contained 46.6 per cent of insured workers in employment, by June 1938 their percentage had risen to 53.9, while there had been corresponding declines in the rest of Great Britain. There was, in fact, a considerable movement of population out of the declining and into the expanding areas, though, as we shall see, large pools of unemployed remained in the old industrial regions.

Thus Britain's industrial balance was now tilting increasingly towards the south and east—a reversal of the movement associated with the 'first industrial revolution'. That earlier revolution, based on coal, iron, steam and textiles, heavily concentrated in the northern counties, had now spent its force, leaving depressed industrial areas that were not attractive to new industry, with the immense problems of scrapping and rebuilding, the stagnation of unemployed specialized labour, the widespread poverty and general air of dereliction and gloom. In the 'second industrial revolution', based on electricity, oil, motor manufacture, road transport and consumer goods trades, coal ceased to be such a strongly locational force, and factories could be built in other areas, employing the light-industrial skills of London, Birmingham, etc., or cheap unskilled (often female) labour in mechanized production and being also near to the huge and prosperous metropolitan market; in such growth areas, moreover, there was rapid expansion of building and all the various trades and services catering for a growing population with rising incomes, so that growth had a cumulative snow-ball effect. Thus, while many towns in the depressed areas had stagnant or declining populations, those in Greater London and the midlands mushroomed during this period; between 1923 and 1937 the insured working population of London and the two southern regions rose by nearly half, in the midlands by about a third, but in the rest of Britain by only about 10 per cent.

The striking contrast between the depressed northern and western half of the country and the prosperous southern and midlands half illustrates how decline and unemployment accompany growth in a dynamic changing economy. While old staple industries and areas decayed, others developed rapidly, so that overall production and productivity increased substantially, thus raising national and *per capita* income and the general standard of living (see pp. 263–4, 272). Such restructuring was a necessity of changing technology and markets, just as old handicrafts and local industries had been inevitable casualties of the 'first indus-trial revolution'. Unemployment was technological as well as structural, result-ing from increased labour-saving mechanization and rationalization, scrapping of outdated machinery and plant, concentration of production in larger more efficient factories, fuel-saving economies and switching to alternative sources of fuel and power. At the same time, foreign competition and international cyclical fluctuations also seriously affected British industry, throwing large numbers out of work in the slumps of the early 1920s and early 1930s, especially in the heavy capital goods industries of the north and west.

Change and growth in the inter-war years, therefore, were accompanied by a persistently high level of unemployment. Before the war, unemployment had averaged about 5 per cent, fluctuating between 1 or 2 per cent in booms and about 10 per cent in slumps (though with considerable industrial and local variations); but in the inter-war period—after a brief post-war boom, when it was only about 2 per cent—it averaged about 14 per cent of all insured workers, falling little below 10 per cent in the best years (1924, 1927, 1929, 1937) and rising to nearly 23 per cent in the worst (1931–2). From 1921 onwards there were never less than a million unemployed, and in 1931–2 there were nearly three million. Even in the expanding industries, unemployment was heavier than in the pre-war period, while in the depressed industries it reached catastrophic proportions: in June 1932, for example, 58.6 per cent were unemployed in shipbuilding, 47.7 per cent in iron and steel, 40 per cent in coal-mining, 30.4 per cent in cotton, 27.8 per cent in general engineering and 26.4 per cent in woollen and worsted.

The disparities in unemployment between industries gave rise to similar regional differences, according to industrial localization. There was a marked contrast between the relatively low levels of unemployment in the southern part of the country and the very high levels in the northern and western parts; even in the midlands, unemployment was much higher than in the south-east. The much higher levels of unemployment in the north and west reflected the heavy regional concentrations of the old depressed industries in those areas. Between 80 and 90 per cent of the cotton industry, for example, was concentrated in Lancashire and Cheshire, 70 to 80 per cent of woollen and worsted in the West Riding and 50 to 60 per cent of shipbuilding in Northumberland and Durham and on Clydeside, with similar though more scattered concentrations of coal, iron and steel in the northern and midland regions. In some districts dominated by a single basic industry, especially coal and shipbuilding, up to 70 or 80 per cent of insured workers were unemployed in the slump of the early 1930s. On the other hand, there were towns in the north and west with more varied and relatively prosperous industries in which unemployment was relatively light, while conversely there were pockets of depression even in the southern areas, in places where local industries were declining. In general, however, the regional industrial contrasts we have previously observed were reflected in the unemployment figures, for the new industrial growth took place most vigorously outside the old industrial areas and did not provide enough alternative employment in those areas to compensate for the declining industries.

REGIONAL DISTRIBUTION OF UNEMPLOYMENT, 1929–37

Region	July 1929	July 1932	July 1937
London	4.7	13.1	5.5
South-eastern	3.8	13.1	5.0
South-western	6.8	16.4	6.2
Midlands	9.5	21.6	7.0
North-eastern	12.6	30.6	11.3
North-western	12.7	26.3	12.9
Scotland	11.2	29.0	16.1
Wales	18.8	38.1	19.9
Great Britain	9.7	22.9	9.9

Source: Ministry of Labour Gazette.

Consequently, there was a considerable movement of population out of the depressed areas into the growth regions. Between 1923 and 1936 the three southern regions attracted over 1.1 million migrants, while there were correspondingly heavy losses from northern England, Wales and Scotland. From 1928 onwards such movement was facilitated by financial assistance from the Ministry of Labour, under an industrial transfer scheme, which also included the setting up of industrial training and rehabilitation centres; but, of the few hundred thousand who took advantage of the scheme, many returned home and others could not find work. Only the most active and enterprising would move into other areas and jobs, while the majority were deterred by the problems of re-training and rehousing, by distance and cost, and were reluctant to leave their local neighbourhoods; this human inertia was encouraged by unemployment benefit and public assistance. The situation was made more difficult by the growth of population, without a corresponding increase in employment, so that there was a considerable overall labour surplus, while an increasing proportion of older workers tended to restrict mobility and redeployment (see p. 273). Stagnant pools of unemployed demoralized labour therefore tended to accumulate, especially in the depressed areas, including many men who had been out of work for years.

It gradually became obvious that the old basic industries were in long-term decline and that consequently chronic unemployment in the depressed areas could only be relieved by the introduction of new industries. To some extent this did occur, especially in areas like the Manchester and Merseyside regions, with a pre-existing variety of industries such as engineering, metal manufactures, chemicals, brewing, printing and clothing, as well as cotton manufacture; but other more specialized areas tended to be neglected. Eventually, therefore, the Government was forced to intervene, with 'Special Areas' legislation in 1934–7, under which Commissioners were appointed to encourage more diversified industrial development in the four specially depressed areas of central Scotland, south Wales, west Cumberland and Tyneside with part of Durham. Financial support could be given to firms setting up in those areas, including contributions towards rents, rates and taxes, and 'trading estates' were established providing factory buildings for such firms, together with all public services; the main schemes were at Hillington, Treforest and Team Valley, with minor ones elsewhere. Preference was also given to the special areas in placing Government contracts, and foreign firms were encouraged to settle there. But these schemes did not make much impact on unemployment in the depressed areas: the Commissioners' grants totalled only £17 million by the end of 1938, only 12,000 jobs were created on the industrial estates and it proved difficult to attract firms into such areas. Migration did more to relieve unemployment, which was also reduced in the later 1930s by general trade recovery and by the rearmament programme, which particularly benefited the heavy industries. At the end of the period, however, unemployment in the northern and western regions of Britain still remained two to three times as high as in the rest of the country.

In other ways, monetary and fiscal policy may actually have contributed to unemployment in this period, as with over-valuation of the pound and 'dear money' after 1925 and deflationary policies (public expenditure cuts and increased taxes) in the slumps, especially in the early 1930s. On the other hand, devaluation and 'cheap money', together with tariff protection and subsidies, helped to bring about subsequent recovery (see pp. 268–9). In general, however, governmental policy was of comparatively minor effect in the profound structural and technological changes of these years. No government, in fact, could have done much about the massive decline of the old export trades or of industries hit by new technology, and the regions in which those industries were so heavily concentrated were bound to suffer: indeed, Government policy in regard to 'rationalization', aimed at increasing efficiency by amalgamations and removal of surplus capacity, tended to increase unemployment (see p. 289). It is a modern fallacy to think that governments can maintain 'full employment', together with industrial flexibility and competitive efficiency. Unemployment was the inevitable accompaniment of fundamental readjustments and renewed growth in British industry. It might have been better to have spent more on industrial redevelopment rather than on mere relief payments to the unemployed—though these helped to sustain the level of consumption—but, as it was, Britain's record in increasing industrial production and productivity, especially in the 1930s, compared well with that of other countries (see p. 264) and also with her own pre-war situation, when a lower level of unemployment had been accompanied by structural rigidities, low rates of growth and rapid relative decline. Keynesian ideas—only just emerging in the early 1930s—would have involved increased public expenditure, financed by budgetary deficits and borrowing, but they were concerned with relieving cyclical rather than structural unemployment, and it is very doubtful whether politicians and civil servants would have been more capable than industrialists in long-term allocation of capital resources.

Changes in industrial organization*

In both depressed and growing industries during these years, technological and commercial forces accelerated organizational changes, as mergers, combines and 'rationalization' schemes were devised to achieve economies of large-scale production and distribution, to eliminate excess capacity and to suppress or control competition by regulating output and prices. There was nothing new in these developments, which had become widespread from the 1880s onwards (see pp. 245–55), but the greater difficulties of the inter-war years stimulated such schemes, which were now, moreover, encouraged or even imposed by Government, as faith in free competition weakened and fears of monopoly subsided.

Government intervention was at first most strongly marked in the organization of public utilities—in rail and road transport, civil aviation, electricity supply and radio broadcasting—and then in overseas trade, with the return to tariffs, import quotas and exchange controls (see pp. 266–9). But it was soon extended

---

* In this section we shall be looking only at the general features of changing industrial organization. More detailed consideration of particular industries and firms referred to here will be found in Chapters 17–19.

to industry, which was not only encouraged by protective duties, subsidies, loan guarantees and derating, but also in some cases forced into 'reorganization' schemes. Such direct intervention, however, was confined almost entirely to the depressed industries of coal, shipbuilding, iron and steel and cotton, where it became essential to rationalize industrial structures by removal of redundant, obsolete, high-cost plant and concentration of production in the largest and most efficient units. Such reorganization was strongly advocated by the Royal Commission on the Coal Industry (1925), the Balfour Committee on Industry and Trade (1928), the Economic Advisory Committee in its report on the cotton industry (1930) and the Liberal Industrial Enquiry (1928). Some progress in this direction was achieved by voluntary amalgamations and combines along pre-war lines, with help from new financial bodies such as the Bankers' Industrial Development Company and the Securities Management Trust (a subsidiary of the Bank of England); in this way the Lancashire Cotton Corporation (1929) and National Shipbuilders' Security (1930) were assisted in schemes for scrapping surplus capacity. Such schemes were also encouraged by tax concessions in the Finance Act of 1935. But Government compulsion was eventually required in the 1930s to bring about reorganization of the depressed industries. In coal-mining, Acts were passed in 1926, 1930, and 1938 to bring about amalgamations and pit closures, under a central Coal Mines Reorganization Commission (1930), while national and district machinery was also established to regulate output and prices. The Cotton Industry Reorganization Act (1936), with its Spindles Board, had the similar object of scrapping redundant spinning machinery, and in 1939 a statutory price-fixing scheme for yarns was introduced. In the iron and steel industry, tariff protection was made dependent on central reorganization, leading to the establishment of the British Iron and Steel Federation (1934). In shipping and shipbuilding, loans were tied to scrapping, and under the Sugar Industry Reorganization Act (1935) payment of a subsidy was made conditional on amalgamation of beet-sugar factories into the British Sugar Corporation.

These measures, however, were not always very successful in achieving their objectives—in the coal industry, for example, amalgamations proceeded very slowly—and they were also inconsistent, since cartel schemes for control of output and prices, as in the coal and iron and steel industries, tended to support the existing industrial structure and thus to impede moves towards rationalization, involving elimination of capacity. The most that can be said for Government policy is that it may have assisted in a more orderly run-down of the old basic industries.

In other expanding industries, no State assistance or control was needed, since they did not have to cope with such great problems of declining markets, redundancy and reorganization. But, with continuing technological advances, increasing capital investment, manufacturing diversification, market expansion and new methods of managerial control, there was a *general* tendency towards larger-scale production, bigger companies, mergers, combines and rationalization. These developments led to a further concentration of British industrial production, following the earlier trend towards what Hannah has called 'the modern corporate economy of large-scale firms'. 'The share of net output in manufacturing industry accounted for by the hundred largest enterprises in 1909 has been estimated at 15 per cent: by 1935 it had increased to 24 per cent, and by 1970 . . . [nearly] one-half of manufacturing net output was accounted for by these giant enterprises.' The inter-war growth of large enterprises is also illustrated by the fact that, whereas in 1907 there had been only seven companies with a market capitalization of over £8 million, there were 25 such companies by 1924 and 61 by 1939. (As share prices had only doubled between 1907 and 1939, substantial real growth had occurred.) The large companies also became much bigger: I.C.I., for example, had an initial capital of £65 million and, like other big companies, it continued to expand both by internal growth and by absorption or elimination of smaller competitors. Small firms were still much the most numerous but accounted for a steadily declining proportion of total assets, employment and output.

This increasing industrial concentration was closely associated with the continuing trend towards larger-scale joint-stock company organization, resulting from the growing capital requirements of modern industry. There were still a great many individually owned firms or partnerships, but more and more became incorporated. The number of private companies soared from less than 50,000 in 1914 to about 145,000 in 1939, but they were mostly small and altogether accounted for less than a third of total joint-stock capital. Larger public companies increasingly predominated: as new formations were balanced by mergers, the total number remained about the same—some 14,500 in 1939 compared with 14,270 in 1914—while the average company grew greatly in size. Such companies were mainly responsible for the increasing concentration of employment and output, revealed in the 1935 Census of Production (Leak and Maizels). The Census data related only to firms employing more than 10 persons, of which there were 53,217, with a total employment figure of 7,203,057; in addition, there were 204,151 firms employing not more than 10, but they were estimated to have an aggregate employment of only 826,700 or about 10 per cent of the whole industrial labour force. Including firms of all sizes, the 'average firm' employed only 31 persons, but this figure is misleading, because it obscures the growing economic predominance of large firms. Of those included in the Census, about 60 per cent employed fewer than 50 persons but accounted for only one-ninth of total employment, while more than half the workers were employed by 2,280 large firms, or less than 5 per cent of the total, employing 500 or more persons; at the top end of the scale, there were some giant firms employing up to 50,000 or even more.

SIZE OF FIRMS, 1935

Size	Firms		Total persons employed	
(persons employed)	*Number*	*%*	*Number*	*%*
11– 24	17,609	33.1	304,113	4.2
25– 49	14,147	26.6	491,696	6.8
50– 99	9,459	17.7	656,237	9.1
100– 499	9,722	18.2	1,993,241	27.7
500– 999	1,270	2.4	878,764	12.2
1,000– 4,999	909		1,759,928	
5,000– 9,999	70		479,416	
10,000–19,999	21	2.0	283,743	40.0
20,000–49,999	8		214,507	
50,000+	2		141.412	
Total	53,217	100	7,203,057	100

Source: H. Leak and A. Maizels, 'The Structure of British Industry', *Journal of the Royal Statistical Society*, Vol. CVIII (1945), Table 1, p. 144.

Overall industrial concentration was, in fact, even greater than these figures indicate, because many firms, though operating under their own name, were not independent but were owned or controlled by larger business enterprises, some of which had become multi-plant multi-firm complexes, as a result of horizontal and/or vertical mergers; this trend was also associated with multi-product diversification, as large companies spread their interests into several trades, though some remained specialized.

The growth of large businesses was also associated with the growth of large plants. The size of works, factories, shipyards and mines had gradually increased, as we have seen, with power-driven mechanization, and big businesses tended to predominate in those industries where such large-scale production had developed, while small firms were most numerous where craft manufactures still survived. These correlations were clearly evident in the 1935 Census of Production. Large firms accounted for the greater part of employment and output in those industries with relatively high proportions employed in large establishments (with 500 or more workers), such as coal mining, iron and steel, shipbuilding, mechanical and electrical engineering, motor, cycle and aircraft manufactures, heavy chemicals, rayon, rubber, cement, chocolate, biscuits, tobacco and newspaper printing, in which massive concentrations of capital and labour were required for large-scale mechanized production and in which firms also tended to expand by establishing or acquiring several plants, by horizontal and/or vertical integration—thus achieving further economies of scale. But in a wide range of other industries—including textiles and clothing, leather and footwear, grain-milling and baking, many chemical manufactures, soap, pottery and glass, building, brick-making, timber and wood-working, numerous small metal manufactures and general printing—although large works existed, small and medium plants predominated, for a variety of technical and commercial reasons, such as limited mechanization, multiplicity of products, process specialization and localized markets; in some of these industries, small firms with no more than 10 workers were still very numerous, practising traditional crafts. The 1935 Census showed that such small-scale production was now of relatively minor importance, but it also demonstrated that only a minority of the total labour force was employed in large works: of those in manufacturing establishments with more than 10 workers, three-quarters were in plants with 100 or more workers, but little more than a third in those with 500 or more and just over a fifth in those with 1,000 or more, according to Armstrong and Silberston.

It was in industries where large-scale production and large businesses predominated that there was the strongest tendency towards monopoly or oligopoly. Leak and Maizels calculated the 'degree of concentration' or concentration-ratio in each industry according to the proportion of employment or output controlled by its three largest units. They found that, out of 249 trades in 1935, there were 33 (with 7 per cent of the total labour force) in which the employment concentration was 70 per cent or more, while production of a much larger number of more specialized products was also highly concentrated. Such high concentration was most strongly marked in the chemical and electrical trades, in some branches of metals and mechanical engineering and also in sewing cotton, rayon, rubber, glass, cement, matches, cigarettes, chocolate, sugar, spirit distilling, seed-crushing, wallpaper, soap and margarine, gramophones and records, photographic apparatus and films. This concentration resulted very largely from pre- and post-war mergers or combines, aimed at acquiring monopolistic or oligopolistic control, regulating output and prices and removing surplus capacity. In the great majority of trades, however, the concentration was much lower: it was less than 10 per cent in such important trades as cotton weaving, woollen and worsted, tailoring, dress-making and millinery, hat and cap, leather, boot and shoe, general engineering, brass manufactures, coal-mining, building and contracting, timber and furniture, printing and bookbinding, pottery, baking and confectionery, which together accounted for about 40 per cent of total employment. Two-thirds of all workers were in trades where the degree of concentration was below 30 per cent; for all trades, the weighted average was 26 per cent.

The danger of monopolistic or oligopolistic control by a handful of firms was thus confined to a relatively small number of products, particularly in the newer industries, where technical and marketing factors tended towards production in a few large units. In addition, however, there was a large number of trades, accounting for over a quarter of total employment, with concentrations between 30 and 70 per cent, in which a few large firms might well play a preponderant role. Moreover, some of the biggest concerns, such as I.C.I., Unilever, General Electric, Vickers, and also the C.W.S., figured among the three largest producers in several interrelated trades. On the other hand, large-scale production does not necessarily lead to a high level of concentration, as demonstrated in coal-mining and mechanical engineering, in which there was a large number of big firms. And even where concentration is high, there may be strong competition between the few dominant firms, though possibilities of collusion are, of course, greatest in such cases. Moreover, 'monopoly profits' may be accompanied by reduced prices as a result of cost-reducing economies of scale.

'Big business' was not, in fact, simply a product of monopolizing tendencies but mainly of technical and commercial pressures towards larger-scale production and distribution. The growth of large companies was also accompanied and facilitated by managerial innovations, making possible their more efficient operation, without which, indeed, growth would have brought increasing *dis*economies, through unwieldy structures, with inadequate integration, co-ordination and control. Such innovations, however, were rather slow and patchy in this period, as before 1914 (see pp. 252–3). In a few of the largest combines, such as I.C.I., a multi-divisional structure was developed on a regional or product basis, combining decentralized manufacturing and marketing operations with central control over general policy and finance; but most were rather loosely run confederations, with a holding company structure and minimal control over subsidiaries. In smaller and medium-sized companies, on the other hand, direct centralized control was still possible. In most sizeable companies, functional specialization was developing, with separate departments for production, purchasing, marketing, accounting, research, personnel, etc., together with hierarchical managerial structures. Managerial control was also greatly facilitated by increasing use of such technical aids as telephones, accounting machines, typewriters and other office machinery.

Many large companies and combines had emerged before the First World War but had tended in many cases to be cumbersome conglomerates. It was because of the increasing awareness of such deficiencies that new managerial structures and methods were developed, with greater emphasis on managerial recruitment and training. Moreover, although mergers and take-overs took place more numerously than ever, especially in the 1920s, they tended to be more gradual and piecemeal, by contrast with the ramshackle multi-firm combines of the pre-war period; thus new acquisitions could be digested and integrated. There were, of course, some dramatic mergers such as those of Imperial Chemical Industries (1926), Associated Electrical Industries (1928) and Unilever (1929), but these were based on large pre-existing concerns—Brunner Mond, Nobels, United Alkali and British Dyestuffs in the first case, British Thomson-Houston, Ediswan and Metropolitan–Vickers (formerly British Westinghouse) in the second, Lever Brothers and their Dutch counterparts in the third—which had themselves expanded by earlier mergers. Other large companies developed, as in the past, mainly by internal growth, especially in new and expanding industries— Courtaulds and British Celanese in the rayon industry, for example, and Austin and Hercules in the motor and bicycle manufactures. But many of the largest companies and combines had already appeared on the scene before the First World War and continued to grow, both internally and by mergers, in the inter- war years.

Family names still remained prominent in many of the largest companies, both old and new, such as Armstrong–Whitworth, Vickers, John Brown & Co., Stewarts and Lloyds, Guest, Keen and Nettlefold, Baldwin's and Thomas's (in iron and steel, engineering, shipbuilding, tinplate, etc.); Horrocks and Courtaulds (textiles); Wedgwoods (pottery); Pilkingtons (glass); Boots (phar- maceuticals); Fisons (fertilizers); Dunlops (rubber); Austin, Morris and Rootes (motor manufacture); Lucas and Smith's (car components, instruments, etc.); Parsons and Ferranti (electrical engineering); Renold (transmission chains), Turner and Newall (asbestos); Crosse & Blackwell, Reckitt and Colman (food processing), Ranks and Spillers (flour-milling), Cadburys, Rowntrees and Frys (chocolate), Tate and Lyle (sugar-refining); and also, of course, the great family brewing firms (see p. 249). In some of these, owner control still strongly survived, but frequently such companies grew by taking over or merging with other firms, and there was an increasing tendency towards diffusion of share ownership, combined with professional managerial operation. There was a trend in large companies, in fact, towards a much more impersonal more bureaucratic struc- ture and image, particularly evident in mergers and expressed in corporate names, like the older Calico Printers' Association (and other textile combines), Imperial Tobacco, Portland Cement Manufacturers, Distillers, Wallpaper Manufacturers, etc., together with new combines such as Imperial Chemical Industries, Unilever, English Electric, Associated Electrical Industries, Elec- trical and Musical Industries, United Steel Companies, English Steel Cor- poration, Consolidated Tin Smelters, Imperial Smelting Corporation, Tube Investments, Allied Ironfounders, Lancashire Cotton Corporation, Textile Machinery Makers, Metal Box Company, English China Clays, British Plasterboard, British Match Corporation, British Sugar Corporation and Allied Newspapers. Behind these impersonal façades of 'managerial capitalism', how- ever, family capital and personnel, or family trusts, often remained important, while individual personalities were still of crucial significance, as Reader has emphasized, even in the professional operation of large bureaucratic corporations, as the examples of Harry McGowan in I.C.I. and Francis D'Arcy Cooper in Unilever demonstrate. Moreover, though scientific-technical research and development, requiring increasing capital investment, also tended to be carried out mainly in large companies, it must not be forgotten that innovative ideas originate in individual minds, that the success of research teams depends on the quality of leadership and that many inventions continued to be made by individuals or small firms, as Jewkes and others have shown.

On the other hand, the waning of family control and the increasing importance of outside institutional investors, such as banks and insurance companies, supplying short- or long-term capital, were significant in bringing about industrial reconstruction, as illustrated by the interventions of the Bank of England and commercial banks in the steel, shipbuilding and cotton industries. The infusion of foreign enterprise and capital also became more important, especially by American companies in the new industries, as in the electrical industry (for example, the American G.E.C., through control of A.E.I.), in motor manufacture (Fords, with their British subsidiary, and General Motors, through acquisition of Vauxhall), in oil (Anglo-American Oil, etc.), in soap and chemicals (Procter and Gamble, Colgate–Palmolive, Monsanto), in domestic electrical appliances (Hoover), in office machinery (Burroughs and Remington Rand) and in photographic equipment (Kodak), while in sewing and boot- and shoe-making machinery American predominance continued to be exercised by Singers and the United Shoe Machinery Company respectively. Many of these American firms had established themselves in Britain before the First World War, but now expanded their activities. Developments in 'scientific management' were also largely of American origin.

The increasing scale of industry, with its tendency towards oligopoly or even monopoly, was also associated with an extension of trade associations or cartels (see pp. 254–5), which became much more numerous during these years. Moreover, just as many of the big companies were becoming increasingly multinational, with factories or agencies in many foreign countries, so too were international cartels more widely organized for regulating markets and prices. Although the State now encouraged industrial combines, especially in the depressed industries, there were obvious dangers of restrictive practices, especially after the return to protection, reducing foreign competition. British businessmen in this period have, in fact, been criticized for being mainly concerned with suppressing competition and keeping up profits by controlling output, sales and prices, rather than with improving technical and organizational efficiency and thus reducing costs. But in view of the evidence of structural change and increased productivity during these years, such criticism would appear to be exaggerated. 'Rationalization' was not, in fact, just old monopoly writ large and made respectable: by eliminating smaller works and obsolete plant and by concentrating production in larger more efficient units, by undertaking much more research and development and by larger-scale commercial operations, it brought about substantial cost and price reductions, thus benefiting consumers and also making British industry more vigorously competitive with foreign rivals. It was a gross exaggeration to declare in 1937, as Lucas did, that 'free competition has nearly disappeared from the British scene'. In most industries there was still a considerable degree of competition, new firms could enter, or existing firms could diversify into new markets, while others declined or went bankrupt, and, despite growing State intervention, private enterprise was still flourishing, especially in new technological fields, where the profit motive still provided a stimulating and beneficial incentive to production of new and cheaper products.

17

The Old Heavy Industries

We have seen, in Chapter 16, that there was no simple contrast between old (declining) and new (growing) industries during the inter-war period. The performance of the old industries varied from sorry decline to rapid growth, while the new industries grew at varying rates, in some cases (such as chemicals) rather slowly. There are also problems of classification by age: neither gas nor water supply was new, for example, though usually grouped with electricity in that category, and the chemical industry was also old-established, though developing newer branches such as synthetic dyestuffs, plastics and pharmaceuticals, while viscose or rayon (artificial silk) became a flourishing new branch of the old textile manufactures. A clearer distinction was between what may be called 'depressed' and 'growing' industries. The distinction is stronger in comparing 1913, rather than 1920, with 1938 (see the table on p. 277), and this is a more valid comparison—even though 1913 was a peak pre-war year—because 1920 was distorted by the war and post-war situation. On that basis, the depressed industries stand out as those in which output was declining or stagnant, or only slowly growing, and in which employment was falling sharply, while unemployment was exceptionally heavy. These were all old industries —mainly the old 'basic industries'—of which the most depressed were coal, shipbuilding and textiles, which never regained their pre-war outputs, while iron and steel and mechanical engineering experienced mixed fortunes, growing gradually overall but with massive fluctuations and declining employment. These had been the major export industries of the nineteenth century—indeed they still were in 1938 (see p. 282)—but they now suffered severely from the growth of tariff-protected foreign industry and declining world trade, as well as from the competition of other products. The growing industries, however, comprised not only new ones, such as the motor, aircraft, electrical and rayon manufactures, together with new chemicals, but also many old industries, including building and allied trades (bricks, tiles, cement, timber, glass, etc.), furniture, non-ferrous metals, foodstuffs, tobacco, paper and printing, all of which were expanding rapidly in output, though less rapidly in employment, while others, such as clothing and leather, grew more slowly, with comparatively little change in numbers employed. All these growing industries were catering predominantly for the home market; though some increased their exports, they were far less orientated towards overseas trade than the old depressed basic industries. Even in the latter industries, however, productivity was improved by technological innovations, rationalization and reduction of labour forces, though these necessary changes added to their unemployment.

In the following chapters we shall trace the main developments in these major industries, but first their increasing interdependence must be emphasized. Such interdependence, of course, had long existed—between coal, iron and engineering, for example, between these industries and railway and steamship building, between engineering and power-driven mechanization in textiles, etc., between chemicals and dyeing, bleaching and calico-printing, between coal, gas and chemicals, between chemicals, glass, pottery, soap and other industries. During the inter-war years, such inter-industrial relationships were multiplied and extended by technological innovations and business expansion. The growth of new forms of power and fuel (electricity and oil), for instance, had even more widely pervasive effects on industry and transport than the earlier coal-and-steam revolution, stimulating further mechanization and growth of engineering, together with new electro-chemical and electro-metallurgical processes, and creating new industries such as electrical engineering and motor and aircraft manufactures, with new requirements for metals, rubber, glass and a host of accessories, while at the same time the chemical industry was producing new materials. As industrial firms grew in size, they integrated vertically and horizontally, whilst also diversifying their activities, so that giant companies such as I.C.I., Unilever, Vickers and General Electric developed very wide-ranging interests. In the following chapters, therefore, while looking first at the old industries—depressed, slow-growing and rapidly expanding—and then at the newer industries, we shall constantly observe their interrelationships.

The coal industry

Coal's predominance was gradually reduced in the inter-war period. Total United Kingdom output, which had risen to 287 million tons in 1913, never regained that level, gradually declining, though with marked fluctuations, to 227 million tons in 1938. The industry remained of massive importance: it still fired furnaces and boilers in many industries, it still powered engines, railway locomotives and steamships, and provided fuel for domestic fires, gas for lighting and cooking, and tar by-products for the chemical industry; it was also the main fuel for electric power stations. But it was increasingly challenged by alternative fuels and forms of power, as oil and electricity were now more extensively introduced. Though railways were still mostly run by steam, the rapid introduction of oil-firing and diesel engines into shipping seriously reduced demand for coal, the Welsh steam-coal trade being particularly badly hit. At the same time, oil and gas came into more widespread use, for both power and fuel, while electricity increasingly revolutionized factories. The growing consumption of coal in gas-works and electric power stations only partially compensated for its decline elsewhere, especially as fuel-saving economies were introduced in these and other industries, such as iron and steel. The home market therefore stagnated at around 185 million tons. Exports, however, were seriously reduced, declining from nearly 100 million tons (including bunker coal) in 1913 to about 50 million in 1938, not only for the reasons just mentioned but also because of growing foreign coal production and competition in overseas markets, especially in Europe from Germany and Poland. Britain's share of world coal production declined from 25 to 19 per cent between 1913 and 1937, while her share of world exports (including bunkers) fell from 55 to 40 per cent. To some extent these declines may have resulted from higher costs and relative inefficiency in British mining, but they were largely beyond the industry's control, in conditions of stagnating world demand for coal and industrial protection in other countries.

Declining production and exports were mainly responsible for reducing the number of men in coal-mining from over 1.1 million in 1913—rising to nearly 1.25 million in the immediate post-war boom—to less than 0.8 million by 1938 (many of whom were out of work). But this reduction was also caused by increasing mechanization, so that employment fell more than total output. The percentage of coal cut by machinery rose from 8 to 59 per cent between 1913 and 1938, and there was a similarly striking increase in the use of mechanical conveyors. Thus productivity, which had been steadily falling in the pre-war decades, now rose from 260 tons per man employed in 1913 to over 300 tons annually in 1937–8. These technological developments, of course, while increasing efficiency, added to unemployment among miners.

Declining output and employment in the coal-mining industry were accompanied by falling prices and profits, pit closures, redundancies, wages-cuts and strikes, most notably in 1921 and 1926, when they occasioned the general strike. A good deal of blame has been placed upon the mine-owners and upon the structural deficiencies of the industry, with its multiplicity of competing colliery undertakings (see p. 171), but it is doubtful whether, under the existing economic circumstances, much more could have been done to prevent gradual decline. Schemes were, however, introduced to rationalize the industry's structure and operations. Following the recommendations of the Samuel Commission of 1925, the Mining Industry Act of 1926 sought to bring about amalgamations, but with little success. Several voluntary mergers took place, however, and cartels were organized in some districts in the late 1920s, leading to the Coal Mines Act of 1930, which set up a compulsory cartel scheme for the whole industry, to regulate output, sales and prices through central and district organizations of colliery owners, together with a Coal Mines Reorganization Commission to promote and even enforce amalgamations. It met with great difficulties, however, because of price competition between districts and opposition by coal-owners to amalgamation. In 1936, therefore, a centralized selling scheme was introduced, and in 1938 a new Coal Act was passed, which, in addition to providing for the nationalization of mining royalties, set up a new Coal Commission, which would have been able to carry through compulsory amalgamations, though under a complicated legal procedure, had not war intervened.

Meanwhile, however, numerous voluntary mergers had brought about further industrial concentration, so that by 1937, though there were still about a thousand colliery undertakings, 129 produced 77 per cent of total output. Undertakings varied in size from large companies such as the Powell Duffryn Associated Collieries, with scores of mines and 30,000 to 40,000 men, to small units with only a dozen miners. Mines similarly varied, but, though small ones were still very numerous, about four-fifths of total output came from those with 500 or more workers.

Despite wide variations in the size and efficiency of collieries, however, the system of output restriction and price controls, under the 1930 Act, protected all alike. This ran contrary to the other part of that Act, encouraging or compelling amalgamations, with the object of eliminating smaller (and, as it was believed, less efficient) units and achieving the economies of large-scale production. But, as Buxton has demonstrated, there was no general correlation between the size and efficiency of mines: variations in mechanization, productivity, costs and profits depended on differing geological conditions and markets, as well as on size. Criticism of British colliery owners for their resistance to reorganization has therefore been grossly exaggerated: there were perfectly rational economic and technical factors underlying the complex structure of the industry. The labour conflicts were also understandable, in a situation where falling demand and prices, on the one hand, and relatively high wage-rates, on the other, were seriously squeezing profits and investment. These factors, moreover, largely accounted for the lower level of mechanization in British collieries compared with Germany, Poland and Holland. It may be argued that, instead of fixing output quotas and prices, coal-owners might have collaborated in greater efforts to get rid of surplus capacity and increase efficiency, but this would have involved immense difficulties of agreeing on closures, according to differing geological, technical and economic factors, not simply related to size, in an industry with deep-rooted traditions of district and colliery competition. And unemployment, of course, would have been even higher.

Iron and steel and non-ferrous metals

The iron and steel industry experienced striking fluctuations in this period. The immense stimulus of the war and post-war boom left it with a heavy burden of surplus capacity and over-capitalization, as output slumped massively in the early 1920s; then, after rising gradually and unsteadily to another peak in 1929, it plunged once more in the great depression of the early 1930s; the subsequent recovery was strongly sustained up to 1937, with output rising well above that of 1929, but there was a sharp recession in 1938, soon reversed, however, by the Second World War.

UNITED KINGDOM PIG-IRON AND
STEEL OUTPUT, 1913–39
(million tons)

Year	Pig-iron	Steel
1913	10.26	7.66
1917	9.32	9.72
1920	8.03	9.07
1921	2.62	3.70
1929	7.59	9.64
1932	3.57	5.26
1937	8.49	12.98
1938	6.76	10.40
1939	7.98	13.22

Source: G. C. Allen, *British Industries and their Organization* (1951), pp. 118–19.

Britain's share of world steel output, which had declined to 10.2 per cent by 1913, continued to fall in the 1920s to 8.1 per cent in 1929 and 7.6 per cent in 1931; but by 1937 it had risen to 9.7 per cent. Steel cannot, therefore, be classed as a declining industry: although demand was falling from railways, shipbuilding and the older branches of engineering, it was growing from newer branches of engineering, from the motor, cycle, aircraft and electrical industries, from building and construction and from the canning industry, and by the later 1930s it was also reviving in the older industries, with industrial recovery and rearmament. Domestic consumption of steel, which had been just over 5 million tons a year in 1910–14, rose to 10.6 million by 1935–8.

Decline did occur, however, in other branches of the iron and steel industry and especially in the export trade. The domestic output of iron-ore, which had reached 16 million tons in 1913, never recovered to that level; in 1937, the best inter-war year, it rose to just over 14 million, but was generally much lower. Britain did not, however, become more heavily dependent on foreign ore imports, which remained less than half the home tonnage and did not reach the pre-war annual average of nearly 7 million tons until 1937. Declining ore consumption was associated with a considerable reduction in pig-iron output, as the above table shows; even the $8\frac{1}{2}$ million tons of 1937 was nearly two million below the 1913 figure. This resulted partly from the continuing substitution of steel for cast- and wrought(bar)-iron and also from the greatly increased use of scrap in steel furnaces; output of puddled bar-iron, which had fallen from around 3 million tons annually in the early 1870s to 1.2 million in 1913, dwindled into insignificance in the inter-war years, being only 54,000 tons in 1938.

The declining production of pig- and bar-iron was also caused by the fall in foreign demand for what had once been the main exports of the British iron industry. Exports of pig-iron and ferro-alloys, for example, dropped from 1.12 to 0.1 million tons between 1913 and 1938. During the 1920s, by contrast, overseas markets for steel manufactures (plates, sheets, tubes, etc.) expanded considerably, so that total iron and steel exports of 4.4 million tons in 1929 were nearly up to the pre-war level, though less than those of France, Germany and Belgium. In the slump of the early 1930s, however, there was a general collapse, total exports dropping below 2 million tons, and though they slowly recovered to 2.6 million by 1937, they fell back again in 1938 and remained much lower than those of Germany, Belgium and the United States. Imports, moreover, continued to be considerable, especially of cheap basic Bessemer semi-manufactured steel for the finishing trades. After having risen sharply to 4.4 million tons in 1927, double the pre-war figure and surpassing exports, they fell to less than a million by 1933, as a result of the slump and import tariffs (see pp. 304–5), but recovered thereafter, and though still well below 2 million in the late 1930s, they were not far behind export tonnages.

These difficulties in overseas trade, however, were more than counterbalanced by expansion of the home market. And under such pressures of foreign competition and domestic demand, considerable changes were made in the technology, structure and organization of the industry. The biggest technical changes, already under way before the war, were from acid to basic steel, and from the Bessemer to the open-hearth process; in Britain (though not on the Continent), Bessemer converters had almost disappeared by the early 1930s, though basic production was revived in the following years. Electric furnaces came slowly into use, mainly in Sheffield for producing special steel alloys for which they largely displaced the old crucible process. The change to basic steel was associated with a further shift in geographical location, towards the east midlands phosphoric ores, mainly in Lincolnshire and Northamptonshire, which by the late 1930s were producing three-fifths of total ore output, while production in older areas, such as the north-east (Cleveland), north-west, west midlands and Scotland steadily declined. Blast furnaces tended increasingly to be located on these ore-fields, notably at Corby and Scunthorpe, so that between 1913 and 1937 the east midlands increased their proportion of pig-iron output from 16 to 38 per cent, while all the other areas except south Wales experienced relative or even absolute decline. In steel, however, the shift was much less marked: though production increased considerably in the east midlands, their proportion of total output in 1937 was only 13 per cent, and there were still major centres in the north-east, the Sheffield area, south Wales and Clydeside, with minor centres elsewhere.

UNITED KINGDOM STEEL PRODUCTION
(thousand tons)

Year	Bessemer		Open-hearth		Electric	Total
	Acid	Basic	Acid	Basic		
1913	1,048.8	551.9	3,811.4	2,251.8	—	7,663.9
1920	586.6	375.5	3,379.7	4,579.6	89.1	9,067.3
1929	559.1	0.1	2,450.6	6,488.2	86.8	9,636.2
1939	232.8	701.6	2,157.1	9,704.8	292.0	13,221.3

Source: Allen, op. cit., p. 119. The totals after 1913 include some additional small items.

Important cost-reducing technological advances were also made during this period. The average annual output of blast-furnaces, for example, rose from 30,000 tons in 1913 to 83,000 tons by 1937; they were not only increased in size but also in efficiency, by mechanical charging and fuel economies, considerably reducing consumption of coke per ton of pig-iron produced. At the same time, the old beehive coking ovens were largely replaced with by-product recovery plant. Increased integration of coke-ovens, blast-furnaces and steelworks also produced economies in transport, handling and fuel consumption: molten pig-iron could be passed direct from blast-furnaces to steel furnaces, and the steel ingots could then be taken hot to the rolling mills, while coke-oven and blast-furnace gases could be used in boiler-plant or furnaces or in internal-combustion engines to generate electricity for driving mills; the increasing scale of production also made possible the introduction of continuous rolling. Consequently, there was a substantial increase in productivity: output per man in blast-furnaces, for example, rose by about 50 per cent between 1924 and 1937. This meant, of course, that, while output was increased, the labour force was reduced and technological unemployment was added to that caused by trade depression (see pp. 276–8 for statistics of employment, output and productivity).

Despite these technological advances, however, there is evidence of what Burn called 'retarded development' in the British industry. Technical units (blast-furnaces, etc.), plants and firms were still much smaller than in the United States and Germany, mainly because of relative slowness in integration and concentration. Thus although by 1932 ten vertical groups controlled 47 per cent of pig-iron capacity and 60 per cent of steel capacity, the degree of concentration was much less than in America and Germany. In Burn's view, the industry was still dispersed in too many relatively small units, each producing too many products, inadequately utilizing the economies of large-scale production and often badly sited in relation to ore supplies, whether home-produced or imported.

Concentration in the industry, however, was a very difficult and inevitably gradual process, going back long before 1914 and involving firms in closely related industries such as engineering, shipbuilding, armaments and manufactures of tinplate, tubes, nuts and bolts, etc., among which there had been earlier amalgamations. The large companies that had thus developed continued to expand during the war, with more mergers, of which the United Steel Companies in 1918 was the most notable example, combining firms in the Sheffield, Scunthorpe and Workington areas. Further amalgamations and rationalization took place after the war, especially in the late 1920s and early 1930s, under pressure from, and with the assistance of, the joint-stock banks and the Bank of England (the Securities Management Trust and Bankers' Industrial Development Company), involving financial reconstruction, writing off capital, etc., as well as closures of surplus plant. The high-grade heavy-steel interests of Vickers, Armstrong–Whitworth and Cammell Laird were concentrated in the English Steel Corporation, while several other companies controlled by Armstrong–Whitworth in Lancashire formed the nucleus of the Lancashire Steel Corporation, involved particularly in wire-making; at the same time, John Brown and Thomas Firth made a similar merger in Sheffield, and a few years later Firth–Vickers Stainless Steels Ltd. was formed to combine the interests of Firth–Brown with those of the English Steel Corporation in that special field. Similarly, in the north-east, the merger of South Durham with Cargo Fleet (in the Furness Withy group) was followed by that of Dorman Long and Bolckow Vaughan; in Scotland, Colville's acquired a dominant position by taking over Dunlop's and other Scottish companies and also by securing the plates, sections and rails business of Beardmore's and Stewarts & Lloyds; in south Wales and the midlands, Guest, Keen & Nettlefolds (who had previously acquired Lysaght's) merged with Baldwin's, while Richard Thomas's and Stewarts & Lloyds continued to expand in their respective tinplate and tube manufactures.

Thus, by limited regional consolidations and product specialization, by financial reconstruction and also by participation in numerous local and sectional associations for control of prices, iron and steel firms tried to cope with slump and foreign competition. Their efforts were supported in 1932 by the imposition of a $33\frac{1}{3}$ per cent tariff, as recommended by the Import Duties Advisory Committee, on condition that some central scheme of 'reorganization' and technical redevelopment would be carried through. This led to the establishment of the British

Iron and Steel Federation in 1934, with quasi-monopolistic powers for regulating prices, controlling competition and supervising reorganization plans. By getting the tariff raised temporarily to 50 per cent in the following year, it was able to secure, by agreement with the European Steel Cartel, a quantitative restriction on imports and agreed export quotas. It also established the British Iron and Steel Corporation to undertake the centralized purchase of imports of pig-iron, steel and scrap. Thus protected, however, the Federation tended to become mainly concerned with controlling competition, raising prices (though only on approval by the Import Duties Advisory Committee) and subsidizing high-cost producers by means of general levies rather than with industrial rationalization, which would require closures of obsolete and surplus plant, concentration on the most favourable sites and technological integration and modernization. Social and political pressures, moreover, resulting from concern over unemployment, hindered plans for relocation, while companies and sectional associations remained strongly independent.

Nevertheless, considerable changes were made by progressive firms, supported by the banks, in the period up to 1939, with further mergers, interlocking agreements and co-operation between leading companies, while large numbers of old coke-ovens, furnaces and mills were scrapped and new integrated installations were built—notably the steel and tube-making plant of Stewarts & Lloyds at Corby, the new plants at Appleby-Frodingham (United Steel) and Cardiff (Guest, Keen and Baldwins), the continuous wide-strip mills at Ebbw Vale (Richard Thomas) and Shotton (John Summers)—so that output and productivity rose rapidly with trade recovery. Much more scientific and technical research was carried out under the auspices of a new Industrial Research Council (1929), together with the Federation and the Iron and Steel Institute, as well as by individual companies. No doubt reorganization was still incomplete, and the industry still lagged behind its strongest competitors, but critics such as Burn appear to have overemphasized its shortcomings by comparison with the substantial advances made, under conditions of great difficulty.

The problems of the iron and steel industry were very closely related to those of other heavy industries with which it was associated. Ownership of collieries by iron and steel firms remained common, while many were also involved in engineering and shipbuilding, so that difficulties in those industries, especially in export markets, directly affected the iron and steel industry. Some firms, such as Dorman Long, Bolckow Vaughan, United Steel and Colvilles, were engaged predominantly in the heavy steel-making processes, producing billets, bars, rails, plates, sheets, etc., but others had major interests in the steel-consuming industries: Stewarts & Lloyds in tube-making for example; Guest, Keen & Nettlefolds in engineering, nuts, bolts and screws; John Brown & Co., Cammell Laird and Furness Withy in shipbuilding; Vickers and Armstrong–Whitworth (combined in

Vickers–Armstrong) in engineering and armaments, as well as shipbuilding. Some of these interrelationships will be referred to in other sections, but this is an appropriate point at which to note the increasing integration of steel-making and tinplate manufacture.

Up to 1914, the tendency had been towards separation: tinplate firms, heavily concentrated in south Wales, were mostly 'pure' tinplate producers—numerous small independent firms, who bought bars from the Siemens open-hearth steel-works in that area, though larger concerns, such as Richard Thomas & Co. and Baldwins, had their own steel-making plant. Britain remained the world's largest tinplate manufacturer and dominated the export trade. During the war, however, the United States surged ahead, while British production and exports were drastically reduced, and although the industry gradually recovered in the post-war years, it was faced with great difficulties, especially in the slump periods.

BRITISH TINPLATE PRODUCTION
AND EXPORTS
(thousand tons)

Year	Production	Exports
1912	848	481
1917	410	190
1920	611	389
1921	327	240
1929	880	605
1931	717	412
1937	958	479
1939	610	338

Source: Minchinton, op. cit., pp. 140, 163.

Nevertheless, during the 1920s the British industry held its own, retaining just under a third of world production and nearly two-thirds of world exports in 1929. The situation changed considerably, however, in the 1930s, when world trade was hit by the slump and protectionist restrictions. The British steel tariff deprived the independent tinplate manufacturers of cheap bar imports and stimulated foreign production and competition, so that the industry was forced to participate in an international cartel; exports never recovered to the volume of 1929 and fell to well below half the world total, while Britain's export lead was increasingly challenged by the United States and Germany. On the other hand, production for the home market greatly increased, especially with the growth of the canning and container industries (see pp. 315–6, 330). Britain therefore remained second only to the United States in world output and well ahead of any other country.

It was only very gradually, however, that the traditional structure of small technologically conservative firms was altered, and the industry lagged considerably behind that of the United States, where the continuous hot-strip mill and cold-reduction process were developed to meet rapidly growing demands from the motor-car and canning industries. In south Wales there was a great deal of surplus and obsolete capacity, which was only slowly reduced as the large firms such as Richard Thomas & Co., Baldwins and the Briton Ferry Steel Company acquired increasing control; in 1937 there were still 34 firms in the industry, though Thomas's alone had 224 out of the 518 mills. These larger firms had their own steelworks, so that the industry became more closely integrated into iron and steel, but full technical integration was not achieved until Thomas's continuous strip mill—the first in Britain—came into production in 1938, with coke-ovens, blast-furnaces, open-hearth steel furnaces, hot-strip mill and cold-reduction plant on the same site. Until then, production was entirely in traditional 'pack-mills', though improvements had been made in mechanical handling, pickling and tinning.

The tinplate and other non-ferrous metal manufactures had, of course, originally been based on domestic ore resources, but, from the late nineteenth century onwards, there was a growing influx of foreign ores or semi-manufactured metals. Mining of tin and copper ores in Cornwall, Devon and other areas, which had collapsed between 1870s and 1914 (see p. 178), declined to almost negligible proportions in the inter-war years. Lead mining, on the other hand, after continuing to decline in the 1920s, experienced a sharp recovery in the early 1930s to nearly 70,000 tons (compared with 25,000 before the First World War), but production fell back to well below 40,000 later in that decade, and comparatively little is now mined in Britain. Imports of copper and lead came to be entirely in semi-manufactured form, ore imports dwindling completely away, but the reverse development occurred with tin and zinc ores and concentrates, which were increasingly processed in this country in a few large smelting and refining plants, by the Consolidated Tin Smelters (1929) at Bootle (Lancashire) and North Ferriby (Yorkshire) and by the Imperial Smelting Corporation (1916) for zinc at Swansea and Avonmouth. Output of non-ferrous metals and manufactures, as we have seen, increased rapidly in the inter-war period (see pp. 227–9), as demand grew from the new motor and electrical manufactures, as well as from the traditional metal-working and building trades.

Aluminium also came increasingly into use, after development of the electrolytic process from the late nineteenth century onwards (see p. 179). It proved very suitable not only for domestic pans, etc., but also in breweries, dairies and chemical plant and in the aircraft, motor, electrical and container industries, where the lightness, strength and durability of its alloys were great advantages. But, although the British Aluminium Company had been established in 1894, production of the metal only grew slowly in this country, from 10,000 to 25,000 metric tons between 1913 and 1939; by the latter date consumption had reached 90,000 tons, imports coming in from cheap hydro-electric producers in Europe and North America, under the control of an international cartel.

Shipbuilding

The shipbuilding industry displayed, in an accentuated form, the same depressing features in the inter-war period as the coal, iron and steel industries, with which it was closely associated. The general depression in such areas as northeastern England and Clydeside, in fact, derived mainly from that in shipbuilding. The industry's problems stemmed firstly from its massive pre-war predominance or over-commitment—it was still building three-fifths of world tonnage in 1913—and from the effects of the war, which, while necessitating a great increase in capacity to replace merchant shipping sunk by enemy submarines and to build more warships, at the same time stimulated other countries, such as the United States and Japan, greatly to develop their shipbuilding industries. Moreover capacity was still further increased in the post-war replacement boom, in which shipbuilding firms, like those in iron and steel, became heavily over-capitalized, with burdensome commitments on debentures and bank loans. By 1920 it was estimated that Britain had a shipbuilding capacity of 3 to 4 million tons (gross), nearly twice the pre-war peak output (1.93 million gross tons) in 1913 and vastly greater than the tonnage launched in any inter-war year. This grossly excess capacity, with its associated over-capitalization, therefore hung like a millstone round the neck of the industry in this period.

UNITED KINGDOM AND WORLD SHIPBUILDING OUTPUT, 1913–38
(gross tonnage launched in thousand tons)

Year	United Kingdom	World	United Kingdom percentage
1909–13 (average)	1,522	2,589	58.7
1920	2,056	5,862	35.1
1923	646	1,643	39.4
1924	1,440	2,248	64.0
1926	640	1,675	38.3
1929	1,523	2,793	54.5
1933	133	489	27.2
1938	1,030	3,034	34.0

Source: L. Jones, *Shipbuilding in Britain* (1957), p. 64.

The statistics of inter-war output show several short- and long-term features. It is clear that the difficulties of the shipbuilding industry were not confined to

Britain—in fact, British experiences fitted into a general pattern, marked both by severe cyclical fluctuations and by long-term decline and stagnation, after the great post-war boom. The short-term fluctuations were related, of course, to the general cyclical swings, always most pronounced in the heavy capital goods industries such as shipbuilding. The depressing long-term situation was also related to wider economic factors, particularly to the inter-war depression of world trade (see pp. 264–5), which resulted in a large amount of shipping being redundant, laid up or scrapped, so that the demand for new ships inevitably declined; at the same time, naval shipbuilding, which had been boosted to over half a million tons (displacement tonnage) by 1918, was greatly reduced, almost to nothing in the early 1920s and below 50,000 in most years thereafter, until the late 1930s, when rearmament brought it above 100,000 tons in 1937. It is noteworthy, however, that, even after the great collapse of the post-war boom, British shipbuilding maintained its position relatively well in the 1920s, with outputs in the best years, 1924 and 1929, about up to the pre-war average, though well below that of 1913, and with the same proportion of world output. Catastrophe came, however, in the huge slump of the early 1930s, with production almost at a standstill, and, despite gradual recovery later in that decade, output never reached the earlier figures, and Britain's share of world output declined to about a third, though she still remained the biggest ship-builder. The number of insured workers in the industry was halved in the inter-war period, from about 350,000 at the height of the post-war boom to 175,000 in 1938, nearly a quarter of whom were unemployed.

During this period, therefore, the shipbuilding areas such as Clydeside, the north-east, Barrow, Merseyside and Belfast were probably the worst hit in the country, with idle or only partially active yards and massive unemployment. Even in the busiest years the industry was barely utilizing half its capacity, while in the slumps, especially in the early 1930s, the proportion of men out of work rose to unprecedented heights, averaging over 60 per cent in 1932–3; at Jarrow, following the closure of Palmer's once-great shipyard, it was as high as 80 per cent. The industry was therefore driven into financial and structural reorganization: in the later 1920s many millions of pounds were written off capital, and efforts were made to consolidate through amalgamation, most notably in the merger of Vickers and Armstrong–Whitworth in Vickers–Armstrong (1928), followed by consolidation of their steel interests and those of Cammell Laird in the English Steel Corporation (see p. 304). By the end of that decade, however, when the great slump started, it became obvious that more drastic collective action would have to be taken in order to eliminate redundant capacity, concentrate production and reduce costs. As in the iron and steel industry, moreover, the Bank of England and large joint-stock banks were compelled to safeguard their interests by providing assistance for such reorganization. With the backing, therefore, of the Bankers' Industrial Development Company, an organization called National Shipbuilders' Security Ltd. was established in 1930, to buy up and dismantle redundant or obsolete yards with loan funds thus provided. Nearly all shipbuilding firms subscribed to its shares, undertaking to pay off the loan with a levy of 1 per cent on sales of new ships. By 1937, yards with an aggregate capacity of about a million tons, belonging to twenty-eight firms, including some famous ones, had been closed down in this way and the industry's total capacity had been reduced to about $2\frac{1}{2}$ million tons (gross)—a drastic but inevitable reduction.

By the later 1930s, with trade revival and rearmament, this run-down was halted, though there was still much surplus capacity and heavy unemployment. The industry recovered very slowly, and its relative position deteriorated. This was partly because of falling home demand, with the decline of the British merchant fleet, which was faced by growing competition from many countries. British mercantile tonnage fell from 18.9 to 17.8 million gross tons between 1914 and 1938, while world tonnage rose from 45.5 to 66.9 million; though the British fleet was still by far the biggest, twice the size of the American, the nearest rival, it had declined from about 42 to 27 per cent of the world total. Moreover, foreign ships were often more up-to-date: British shipowners were relatively slow, for example, in adopting diesel-engined ships—only a quarter of the British fleet used diesel propulsion by 1939—and they similarly lagged in tankers. To some extent British shipping was handicapped by the considerable assistance given by foreign governments to their shipping and shipbuilding industries, in the form of subsidies, loans and tax relief. Some State help was also given in Britain, which indirectly benefited shipbuilders, such as the Shipping (Assistance) Act of 1935, offering tramp owners loans on favourable terms for 'scrap-and-build' schemes, but this was little utilized because of a direct subsidy on freight rates, which discouraged scrapping, though it stimulated new building. Similar Government aid was also given to the building of two large new liners, the *Queen Mary* and *Queen Elizabeth*, on condition of the merging of the Cunard and White Star lines. But much more help was given by various foreign governments to their national maritime industries. This also contributed to the decline in export orders. The tonnage of British ships built for foreign registration, which had averaged 340,000 tons annually in 1909–13, rose to two or three times that figure in the post-war boom and, though declining sharply thereafter, recovered in the later 1920s to nearly twice the pre-war figure in 1930; but collapse then followed, export orders almost disappearing in the early 1930s and not rising above 200,000 tons again till 1938.

The deterioration in the 1930s cannot, however, be entirely attributed to the state of world trade and foreign protection, but was also caused by inherent weaknesses in the British shipbuilding industry, which has been criticized for its relative inefficiency in comparison with more modern foreign yards, for its cramped sites and outdated equipment, and for its slowness in changing from riveting to electric welding, from coal to oil fuel, from reciprocating engines to turbines and from steam to diesel or motor-ships (though a good deal of the blame must be attached to the shipping companies). Certainly the industry's productivity increased at a rate that was slower than average in the inter-war years (see p. 278). No doubt the times were unfavourable to capital investment and modernization, but shipbuilding firms appear to have been conservatively lethargic, both technologically and commercially, compared with more vigorous foreign competitors. During this period, in fact, despite the stagnation of international trade, a technological revolution was occurring in shipbuilding—steam turbines were more rapidly introduced, while the proportion of world tonnage using oil for raising steam and in diesel engines rose from 3.4 to 54 per cent between 1914 and 1939—and in this new age Britain did not have the established leadership and advantages she had enjoyed in the earlier period of coal and reciprocating steam engines; indeed, her massive investment in older equipment and skills had a strong retarding influence.

The industry was dominated by the handful of large firms that had grown by amalgamation before and after the First World War—John Brown & Co., the Lithgow Group, Harland & Wolff, Swan Hunter & Wigham Richardson, Cammell Laird and Vickers–Armstrong—controlling numerous yards, heavily involved in steel and engineering and employing many thousands of workers. The 1935 Census of Production showed that, although there were hundreds of small shipbuilding and repairing establishments, nearly three-fifths of the labour force in the private shipbuilding industry were in 34 large shipyards, each employing 500 or more workers. The growth in the size of ships, especially passenger and cargo liners, tankers and warships, led to heavy concentration in the large yards of the big companies, while the numerous smaller shipbuilders were engaged in production of tramp ships, coasters, trawlers, tugs, boats and barges. In general, however, there was inadequate specialization and concentration of production on particular types of ships, which could have achieved economies of scale. Strong traditional ties between the bigger shipowners and shipbuilders seem to have encouraged conservative complacency, though by the late 1930s some shipping firms were placing more orders abroad, where costs were lower. In exports of new ships, in fact, Germany far surpassed Britain in those years and Japan was also rapidly increasing her output, while Britain's imports were almost as much as her exports. It was inevitable, especially when other countries were pursuing such autarchical policies, that Britain should lose the overwhelming shipbuilding predominance she formerly had, but her competitive weakness in export markets was indicative of financial, structural and technological deficiencies, to which higher labour costs and trade-union demarcations contributed.

Engineering and small metal manufactures

Many branches of engineering, especially the traditional heavy engineering of the nineteenth century, were among the depressed basic industries of the inter-war years, experiencing severe contractions of output and employment in the slumps and generally declining over the whole period. With the development of new forms of power and transport and the decline of railways, shipbuilding and textiles, there was a falling demand for reciprocating steam engines (industrial, locomotive and marine) and for textile machinery. At the same time, however, the 'second industrial revolution' led to the rapid growth of new sectors, concerned with turbines and diesels, electrical engineering and motor and aircraft manufactures, while the continued spread of mechanization provided a general stimulus to engineering. Employment in the established branches of mechanical engineering declined—as a result of labour-saving technological advances, as well as of depression in the old sectors—but production showed a moderate increase, and productivity rose at well above the average industrial rate, while in electrical engineering and in the motor and aircraft industries both employment and output grew rapidly (see pp. 267–9 for the figures).

Many old and famous firms still survived, specializing in their various fields—Hick, Hargreaves in steam engines, for example; Galloways and Babcock & Wilcox in boiler-making; the North British Locomotive Company, Nasmyth Wilson and Beyer Peacock in railway locomotives; Dobson & Barlow, Mather & Platt and Platt Bros. in textile machine-making; Armstrong–Whitworth in general engineering, armaments, etc.; Marshalls, Ruston & Hornsby and Ransomes in agricultural engines and machinery—but those who stayed in steam tended to find themselves in increasing difficulties, while the more enterprising, who switched to diesel or electric engines, or to machinery for the new and expanding industries, were able to find a new lease of life. Such transitions, however, presented great difficulties to firms located in the older centres of industry, catering for declining trades and with specialized technical expertise, equipment and labour. The difficulties of diversifying are strikingly illustrated by the case of Vickers, who had already by 1914 spread their interests not only from steel into armaments, engineering and shipbuilding but also into motor manufacture (by acquiring the Wolseley Company) and who further expanded during the war and post-war boom into aircraft and submarines and also into railway carriages and wagons and electrical engineering (Metropolitan–Vickers, see p. 358). During the later 1920s, however, Vickers were forced to dispose of their new acquisition in automobiles, electrical engineering, etc., and to consolidate their interests in the older fields by merger with competitors such as Armstrong–Whitworth and Cammell Laird; though they thus acquired control of Vickers–Armstrong, Metropolitan–Cammell and the English Steel Corporation (see p. 304), their difficulties in these older industries, as well as the technical and managerial problems of diversification, forced them to abandon their new ventures. It is not surprising, therefore, that many lesser firms failed to make such a transition.

Despite the widening range of new technology, in fact, mechanical engineering of the more traditional kind still formed the biggest section of the industry, classified in the Ministry of Labour's statistics as 'General Engineering', with 614,000 insured workers in 1937, to which we can add marine engineering (54,000), the building of railway coaches and wagons (51,000) and constructional engineering (40,000), as well as numerous other iron-founding and metal-working trades.* Electrical engineering, together with electrical manufactures and contracting (totalling 334,000), vehicles, cycles and aircraft (352,000), however, were now major growth industries and will, therefore, be considered separately in later sections; employment in these industries had approximately doubled since 1923, compared with stagnant or declining numbers and heavy unemployment in the older branches of engineering, though the latter were still of major importance at the end of this period. The newer branches of engineering, however, had more automatic or semi-automatic machinery, enabling them to make more use of semi-skilled and female labour, and they did not generally develop in the old heavy engineering areas.

Mechanical engineering was really an agglomeration of numerous separate trades, many of them highly specialized. In addition to the specializations in prime movers and boilers for industries, railways and ships and also in machine-tools, there were many different branches of machine-making for particular industries, as well as specialized manufacturers of pumps, cranes, lifts, weighing machines, etc. There was also wide variety in the sizes of firms in this industry, ranging from small repair shops to giant companies with interests in many branches of engineering, as well as in iron and steel, shipbuilding and other trades. The 1935 Census of Production showed that nearly three-fifths of the workers in mechanical engineering were employed by firms with 500 or more employees, mostly in large establishments, but the concentration ratio was low, as there were between two and three hundred firms of that size, together with several thousand smaller ones; the three largest concerns, together employing nearly 36,000, accounted for only 8 per cent of the total labour force, according to Leak and Maizels. Some branches of engineering, however, notably the manufacture of sewing and boot- and shoe-making machines, were dominated by one or two large firms, such as Singers and the British United Shoe Machinery Company, both American subsidiaries.

These various branches of engineering were of increasing importance in

---

* The figures are of all insured workers, aged 16 to 64, including unemployed, in Great Britain and Northern Ireland, from E. Allen, 'The Engineering Trades', British Association, *Britain in Recovery* (1938).

export trade, together with motor vehicles and electrical manufactures, while textiles and coal declined (see p. 282). But though the pattern of Britain's exports was thus being changed, with the changing structure of world trade, her share in exports of general engineering products declined markedly between 1913 and 1937, and Tyszynski'has attributed this mainly to competitive weakness, especially in the expanding sectors. Britain had already lost the lead in this field to Germany by 1913 and was also overtaken by the United States in the inter-war period, but though her share of world trade in these products fell from 28.1 to 20.8 per cent between 1913 and 1929, it improved somewhat in the 1930s to 21.5 per cent in 1937; in absolute terms, however, exports were reduced by the general trade depression, only declining less than those of other countries. There was consequently a swing towards production for the home market, especially after introduction of tariff protection in 1932. The situation was worst for those sectors such as textile machine-making and locomotive manufacture that had been heavily dependent on exports and for which domestic demand was declining; those producing machinery for the expanding domestic industries, on the other hand, did relatively well.

EXPORTS OF INDUSTRIAL EQUIPMENT, 1913–37
(£ millions)

Country	1913	1929	1937
United Kingdom	30.4	46.6	42.0
Germany	40.5	64.7	58.5
United States	22.7	73.8	59.9
World	108.3	223.8	195.6

Source: Tyszynski, op. cit., Tables II, III and IV. Excluding railway rolling stock, electrical engineering, motor vehicles, etc. and agricultural equipment.

The most crucial sector of engineering was the machine-tool trade, producing equipment for all machine-making industries, but the British performance was relatively weak in this field. Output of machine-tools, which had totalled 78,000 tons (£2.9 million) in 1907, was considerably boosted by the war but dropped heavily in the post-war slump and remained far below the pre-war volume until the late 1930s, when it rose sharply to 87,000 tons (£14 million) in 1938; over the whole period its growth was very modest and was outclassed by that of Germany and the United States. This was particularly evident in the export field: even before the war Britain's machine-tool exports were only a quarter of Germany's and less than a third of those of the United States, and throughout most of this period her position deteriorated. In most years Germany and the United States held three-quarters or more of the international market, while Britain found difficulty in retaining one-tenth; Germany alone exported more machine-tools than Britain actually produced, and in the late 1930s imports into Britain considerably exceeded exports, despite protective tariffs.

There were considerable technical improvements in machine-tools during these years, such as the use of tungsten-carbide in high-speed cutting tools, electric and hydraulic drives and simplifications in design and operation, but the small scale of most British machine-tool firms precluded standardized mass-production and intensive marketing methods, so that the industry remained competitively weak, though there were some large up-to-date vigorous firms such as Herbert's. In 1935, over half the establishments in the industry employed less than 100 workers each—over a third less than 50—and only ten had more than 500, while the three largest firms (together employing less than 6,000) accounted for little more than a quarter of the total labour force. The small firms tended to carry on with traditional production methods and products, though even in America machine-tool firms were not generally very large. The industry was affected, of course, by falling home demand in the old declining industries, but seems to have been lethargic in meeting demand from the new industries and export markets. Most special-purpose machine-tools for the motor industry, for example, were imported from the United States.

The increasing adoption of mechanical methods of production in numerous small metal manufactures brought what had formerly been handicrafts within the sphere of engineering, using power-driven machinery for hammering, stamping, pressing, cutting, drilling and grinding operations. In the Birmingham and Black Country trades, for example, though small workshops still survived in the inter-war period, the production of all kinds of iron and brass hardware, hollow-ware and plated manufactures was now concentrated mainly in factories; and similarly in the Sheffield cutlery, hand-tool, file and saw trades, mechanized factory production was increasingly displacing traditional handicraft methods and small masters, though the latter were still numerous and most firms were small or medium. There was a widening market for such products with the expansion of the building and household goods trades, including also gutters, pipes, stoves, grates and other general iron-founding products, while the growth of the motor industry created new demands for numerous metal accessories. Watch- and clock-making, on the other hand, which had revived during the war on a mass-production basis, tended to decline afterwards in face of foreign competition, though some firms such as Smith's expanded. The general growth is shown in the rising output indices of miscellaneous metal manufactures and also of non-ferrous metals (see pp. 276–8), including aluminium, which was tending to displace tinplate and enamelled ware in domestic utensils. Tinplate, on the other hand, was in increasing demand for the canning and container industries; the Metal Box Company, by a succession of mergers, became the largest producer of tinplate containers in Europe, mass-producing cans, tins and boxes for a great variety of trades.

Employment in these various metal-working manufactures amounted to well over half a million by the late 1930s, but had grown little during this period because of increasing mechanization (see p. 276). There were now scores of firms employing over 500 workers, but in most trades they accounted for only a fifth to a third of total employment, the great majority of works and firms being small or medium-sized. Nevertheless, competition and surplus capacity tended to bring about mergers, such as Allied Ironfounders (1929) and Federated Foundries (1935) in the light foundry trade, including domestic iron pipes and fittings.

18

Traditional Consumer Goods Trades

During this period, as we have seen, there was a considerable rise in average real incomes, which stimulated increased expenditure on consumer goods. This was reflected, for example, in the small metal manufactures referred to in the previous chapter, including cutlery, kitchen utensils, nickel- and silver-plated wares, clocks and watches, sewing machines and many other commodities, now increasingly being mass-produced in factories. In this chapter we shall look at other traditional consumer goods trades—textiles, clothing, boot-and-shoe, food, drink, tobacco, printing, building and allied trades—that were still of basic importance and employing large numbers of people. Though some of these, notably textiles, declined, this was primarily caused by collapse of exports, while most of the others, catering predominantly for the home market, experienced substantial growth and prosperity. Consumption of food and clothing was rising considerably, while the great building boom was associated with increasing demands for floor coverings, furniture and other household goods.

Textiles

Textiles, for centuries the great staple of Britain's manufactures and exports, though declining in relative importance before the First World War, had still continued to grow, maintaining their predominance in overseas trade. During and after the war, however, they experienced the trauma of absolute contraction: employment, production and exports all fell sharply, so that their relative decline became more striking (see pp. 276–82). The main cause of this deterioration was the collapse of the export trade, especially in cottons, as a result of the growth of foreign industry, protection and competition and the changing structure of world trade. Nevertheless, textiles were still of major importance at the end of this period: in 1938 they had well over a million insured workers—more than the combined total in vehicle and electrical manufactures—and they contributed nearly a quarter of the total value of domestic exports. While the major industries of cotton and wool declined, together with linen, jute and lace, others such as carpets, hosiery, knitwear and rayon grew substantially, mainly on the basis of a thriving home market. (Rayon is included in Chapter 19, with the new industries, but its importance in the changing pattern of textile manufactures should be remembered.)

Until 1914, the British cotton industry, the 'leading sector' in the 'first industrial revolution', had retained an extraordinary world predominance, especially in exports (see p. 204), but in the inter-war years it collapsed dramatically, and Lancashire came 'under the hammer'. The figures of raw cotton consumption output and exports starkly demonstrate this rapid decline, showing that it was entirely attributable to the huge fall in exports, mostly of cloth; the home market, in fact, gradually expanded (imports remaining negligible). Cotton exports were reduced from over four-fifths to much less than half of total production, and from a quarter to little more than a tenth of total domestic exports (see p. 282), while the number of workers in spinning, doubling and weaving fell from 622,000 in 1912 to 393,000 in 1938, many of whom were unemployed. (The 1938 figure is for insured employees, aged 16 to 64.) Over two-fifths of insured workers in the industry were out-of-work in 1931 and about a quarter during most of the rest of that decade.

UNITED KINGDOM COTTON INDUSTRY, 1912–38

Year	Raw cotton consumption (million lb)	Yarn (million lb)		Piece goods (million sq. yds)	
		Production	Exports	Production	Exports
1912	2,142	1,983	244	8,050	6,913
1924	1,369	1,395	163	6,074	4,444
1930	1,272	1,047	137	3,500	2,472
1937	1,431	1,377	159	4,288	2,000
1938	1,109	1,070	123	3,126	1,494

Source: R. Robson, *The Cotton Industry in Britain* (1957), Appendix; Board of Trade Working Party Report, *Cotton* (1946). The 1912 figures for piece goods are in linear yards, but the difference is negligible. The figures for the 1930s include small quantities of spun rayon and mixtures.

No doubt the causes of this collapse can be traced back long before 1914, to the industry's massive over-commitment, based on early technological supremacy. As other European countries and the United States eventually developed their own industries, British exports had still been able to expand into other parts of the world, especially in India and other relatively undeveloped countries; despite the early growth of cotton manufactures in India and Japan, expansion had continued right up to 1914, though at a slower rate and with signs of technological stagnation. The war, however, hit the industry severely, causing manpower shortages, curtailment of raw cotton imports and loss of export markets, stimulating production in other countries; piece goods exports fell from 7,075 million linear yards in 1913 to 3,523 million in 1919. And after the brief post-war boom, in which cotton, like other industries, over-expanded in hopes of returning to the pre-1914 'normal', the industry was left with a great burden of excess capacity and over-capitalization, in a situation of gradually shrinking overseas trade. Exports were halved again in the slump of the early 1930s and, though recovering slightly thereafter, fell to even lower levels in 1938–9.

The greatest single loss was that of the Indian market, mainly as a result of the rapid growth of the Indian home industry, but also through Japanese competition. In the years 1909–13, Indian imports had averaged 2,741 million linear yards, almost all from the United Kingdom, but by 1938 they had fallen to 724 million square yards, of which little more than a third came from this country and most of the rest from Japan; British exports to India were only a tenth of the pre-war figure. In other eastern markets and elsewhere, Lancashire also suffered heavy losses. The general situation was, in fact, extremely unfavourable: while world production was increasing, world trade in cotton goods had by the late 1930s declined to two-thirds of the pre-war level, as countries expanded their own manufactures and restricted imports by protective measures. But not merely did the British industry's proportion of world production (as measured by raw cotton consumption) fall from one-fifth to less than one-tenth; its share in the shrinking volume of world trade also sharply declined, from nearly three-fifths to little more than a quarter, as a result of strong foreign competition, especially from the Japanese. In fact, while Britain's cotton exports were declining catastrophically, Japan's were rapidly increasing, so that by the late 1930s they accounted for two-fifths of the world volume.

To a very large extent, Lancashire's decline was inevitable, as other countries expanded and protected their domestic industries and as competition for diminishing world trade grew fiercer, but it was also caused partly by internal deficiencies. Lancashire blamed its losses mainly on competition by cheap Eastern labour, but the exports of other European countries did not fall to anything like the same extent, and there is evidence that productivity in the British industry was rising very slowly by comparison with Japan and the United States. Of course, it had to bear a greater burden of excess capacity, so that, despite heavy scrapping, plant was constantly under-utilized and short-time working frequent, causing higher unit costs, while chronic over-capitalization made it difficult to reorganize and re-equip the industry, especially in such depressed conditions. There was therefore little technological change, much antiquated machinery still remaining in use. The number of mule spindles was drastically reduced, from 45 million in 1912 to 27 million in 1937 but still considerably outnumbered ring spindles, which remained at between 10 and 11 million. The number of traditional power-looms was also reduced from 786 to 505 thousand, but there were still only 16 thousand automatics in 1937. As before 1914, Lancashire tended to concentrate on production of finer yarns and fabrics, which fared better than the coarser sections, but competition was also increasing in better-quality goods.

After the return to protection, the industry secured tariff preferences in the Dominions, while quota restrictions were placed on colonial imports and trade agreements were negotiated with a number of European and South American countries, but, though these somewhat checked the decline of exports, they did comparatively little to compensate for the huge losses elsewhere. There was consequently greater concentration on the home market, with expansion of the clothing trades; spinning firms also found growing markets for their yarns in other manufactures, such as hosiery and tyres, while weaving firms turned increasingly to rayon and mixed fabrics. But the only long-term solution to the industry's problems was a massive reduction in capacity, by scrapping redundant and obsolete plant and by concentration of production in the most efficient mills. As in other industries, efforts were made to achieve this by collective organization, but the structure of the cotton industry, with its multiplicity of firms—some 3,000 in 1924—and its sharply demarcated sections of spinning, weaving, finishing and merchanting, made reorganization extremely difficult. Moreover, the usual cartel methods of output and price controls would not be effective in an industry suffering from loss of export markets: only by increased efficiency might foreign competition be met.

The most notable schemes were those introduced in the spinning section. A Cotton Yarn Association organized in 1927 in the depressed American (coarse- and medium-spinning) section, to fix minimum prices and output quotas, soon broke down, but was followed in 1929 by the Lancashire Cotton Corporation, established in that same section with the assistance of the Bank of England and the Bankers' Industrial Development Corporation. This was a massive merger, embracing eventually nearly a hundred firms and acquiring some 9 million spindles, and despite serious managerial and financial difficulties it managed to scrap half this capacity by 1939 while modernizing the remainder. In the smaller Egyptian or fine-spinning section, the banks set up the Combined Egyptian Mills Ltd., also in 1929, which bought up 3 million spindles. Despite these voluntary schemes, however, the spinning section continued to be depressed by surplus capacity, so in 1936 the Government finally intervened with the Cotton Industry Reorganization Act, based, like the shipbuilders' rationalization scheme, on the principle of a 'reconstruction levy'. It set up a Spindle Board, with powers to buy up redundant spindles—estimated at 13½ million—by means of loan funds, to be financed by an annual levy. By 1939 it was about half-way to its target, when a more comprehensive scheme, applying to all sections, was introduced by another Act, which set up a Cotton Industry Board, for regulating output and prices as well as for reducing capacity, but the outbreak of war prevented its functioning.

Meanwhile, in the weaving section, with its more numerous and smaller firms, unorganized market forces were bringing about a considerable reduction in the number of looms (see p. 320), though, as in spinning, there was still much redundant plant at the end of this period. In the finishing sections, there were already strong combines, such as the Bleachers', Dyers', and Calico Printers' Associations (see p. 250), which were able to take more effective action in closing works, scrapping machinery, concentrating production and modernizing plant, though not without serious difficulties; the Calico Printers' Association, for example, paid no ordinary dividend throughout the 1930s, while many small firms went out of business; price controls broke down, and competition was fierce. In the textile-finishing trades generally, including all bleaching, dyeing and printing, the number of insured workers fell from 121,000 in 1924 to 94,000 in 1939.

The wool textile industry suffered much less than cotton did during this period, mainly because it was far less dependent on exports. In the pre-war period, the export trade, especially in worsteds, had been declining (see p. 207) and accounted for less than half the total production. Consequently, though exports were further reduced during the war and inter-war years, the decline was nothing like so catastrophic as that in cotton. Moreover, though similarly faced with a declining volume of world trade, as other countries developed and protected their own industries, British woollen and worsted manufacturers succeeded in increasing their proportion, by switching to new markets and to lighter higher-quality goods; with 30 per cent of the international trade in yarns and nearly 50 per cent in tissues in the late 1930s, Britain was still the largest exporter of wool products. Quantitatively, however, exports had declined considerably and were now only about a quarter of total output.

THE BRITISH WOOL TEXTILE INDUSTRY, 1912–37

Year	Tops (million lb)		Yarns (million lb)		Tissues (million sq. yds)	
	Production	Exports	Production	Exports	Production	Exports
1912	304.5	41.9	565.1	87.0	572.5	225.9
1924	285.5	41.1	554.5	65.9	440.0	221.5
1930	224.5	28.8	385.9	49.6	324.1	113.7
1935	307.5	55.9	543.0	50.7	412.9	109.9
1937	278.5	40.2	565.8	41.4	445.5	122.8

Source: Allen, op. cit., pp. 243–4. The export figures for 1912 are the average of 1909–13.

Both woollens and worsteds suffered in this decline; though exports of worsted tops remained buoyant, those of woollen and worsted yarns and tissues fell to half their pre-war volume. But total production did not decline to the same extent, rising substantially in the recovery of the 1930s. This revival was based mainly on the home market, in which protective tariffs soon reduced imports of tissues from 50 to 7 million square yards, and in which there was a growing demand from the clothing, hosiery, knitwear, furnishing fabric, carpet and rug trades; by the late 1930s nearly half the yarn output was going to the hosiery industry or to hand knitters, while rayon and other materials were being used in cloth manufactures. Output of tops and yarns thus recovered to pre-war volumes, though tissues were still at a considerably lower level, as a result of the decline in exports; all sections, however, experienced a sharp fall in 1938. By that date the number of insured workers in the industry had fallen from 269,000 in 1923 to 216,000; a third of the labour force was unemployed in 1931 and the percentage only fell slowly thereafter.

The industry was still located mainly in the West Riding, though the West of England, the Scottish Border counties, the Hebrides and other areas still retained their distinctive products. Little change occurred in organization; there were a few large amalgamations, but hundreds of small and medium firms still existed, vertically integrated for the most part in woollens, horizontally specialized in worsteds, still with much the same localized varieties. In 1935 over half the establishments employed less than 100 persons, and over half the labour force was in those with fewer than 300. Combines had earlier developed in the combing and dyeing trades (see p. 250), in which there were fewer and bigger factories, but competition remained intense in other branches. There was little technological improvement, however, much old machinery remaining in use and productivity rising slowly; in this respect the industry does not appear to have done any better than cotton. Suffering less from declining exports, however, the West Riding was not forced into reorganization and scrapping like neighbouring Lancashire, though it had to be adaptable to changing markets and fashions.

The carpet industry, using mostly woollen and worsted yarns, together with jute, cotton and other materials, expanded considerably during this period, mainly on the basis of rising home demand. Output nearly doubled between 1924 and 1937, from 21.6 to 40.6 million square yards, though exports stagnated at 6 to 7 million (dropping to half that figure in the slump of the early 1930s); declining from about a third to a sixth of total production, they went mainly to the Empire, while imports were reduced far below exports by protection. The labour force grew from about 25,000 to 30,000 over the same years, with substantial increases in productivity. The industry was located mainly in Kidderminster and the West Country (for example Axminster and Wilton), the West Riding and neighbouring Lancashire and west-central Scotland. Carpet firms were mostly fairly large, averaging well over 500 workers, and in 1939 over 60 per cent of the labour force were in ten companies, each with 1,000 or more employees; but there were no very powerful combines.

Flax, hemp and jute manufactures were, from the late nineteenth century onwards, already feeling the effects of foreign competition and tending to stagnate (see pp. 209–11). During the war and post-war period, stagnation turned to decline and depression, as a result of falling exports. Exports of linen piece goods, for example, fell from an average of 205 million yards in 1910–13 to 75 million in 1936–8, while those of yarns likewise declined; most of this fall occurred during the war and the industry never recovered its pre-war trade. Exports of jute manufactures (sacking, cloth, carpets, etc.) similarly collapsed, under competition mainly from Calcutta mills, at the source of the raw material and employing much cheaper labour; whereas in the late nineteenth century the industry was exporting about 75 per cent of its output, the proportion never reached 20 per cent in the 1930s and by 1938 there was an import surplus. Both these industries were driven increasingly to dependence on the home market and to production of higher-quality goods; tariff protection encouraged this tendency in the 1930s, though it provided no safeguard for the jute industry against Indian imports. Production did not fall to the same extent as exports, but labour forces were reduced, and there was heavy unemployment in Belfast and Dundee, where these industries were strongly localized: the number of insured workers in the linen industry fell from 83,000 in 1924 to 74,000 in 1938, in the jute industry from 41,000 to 28,000, but in hemp, rope and twine manufactures there was only a slight fall, from 21,000 to 19,000.

The lace trade presents much the same depressing features in this period. After being hit by the war, the industry never recovered its pre-war level of exports, which had been £4.1 million, or nearly two-thirds of total output, in 1912, but declined to an annual average of only £1.7 million, or about a third of total production, in 1936–8. As in other textile trades, this decline was caused largely by the growth of foreign industries, tariffs and competition, but changes in fashion—in women's dress, curtains and other furnishings—also reduced the demand for lace. The industry was similarly driven into increased dependence on the protected home market in the 1930s, and on trade with the Dominions, helped by preferential duties. Many firms failed in the slump, and there was a great deal of redundant capacity. Employment in the industry had fallen to about 14,000 by 1939, little more than a third of the pre-war figure. There was some increase in output per operative, but no very striking change in either technology or organization. A great deal of old machinery was still used—the traditional bobbin-net, leavers and other machines—producing plain and patterned goods. Production was still predominantly small-scale (two-thirds of the establishments in 1935 had less than fifty workers), because of the great variety of specialized products and designs in this fickle fashion trade, though plain net was mostly mass-produced by a few large concerns; there were also numerous specialized finishing and merchanting firms, as in other textiles. The industry remained highly localized in the Nottingham district, though with some dispersion into mid-west Scotland and with Heathcoat's famous firm still at Tiverton. The greater part of output was still of cotton goods, but silk also continued to be used, while artificial silk or rayon was becoming increasingly important.

The hosiery and knitwear industry, also located mainly in the east midlands and now almost entirely in factories instead of framework-knitters' cottages, was relatively prosperous during this period. It was much less dependent than other textile trades on foreign markets and benefited from the increasing home consumption of its products, resulting partly from the general rise in real incomes and partly from changes in fashion. There was a greatly increased demand for women's silk and rayon hose, for men's woollen socks, for cotton and rayon underwear, sports shirts, etc., for woollen outerwear (jumpers, cardigans and pullovers) and for gloves and knitted fabrics generally. In 1935 about half the production was of wool, but that of cotton, silk and rayon was increasing more rapidly, especially for underwear and stockings—a reversal of the pre-war trend. Increasing output was reflected in the growth in the number of insured workers from 93,000 in 1924 to 121,000 in 1939 (together with about 13,000 boys and girls aged 14 to 15 and an uncertain number of domestic out-workers, probably numbering several thousand); over four-fifths of this labour force were females. There were no fundamental technical changes in the industry but numerous minor improvements were introduced, such as the interlock process (particularly important for underwear manufacture), more automatic machinery (requiring less skilled labour) and faster knitting, together with high-speed sewing machines for making-up, electric rotary cutters for cutting-out, and machine pressing and calendering, as well as improvements in dyeing. Most of the more complicated machines, however, such as those for making fully-fashioned goods, were imported from Germany and the United States.

Leicester, rather than Nottingham or Derby, was now the main centre of the industry, but factories were increasingly set up in small towns and villages in those counties, where plenty of cheaper semi-skilled female labour was available (for example wives and daughters of men employed in mining or boot- and shoe-making). For the same reason, factories were also established in Lancashire and surrounding areas, employing redundant female cotton workers, and the industry also spread into the Greater London areas, drawn by the huge metropolitan market; Hawick and other Scottish centres also remained significant, especially in woollen goods. As in the lace trade, small establishments and firms abounded, since the initial capital requirements were very modest, while the diversity and specialization of products and changing fashions were unfavourable to large-scale standardized manufacture, except in plain goods. Of the aggregate number of establishments in 1935 (including those employing 10 or less), three-fifths employed fewer than 50 persons, though they only produced a tenth of total output; over half the labour force was in establishments with less than 300. On the other hand, there were a few factories with over 1,000 workers and a handful of large firms each employed several thousand. The larger firms tended increasingly to supply branded (trade-marked) and advertised goods direct to retailers, especially to chain and department stores, while the smaller firms were still dependent on wholesalers. Though the industry is usually classified with the textile trades, it may also be regarded as part of the clothing industry, since the greater part of its output is of finished goods; in addition to supplying knitted fabrics to the light clothing trades, most hosiery firms had their own making-up and finishing departments, though dyeing was mostly a separate specialized trade.

Even before the First World War the hosiery industry had experienced strong foreign competition—imports exceeding exports—and in the inter-war years it shared, though to a lesser degree, in the export difficulties of textiles generally. In 1924 exports accounted for about 15 per cent of total production, but by the late 1930s they had fallen to less than 7 per cent; in value they fell from over £12 million to about £2½ million, the most striking decline being in woollen goods, especially stockings, the main export. On the other hand, tariffs protected the home market from 1932 onwards, so that imports, especially of cotton goods, were sharply reduced; in the late 1930s they averaged £2½ million annually, mainly of silk and rayon stockings. By that time over nine-tenths of the expanding home market was held by British products. There was a good deal of surplus capacity and obsolete machinery in the industry, while unemployment averaged 6 to 8 per cent even in the good years and rose to about 20 per cent in 1931, but the situation was nowhere near as bad as in other textiles, so despite talk of reor-ganization, nothing was done; amalgamations were few and firms remained highly individualistic, though participating in trade associations.

Clothing and footwear

We have already noted that the hosiery and knitwear trades, traditionally classified with textiles, were considerably extending the range of their products, in both underwear and outerwear, as well as in the new rayon or artificial silk stockings, and were thus becoming more like a section of the clothing trades. The latter, however, did not experience such vigorous growth in this period. Together with textiles, they were in general badly hit by the war: the total number of people in the clothing trades (including boot-and-shoe manufactures), according to the Census figures, fell from 1,257,000 in 1911 to 917,000 in 1921, while Lomax's index shows production in the industry declining from 116.8 in 1913 to 70.9 in 1918 (1924 = 100). Recovery was only slow and gradual in the inter-war years. The production index rose very steadily, however, unaffected by the slump of the early 1920s and only falling slightly in that of the early 1930s, so that by 1937 it had reached 131.0, though dropping back in 1938 (see p. 277). Compared with pre-war, therefore, the overall rise in output was very modest, but there had been a substantial recovery from the low war-time level. Employment, on the other hand, did not recover, but gradually declined to 814,000 in 1938 (see p. 276), and though the clothing trades were not so badly affected by economic depression as the heavy industries or textiles, there was a persistent pool of unemployment; in tailoring, for example, it averaged about 10 per cent in the 1920s, rising to 18 per cent in the early 1930s and still averaging 14 per cent in the latter half of that decade.

This industry, of course, like the building trades, tended to employ a good deal of casual seasonal labour, though these were mostly women, many still working at home, so there was always a reserve of such labour. At the same time, however, the steady decline in employment, in contrast with rising production, was caused by more rapid changes in technology and organization, such as had been occurring before the war, with increasing use of power-driven cutting, sewing and other machines in factories, producing not only ready-made goods (suits, costumes, dresses, shirts, etc.) but also made-to-measure (wholesale bespoke) clothing, distributed through multiple retail shops along lines developed by firms such as Hepworth's, Burton's and Price's (the 'Fifty-Shilling Tailors'), all of Leeds. Ready-made factory clothing was also increasingly supplied direct to large department and chain stores, such as Lewis's and Marks & Spencer's, though women's clothing was still sold largely through small retail shops. Traditional retail bespoke tailoring, or hand tailoring, still survived for more expensive suits, but was rapidly being overwhelmed by cheaper factory goods, as these were steadily improved in manufacture, quality and style, under the stimulus of rising consumer expenditure.

By 1939 Burton's were employing 10,000 workers in Leeds and a further 1,500 in Lancashire, but there were still large numbers of small workshops and out-workers in London, Leeds and Manchester, the main centres of the industry. In 1935 there were nearly 20,000 firms employing not more than 10 persons in tailoring, dress-making, millinery, etc., while of the 5,000 or so establishments with more than 10, well over three-fifths had less than 50; altogether these numerous small firms employed over a third of all workers in the industry, while the 78 large establishments employing 500 or more persons accounted for only a fifth. The few large clothing firms employing thousands of workers were not only vastly outnumbered by the small fry, but employed only a small proportion of the total labour force.

A similar situation existed in the hat-making and millinery trades, centred mainly in the Stockport–Denton distict in the north and in Luton and London in the south. The making of men's felt hats in the former area was now mostly mechanized, but, although there were a few large factories, most were small, while in the ladies' hat trade in the south, and especially in the millinery trade, still largely unmechanized, small units were general, and domestic production still survived.

Production of clothing was predominantly for the home market. Exports, which had been increasing before the war, stagnated in the 1920s, after a brief post-war boom, and then fell in the 1930s to a level well below that of the pre-war years, averaging less than £9 million annually in 1936–8.

Employment and production in the boot-and-shoe industry followed much the same course as in the clothing trades. While production gradually rose after the war-time slump, employment tended to fall, as productivity was increased by further mechanization. The number of insured workers in the industry declined from 142,000 in 1924 to 135,000 in 1939, while the proportion of female labour increased. Of the 1939 total, it was estimated that some 28,000 were employed in repairing, mostly in thousands of small cobblers' shops. Even in manufacturing establishments, the bulk of production remained in the hands of small and medium firms, between which there was strong competition: in 1935, there were nearly 1,800 such establishments, of which over half employed no more than 10 persons, while there were only 45, or less than 3 per cent, with 500 or more workers, though these accounted in aggregate for nearly a third of total employment. Most of the machinery was leased from the American-controlled British United Shoe Machinery Company, so that it was fairly easy for small firms to set up, and the optimum size of firm in this industry was not very large; though numerous specialized machines had been introduced for the highly subdivided processes, they had to be worked in balanced teams, while varied sizes and patterns and changing fashions tended to preclude long production runs.

The industry remained concentrated mainly in Northamptonshire and Leicestershire, which together accounted for over half the total output, the former specializing in men's and the latter in ladies' footwear. Lesser centres still existed in London, Norwich, Bristol, Stafford, Leeds and other areas, while the Rossendale district of Lancashire rapidly developed a trade in slippers and cheap shoes; as in the hosiery manufactures, boot and shoe factories tended increasingly to be set up in the small towns and rural areas of the east midlands, where cheaper labour could be employed on semi-automatic machines and where rates were also lower. Many of the larger manufacturers, as we have previously seen, had set up their own distributing chains of retail shops; others, specializing in branded footwear, sold direct to retailers, both multiple and individual, while smaller firms still supplied goods mostly to wholesalers. As in the clothing trades, production was increasingly concentrated on the home market; exports, which in 1924 totalled nearly a million pairs, or about 14 per cent of production, fell to only a third of that figure, or little more than 3 per cent of production, by 1939; whereas imports, which had been only a fifth of exports at the former date, were rising towards the same level by the late 1930s, mainly in women's shoes.

Leather still remained the basic material for boots and shoes, but rubber soles were increasingly introduced, while for special products such as wellingtons, plimsolls, sports shoes and industrial footwear, rubber was more extensively used by firms such as Dunlop and Pirelli. Just before and during the Second World War, moreover, experiments were being made not only with synthetic rubbers but also with new plastics. There was comparatively little change in the leather trades (tanning, dressing, saddlery and other manufactures) during this period, production remaining predominantly small-scale and output growing slowly (see pp. 277–8): hence the search for substitute materials. There were some 2,800 firms in these trades in 1935, of which nearly 2,000 employed no more than 10 persons, while about three-fifths of the total labour force of 58,000 were in establishments with less than 100 workers; only three firms employed 500 or more.

Food, drink and tobacco

The rise in living standards was demonstrated much more strongly in the food, drink and tobacco trades than in clothing. Aggregate employment in these trades rose substantially, with comparatively slight checks in the slumps of the early 1920s and early 1930s, and by 1938 the food and tobacco manufactures had more than doubled their output by comparison with pre-war; the drink industry on the other hand, actually declined in both output and productivity—it would appear that consumers were changing their patterns of expenditure and spending less on beer and more on other things (see pp. 276–9). A similar effect is also visible in the flour-milling and baking industries, as *per capita* consumption of flour and bread tended to fall with rising living standards and more varied diets. Output of flour in 1938 was about the same, 3.9 million tons, as in 1907, but this was produced by a considerably smaller number of mills. Although in 1935 there were still well over 2,000 small grain-milling establishments, employing no more than 10 persons, over three-quarters of the total labour force of 39,000 were in the 500 or so larger mills, of which one-seventh, each with 100 or more workers, accounted for nearly half the total. The greater part of production, in fact, came from the big new mills built in the major ports or on main rivers, milling mostly imported wheat, though many small country mills still survived, milling a higher proportion of home-grown wheat, especially for biscuit manufacture and also for local bakers and confectioners, as well as supplying feeding stuffs to local farmers. The big mills were highly mechanized, electrified and largely automated, from their suction elevators and great storage silos, through the preliminary screening, washing and drying processes, to the actual roller-milling, dressing, grading and bagging operations; even the largest mills had only a few hundred employees. Increased efficiency in milling plant was achieved by some outstanding British engineering firms specializing in this field, such as Simon's (Stockport), Robinson's (Rochdale) and Turner's (Ipswich).

After war-time expansion, the industry was left with considerable surplus capacity, and in the consequently fierce competition many of the older smaller mills were driven out of production, so that in 1929 the larger concerns were able to establish a powerful cartel, the Millers' Mutual Association, eventually embracing almost the whole trade, except the C.W.S. This monopoly organization fixed output quotas and raised funds by levies to buy up and close down redundant mills (through a subordinate Purchase Finance Company), while prices were regulated through the Millers' National Association; it proved very successful during the 1930s in reducing capacity and raising profits, while also increasing efficiency and reducing costs. Technological and commercial factors also led to the growth of large milling concerns, of which the three biggest—Ranks, Spillers and the C.W.S.—came to control about two-thirds of the country's total flour output. There was a strong tendency for these and other large companies, such as Hovis and McDougalls, to acquire control of numerous smaller firms, some of whose mills they closed down, while modernizing and extending others and also building large new mills, mostly in the big ports.

There was also a tendency, though not yet very strong, for milling companies to acquire control of baking outlets—like brewers with their tied houses—but the large-scale movement of the big millers into baking did not occur until after the Second World War, to counteract the growth of Garfield Weston's Allied Bakeries group. In general, however, the baking trade still provided opportunities for the small producer–retailer, though larger mechanized units were growing steadily and squeezing out or absorbing small firms. There were still 25,000 to 30,000 bakery concerns at the end of this period, mostly small family bakers, who were still producing about 60 per cent of all the country's bread, as well as often making confectionery. But large bakeries, or bread factories, were developing with a high degree of mechanization and automatic control of weights, temperatures, etc.—equipped with flour-sifting, dough-mixing, dividing and moulding machines, travelling-band ovens, heated by gas, oil or electricity, and slicing and wrapping machines for the finished loaves. Even small bakeries had some mechanical equipment, but they generally still relied on more traditional methods and on quality rather than quantity, in their smaller local markets. The big bakeries, on the other hand, like the big flour-mills, were able to extend their markets by mass-production, lower costs and motor transport.

During this period, however, people were generally tending to eat less bread and more of other manufactured foods—more breakfast cereals, biscuits, cakes and confectionery, for example, and more bottled, canned and packaged foods, in an ever-widening variety of jams, marmalade, fruits, pickles, sauces, potted meats, fish, vegetables, soups, condensed milk, margarine and sausages. These developments were made possible by mass-production of bottles by the glass industry, of tins and cans by the tinplate and container industries, and of packets and wrappers by specialized machines in the various food-processing manufactures or in the paper, cellophane and printing industries. The growth of the canning industry was particularly striking. With assistance from the Ministry of Agriculture, a National Food Canning Council was established in 1925 by the canners and tinplate manufacturers, while fruit and vegetable growers were encouraged to produce for this market, and popular prejudice against canned food was gradually overcome. The introduction of automatic can-making and canning machinery greatly increased output (see p. 306 for links with the tinplate industry). Between 1924 and 1935 the number of canning factories soared from only half a dozen to about eighty, while output rose from 53,500 to 251,200 tons, though imports (especially of tinned fruit, meat and fish) still accounted for the bulk of consumption and the British industry was small by comparison with that of the United States.

In all these food manufactures, too numerous to deal with in detail here, the trends were strongly towards larger-scale mechanized factory production and industrial concentration in the hands of a few large firms, which have become household names in modern Britain: Huntley & Palmer's, Macfarlane's and McVitie's in biscuits, for example; Unilever (with subsidiaries such as Walls, MacFisheries and Bird's Eye) in margarine, sausages, ice-cream and other food products; Crosse & Blackwell, Heinz, Reckitts and Colman in a variety of bottled and tinned foods; Bovril and Oxo in meat extracts; Cadbury's and Rowntree's in chocolate; Chivers, Robertson's and Hartley's in fruits, jams, etc.; Tate & Lyle in sugar-refining; and the C.W.S. in several of these industries. Many thousands of workers were employed in the large factories of such firms, and the growth of the food, drink and tobacco manufactures in general was reflected in the figures of total employment, rising towards 800,000 by the end of this period, despite increasing mechanization (see p. 276). Nearly two-fifths of the total labour force in these trades in 1935 were employed by 162 firms with 500 or more workers, while in particular manufactures, such as those of biscuits, cocoa and chocolate, sugar, margarine, and tobacco, the proportion was much higher; in some, moreover, the three largest firms controlled up to three-quarters or more of total output, in striking contrast with the tens of thousands of small bakers and confectioners.

Among those growing industries, however, as we have previously noted, the brewing industry tended to decline, partly because of the changing pattern of consumer expenditure and partly because of increasing beer duty, higher prices and licensing restrictions. United Kingdom output of beer, which had been 36 million standard barrels in 1914, was only half that figure in 1938, of which less than 1½ per cent was exported. Under these circumstances, and with the development of motor transport, the larger, technically more advanced and lower-cost breweries sought increasingly to expand their markets, to take over smaller concerns, to extend the tied-house and off-licence system and to develop national advertising of their bottled beers, on which profit margins were higher than for draught beers. Thus the great brewing companies gradually established an 'oligopoly situation', to quote Vaizey, while smaller local breweries tended to be squeezed out or taken over and closed down, as part of the process of rationalization, to remove surplus capacity; there were also several important amalgamations of big companies, notably Bass and Worthington in 1927 and Ind, Coope and Allsopp's in 1934, while strong regional as well as national companies similarly developed. But the industry still remained largely traditional, with strongly entrenched family interests even in the biggest companies, while local breweries had by no means disappeared, hundreds still surviving at the end of this period; the total number of breweries (plants), however, was reduced from over 4,000 in 1914 to less than 900 in 1939, while the number of firms was reduced even more. Nevertheless, the industry was not very highly concentrated: in 1935 firms with more than 500 workers accounted for little more than two-fifths of total employment in brewing and malting, and the three largest firms, together employing about 8,700, accounted for only 15 per cent. There were no very striking technical advances, apart from economies of scale, though scientific control of brewing processes continued to be developed.

In the distilling (whisky and industrial alcohol) trade, by contrast, there was a high degree of concentration, as the Distillers' Company further extended its control by acquiring Johnnie Walker and Buchanan–Dewar in 1924, thus dominating the industry; they pursued a similar policy in the gin trade by acquiring Gordon's, Burnett's and Booth's, as well as by diversifying into chemicals, bottle-making and other activities. Many of the brewers, too, went into bottling and also began to acquire interests in the growing soft drinks trade (mineral waters and fruit drinks), though there was rivalry in this field from established firms such as Schweppes.

Along with beer, spirits and other stimulants, tobacco was ceasing to be regarded as a luxury and was becoming practically a necessity for a large part of the population, as consumption soared in the years before the grave health hazards were recognized. Output more than doubled between 1913 and 1938, as cigarettes rapidly displaced pipe tobacco, production being concentrated mainly in the factories of the Imperial Tobacco Company in Bristol, London, Liverpool, Nottingham, Glasgow and elsewhere. But this combine, though making very high profits, did not have matters all its own way, as competition grew from independents such as Gallaher's (of which, however, it acquired secret control in 1932), Carreras, Godfrey Phillips and others, and a 'tobacco war' developed; but this was ended by an oligopolistic agreement in 1933, which established control of prices and brand specifications. The industry provides another outstanding example of the increasing tendency towards standardized mass-production of branded packaged consumer goods, sales of which rocketed with rising incomes and heavy advertising.

Printing and allied trades

Men did not, however, live by bread, beer and tobacco alone, and in this period the provision of mental fare was greatly increased by the flow of newspapers, periodicals and books from the printing presses. Production in the paper, printing and publishing trades nearly doubled between 1913 and 1938, while employment also rose substantially, to nearly half a million, comparatively little affected by economic depressions (see pp. 276–8); in the depths of the slump in the early 1930s, unemployment, at 11 per cent, was only half the general average. Newspapers, magazines and books for the millions were now being produced, to inform and entertain, and there was also an increasing demand for paper and printing in industry and commerce, public administration and education, while the industry enjoyed a large degree of natural protection against imports. The industrial revolution in the printing trade therefore continued: linotype and monotype machines were more extensively introduced, though thousands of hand compositors still survived; new and faster presses were developed, both flat-bed and rotary, together with new processes in photogravure, aniline and lithographic printing, revolutionizing colour-printing especially, while new multiple-process machines were also developed to make and print paper or cellophane bags, wrappers, cartons, cigarette packets, toffee papers, etc., so that the volume and variety of production were greatly increased.

Despite all this mechanization, however, the great majority of firms in the printing and allied trades were still small. In 1935, there were nearly 11,000 firms, nine-tenths of which employed less than 50 workers; but these comprised in aggregate less than a quarter of the total labour force, while 123 firms, each with 500 or more workers, accounted for over a third. In paper-making and in the printing and publishing of newspapers and periodicals, large-scale production predominated, and there were also some big book-printing and publishing concerns, so that large companies with thousands of employees contrasted strikingly with the numerous petty printing and bookbinding establishments. The most outstanding growth of large-scale organization was that of national newspaper 'chains' or combines, such as Northcliffe Newspapers, Allied Newspapers and Provincial Newspapers, paralleled in periodical publishing by the Amalgamated Press, Iliffe & Co., etc; though many small local newspapers, especially weeklies, still survived, they were being rapidly taken over, while the London dailies (some also printing in Manchester) tended increasingly to predominate, with soaring circulations, so that the total number of newspapers declined. Magazines, periodicals and books, on the other hand, multiplied, and there was an accelerating exodus of large London firms into the provinces, where wages and rates were lower. Though London was still the great centre of the trade, printing was very widespread, in offices large and small, mostly small, all over the country.

In paper-making, the earlier trend towards concentration in bigger mills and businesses continued. While old-established firms such as Dickinson's and Lloyd's continued to expand, there were now other large concerns, including groups or combines, such as Bowater's, the Reed and Inveresk groups, Wiggins Teape and Thames Board Mills, with factories in various parts of the country. The industry was increasingly concentrated in Kent and Lancashire, new mills frequently being built on rivers and estuaries, for import of raw materials, and also with good supplies of pure water and in proximity to large urban-industrial markets. The industry benefited not only from the growth of printing but also from the packing and wrapping revolution in the consumer goods trades.

Building and allied trades

That growth in the inter-war period was not confined to the new industries is most strikingly demonstrated by the building and allied trades. According to Lomax's index, production in building and contracting rose at 5.4 per cent per annum between 1920 and 1938, or double the rate for all industries, increasing by more than two and a half times over the whole period, a rate of growth exceeded only by that of motor vehicles; output of building materials doubled over the same period (see pp. 276–9). Employment in building and contracting also rose substantially—from 927,000 in 1920 to 1,266,000 in 1938—though the increase was much less than that in production, which was raised by improved productivity, as well as by increased man-power. To this growing number we should add those employed in producing an increasingly wide range of building materials: bricks, stone, cement, concrete, plaster, tiles, slates, pipes, woodwork, glass, nails, screws, metal fittings, paint, etc. Employment in all these building and allied trades rose to about 15 per cent or more of total industrial employment.

Investment in building, accounting for about half the total domestic fixed-capital formation, followed a strong upward course, tending to remain relatively high even during the slumps and thus having a stabilizing influence on the economy. During the early 1920s, as in the pre-war period, non-residential building predominated, but from 1925 onwards, and especially in the economic recovery of the 1930s, house-building took the lead; in 1934–8 investment in housing (measured at constant prices) was nearly three times as high as in 1920–4, while in building generally (including housing) it was not quite double. But all this building activity did not prevent heavy unemployment in the industry: averaging over 12 per cent in 1923–9, it rose to 30 per cent in the slump of the early 1930s and only fell slowly thereafter, averaging nearly 16 per cent in 1937–8. Considerable numbers of unskilled labourers were recruited into this growing industry on a casual seasonal basis, so that there was a persistent pool or reserve of unemployed or only partially employed labour.

Various factors stimulated building expansion during this period. There was a large backlog to be made up from earlier years, when the number of dwellings built had failed to keep pace with the growth of population, while urban slum clearances had made very slow progress; this situation had been worsened by the almost complete cessation of house-building during the war. In the inter-war years, moreover, falling death and birth rates brought about increases in the numbers of adults and smaller families, requiring more houses, while the substantial rise in real incomes, especially of the middle and better-off working classes, had qualitative as well as quantitative effects, increasing demand not only for more but for better houses. Increasing numbers of people could now afford to buy their own homes, while private building of rented houses was encouraged in the 1920s by Government subsidies. Such subsidies also stimulated council-house building by local authorities, which provided additional subsidies from the rates. During the 1930s, however, Government aid was concentrated on local authority slum-clearance schemes, leaving private enterprise, unassisted, to provide all other accommodation; the housing boom of that decade was thus brought about mainly by private building of unsubsidized houses, mostly for sale to owner-occupiers but also for renting. 'Cheap money' (low interest rates) also provided a powerful stimulus, mainly by reducing capital costs and mortgage rates and also by making investment in rented property relatively more attractive. Reductions in other building costs, such as materials and labour, also contributed to lower house prices. At the same time, the rapid growth of building societies provided increased mortgage funds for house purchases. The development of motor transport stimulated suburban building, especially in the Greater London and Midlands areas, with rapidly growing industries.

Between 1920 and 1939, over 4⅓ million houses were built, of which less than a third were local authority houses; during the great building boom of the 1930s especially, private building predominated. The annual rate of building rose from only about 100,000 houses in the early 1920s to well over 200,000 in the second half of that decade and then to an average of over 350,000 from 1934 onwards. At the same time, many houses were repaired and renovated. Non-residential building was also at a high level during this period; even during the 1930s boom it was not far below that of house-building. The pattern of industrial building (factories, warehouses, etc.) was shaped, of course, in its timing and distribution by the general trade cycle and by variations in the growth of particular industries and areas. The building of shops, offices and hotels reflected the rising importance of the service industries, while the growth of the public sector was demonstrated not only in council-houses but also in schools, libraries, hospitals and other public buildings.

The industry's rapid rate of growth, however, was achieved without any revolutionary changes in technology or organization. There was a striking increase in the number of firms, since the limited fixed-capital requirements and easy credit facilities continued to make entry easy. The Census total of about 50,000 firms in 1924 rose to 76,000 in 1935, and of the latter total about seven-eighths employed 10 men or less, though they accounted for less than a quarter of total employment; at the other end of the scale, there were 31 large builders and general contractors, each employing over 1,000 men, though also sub-contracting extensively to specialist firms. A considerable proportion of the small firms were engaged only on jobbing repairs and sub-contracting, but many went into house-building; the industry was highly competitive, speculation rife and bankruptcy common. Of the industry's labour force, about half were now unskilled or semi-skilled labourers, the other half skilled tradesmen (bricklayers, carpenters, painters, plumbers and glaziers, plasterers, masons, slaters and tilers), still practising their traditional handicrafts, especially in house-building, largely untouched by mechanization. In large-scale non-residential building and contracting, on the other hand, and also in building large blocks of flats or tenement houses, labour-saving equipment was now commonly used, including mechanical cranes and hoists, steam shovels, hydraulic and pneumatic riveters, cement mixers, wood-working machinery and paint sprays. In large industrial and commercial buildings, moreover, new structures—steel frames, reinforced concrete, artificial stone and expanses of glass—often in standardized prefabricated form, were widely introduced. Even in house-building, there was growing use of prefabricated standard fittings, such as doors, window-frames and cupboards, gutterings, drain-pipes and sanitary ware, produced by the wood-working, iron-founding and other trades.

It was, in fact, on the materials side that building costs were most considerably reduced in this period, with large-scale production of Fletton bricks, concrete tiles, asbestos-cement sheet, fibre- and plaster-board, together with the general introduction of rotary kilns for cement making and the development of continuous mass-production glass-making, while in clay, sand, gravel and chalk pits and in stone and slate quarries, mechanical equipment was extensively introduced. In some of these supply industries, by contrast with the building trades themselves, large-scale production was predominant, as illustrated by the Associated Portland Cement Manufacturers (who strengthened their position by acquiring control of rival groups and companies in the 1930s), the London Brick Company (Fletton bricks), the Marley Tile Company (cement tiles), Pilkingtons (sheet glass) and Turner & Newall (asbestos cement). There were also numerous trade associations for regulating prices, though competition had by no means been eliminated; mass-production brought substantial cost reductions, but more might have been passed on to consumers.

It is obvious from these references to so many other industries how important the building industry was to general economic growth in this period, especially in the recovery of the 1930s. Moreover, in addition to its direct demands for building materials, it indirectly stimulated industries such as electricity, gas and water supply, wallpaper, furniture and other household consumer goods trades, while it was also closely related to suburban road-building and transport developments. Though an old and still largely traditional handicraft industry, it had widely pervasive effects in stimulating general industrial and technological development. Being entirely a domestic industry—though most of the timber and some bricks, tiles and other materials were imported—its growth was characteristic of the increasing industrial concentration on the home market in this period.

It is clear, indeed, from this survey that during these years the traditional domestic consumer goods trades were still growing and important. But with rising incomes and technological innovation, many other products were now pouring onto the market from the newer industries, as we shall see in Chapter 19. From the chemical and allied trades came ever-increasing quantities and varieties of soaps, washing powders, toothpastes, dyes, paints, pharmaceuticals, cosmetics, rubber manufactures and photographic films; the electrical industry produced a widening range of light fittings, heaters, clothes-irons, cookers, vacuum-cleaners, washers, radios and gramophones; while the cycle, motor-cycle and car industries provided unprecedented personal mobility. More notable, indeed, than the increasing quantities of consumables (food, clothing, etc.) was the rapidly growing output of consumer durables or capital goods (houses, household equipment, cars, etc.), visible signs of rising average income and wealth. Not all sections of the population, of course, shared equally in this increasing consumption—most of the more expensive consumer capital goods went to the middle and better-off working-class families, especially in the more prosperous areas—but there can be no doubt that widespread increases in consumption accompanied and stimulated rising rates of industrial production.

19

The New Industries

None of the industries dealt with in this chapter was entirely new—indeed some, such as glass, pottery and soap, were very old and are only included here because of their relationships with chemicals. Several branches of the chemical industry, moreover, were long-established, but others, such as synthetic organic products, were distinctly novel or now more rapidly developing, like the motor and electrical manufactures with which they are generally associated in the 'second industrial revolution'. Rayon is also included, because it falls into the same category; though classified industrially with textiles, it is differentiated by its chemical basis and rapid modern growth as the first 'man-made' fibre. Such distinctions, however, should not be over-emphasized, since many new processes and products, as we have seen, were also being developed in the old industries; we have included aluminium, for example, with other metals, and canning with consumer goods, though both were relatively new (see pp. 307–8, 330).

The chemical and allied trades
The chemical industry, though generally regarded as among the new science-based growth industries of the twentieth century, had long been engaged in manufacturing alkalis, acids, bleaching powder, dyestuffs, explosives, fertilizers, etc., and its growth in the inter-war period was only modest by comparison with that in new industries, such as motor and electrical manufactures, or in many old industries—in fact its growth, in both production and productivity, was well below the general average rate in British industry during this period. Employment in the chemical and allied trades increased very slowly—stagnating in the 1920s but rising in the 1930s—and in 1938 it accounted for only 1.3 per cent of total employment, or 2.9 per cent of industrial employment. And though these trades have always been capital-intensive, with relatively large quantities of plant tended by relatively small numbers of workers, their contribution to gross

national product in 1935 was only 2.1 per cent, having risen from 1.1 per cent in 1907 (see pp. 276–80). The really striking growth of chemicals, in fact, has taken place since the Second World War, and some of the sources of that growth, as in petrochemicals and synthetic products (textile fibres, plastics, detergents, etc.), had not previously been exploited on a massive scale or were only just beginning to be developed. In the inter-war years, though new developments and growth certainly occurred, the industry was affected by declining demand for some of its products, notably in textiles, while chemical exports also stagnated (see p. 282) and were still only half the value of Germany's in 1937.

The First World War greatly stimulated certain branches of the chemical industry. There was a huge increase, of course, in output of explosives, by Nobel's and other chemical firms and by Government factories, necessitating a great expansion in production of concentrated sulphuric and nitric acids for making nitro-explosives, and also in production of coal-tar derivatives—phenol for lyddite (picric acid) and toluene for TNT—together with ammonium nitrate (produced from Chilean nitre or sodium nitrate), for mixing with TNT in the explosive amatol; the dependence on Chilean imports also induced experiments with the Haber process for ammonia synthesis, 'fixing' atmospheric nitrogen, which led to Brunner Mond's great (though financially disastrous) post-war venture at Billingham, for production of synthetic nitrogenous fertilizer. Closely allied to explosives manufacture was that of synthetic dyestuffs, also from coal-tar distillates, and, though explosives manufacture had priority, measures also had to be taken to develop the dyestuffs industry, because of the pre-war dependence on German imports; these culminated in the Government-sponsored British Dyestuffs Corporation of 1919, merging the wartime British Dyes (centred on Read Holliday's) and Levinstein's, the main firms in this field. Moreover, just as the war hastened introduction of the contact process for sulphuric acid manufacture, so too was electrolytic production of chlorine stimulated, though the increased demand for gas warfare did not make up for reduced consumption in textiles, etc.

With the ending of the war, of course, production of explosives was rapidly reduced, while the inter-war depression of some of the major peace-time industrial consumers seriously affected markets for other chemical products. The decline of textiles, for example, especially of cotton, reduced their demand for soda, bleaching power, acid sours and dyestuffs. Other established users, however, such as the soap, glass, paper, metals, pharmaceuticals and agricultural fertilizer maufactures, continued to increase their consumption, while new industries such as rayon, transparent paper (cellophane) and plastics provided new markets. But though production of synthetic organic chemicals (dyestuffs, fibres, plastics and pharmaceuticals) was gradually increasing, the greater part of output was still of the established heavy inorganic products. Demand for these, however, tended to stagnate: output of sulphuric acid, for example, which had reached nearly 1.2 million tons in 1914, rising to nearly 1.4 million during the war, collapsed to less than 0.6 million in the post-war slump of 1921 and was still barely 1.1 million in 1939, nearly two-thirds of which was still produced by the old lead-chamber process. (Compare this with the increase to over 3.1 million tons by 1964, nine-tenths by the contact process—an illustration of the inter-war lag, by contrast with more recent growth.)

Coal-tar, cellulose (wood pulp, etc.) and fermentation alcohol continued to be the main sources of organic-chemical raw materials. Oil was mostly imported in a refined state and the massive growth of the petrochemicals industry did not occur until after the Second World War, when the oil companies established refineries here (see p. 342). The production of synthetic organic-chemical materials, as we have seen, had started in the late nineteenth and early twentieth centuries, with synthetic dyestuffs, celluloid, viscose (rayon) and bakelite (phenol–for-maldehyde), and these continued to be the main products in this field in the inter-war period. Under specially protective legislation, the synthetic dyestuffs industry continued to grow rapidly (see p. 266), output rising from 5,000 tons in 1913 to 29,000 by 1937, by which time imports accounted for only 5 per cent of home consumption, while exports were over twice as great in quantity, though slightly less in value. Synthetic pharmaceuticals, similarly protected and closely related to synthetic dyestuffs, also developed strongly. In both these areas, the former German predominance was considerably reduced. Rayon pro-duction—classed with textiles manufactures, though based on industrial-chemical processes—likewise increased rapidly during these years, but it was not until after 1939 that production of other synthetic fibres such as nylon and terylene was developed (see pp. 343–5). Celluloid and bakelite continued to find growing markets, while similar amino-plastics were also developed, for use in the electrical, radio, car and other manufactures. In the 1930s new synthetic poly-mers such as perspex, polystyrene, polythene and polyvinyl chloride were pro-duced, but these had hardly got beyond the development stage by the end of this period and the rapid expansion in production of such materials—the growth, in fact, of a large plastics industry—did not occur until after 1939, in close associ-ation with petrochemicals. In the discovery and development of some of these organic-chemical materials—notably rayon, perspex, polythene and tery-lene—British science and technology played an outstanding role, but in terms of output these products were as yet relatively unimportant by comparison with the traditional inorganic chemicals. Links between the inorganic and organic sides of the industry were formed by the development of various chloro-hydrocarbons—an outlet for chlorine following decline of bleaching powder production—and sizeable quantities of these were being produced by the end of this period for a variety of industrial uses, especially as solvents. But massive development of the new heavy organic chemical industry still lay in the future, in man-made fibres, plastics and other synthetic products.

The most outstanding event in the inter-war chemical industry was the creation in 1926 of Imperial Chemical Industries Ltd., by the merging of Brunner Mond's, the United Alkali Company, Nobel Industries and the British Dyestuffs Corporation. These concerns were themselves products of earlier mergers, mainly in alkalis, acids and other heavy chemicals, explosives and synthetic dyestuffs, but only by this more comprehensive amalgamation could the British industry stand up to the scientific, technological, financial and commercial strength of the giant chemical combines of Germany and the United States. With an initial authorized capital of £65 million, it was by far the biggest merger in British industry, and its various groups or divisions eventually embraced almost all the main branches of chemical production, including not only those forming the original base but also others such as fine chemicals, pharmaceuticals, fertilizers, metals, paints, leathercloth and plastics. Moreover, the company continued to expand its interests in the following years, with further mergers such as that of the Salt Union in 1937. It was able to carry through a vigorous policy of rationalization, research and development, to establish overseas subsidiaries and to negotiate internationally on markets, prices and patents. But I.C.I. did not acquire an industrial monopoly. Undoubtedly the company held a very powerful position, but it by no means dominated the whole British chemicals industry and there were limits to the extent to which it could exploit its power. It controlled only about a third of the industry and there were many other important firms, either in the chemical industry itself or in closely allied industries, with capacity and potential for increased chemical production: Laportes, Tennants, Fisons, Albright & Wilson, British Drug Houses, Boots, Beechams, Turner & Newall, British Oxygen, Imperial Smelting, Distillers, Unilever, Courtaulds, Pilkingtons, Dunlop, Anglo–Persian Oil (now British Petroleum), Shell and various coke and tar-distilling concerns, as well as subsidiaries of American and Swiss chemical companies.

This was certainly an industry in which big firms tended to predominate, because of the heavy capital requirements for plant, materials, research and development, and the economies of large-scale integrated production. In 1935, firms employing 500 or more workers accounted for nearly half the labour force. But there were many hundreds of small and medium firms, specializing in particular chemical products. The degree of concentration was highest—as high as 70 or 80 per cent or more—in alkalis, dyestuffs and explosives, in which I.C.I. almost had a monopoly, but was much lower in coal-tar products, fertilizers, fine chemicals, pharmaceuticals, paints and lacquers.

Production was also highly concentrated in certain chemically related trades, such as soap and margarine manufacture, seed-crushing or oil-milling, spirit distilling, rubber tyre manufacture, flat-glass making, match-making and refining of non-ferrous metals. In the soap and margarine trades, the creation of Unilever Ltd. in 1929 paralleled that of I.C.I., with ramifications also into oil-milling, chemicals and food-processing. While hard-soap consumption continued to rise steadily with living standards, that of washing powders and flakes soared; production of synthetic soapless detergents, however, was only in an experimental stage and did not reach large-scale production until after the Second World War, in association with petrochemicals. In soap making, however, and also in oil-milling (producing vegetable oils not only for soap, margarine and cooking but also for paints, linoleum, etc., together with cattle foods), Unilever did not have things all their own way but had to face strong competition from Hedley's (Procter & Gamble), Colgate–Palmolive, Bibby's and the C.W.S., while in their related chemicals manufactures of caustic soda, silicate and related products (mainly by Crosfields, their subsidiary), relationships had to be carefully maintained with I.C.I. and also with powerful German and American concerns. Similarly in food-processing, as we have seen, there were other strong competitors (see p. 330).

The Distillers' Company similarly extended its interests from whisky into industrial alcohol and its various hydrocarbon derivatives, used in making solvents and plastics. In rubber manufactures, especially that of motor tyres, now rapidly expanding in the road transport revolution, Dunlop's also held a powerful position and tended to diversify into chemicals for production of synthetic materials for footwear and sports products; but they too were faced by powerful European and American competitors, such as Pirelli, Michelin, Goodyear and Firestone, with subsidiaries in Britain. Pilkington's likewise acquired predominance in the flat-glass industry—also booming with motor manufacturing and building—as they took over their old rivals, Chance's, and other competitors; but they continued to draw their alkali supplies from I.C.I. Their increased size and capital resources enabled them to develop continuous 'flow' production of plate glass and a similar 'flat-drawn' process for sheet glass, together with new products such as Triplex safety-glass and fibreglass, closely associated with the developing plastics industry (and hence involving delicate agreements with I.C.I.). Like I.C.I., Unilever, Dunlop's and other large firms, they developed on an international scale but still had to face strong foreign competition, especially Belgian, though protection was provided in the home market from the early 1930s onwards. In the glass industry generally, however, while large-scale production predominated—firms with 500 or more workers accounting for three-fifths of total employment in 1935—the three biggest concerns, with an aggregate of over 15,000 workers, employed only a third of the total. There were a number of sizeable bottle-making concerns, but production of domestic and fancy glassware was on a smaller scale, still struggling against foreign competition. That the industry was generally expanding, however, is indicated by the growth in the number of insured workers from 44,000 in 1923 to 54,000 in 1938.

The British Match Corporation, formed in 1927, centred on Bryant & May and dominating production of safety matches, also had chemical interests, and so did Albright & Wilson, who supplied phosphorus for this industry but were gradually diversifying. Similarly in non-ferrous metals, the British Aluminium Company (1894) and the Imperial Smelting Corporation (1916, in zinc), while predominating in their particular fields, also tended to develop wider chemical-metallurgical interests. In fact, there were no bounds to the complex and ever-changing scientific, technical and commercial inter-relationships in the chemical and allied industries. Potentially the most important were those of the great oil or petroleum companies, Anglo-Persian, Shell, Burmah and others, but until after the Second World War their activities in Britain were confined mainly to import-ing and distribution. Imports of crude oil for refining gradually rose from an annual average of 0.9 million tons in the early 1920s to 2.1 million in the late 1930s, but were still far below the level of refined imports, which rose from 3.8 to 8.9 million tons over the same period. About three-fifths of consumption was in transport, mainly in motor vehicles and ships, and the remainder was used for industrial power (diesel engines) and fuel (for steam-raising or in furnaces), and also for lubricants, bitumen (asphalt), heating and lighting, with only a tiny proportion refined into chemical products. But, as we have seen, the stage was set for massive development of synthetic manufactures based on petro-chemicals, in which the oil companies would play an increasingly important role.

Another new industry, though with roots stretching back into the nineteenth century, was that of photographic chemicals, plates, films and cameras, with leading firms such as the American Kodak subsidiary and Ilford's. Despite protection, however, it still remained inferior to that of Germany in both chemicals and optical glass.

Many of these industries, of course, both old and new, though closely linked to chemicals, either through raw materials requirements or by the chemical charac-teristics of their processes, nevertheless retained a separate identity. This was particularly true of one of the oldest industries, that of pottery manufacture, in which, despite chemical and mechanical innovations, established family firms and craft traditions were still strong. Among the leading names, those of Wedgwood, Copeland, Minton, Ridgway, Doulton, Twyford and many others still stood out and the industry remained heavily concentrated in the north Staffordshire Potteries. There were still hundreds of small and medium firms, together with some large ones; establishments with 500 or more workers accounted for much less than a third of the total labour force of 70,000 in 1935, and the three biggest firms together employed only about 6,300 or 9 per cent of the total. The Board of Trade Working Party on the industry in 1946 commented particularly on the age of its buildings and equipment, the strong influence of craft traditions and the slowness of technical change. Though power was now generally applied to the processes of preparing the clay and other materials and to jolleys and jiggers for making the pottery, much manual labour, skilled and unskilled, was still required; very little use was made of automatic or semi-automatic machinery like that used for mass-production in the United States, and the old coal-fired bottle-kilns still predominated—in 1938 there were still 2,000 of these, but less than a hundred gas, oil and electric tunnel-kilns of the 'continuous' type. The modern revolution in British pottery manufacture has occurred since the Second World War.

The industry experienced mixed fortunes in the inter-war period. Exports, badly hit by the First World War, recovered in the 1920s to the pre-war figure of over £3 million by 1929 but were halved in the following slump and were still only £2.4 million in 1938. The overseas trade in domestic pottery or tableware was seriously affected, but with protection in the early 1930s, rising living standards and the boom in the building and electricity trades, the home market expanded not only for crockery, ornaments, etc., but also for glazed sanitary ware, tiles and electric insulators, in which larger-scale mass-production methods were introduced. Consequently the number of insured workers in the industry rose from 72,000 in 1923 (the same figure as pre-war) to 82,000 by 1938; but this increase was almost entirely in females, while unemployment rose to over 36 per cent in 1931–2 and only fell very slowly thereafter.

Rayon

Rayon or artificial silk provides a striking example of new growth grafted onto old manufactures, as it came rapidly into widespread use not only in hosiery manufactures but also in textile fabrics generally. Rayon production was basically chemical, converting wood pulp and cotton linters into viscose or acetate materials, but as these were then processed into yarn and staple fibre for textile manufactures, in which the rayon producers were also intimately involved, the new industry was classified among textiles rather than chemicals. Rayon yarns and staple fibre were frequently mixed with cotton, wool or silk, while materials made entirely of rayon were also increasingly produced; with technical developments, the quality of rayon was much improved, while its price was greatly reduced, so that it tended to displace not only natural silk but also other textiles. Production of real silk goods stagnated in this period, despite the stocking trade and restoration of tariff protection; imports of piece goods remained substantial, averaging nearly 25 million square yards in the late 1930s, of which Japan supplied over half. Rayon, however, was increasingly substituted for silk, and to some extent for other textiles, especially in women's stockings and underwear, and also, mixed with cotton and wool, in various lighter more attractive woven fabrics. In the late 1930s about three-quarters of rayon filament yarn went to be woven, into either pure rayon or mixed fabrics, while most of the remainder was taken by the hosiery and knitwear trades; the greater part of rayon staple fibre went to cotton-spinning mills. The larger rayon producers, however, were also integrated into textiles, with their own spinning, weaving and knitting factories.

The pre-war viscose process, pioneered by Courtaulds, predominated throughout this period, but production of cellulose–acetate yarn was developed during and after the war, mainly by British Celanese, and accounted for over a third of rayon yarn output in the late 1930s; the cuprammonium process was not much used in this country. Another major development was that of 'staple fibre', or 'artificial cotton wool', consisting of rayon filaments cut into short lengths (staples), which could be used on ordinary spinning machinery, together with natural fibres; production rapidly increased in the 1930s. Total United Kingdom output of rayon yarn and fibre soared from less than 4 million lb in 1918 to nearly 170 million lb in 1939, of which two-thirds was continuous filament yarn (viscose and acetate) and one-third staple fibre (nearly all viscose). Output was scarcely affected by the slump of the early 1930s, though some of the weaker firms that had sprung up in the preceding boom then collapsed. The total number of insured employees in silk and artificial silk manufactures more than doubled between 1923 and 1938, from 37,000 to 77,000, mainly as a result of the rapid growth of the rayon industry, in which by the latter date about half that total was employed.

Courtaulds continued to predominate in the British rayon industry with factories in the west midlands, Lancashire, Flintshire and elsewhere, while also establishing subsidiaries in the United States, Canada, Europe and India. By 1939 they had an issued capital of £32 million, were employing nearly 20,000 in rayon production in this country and accounted for two-thirds of the total British output. Their only comparable rival (whom they were to absorb in 1957) was British Celanese, the dominant acetate producer, with capital of £13½ million and large works near Derby. There were nine other United Kingdom rayon producers (including several foreign subsidiaries), but they were pygmies by comparison with these giants, though large by most other standards, with capitals of up to £1½ million. Only very large concerns could provide the necessary financial, technical and commercial resources for this capital-intensive high-technology industry, in competition with powerful foreign rivals. Moreover, despite suggestions of monopoly practices and Courtaulds' initially high profits, it must be pointed out that there was strong internal and external competition, and though by the late 1930s firmer collusion was being achieved, both nationally and internationally, prices had meanwhile been greatly reduced, to the obvious benefit of consumers.

Despite the impressive growth figures, however, Britain lost her early lead in world rayon output, as other countries more rapidly expanded their production. Her share gradually declined from about 20 per cent in the early 1920s to 8 per cent by the late 1930s, by which time British output was only a third of that of Germany and Japan and half that of the United States and Italy. Consequently, yarn exports, which had grown quite strongly in the 1920s, to an average of 8 million lb annually in 1926–8, or 20 per cent of production, stagnated in the 1930s, declining to about 10 per cent, mostly going to the Dominions and other non-European markets, though towards the end of that decade exports of staple fibre were rising very sharply, especially to the United States. Piece goods did better, averaging 70 million square yards annually in 1936–8, nearly half of pure rayon and the rest mixed fabrics, again mainly to preferential Dominion markets. Imports of yarn, on the other hand, which had been rising very sharply in the early 1920s, were reduced by tariff protection in 1925, averaging only about a fifth of exports in the 1930s; imports of piece goods were about a third of exports. Even this new and rapidly growing industry, however, was driven by foreign competition and tariffs into concentrating on the home market, though there is evidence of technological sluggishness and higher costs by comparison with foreign producers. Courtaulds and British Celanese, however, had important interests in the American and European rayon industry—notably Courtaulds' American Viscose Corporation—supplying those markets from within tariff walls.

Another vista opened at the end of this period, with the Courtaulds–I.C.I. joint venture in 1940, British Nylon Spinners Ltd., to develop this new synthetic fibre—though a product of American research—followed by the British discovery of terylene in 1941, in the laboratory of the Calico Printers' Association, thus initiating production of the first wholly man-made fibres and bringing the textiles and chemical industries into even closer relationships.

Motor and aircraft manufactures

The British motor industry, a slow starter in the pre-1914 period, lagging behind France, Germany and the United States, expanded rapidly in the inter-war years, so that by the late 1930s it was second to the giant American industry in output and exports. During the First World War, production was switched to military vehicles and armaments, but the industry quickly recovered after the war, and by 1922, despite the slump, total output of cars and commercial vehicles had risen to 73,000, over twice the figure for 1913. By 1929 it had reached 239,000 and, after falling slightly in the great depression, soared upwards again to a peak of 508,000 in 1937, though dropping back considerably in 1938–9. While the United States produced nearly ten times as many cars as Britain in 1937, German output in that year was only just over three-fifths, the French only two-fifths, of that of the

British industry, which outdistanced its European rivals in the 1930s. Production was mainly for the home market, rapidly expanding with rising incomes and protected against foreign competition; the wartime McKenna duty of 33⅓ per cent, imposed on cars and components in 1915, was continued throughout the inter-war period, apart from a brief interval in 1924–5, and was extended in 1926 to commercial vehicles and parts, so that the industry was able to grow behind this protective shield and by the late 1930s was supplying 97 per cent of the domestic market. At the same time, exports were gradually increased: the 1913 figure was not exceeded until 1924, when about 13,000 vehicles were exported, but the number then rose sharply to 42,000 by 1929 and, after slumping in the early 1930s, increased to 98,500 in 1937, nearly a fifth of production in that year; by value their share of the world market was raised from about 7 to 14 per cent between 1929 and 1937, well above that of any other European country, though only between a quarter and a fifth of the American. They were then three times as great as imports, going mainly to Empire countries, in which they enjoyed tariff preferences. The 1930s also saw the beginnings of an export trade in tractors, rising to 11,000 by 1937.

The motor-cycle industry, by contrast, after booming in the 1920s and dominating world exports, fell away in the 1930s. Output doubled in the first post-war decade to 146,000 (exports 62,000) in 1929, but fell by nearly two-thirds in the slump and averaged only 74,000 (exports 22,000) annually in 1936–8. This decline was caused partly by the substitution of cheap cars for motor cycles in the home market, but mainly by the collapse of exports with the growth of foreign manufactures. The pedal-cycle industry, on the other hand, displayed remarkable resilience, recovering rapidly from the slumps and expanding very strikingly over the whole period: by 1937 output had topped two million, more than treble the 1907 figure, while exports rose even more strongly, accounting for over two-fifths of complete cycles produced in 1937*.

Figures simply of the number of motor vehicles produced are somewhat misleading, because great changes were made in their styles, construction, power and performance. The most important general development was the adoption of American assembly-line methods for mass-production of cheaper saloon cars, by Morris, Austin and other leading British makers, as well as by American subsidiaries in this country. Before 1914 cars had been expensively engineered products for the wealthy, but in the inter-war period the market was greatly widened by labour-saving mechanization and standardization: by using special-purpose machine-tools (automatic gear-cutters, multiple cylinder-borers, milling machines, etc.), by die-pressing of body parts and paint spraying,

---

*I am grateful to Dr A. E. Harrison, of the University of York, for supplying information on the motor- and pedal-cycle manufactures.

by buying in mass-produced components and by continuous flow production, bigger manufacturers were able to achieve large reductions in costs and thus to tap potential demand among the middle and better-off working classes, by producing smaller standardized cars, which were also cheaper to run under the existing system of taxation on horse-power and petrol. The average factory value of private cars in Britain fell from £308 in 1912 to £259 in 1924 and £130 in 1935–6, while similar though less dramatic reductions occurred in the prices of commercial vehicles, as a result of larger-scale production for a rapidly growing market. While more and more cars were used for business and private purposes, vans and lorries brought about a commercial transport revolution; at the same time, there was a rising replacement demand, as vehicles were worn out and scrapped. By 1939 the number of licensed cars had risen to over two million, that of goods vehicles to nearly half a million.

In the early years of the motor industry, hundreds of firms had mushroomed into existence, mostly small and short-lived, and in 1914 only a handful were producing more than a thousand vehicles annually. After the war, scores of new firms entered the industry, but many failed in the slump of the early 1920s, and from then onwards there was a strong trend towards concentration of output in the more technically and commercially progressive firms, which expanded by mass-production methods. In 1922 there were 96 car firms, but these were reduced to 41 by 1929, when about three-quarters of total output was produced by the 'Big Three'—Morris (63,000, or 35 per cent), Austin (46,000, or 25 per cent) and Singer (28,000, or 15 per cent)—followed at a considerable distance by Ford, Standard, Hillman, Humber, Vauxhall and others. Already there was a tendency towards amalgamation: Sunbeam, Clément–Talbot and Darracq combined in the early 1920s; Morris took over Wolseley (previously acquired by Vickers) in 1927, after having earlier integrated several firms making engines, radiators, carburettors and other components; a Hillman–Humber–Commer combination was formed in 1928, while the American giant General Motors acquired Vauxhall and thus gained entry into the British motor industry.

During the 1930s, though the number of car-makers was further reduced, the 'Big Three' failed to maintain their predominance and by 1939 over 90 per cent of output was in the hands of the 'Big Six'—still including Morris (Nuffield) and Austin (with 26.6 and 17 per cent of the car market respectively), together with Ford (17.8 per cent), Vauxhall (10.1 per cent), Rootes (9.6 per cent) and Standard (9 per cent), while Singer had declined. The Rootes group had acquired not only Hillman–Humber–Commer but also Sunbeam and Clément–Talbot, but the other firms grew mainly by internal expansion, though Nuffield absorbed Riley Motors in 1938. The growing American involvement—following the opening of Ford's new Dagenham factory in 1931 and General Motors' acquisition of Vauxhall—was a notable feature of this decade. The number of car-making firms had been reduced to 33 by 1939, but these included companies owned or controlled by others—for example, the Nuffield Organization comprised four companies (Morris, M.G., Riley and Wolseley), the Rootes group three (Hillman, Sunbeam–Talbot and Humber), and the B.S.A. group three (B.S.A., Daimler and Lanchester)—so that there were only about twenty independent firms. These included specialist makers of high-quality cars such as Rover, Jaguar, Armstrong Siddeley and Rolls Royce (which had absorbed Bentley), produced in much smaller numbers by more traditional engineering methods.

Despite increasing business concentration, however, the industry was still producing a large number of models—136 in 1939, with different engine and body sizes, etc., though many components could be used interchangeably in different models. By such variety, manufacturers sought to cater for different pockets and tastes, in a competitive situation. No doubt there could have been more cost-reducing standardization, with longer production runs in fewer and larger factories, but the industry has perhaps been unfairly criticized by comparison with the American, which had a far bigger mass market.

The large car-manufacturing firms also produced most of the light commercial vehicles (vans, light lorries, etc.), by similar mass-production methods. In 1938, for example, Nuffield (Morris), Ford and Vauxhall (Bedford) accounted for over 70 per cent of the total number of commercial vehicles manufactured. But from the beginning there were numerous specialist producers of heavier vehicles and by the 1930s Leyland, A.E.C., Albion, Dennis, Thorneycroft, Scammell and Guy were outstanding. In that decade, moreover, as the heavy-oil diesel engine began to supersede the light petrol type for such vehicles, other firms such as Atkinson, Foden, E.R.F. and Seddon also entered this field, the first two transferring from the earlier manufacture of heavy steam vehicles. Because of the wide variety of types produced, according to customers' requirements, mass-production techniques were inappropriate; such firms, like the specialist car-makers, relied mostly on basic multi-purpose machine-tools, operated by skilled labour.

The car industry tended to become increasingly concentrated in the west midlands and south-east. The early Scottish firms soon died out, while Manchester lost Ford's to Dagenham and Rolls Royce to Derby. The Coventry–Birmingham–Wolverhampton area, with the great variety of its metal-working and components manufactures, remained the great hub of the industry, but London and other centres attracted such firms as Ford (Dagenham), Vauxhall (Luton) and Morris (Cowley, Oxford), in proximity to the metropolitan market, but with land and labour available for large mass-production factories, in which semi-skilled workers could be employed. The manufacture of heavy commercial vehicles, on the other hand, with its greater reliance on traditional heavy engineering, was located mainly in Lancashire and north Cheshire, and to a lesser extent in London and the Home Counties.

The growth of large-scale production, especially in car manufacture, was reflected in the employment figures for both factories and firms. In the motor and cycle industry as a whole by 1935, nearly three-quarters of the labour force were in plants employing 500 or more workers, and the largest firms were each employing 15,000 to 20,000. Despite this increasing scale of production, however, a large proportion of motor-manufacturing requirements were supplied by other industries and by closely associated specialist producers of components; bought-out components, in fact accounted for about 60 per cent of total costs. The steel industry supplied the basic sheet, strip, casting and forging materials, while considerable quantities of non-ferrous metals, timber and other materials were also needed; glass was required for windscreens, windows and lights; rubber for tyres, hoses and insulation; asbestos for brake linings; leather, cloth and plastic for upholstery; paints for body finishes; hydraulic equipment for fuel and water pumps and brakes; and a wide variety of electrical components for ignition and lighting, including carburettors, dynamos, magnetos, distributors, plugs, starting motors and batteries. Motor manufacturing was, in fact, largely a massive assembly industry and the growth of large car firms was closely associated with that of large components manufacturers, such as Pressed Steel, Briggs Motor Bodies, Fisher and Ludlow and Mulliner's (body-building), Herbert's and Archdale's (machine-tools), Renold and Coventry Chain Co. (transmission equipment); Lucas and Smith's (electrical components); Ferodo and Girling (brakes and hydraulics), Dunlop (tyres), Pilkington and Triplex (glass), I.C.I. (paints and leathercloth), together with numerous other specialist manufacturers of ball-bearings, plugs, etc.

Because of these innumerable linkages, it is difficult to provide any precise figure for employment in the motor industry, since it is almost impossible to define its boundaries. Statistics collected by the Society of Motor Manufacturers and Traders in 1937, from hundreds of firms engaged not only directly in motor manufacturing but also in making bodies and components, suggest an employment figure of nearly 300,000, but this by no means included all those involved in producing materials and parts, nor the growing numbers employed in sales, servicing and repair. With such widespread industrial ramifications and with its equally pervasive effects on transport of goods and people, motor manufacturing was of central importance in the 'second industrial revolution'.

There was a similar growth of large-scale production in the motor- and pedal-cycle manufactures, closely associated with the car industry. In motor cycles, large concerns such as the Birmingham Small Arms Company (B.S.A.) and Associated Motor Cycles (comprising Matchless, A.J.S. and Sunbeam) were becoming increasingly predominant by the late 1930s and were subsequently to take over such famous firms as Norton, Ariel and Triumph. In pedal-cycles, the Hercules, Raleigh and B.S.A. companies were similarly outstanding, growing almost entirely by internal expansion, while Tube Investments extended their interests in the cycle trade by acquiring control of firms manufacturing steel tubing and components; Hercules were particularly notable for pioneering flow-production of cheap popular bicycles. In both motor- and pedal-cycle manufactures by 1935, there were factories employing thousands of workers, and the three largest firms in each trade accounted for about two-thirds of the labour force, still located predominantly in the Coventry–Birmingham–Wolverhampton, London and Nottingham areas.

Aircraft manufacture was closely related to the motor car industry, being also based on development of the piston-driven petrol engine, so that some firms such as Rolls Royce, Napier, Bristol, Armstrong Siddeley, Armstrong–Whitworth and Vickers were involved in both industries. The First World War caused a great expansion of this infant industry and though it declined immediately afterwards, with the collapse of military demand and with availability of war-surplus aircraft, many firms, in addition to the aforementioned, survived this post-war slump, including such famous names as Handley Page, Fairey, Gloster, De Havilland, Avro (A. V. Roe), Short Bros., Saunders–Roe, Westland, Blackburn, Boulton & Paul and Hawker. Like the motor industry, it soon came to be organized on a large scale: by 1935 fifteen establishments, each employing 1,000 persons or more, accounted for over three-quarters of total employment in the aircraft industry, and the three largest firms together employed about 16,500, or nearly half the labour force. But, with a total of only 35,000, it could not yet be classed as a major industry, and only with rearmament in the late 1930s did it begin to grow rapidly.

Civil aviation developed slowly in the inter-war years. Though passenger-miles flown on British airlines rose from 3 to 53 million between 1925 and 1938, this increase was almost insignificant by comparison with the enormous growth after the Second World War (the figure for 1965, for example, was 7,417 million). Dependent on public subsidies, the commercial airlines were amalgamated into Imperial Airways in 1924, while several others in the slowly developing internal and European services were combined into British Airways in 1935, similarly subsidized, and the two companies were finally nationalized in 1939 and brought together in the British Overseas Airways Corporation. In addition to demand from these airlines, the growth of private flying clubs and exports also provided markets, but most aircraft manufacturers remained heavily dependent on Air Ministry orders, which, however, being shared out among the numerous companies, tended to discourage rationalization, large-scale standardized production and technical innovation. For most of the inter-war period, old-fashioned fabric-covered biplanes continued to predominate, and it was not until rearmament in the late 1930s that metal-skinned monoplanes, with retractable undercarriages, more powerful engines and variable-pitch propellers, began to be vigorously developed.

There were some amalgamations and growth of larger-scale production, such as Vickers' take-over of Supermarine in 1928 and the mergers in 1934–5 between Armstrong Siddeley, Armstrong–Whitworth, Avro, Hawker and Gloster that led to the formation of the Hawker Siddeley group. This group, like the Bristol, De Havilland and Blackburn companies, manufactured aero-engines as well as airframes, but most of the other aircraft companies confined themselves to the latter, buying-out engines and other components, such as wheels, under-carriages, hydraulic systems, instruments, etc., from specialist manufacturers, in the same way as car firms in the motor industry. Rearmament and the creation of 'shadow factories' in the late 1930s led to the involvement of outside firms, such as English Electric, Metrovick and other electrical and mechanical engineering and motor-manufacturing companies, as the industry entered an era of prodigious expansion.

Electrical supply and manufactures

The rapid spread of electric power in factories and homes during the inter-war period was only rivalled in revolutionary importance by the growth of motor and aircraft manufacturing. It is therefore generally imagined that this new electrical age witnessed the waning of steam power, on which the 'first industrial revolution' had been based. In an important sense, of course, this is true, with the declining use of steam engines for direct driving of machinery, but electrical power was itself based on steam, except where hydro-electric generation was possible. In Britain electricity was produced predominantly by steam-driven generators—at first with reciprocating steam engines and then with increasingly powerful steam turbines, pioneered by Parsons. Throughout this period, moreover, the main fuel for steam-raising continued to be coal, though oil-firing was being developed, and even in modern nuclear power stations this new form of energy is utilized simply to produce heat for the boilers of steam turbines. Thus steam still remains the medium for conversion of heat into mechanical energy.

The 1930 Census of Production reveals the changing pattern of the United Kingdom's power resources in the inter-war period. (Horse-power statistics are not available from the 1935 Census.) The total capacity of the various types of prime movers, in all trades and electricity supply undertakings, was 21.2 million horse-power, or twice that of 1907 (see pp. 168–9), though the capacity 'ordinarily in use' totalled only 17.6 million horse-power, the remainder being 'in reserve or idle'. Over 93 per cent of that capacity was provided by steam engines (reciprocating and turbine), the rest by gas, oil and water engines. By this time steam turbines had become predominant, accounting for nearly three-fifths of capacity, while reciprocating steam engines had declined to little more than a third. Nearly half the total capacity was now in electricity supply undertakings, whereas in 1907 industrial firms had provided the great bulk of their own power, mostly direct from reciprocating steam engines.

PRIME MOVERS IN THE UNITED KINGDOM, 1930
(thousand h.p.)

Prime movers	All trades exclusive of electricity supply undertakings			Electricity supply undertakings		
	Ordinarily in use	In reserve or idle	Total	Ordinarily in use	In reserve or idle	Total
Reciprocating steam engines	5,936.3	1,059.8	6,996.1	94.1	116.4	210.
Steam turbines	2,053.5	851.7	2,905.2	8,294.2	1,351.4	9,645.
Internal combustion engines						
Gas	490.4	140.0	630.4	16.1	5.1	21.
Oil	329.7	62.3	392.0	103.9	6.7	110.
Water engines	104.6	12.2	116.8	143.2	32.8	176.
Others*	4.9	0.4	5.3	—	—	—
Total	8,919.4	2,126.4	11,045.8	8,651.5	1,512.4	10,163.

*Excluding locomotives, road-rollers, etc.

Source: *Fourth Census of Production*, 1930, *Final Report*, Part V, p. 113.

It was in electricity generation that steam turbines had most rapidly increased, especially in electricity supply undertakings, in which they accounted for over 96 per cent of generating capacity in use, compared with under 59 per cent in industry generally, where reciprocating engines, together with gas, oil and water engines, were still widely used both for electricity generation and for directly driving machinery. Total generating capacity (including generators 'in reserve or idle') was now 10.4 million kilowatts—six times that of 1907 (see pp. 169–70)—of which 7.4 million, or nearly three-quarters, was in electricity supply undertakings. The total capacity of electric motors available for driving machinery in all industries, including electricity undertakings, was 11.1 million (9.7 million 'ordinarily in use'), of which well below half was now driven by electricity generated by firms themselves. It is therefore evident that by this time the direct driving of machinery by steam engines and other prime movers was being superseded by use of electric motors, and that industrial firms were increasingly purchasing their supplies of electricity instead of generating their own. The degree of electrification varied considerably between different industries, ranging from 38.4 per cent in textiles to 95.6 per cent in engineering, shipbuilding and vehicles, but overall the proportion was 60.6 per cent.

INDUSTRIAL POWER IN USE IN THE UNITED KINGDOM, 1930*

Trade group	Power applied mechanically	Power applied electrically	Total power	Proportion of power applied electrically
	(thousand h.p.)	*(thousand h.p.)*	*(thousand h.p.)*	*(per cent)*
Factory trades				
Iron and steel	1,205.8	1,469.3	2,675.1	54.9
Engineering, shipbuilding and vehicles	82.4	1,784.7	1,867.1	95.6
Non-ferrous metals	28.4	220.0	248.4	88.6
Textiles	1,505.0	937.8	2,442.8	38.4
Leather	14.7	55.5	70.2	79.1
Clothing	19.2	87.7	106.9	82.0
Food, drink and tobacco	141.5	520.5	662.0	78.6
Chemicals, etc.	127.2	398.7	525.9	75.8
Paper, printing and stationery	128.3	575.8	704.1	81.8
Timber	68.0	193.3	261.3	74.0
Clay and building materials	161.9	358.0	519.9	68.9
Miscellaneous	55.6	332.9	388.5	85.7
Total (factory trades)	3,538.0	6,934.2	10,472.2	66.2
Non-factory trades				
Building and contracting	76.6	111.3	187.9	59.2
Mines and quarries	1,945.3	1,807.7	3,753.0	48.2
Public utility services*	476.6	432.9	909.5	47.6
Total (non-factory trades)	2,498.5	2,351.9	4,850.4	48.5
Total (all trades)	6,036.5	9,286.1	15,322.6	60.6

*Excluding electrical supply undertakings.

Source: Fourth Census of Production, 1930, *Final Report*, Part V, pp. 120–1.

These figures show that the metal trades, coal and textiles were still the great power users, but that other industries were now increasingly becoming power-driven, especially by electricity, which provided a revolutionary new means of transmitting and distributing power. Though experiments had been made with piping steam over very limited distances, in general each steam-powered works or factory required its own engine. Gas and hydraulic power were successfully distributed by mains and pipes in towns, but electricity eventually provided far wider scope. Initially, as we have seen, it was generated on a small-scale, first for individual large houses, public buildings or works, then progressing to schemes for local areas, organized by municipal authorities or private companies; although pioneers such as Ferranti at Deptford and Merz in the north-east had shown the possibilities of large central power-stations and long-distance high-voltage transmission, there were still hundreds of these small local under-takings in 1914 (see p. 195). During the inter-war years, however, although these small-scale characteristics survived in local distribution, electricity came to be produced in larger generating stations and transmitted over the greater part of the country by a 'national grid', so that it was generally available for conversion into heat or light or, by means of electric motors, into mechanical energy for driving machinery. The earlier local industrial dependence on coal was thus largely removed: manufactures tended to become much more widely dispersed, now that electric power could be thus conveyed by cables and wires for use in mechanical or electrothermal or electrolytic processes, though for many furnace operations coal or gas was still used and coalfields continued to exert a strong locational influence on such industries, as well as on the locations of power-stations. At the same time, electricity revolutionized internal factory lay-out and operations, by dispensing with gearing, shafting and belting, as individual machines could now be driven by electric motors. The general environment was also improved by a gradual reduction in the myriads of factory chimneys.

Electricity also came into general use for lighting streets and homes, rapidly displacing gas and oil lamps, as well as in a widening range of domestic appliances (see p. 356). Telephones and wireless sets (radios) similarly mul-tiplied, while the market for electrical equipment was also greatly expanded by the growth of the motor industry (see p. 349). Only in transport did electricity experience a relapse, with the decline of trams; though electric trolley-buses to some extent replaced them, petrol- and diesel-engined motor buses came into much more widespread use, while on the railways steam still predominated, except for the Southern line, electrified in the late 1930s.

Thus electrical engineering and manufacturing expanded rapidly in the inter-war period, as shown in figures of employment and output, though to a lesser extent in exports, because of concentration on the home market (see pp. 274–82). The range of production was vast: from simple cells and batteries to giant turbo-generators and transformers for power-stations; from narrow-gauge wire to massive multi-core cables; from small domestic motors to large power-units for industry and transport, together with a plethora of other products and components.

The basis of all these developments, of course, was the electrical supply system. After wartime experience had demonstrated the necessity for greater co-ordination between the numerous local authority and company undertakings, an Act of 1919 sought to achieve this by appointment of central Electricity Com-missioners and voluntary formation of regional Joint Electricity Authorities, with the aim of interlinking power-stations and organizing larger-scale production and distribution. But progress proved so slow that in 1926 a more far-reaching Act was passed, providing for the establishment of a Central Electricity Board and construction of a 'national grid'; the Board was empowered to concentrate generation in the most efficient stations, which would be linked by high-tension transmission lines, at a standardized alternating frequency and voltage, with control stations in each region. The Board would purchase bulk supplies of electricity from existing generating authorities, control its transmission and resell it to authorized distributors, so that the Act was a compromise between the necessity for an efficient national network and the interests of established under-takings concerned with generation, bulk supply and retail distribution.

During the following years this national plan was steadily brought into oper-ation. The last tower of the grid as initially planned was erected in September 1933, and by the end of 1935 over 4,000 miles of transmission lines were in operation. As larger and more efficient generating stations were developed and interlinked, the total number was gradually reduced; though the reduction took place much more slowly than originally envisaged—from 463 under authorized undertakings in 1927 to 297 by 1947—the bulk of output came from the larger 'selected stations' under the Board's control, numbering about half that total. Regional control stations were also set up and a national control-room was finally established at Bankside in 1938, thus achieving an interconnected national system. Capital investment and construction went on throughout the slump, stimulating the electrical engineering, metals and constructional industries with demands for power-station buildings, heavy generating plant, transformers, switchgear, grid towers, wires, cables and meters. And as the network was extended, consumption of electricity rose spectacularly, with increasing indus-trial and domestic electrification.

GROWTH OF THE ELECTRICITY SUPPLY INDUSTRY

Year	Numbers employed (thousands)	Generating capacity (million Kilowatts)	Units generated (thousand million B.T.Us or Kilowatt-hours)
1921–2	Not available	2.8	3.9
1926–7	48.7	4.7	7.0
1938–9	109.2	9.4	24.8

Source: Sir H. Self and E. M. Watson, *Electricity Supply in Great Britain* (1952), p. 210.

Year	Consumers of electricity	Year	Electric motors in Great Britain (million h.p.)
1920	730,000	1912	$2\frac{1}{2}$
1929	2,894,000	1924	$6\frac{1}{2}$
1938	8,920,000	1930	9
		1936	12

Source: R. A. S. Hennessey, *The Electric Revolution* (1971), p. 177.

Many industrial firms still generated their own electricity, but with the increasing availability and declining cost of public supply—the average price per unit sold was reduced from just over 2d. in the early 1920s to half that figure by 1939—private generation tended to decline. Cost-reducing technical advances were encouraged by larger-scale production and transmission, while the growth and diversification of demand resulted in more economic load-spreading. Despite the integration of supply through the national grid, however, complete standardization had by no means been achieved—there were still D.C. as well as A.C. systems, together with differing frequencies, voltages and tariffs—and there were still over 600 various authorized (statutory) undertakings, of widely differing sizes, involved in generation and distribution, operated by local authorities and companies, while there was also confusion of functions between the Electricity Commissioners and the Central Electricity Board. Proposals for administrative reorganization were therefore being strongly pressed in the late 1930s (for example in the Macgowan and P.E.P. reports), foreshadowing the eventual Nationalization Act of 1947.

The rapid electrification of the inter-war years, however, enormously boosted the electrical engineering industry, leading to the growth of large-scale production by a small number of major firms, producing not only heavy plant such as turbo-generators, transformers, switchgear and motors, together with equipment for electric locomotives, trams and trolley-buses, but also a widening range of domestic electrical goods. The extent of the consumer revolution in this period, however, should not be exaggerated, for although 65 per cent of United Kingdom households were wired for electricity by 1938, this was mainly for electric lighting; the majority had wireless (radio) sets, either mains or battery operated, while electric irons and fires were becoming more common, but, as Corley has shown, only 27 per cent of households had vacuum cleaners, only 18 per cent had electric cookers and a mere 3 per cent had refrigerators and washing machines, the market for such domestic appliances being as yet confined to the better-off.*. Nevertheless, the beginnings of this 'domestic revolution', combined with the rapidly growing demand for electrical equipment in the motor industry, led to a considerable growth of light electrical manufactures, in addition to heavy engineering. Growth was most rapid in the 1930s, as the national grid was completed, coinciding with the house-building boom and the extension of tariff protection, which greatly encouraged the domestic electrical industry, as well as causing foreign firms to manufacture in this country instead of importing. The

---

*In 1939 there were 8.5 million homes wired for electricity, with 6.5 million irons, 2.3 million vacuum cleaners, 1.6 million cookers, 480,000 water-heaters, 360,000 wash-boilers, 150,000 washing machines and 200,000 refrigerators, worked by electricity. P.E.P., *The Market for Household Appliances* (1945). In some appliances there was strong competition from gas (there were about 9 million gas cookers).

establishment of the British Broadcasting Corporation, at the same time as the Central Electicity Board, was followed by a parallel growth of the radio network and a vast increase in popular demand for receiving sets, the number of licences soaring from 1,350,000 in 1924–5 to 8,593,000 in 1937–8; an embryo market for television sets was also developing by the late 1930s.

In all these various fields of electrical engineering, large-scale production soon predominated, though small firms remained numerous, especially in 'wiring and contracting' (installations). In 1935 establishments with 500 or more workers accounted for nearly three-quarters of total employment (then 255,000). But as there were scores of large firms, as well as hundreds of small ones, the three biggest, though together employing over 60,000, accounted for barely a quarter of the total labour force. On the other hand, the concentration-ratio was high in particular branches of the industry: between two-thirds and four-fifths in gramophones, batteries and accumulators, telegraph and telephone apparatus, wireless valves and electric lamps, and about half in wires and cables, heating and cooking apparatus, and electrical machinery. This contrast reflects the fact that, while general electrical engineering predominated, with a considerable number of large firms, there was also a high degree of specialization in certain products, employing relatively much smaller numbers. The 'Big Three' in the industry—Associated Electrical Industries (A.E.I.), General Electric (G.E.C.) and English Electric—covered a very wide range: though weighted towards production of heavy plant for power stations, industry and transport, they were also the leading manufacturers of light bulbs, for example Osram (G.E.C.) and Ediswan and Mazda (A.E.I.), and were extending their interests in domestic appliances and radio. But even in their main fields there were other important firms, such as Parsons, Ferranti, Siemens and Thorn, while more specialized manufacturers were strongly entrenched elsewhere, such as British Insulated Callender's Cables (B.I.C.C.) and Lucas (in electrical equipment for the motor industry), together with numerous firms in domestic appliances, such as Hoover, Belling, Berry, Goblin, Simplex, Radiation, Morphy Richards, Hotpoint, Electrolux, Prestcold and Frigidaire, and also in the interrelated telegraph and telephone, wireless (radio) and gramophone manufactures, including Marconi, Cossor, Mullard (Philips), Decca, Pye, Murphy, Philco, Ferguson, Cable & Wireless, Standard Telephones & Cables, and Electrical & Musical Industries. These firms developed standardized mass-production in the 1930s, as the market for such consumer goods rapidly expanded, and there was an increasing tendency towards industrial concentration in the hands of large multi-product and specialist firms.

As before 1914, foreign capital, technology and enterprise remained very important in the electrical industry. American involvement was particularly strong. A.E.I. was a merger in 1928 of British Thomson-Houston (B.T.H., a subsidiary of the American General Electric)—which had previously absorbed Edison Swan—with Metropolitan Vickers (Metrovick, formerly the American-controlled British Westinghouse)*; the Hotpoint company was their subsidiary in domestic appliances. Moreover, in addition to controlling A.E.I., the American General Electric also acquired a large block of shares in the British G.E.C., which had grown substantially from its late nineteenth-century origins. American Westinghouse similarly, in 1929, secured a considerable stake in the English Electric Company, established in 1919 by a merger of various electrical and mechanical engineering interests, including those of Dick, Kerr & Co. There was much contemporary resentment against this growing (often clandestine) American control, but there were gains from American capital, technology and international market-sharing (cartel) arrangements†. In other branches of the electrical industry, American penetration was equally strong. Standard Telephones & Cables (formerly Western Electric) was a subsidiary of International Telephone & Telegraph. Electrical & Musical Industries, formed in 1931 by amalgamation of the Gramophone (H.M.V.) and Columbia companies, was also American-controlled; so were the Philco and Ferguson radio companies. Hoover Ltd., established in 1919 to market its American parent firm's vacuum cleaners, started production in Britain in the early 1930s. Prestcold and Frigidaire refrigerators were also manufactured by American-controlled companies, the former by Pressed Steel, who thus diversified from making car bodies, though the American interests were sold out in 1935. Other leading foreign concerns were the Dutch company, Philips, and Swedish Electrolux, while Siemens had German affiliations. Electrical manufactures, like chemicals, strikingly demonstrate the international, or multinational, developments in large-scale modern industry, in which, of course, many British companies participated.

Through this infusion of foreign enterprise, as well as by the achievements of British firms, there is no doubt that the electrical industry was much stronger than it had been before the First World War, both in the generation and application of electricity and in manufactures, especially of heavy plant; in light manufactures, mass-production techniques were gradually being developed. With the aid of tariffs, imports of electrical goods were substantially reduced, to between a third and a quarter of exports by the late 1930s. In this, as in other fields, the 'second industrial revolution' was transforming British industry.

---

*The Metropolitan Carriage & Wagon Co. (see p. 185) had acquired control of British Westinghouse during the War, and both were bought by Vickers in 1919, as part of their diversification policy, but they had to dispose of Metrovick in 1928 because of their difficulties in steel and engineering (see p. 312). Considerable rivalry, however, continued between B.T.H. and Metrovick within A.E.I.
†The American General Electric's shareholdings in the British G.E.C., however, were sold in 1935, those in A.E.I. in 1953; the Westinghouse holdings in English Electric were also disposed of soon after the Second World War, when the anti-trust movement in the United States began to have effect.

Select Bibliography

General Works

The following works, relating to the period since 1500, or in some cases since about 1700, are brought together here to avoid repetition in the ensuing sections.

Campbell, R. H., *Scotland since 1707: The Rise of an Industrial Society* (1964).

Chaloner, W. H., and Musson, A. E., *Industry and Technology* (1963), in the *Visual History of Modern Britain* series, ed. J. Simmons.

Cullen, L. M., *An Economic History of Ireland since 1660* (1972).

Deane, P., and Cole, W. A., *British Economic Growth, 1688–1959* (1964; 2nd edn. 1967).

Hoffmann, W. G., *British Industry, 1700–1950* (English trans., 1955).

Landes, D. S., *The Unbound Prometheus: Technological Change and Industrial Development in Western Europe from 1750 to the Present* (1969).

Lythe, S. G. E., and Butt, J., *An Economic History of Scotland, 1100–1939* (1975).

Mathias, P., *The First Industrial Nation: An Economic History of Britain, 1700–1914* (1969).

Mitchell, B. R., and Deane, P., *Abstract of British Historical Statistics* (1962).

Murphy, B., *A History of the British Economy, 1086–1970* (2 vols., 1973).

Pollard, S., and Crossley, D. W., *The Wealth of Britain, 1085–1966* (1968; rev. edn. 1972).

Singer, C., *et al.* (eds.), *A History of Technology*, Vols. III, IV and V (1953–8).

Usher, A. P., *A History of Mechanical Inventions* (rev. edn., 1954).

General Works, 1500–1700

Clapham, J. H., *A Concise Economic History of Britain from the Earliest Times to 1750* (1949).

Clark, G. N., *Science and Social Welfare in the Age of Newton* (1937).

—— 'Early Capitalism and Invention', *Econ. Hist. Rev.*, VI (1935–6).

Clark, P., and Slack, P., *English Towns in Transition, 1500–1700* (1976).

Clarkson, L. A., *The Pre-Industrial Economy in England, 1500–1750* (1971).

—— 'An Industrial Revolution in the Sixteenth and Seventeenth Centuries?' *Melbourne Hist. Rev.*, No. 2, 1962.

Coleman, D. C., 'Industrial Growth and Industrial Revolutions', *Economica*, n.s., XXIII (1956).

—— 'Labour in the English Economy of the Seventeenth Century', *Econ. Hist. Rev.*, 2nd ser., VIII (1955–6).

—— (ed.), *Revisions in Mercantilism* (1969).

—— *Industry in Tudor and Stuart England* (1975).

—— *The Economy of England, 1450–1750* (1977).

Cornwall, J., 'English Country Towns in the 1520s', *Econ. Hist. Rev.*, 2nd ser., XV (1962–3).

Cunningham, W., *Alien Immigrants in England* (1897; repr. with intro. by C. Wilson, 1969).

Davis, K. G., 'Joint Stock Investment in the Later Seventeenth Century', *Econ. Hist. Rev.*, 2nd ser., IV (1951–2).

Davies, M. G., *The Enforcement of English Apprenticeship: A Study in Applied Mercantilism, 1563–1642* (Cambridge, Mass., 1956).

Davis, R., *A Commercial Revolution: English Overseas Trade in the Seventeenth and Eighteenth Centuries* (Hist. Assocn. pamphlet, 1967).

—— (ed.), *English Overseas Trade, 1500–1700* (1973).

Elton, G. R., 'State Planning in Early Tudor England', *Econ. Hist. Rev.*, 2nd ser., XIII (1960–1).

Fisher, F. J., 'Some Experiments in Company Organisation in the Early Seventeenth Century', *Econ. Hist. Rev.*, IV (1932–4).

—— 'Commercial Trends and Policy in Sixteenth-Century England', *ibid.*, X (1940).

—— 'The Development of London as a Centre for Conspicuous Consumption in the Sixteenth and Seventeenth Centuries', *Trans. Roy. Hist. Soc.*, 4th ser., XXX (1948).

—— 'The Sixteenth and Seventeenth Centuries: The Dark Ages in English Economic History?' *Economica*, n.s., XXIV (1957).

—— (ed.), *Essays in the Economic and Social History of Tudor and Stuart England* (1961).

Gough, J. W., *The Rise of the Entrepreneur* (1969).

Habakkuk, H. J., 'Economic functions of English Landowners in the Seventeenth and Eighteenth Centuries', *Explorations in Entrepreneurial History*, VI (1953–4).

Hall, A. R., *The Scientific Revolution, 1500–1800* (1954).

Hartwell, R. M., 'Economic Growth in England before the Industrial Revolution', *Journ. of Econ. Hist.*, XXIX (1969).

Holderness, B. A., *Pre-Industrial England: Economy and Society 1500–1750* (1976).

Hollister-Short, G., 'Leads and Lags in late Seventeenth Century English Technology', *History of Technology*, I (1976).

Hoskins, W. G., *Provincial England: Essays in Economic and Social History* (1963).

Jones, E. L., 'Agricultural Origins of Industry', *Past and Present*, No. 40 (1968).

Kramer, S., *The English Craft Gilds* (New York, 1927).

Mendels, F. F., 'Proto-industrialization: The First Phase of the Industrialization Process', *Journ. of Econ. Hist.*, XXXII (1972).

Nef, J. U., *The Rise of the British Coal Industry* (2 vols., 1932).

—— 'The Progress of Technology and the Growth of Large-Scale Industry in Great Britain, 1540–1640', *Econ. Hist. Rev.*, V (1934–5).

Outhwaite, R. B., *Inflation in Tudor and Early Stuart England* (1969).

Price, W. H., *The English Patents of Monopoly* (Boston, Mass., 1906).

Ramsay, G. D., *English Overseas Trade in the Centuries of Emergence* (1957).

Ramsey, P., *Tudor Economic Problems* (1963).

—— (ed.), *The Price Revolution in Sixteenth-Century England* (1971).

Rees, W., *Industry Before the Industrial Revolution* (2 vols., 1968).

Scott, W. R., *The Constitution and Finance of English, Scottish and Irish Joint-Stock Companies to 1720* (3 vols., 1910–12).

Scoville, W. C., 'Minority Migrations and the Diffusion of Technology', *Journ. of Econ. Hist.*, XI (1951).

Stone, L., 'State Control in Sixteenth-Century England', *Econ. Hist. Rev.*, XVII (1947).

—— 'The Nobility in Business, 1540–1640', in B. E. Supple (ed.), *The Entrepreneur* (Cambridge, Mass., 1958).

—— 'Social Mobility in England, 1500–1700', *Past & Present*, No. 33, April 1966.

Supple, B. E., *Commercial Crisis and Change in England, 1600–1642* (1959).

—— 'Economic History and Economic Underdevelopment', *Canadian Journ. of Econs. and Pol. Science*, XXVII (1961).

Taube, E., 'German Craftsmen in England during the Tudor Period', *Econ. Hist.*, No. 14, Feb. 1939.

Tawney, R. H., *Religion and the Rise of Capitalism* (1926).

Thirsk, J., 'Industries in the Countryside', in Fisher (ed.), op. cit.

Unwin, G., *Industrial Organisation in the Sixteenth and Seventeenth Centuries* (1904; repr. 1957).

—— *The Gilds and Companies of London* (1908; repr. 1966).

—— *Studies in Economic History* (ed. R. H. Tawney, 1927; 2nd edn., 1958; repr. 1966).

Wilson, C., *Mercantilism* (Hist. Assocn. pamphlet, 1958).

—— *England's Apprenticeship, 1603–1763* (1965).

—— *Economic History and the Historian: Collected Essays* (1969).

General Works, 1700–1850

Aldcroft, D. H., and Fearon, P. (eds.), *British Economic Fluctuations, 1790–1939* (1972).

Anderson, B. L., "The Attorneys and the Early Capital Market in Lancashire', in Harris, J. R. (ed.), *Liverpool and Merseyside* (1969), repr. in Crouzet (ed.), op. cit.

Ashton, T. S., *The Industrial Revolution, 1760–1830* (1948; rev. edn. 1966).

—— *An Economic History of England: The Eighteenth Century* (1955).

—— *Economic Fluctuations in England, 1700–1800* (1959).

Berrill, E. V., 'International Trade and the Rate of Economic Growth', *Econ. Hist. Rev.*, 2nd ser., XII (1959–60).

Bowden, W., *Industrial Society in England towards the End of the Eighteenth Century* (2nd edn., 1966).

Buchanan, R. A., *Technology and Social Progress* (1965).

Checkland, S. G., *The Rise of Industrial Society in England, 1815–1885* (1964).

Clapham, J. H., *An Economic History of Modern Britain*, Vol. I (1926).

Cooke, C. A., *Corporation, Trust and Company* (1950).

Court, W. H. B., *A Concise Economic History of Britain from 1750 to Recent Times* (1954).

Crafts, N. F. R., 'English Economic Growth in the Eighteenth Century: A Re-Examination of Deane and Cole's Estimates', *Econ. Hist. Rev.*, 2nd ser., XXIX (1976).

Crouzet, F. (ed.), *Capital Formation in the Industrial Revolution* (1972).

Deane, P., *The First Industrial Revolution* (1965).

—— 'Capital Formation in Britain before the Railway Age', *Economic Development and Cultural Change*, IX (1961), repr. in Crouzet, op. cit.

—— 'The Role of Capital in the Industrial Revolution', *Explorations in Econ. Hist.*, X (1972–3).

See also Deane and Cole, op. cit.

Devine, T. M., 'The Colonial Trades and Industrial Investment in Scotland, *c.* 1700–1815', *Econ. Hist. Rev.*, 2nd ser., XXIX (1976).

Dubois, A. B., *The English Business Company after the Bubble Act, 1720–1800* (New York, 1938).

Evans, G. H., *British Corporation Finance, 1775–1850* (1936).

Eversley, D. E. C., 'The Home Market and Economic Growth in England, 1750–1780', in Jones, E. L., and Mingay, G. E. (eds.), *Land, Labour and Population in the Industrial Revolution* (1967).

Flinn, M. W., *The Origins of the Industrial Revolution* (1966).

Habakkuk, H. J., *American and British Technology in the Nineteenth Century* (1962).

Hartwell, R. M., (ed)., *The Causes of the Industrial Revolution in England* (1967).

—— *The Industrial Revolution and Economic Growth* (1972).

Higgins, J. P. P., and Pollard, S. (eds.), *Aspects of Capital Investment in Great Britain, 1750–1850* (1971).

Hobsbawm, E. J., *Industry and Empire: An Economic History of Britain since 1750* (1968).

Hunt, B. C., *The Development of the Business Corporation in England, 1800–1867* (1936).

John, A. H., 'War and the English Economy, 1700–1813', *Econ. Hist. Rev.*, 2nd ser., VII (1954–5).

—— 'Aspects of English Economic Growth in the First Half of the Eighteenth Century', *Economica*, n.s., XXVIII (1961).

Little, A. J., *Deceleration in the Eighteenth-Century British Economy* (1976). (Actually refers to the second quarter of that century.)

Mantoux, P., *The Industrial Revolution in the Eighteenth Century* (1928; 2nd edn. 1961).

McKendrick, N., 'Home Demand and Economic Growth', in McKendrick (ed.), *Historical Perspectives* (1974).

Minchinton, W. E. (ed.), *The Growth of English Overseas Trade in the Seventeenth and Eighteenth Centuries* (1969).

Moffit, L. W., *England on the Eve of the Industrial Revolution* (1925).

Musson, A. E., and Robinson, E., *Science and Technology in the Industrial Revolution* (1969).

Musson, A. E., *Science, Technology and Economic Growth in the Eighteenth Century* (1972).

Payne, P. L., *British Entrepreneurship in the Nineteenth Century* (1974).

Perkin, H. J., *The Origins of Modern English Society, 1780–1880* (1969).

Pollard, S., *The Genesis of Modern Management* (1965).

—— 'Investment, Consumption and the Industrial Revolution', *Econ. Hist. Rev.*, 2nd ser., XI (1958–9).

—— 'Fixed Capital in the Industrial Revolution in Britain', *Journ. of Econ. Hist.*, XXIV (1964), repr. in Crouzet (ed.), op. cit.

—— 'The Growth and Distribution of Capital in Great Britain, c. 1770–1870', *Third Int. Conf. of Econ. Hist.*, Munich, 1965, I (Paris, 1968).

Porter, G. R., and Hirst, F. W., *The Progress of the Nation* (1912).

Pressnell, L. S. (ed.), *Studies in the Industrial Revolution*, (1960).

Ratcliffe, B. M. (ed.), *Great Britain and Her World, 1750–1914* (1975).

Redford, A., *Labour Migration in England, 1800–1850* (3rd edn., 1976).

—— *The Economic History of England, 1760–1860* (2nd edn., 1960).

Rosenberg, N., 'Factors Affecting the Diffusion of Technology', *Explorations in Economic History*, X (1972–3).

Rostow, W. W., *The Process of Economic Growth* (2nd edn., 1960).

—— *The Economics of Take-Off into Sustained Growth* (1963).

Schofield, R. E., *The Lunar Society of Birmingham* (1963).

Spring, D., 'The English Landed Estate in the Age of Coal and Iron: 1830–1880', *Journ. of Econ. Hist.*, XI (1951).

Tann, J., *The Development of the Factory* (1970).

Thompson, F. M. L., 'Land Ownership and Economic Growth in England in the Eighteenth Century', in E. L. Jones and S. J. Woolf, *Agrarian Change and Economic Development* (1969).

Tranter, N. L., *Population and Industrialization* (1973).

Ward, J. T., and Wilson, R. G. (eds.), *Land and Industry: The Landed Estate in the Industrial Revolution* (1971).

Westerfield, R. B., *Middlemen in English Business, Particularly Between 1660 and 1760* (New Haven, Conn., 1915; repr. 1969).

Wilson, C., 'The Entrepreneur in the Industrial Revolution in Great Britain', *History*, XLII (1957), repr. in *Economic History and the Historian* (1969).

Wrigley, E. A., 'The Supply of Raw Materials in the Industrial Revolution', *Econ. Hist. Rev.*, 2nd ser., XV (1962–3).

General Works, 1850–1914

Aldcroft, D. H., and Richardson, H. W., *The British Economy 1870–1939* (1969).

Aldcroft, D. H. (ed.), *The Development of British Industry and Foreign Competition 1875–1914* (1968).

Ames, E., and Rosenberg, N., 'Changing Technological Leadership and Industrial Growth', *Econ. Journ.*, LXXIII (1963).

Ashworth, W., *An Economic History of England, 1870–1939* (1960).

—— 'Changes in the Industrial Structure, 1870–1914', *Yorks. Bull.*, XVII (1965).

—— 'The Late Victorian Economy', *Economica*, n.s., XXXIII (1966).

Cairncross, A. K., *Home and Foreign Investment, 1870–1913* (1953).

Carter, G. R., *The Tendency towards Industrial Combination* (1913).

Church, R. A., *The Great Victorian Boom, 1850–1873* (1975).

Clapham, J. H., *An Economic History of Modern Britain*, II and III (1932, 1938).

Coppock, D. J., 'The Climacteric of the 1890s: A Critical Note', *Manchester School*, XXIV (1956), commenting on Phelps-Brown and Handfield-Jones, op. cit.

—— 'The Causes of the Great Depression, 1873–1896', *ibid.*, XXIX (1961). See also Saville's comments and Coppock's reply, *ibid.*, XXXI (1963), together with articles by Musson and Coppock, *Econ. Hist. Rev.*, 2nd ser., XV (1962–3) and XVII (1964–5).

Davis, L., 'The Capital Markets and Industrial concentration: The U.S. and U.K., a Comparative Study', *Econ. Hist. Rev.*, 2nd ser., XIX (1966–7).

Deane, P., 'New Estimates of Gross National Product for the United Kingdom, 1830–1914', *Rev. of Income and Wealth*, Series 14, No. 2, June 1968.

Edelstein, M., 'Rigidity and Bias in the British Capital Market, 1870–1913', in McCloskey (ed.), *Essays on a Mature Economy* (1971).

Feinstein, C. H., *National Income, Expenditure and Output of the United Kingdom, 1855–1965* (1972).

Fitzgerald, P., *Industrial Combination in England* (1927).

Frankel, M., 'Obsolescence and Technical Change in a Maturing Economy', *American Econ. Rev.*, XLV (1955). See also Gordon's comments and Frankel's reply, *ibid.*, XLVI (1956).

Hall, A. R. (ed.), *The Export of Capital from Britain, 1870–1914* (1968).

Hannah, L., 'Mergers in British Manufacturing Industry, 1880–1918', *Oxford Econ. Papers*, n.s., XXVI (1974).

—— *The Rise of the Corporate Economy* (1976).

Harley, C. K., 'Skilled Labour and the Choice of Technique in Edwardian Industry', *Explorations in Econ. Hist.*, XI (1974).

Hoffman, R. J. S., *Great Britain and the German Trade Rivalry, 1875—1914* (Philadelphia, 1933).

Jones, G. T., *Increasing Return* (1933).

Kennedy, W. P., 'Foreign Investment, Trade and Growth in the United Kingdom, 1870–1913', *Explorations in Econ. Hist.*, XI (1974).

Kindleberger, C. P., *Economic Growth in France and Britain, 1851–1950* (Cambridge, Mass., 1964).

League of Nations, *Industrialization and Foreign Trade* (Geneva, 1945).

Lee, C. H., *Regional Economic Growth in the United Kingdom since the 1880s* (1971).

Levine, A. M., *Industrial Retardation in Britain, 1880–1914* (1967).

Levy, H., *Monopolies, Cartels and Trusts in British Industry* (English trans. 2nd edn., 1927).

Lewis, W. A., 'International Competition in Manufactures', *American Econ. Rev.*, XLVII (1957).

Macrosty, H. W., *The Trust Movement in British Industry* (1907).

McCloskey, D. N., 'Did Victorian Britain Fail?', *Econ. Hist. Rev.*, 2nd ser., XXIII (1970). See also Aldcroft's 'Comment' and McCloskey's 'Rejoinder', *ibid.*, XXVII (1974).

—— (ed.), *Essays on a Mature Economy: Britain after 1840* (1971).

—— and Sandberg, L. G., 'From Damnation to Redemption: Judgements on the Late Victorian Entrepreneur', *Explorations in Econ. Hist.*, IX (1971–2).

Meyer, J. R., 'An Input–Output Approach to Evaluating the Influence of Exports on British Industrial Production in the late 19th Century', *Explorations in Entrepreneurial History*, VIII (1955–6).

Musson, A. E., 'The Great Depression in Britain, 1873–1896: A Reappraisal', *Journ. of Econ. Hist.*, XIX (1959).

—— 'British Industrial Growth during the "Great Depression" (1873–96)',

Econ. Hist. Rev., 2nd ser., XV (1962–3). See also the subsequent articles by Coppock and Musson, *ibid.*, XVII (1964–5).

Payne, P. L., 'The Emergence of the Large-scale Company in Great Britain, 1870–1914', *Econ. Hist. Rev.*, 2nd ser., XX (1967). See also the work by Payne cited in the previous section.

Phelps-Brown, E. H., and Handfield-Jones, S. J., 'The Climacteric of the 1890s', *Oxford Econ. Papers*, n.s., IV (1952). See also comments by Coppock, op. cit.

Prest, A. R., 'National Income of the United Kingdom, 1870–1946', *ibid.*, LVIII (1948).

Ratcliffe, B. M., op cit. (previous section).

Sanderson, J. M., *The Universities and British Industry, 1850–1970* (1972).

Saul, S. B., *Studies in British Overseas Trade, 1870–1914* (1960).

—— 'The Export Economy, 1870–1914', *Yorks. Bull.*, XVII (1965).

—— 'The American Impact on British Industry, 1895–1914', *Bus. Hist.*, III (1960).

—— *The Myth of the Great Depression, 1873–1896* (1969).

Saville, J., *Studies in the British Economy, 1870–1914* (1965), special issue of *Yorks. Bull.*, XVII (1965).

—— 'Some Retarding Factors in the British Economy before 1914', *ibid.*, XIII (1961). See also his comments on Coppock's article in *Manchester School*, XXXI (1963).

Sayers, R. S., *A History of Economic Change in England, 1880–1939* (1967).

Shannon, H. A., 'The Coming of General Limited Liability', *Econ. Hist.*, No. 6, Jan. 1931.

—— 'The Limited Companies of 1866–1883', *Econ. Hist. Rev.*, IV (1932–4).

Stopford, J. M., 'The Origins of British-Based Multinational Manufacturing Enterprises', *Bus. Hist. Rev.*, XLVIII (1974).

Tyszynski, H., 'World Trade in Manufactured Commodities, 1899–1950', *Manchester School*, XIX (1951).

Utton, M. A., 'Some Features of the Early Merger Movements in British Manufacturing Industries', *Bus. Hist.*, XIV (1972).

Wilson, C., 'Economy and Society in Late Victorian Britain', *Econ. Hist. Rev.*, 2nd ser., XVIII (1965–6), repr. in *Economic History and the Historian* (1969).

General Works, 1914–39

Aldcroft, D. H., *The Inter-War Economy: Britain, 1919–1939* (1970).

—— and Fearon, P. (eds.), *Economic Growth in Twentieth-Century Britain* (1969).

—— and Richardson, H. W., op. cit. (in previous section).

Alford, B. W. E., *Depression and Recovery: British Economic Growth, 1918–1939* (1972).

Allen, G. C., *British Industries and their Organisation* (5th edn., 1970).

Armstrong, A., and Silberston, A., 'Size of Plant, Size of Enterprise and Concentration in British Manufacturing Industry, 1935–58', *Journ. Roy. Stat. Soc.*, Series A, Vol. 128 (1965).

Benham, F., *Great Britain under Protection* (1940).

British Association, *Britain in Depression* (1935).

—— *Britain in Recovery* (1938).

Brown, A. J., *Industrialisation and Trade: The Changing World Pattern and the Position of Britain* (1943).

Burn, D. L. (ed.), *The Structure of British Industry*, (2 vols., 1958).

Compton, M., and Bott, E. H., *British Industry* (1940).

Cook, P. L., and Cohen, R. (eds.), *The Effects of Mergers: Six Studies* (1958).

Dennison, S. R., *The Location of Industry and the Depressed Areas* (1939).

Dunning, J. H., *American Investment in British Manufacturing Industry* (1958).

—— and Thomas, W. A., *British Industry: Change and Development in the Twentieth Century* (1961).

Eveley, R., and Little, I. M. D., *Concentration in British Industry* (1960).

Feinstein, C. H., *Domestic Capital Formation in the United Kingdom, 1920–1938* (1965). See also Feinstein's work cited in previous section.

Florence, P. Sargant, *Ownership, Control and Success of Large Companies: An Analysis of English Industrial Structure and Policy, 1936–1951* (1961).

—— *The Logic of British and American Industry* (1953; 3rd edn. 1972).

Fogarty, M. P., *Prospects of the Industrial Areas of Great Britain* (1945).

—— (ed.), *Further Studies in Industrial Organization* (1948), following Silverman (ed.), op. cit.

George, K. D., *Industrial Organisation: Competition, Growth and Structural Change in Britain* (1971).

Hannah, L., 'Takeover Bids in Britain before 1950', *Bus. Hist.*, XVI (1974).

—— 'Managerial Innovation and the Rise of the Large-Scale Company in Interwar Britain', *Econ. Hist. Rev.*, 2nd ser., XXVII (1974).

—— (ed.), *Management Strategy and Business Development* (1976). See also the work by Hannah cited in previous section.

Heath, H. F., and Hetherington, A. L., *Industrial Research and Development in the United Kingdom* (1946).

Jewkes, J., Sawers, D., and Stillerman, R., *The Sources of Invention* (1958; 2nd edn., 1969).

Kahn, A. E., *Great Britain in the World Economy* (New York, 1946).

League of Nations, op. cit. (in previous section).

Leak, H., and Maizels, A., 'The Structure of British Industry', *Journ. Roy. Stat. Soc.*, CVIII (1945).

Lee, C. H., op. cit. (in previous section).

Lewis, W. A., *Economic Survey, 1919–1939* (1949).

Lomax, K. S., 'Production and Productivity Movements in the United Kingdom since 1900', *Journ. Roy. Stat. Soc.*, Series A, Vol. 122, pt. 2 (1959).

—— 'Growth and Productivity in the United Kingdom', *Productivity Measurement Rev.*, XXXVIII (1964), repr. in Aldcroft and Fearon (eds.), op. cit.

London and Cambridge Economic Service, *The British Economy: Key Statistics, 1900–1966* (1967).

Lucas, A. F., *Industrial Reconstruction and the Control of Competition* (1937).

Maddison, A., 'Output, Employment, and Productivity in British Manufacturing in the last Half-century', *Bull. Oxford Inst. Stats.*, XVII (1955).

Maizels, A., *Industrial Growth and World Trade* (1963).

Milward, A. S., *The Economic Effects of the Two World Wars in Britain* (1970).

Plummer, A., *New British Industries in the Twentieth Century* (1937).

—— *International Combines in Modern Industry* (3rd edn., 1951).

Political and Economic Planning, *Report on the Location of Industry* (1939).

Ridley, T. M., 'Industrial Production in the United Kingdom, 1900–1953', *Economica*, n.s., XXII (1955).

Rostas, L., *Comparative Productivity in British and American Industry* (1948).

Sanderson, J. M., 'Research and the Firm in British Industry, 1919–1939', *Science Studies*, II (1972). See also the work by Sanderson cited in previous section.

Sayers, R. S., 'The Springs of Technical Progress, 1919–39', *Econ. Journ.*, LX (1950). See also work by Sayers cited in previous section.

Silverman, H. A. (ed.), *Studies in Industrial Organization* (1946).

Svennilson, I., *Growth and Stagnation in the European Economy* (Geneva, 1954).

Tyszynski, H., op. cit. (in previous section).

Youngson, A. J., *The British Economy, 1920–1966* (1967).

Specialized Works on Individual Industries

Building and allied trades

Bowley, Marian, *Innovations in Building Materials* (1960).

—— *The British Building Industry* (1966).

Cairncross, A. K., and Weber, B., 'Fluctuations in Building in Great Britain, 1785–1849', *Econ. Hist. Rev.*, 2nd ser., IX (1956–7).

Chalklin, C. W., *The Provincial Towns of Georgian England: A Study of the Building Process 1740–1820* (1974).

Cook, P. L., 'The Cement Industry', in Cook (ed.), *Effects of Mergers* (1958).

Cooney, E. W., 'The Origins of the Victorian Master Builders', *Econ. Hist. Rev.*, 2nd ser., VIII (1955–6).

—— 'Long Waves in Building in the British Economy of the Nineteenth Century', *ibid.*, XIII (1960–1), repr. in Aldcroft and Fearon, op. cit.

Davey, N., *Building in Britain: The Growth and Organisation of Building Processes in Britain from Roman Times to the Present Day* (1964).

—— *A History of Building Materials* (1961).

Lindsay, Jean, *A History of the North Wales Slate Industry* (1974).

Maywald, K., 'An Index of Building Costs in the United Kingdom, 1845–1938', *Econ. Hist. Rev.*, 2nd ser., VII (1954–5).

Parry Lewis, J., *Building Cycles and Britain's Growth* (1965).

Richardson, H. W., and Aldcroft, D. H., *Building in the British Economy between the Wars* (1968).

Robinson, H. W., *The Economics of Building* (1939).

Saul, S. B., 'House Building in England, 1890–1914', *Econ. Hist. Rev.*, 2nd ser., XV (1962–3).

Shannon, H. A., 'Bricks – A Trade Index, 1785–1849', *Economica*, n.s., I (1934).

Chemical and allied trades

Barker, T. C., 'Lancashire Coal, Cheshire Salt and the Rise of Liverpool', *Lancs. & Chesh. Hist. Soc. Trans.*, Vol. 103 (1951).

Barker, T. C., Dickinson, R., and Hardie, D. W. F., 'The Origins of the Synthetic Alkali Industry in Britain', *Economica*, XXIII (1956).

Berry, E. K., 'The Borough of Droitwich and its Salt Industry, 1215–1700', *Univ. of Birmingham Hist. Journ.*, V (1957–8).

Brace, H. W., *History of Seed Crushing in Great Britain* (1960).

Butt, J., 'Technical Change and the Growth of the British Shale-Oil Industry (1680–1870)', *Econ. Hist. Rev.*, 2nd ser., XVII (1964–5).

Calvert, A. F., *Salt and the Salt Industry* (2nd edn., 1929).

Campbell, W. A., *The Chemical Industry* (1971).

Chaloner, W. H., 'Salt in Cheshire, 1600–1870', *Lancs. & Chesh. Antiq. Soc. Trans.*, LXXI (1961).

Chandler, D., and Lacey, A. D., *The Rise of the Gas Industry in Britain* (1949).

Chapman, S. D., *Jesse Boot of Boots the Chemists* (1974).

Clow, A. and N. L., *The Chemical Revolution* (1952).

Cohen, Ruth, 'The Soap Industry', in Cook (ed.), *Effects of Mergers* (1958).

Donnithorne, Audrey G., *British Rubber Manufacturing* (1958).

Falkus, M. E., 'The British Gas Industry before 1850', *Econ. Hist. Rev.*, 2nd ser., XX (1967).

Gittins, L., 'The Manufacture of Alkali in Britain 1779–1789', *Annals of Science*, Vol. 22 (1966).

Haber, L. E., *The Chemical Industry during the Nineteenth Century* (1958).

—— *The Chemical Industry, 1900–1930* (1971).

Hardie, D. W. F., *A History of the Chemical Industry in Widnes* (1950).

—— and Pratt, J. D., *A History of the Modern British Chemical Industry* (1966).

Lindert, P. H., and Trace, K., 'Yardsticks for Victorian Entrepreneurs', in McCloskey (ed.), *Essays on a Mature Economy* (1971).

Miall, S., *A History of the British Chemical Industry* (1931).

Morgan, Sir Gilbert T., and Pratt, D. D., *The British Chemical Industry: Its Rise and Development* (1938).

Mott, R. A., *History of Coke Making* (1936).

Musson, A. E., *Enterprise in Soap and Chemicals* (1965).

Padley, R., 'The Beginnings of the British Alkali Industry', *Univ. of Birmingham Hist. Journ.*, III (1951–2).

Reader, W. J., *Imperial Chemical Industries. A History*, Vol. I, *The Forerunners, 1870–1926* (1970), Vol. II, *The First Quarter Century, 1926–1952* (1975).

Richardson, H. W., 'The Development of the Synthetic Dyestuffs Industry before 1939', *Scottish Journ. of Pol. Econ.*, IX (1962).

Schidrowitz, P., and Dawson, T. R. (eds.), *History of the Rubber Industry* (1952).

Turton, R. B., *The Alum Farm* (1938).

Williams, T. I., *The Chemical Industry Past and Present* (1953).

Wilson, C., *The History of Unilever* (2 vols., 1954).

Clothing trades (for Hosiery, see Textiles)

Brockhurst, H. E., *British Factory Production of Men's Clothing* (1950).

Dobbs, S. P., *The Clothing Workers of Great Britain* (1928).

Dony, J. G., *A History of the Straw Hat Industry* (1942).

—— 'The Hat Industry', in Silverman (ed.), op. cit.

Giles, Phyllis M., 'The Felt-hatting Industry, c. 1500–1800, with particular reference to Lancashire and Cheshire', *Lancs. & Chesh. Antiq. Soc. Trans.*, LXIX (1960).

Newman, P. K., 'The Early London Clothing Trades', *Oxford Econ. Papers*, n.s., IV (1952).

Poole, B. W., *The Clothing Trades Industry* (1920).

Schmiechen, J. A., 'State Reform and the Local Economy: an Aspect of Industrialization in Late Victorian and Edwardian London', *Econ. Hist. Rev.*, XXVIII (1975).

Stewart, M., and Hunter, L., *The Needle is Threaded: The History of an Industry* (1964).

Thomas, Joan, *A History of the Leeds Clothing Industry* (Yorks. Bull., Occasional Paper, No. 1, 1955).

Wray, Margaret, *The Women's Outerwear Industry* (1957).

Coal-mining

Ashton, T. S., and Sykes, J., *The Coal Industry of the Eighteenth Century* (1929; repr. 1964).

Atkinson, F., *The Great Northern Coalfield, 1700–1900* (1966).

Beacham, A., 'Efficiency and Organisation of the British Coal Industry', *Econ. Journ.*, LV (1945).

Benson, J., and Neville, R. G. (eds.), *Studies in the Yorkshire Coal Industry* (1976).

Buxton, N. K., 'Entrepreneurial Efficiency in the British Coal Industry between the Wars', *Econ. Hist. Rev.*, 2nd ser., XXIII (1970). See also Kirby's comments and Buxton's reply, *ibid.*, XXV (1972).

Court, W. H. B., 'Problems of the British Coal Industry between the Wars', *Econ. Hist. Rev.*, XV (1945).

Duckham, B. F., *A History of the Scottish Coal Industry*, Vol. I, *1700–1815* (1970).

Galloway, R. L., *A History of Coal Mining in Great Britain* (1882; repr. 1969).

—— *Annals of Coal Mining and the Coal Trade* (2 vols., 1898 and 1904; repr. 1974).

Griffin, A. R., *The British Coalmining Industry* (1977).

Jevons, H. S., *The British Coal Trade* (1915).

Jones, J. H., Cartwright, G., and Guenault, P. H., *The Coal-Mining Industry* (1939).

Kirby, M. W., 'The Control of Competition in the British Coal Mining Industry in the Thirties', *Econ. Hist. Rev.*, XXVI (1973). See also his comments on Buxton's article, *ibid.*, XXV (1972).

Langton, J., 'Coal Output in South-West Lancashire, 1590–1799', *ibid.*, XXV (1972).

McCloskey, D. N., 'International Differences in Productivity? Coal and Steel in America and Britain before World War I', in McCloskey (ed.), *Essays on a Mature Economy* (1971).

Morris, J. H., and Williams, L. J., *The South Wales Coal Industry, 1841–1875* (1958).

Nef, J. U., *The Rise of the British Coal Industry* (2 vols., 1932).

Neuman, A. M., *Economic Organisation of the British Coal Industry* (1934).

Political and Economic Planning, *Report on the British Coal Industry* (1936).

Smith, R. S., 'Huntingdon Beaumont, Adventurer in Coal Mines', *Renaissance and Modern Studies*, I (1957).

Stone, L., 'An Elizabethan Coalmine', *Econ. Hist. Rev.*, 2nd ser., III (1950–1).

Sweezy, P. M., *Monopoly and Competition in the English Coal Trade, 1550–1750* (1938).

Taylor, A. J., 'Labour Productivity and Technological Innovation in the British Coal Industry, 1850–1914', *Econ. Hist. Rev.*, 2nd ser., XIV (1961–2).

—— 'The Coal Industry', in Aldcroft (ed.), *The Development of British Industry and Foreign Competition, 1875–1914* (1968).

Walters, R., 'Labour Productivity in the South Wales Steam-Coal Industry, 1870–1914', *Econ. Hist. Rev.*, 2nd ser., XXVIII (1975).

Electrical supply and electrical engineering

Appleyard, R., *Charles Parsons* (1933).

Baldwin, F. C. G., *The History of the Telephone in the United Kingdom* (1925).

Ballin, H. H., *The Organisation of Electricity Supply in Great Britain* (1946).

Byatt, I. C. R., 'Electrical Products', in Aldcroft (ed.), *The Development of British Industry and Foreign Competition, 1875–1914* (1968).

Corley, T. A. B., *Domestic Electrical Appliances* (1966).

Dunsheath, P., *A History of Electrical Engineering* (1962).

Hennessey, R. A. S., *The Electric Revolution* (1972).

Hunter, P. V., and Hazell, J. T., *The Development of Power Cables* (1956).

Jones, R., and Marriott, O., *Anatomy of a Merger: A History of G.E.C., A.E.I. and English Electric* (1970).

Kieve, J. L., *The Electric Telegraph* (1973).

Parsons, R. H., *The Early Days of the Power Station Industry* (1939).

P.E.P., *Report on the Supply of Electricity in Great Britain* (1936).

—— *The Market for Household Appliances* (1945).

Randall, W. L., *S.Z. de Ferranti* (1943).

Scott, J. D., *Siemens Brothers, 1858–1958* (1959).

Self, Sir Henry, and Watson, Eliz., *Electricity Supply in Great Britain* (1952).

Sturmey, S. G., *The Economic Development of Radio* (1958).

Whyte, A. G., *The Electrical Industry* (1904).

—— *Forty Years of Electrical Progress: The Story of the G.E.C.* (1930).

Food, drink and tobacco trades

Alford, B. W. E., *W. D. & H. O. Wills and the Development of the U.K. Tobacco Industry, 1786–1965* (1973).

Bennett, R., and Elton, J., *History of Corn Milling* (4 vols., 1898–1904).

Burnett, J., 'The Baking Industry in the Nineteenth Century', *Business History*, V (1962–3).

Burnett, R. G., *Through the Mill* (1945).

Corley, T. A. B., *Quaker Enterprise in Biscuits: Huntley and Palmer's of Reading, 1822–1972* (1972).

Edwards, H. V., 'Flour-Milling', in Fogarty (ed.), *Further Studies in Industrial Organization* (1948).

Lloyd-Hind, H., *Brewing Science and Practice* (2 vols., 1938 and 1940).

Lynch, P., and Vaizey, J., *Guinness's Brewery in the Irish Economy, 1759–1876* (1960).

Mathias, P., *The Brewing Industry in England, 1700–1830* (Cambridge, 1959).

Sheppard, R., and Newton, E., *The Story of Bread* (1957).

Sigsworth, E. M., 'Science and the Brewing Industry, 1850–1900', *Econ. Hist. Rev.*, 2nd ser., XVII (1964–5).

—— *The Brewing Trade during the Industrial Revolution: The Case of Yorkshire* (1967).

Vaizey, J., *The Brewing Industry, 1886–1951* (1960).

—— 'The Brewing Industry', in Cook (ed.), *Effects of Mergers* (1958).

Glassmaking

Barker, T. C., *Pilkington Brothers and the Glass Industry* (1960; 2nd edn., 1977).

——— 'The Glass Industry', in Aldcroft (ed.), *The Development of British Industry and Foreign Competition, 1875–1914* (1968).

Cook, P. L., 'The Flat-Glass Industry', in Cook (ed.), *Effects of Mergers* (1958).

Crossley, D. W., 'The Performance of the Glass Industry in Sixteenth-Century England', *Econ. Hist. Rev.*, 2nd ser., XXV (1972).

Godfrey, Eleanor S., *The Development of English Glassmaking, 1560–1640* (1975).

Guttery, D. R., *From Broad Glass to Cut Crystal: A History of the Stourbridge Glass Industry* (1956).

Kenyon, G. H., *The Glass Industry of the Weald* (1967).

Logan, J. C., 'The Dumbarton Glass Works Company', *Business History*, XIV (1972).

Powell, H. J., *Glass-Making in England* (1923).

Winbolt, S. E., *Wealden Glass: The Surrey–Sussex Glass Industry, 1261–1615* (1933).

Iron and steel

Addis, J. P., *The Crawshay Dynasty: A Study in Industrial Organisation and Development, 1765–1867* (1957).

Andrews, P. W. S., and Brunner, E., *Capital Development in Steel* (1951).

Ashton, T. S., *Iron and Steel in the Industrial Revolution* (3rd edn., 1963).

Birch, A., *The Economic History of the British Iron and Steel Industry, 1784–1879* (1967).

Burn, D. L., *The Economic History of Steelmaking, 1867–1939* (1940).

Burnham, T. H., and Hoskins, G. O., *Iron and Steel in Britain, 1870–1930* (1943).

Campbell, R. H., *Carron Company* (1961).

Carr, J. C., and Taplin, W., *A History of the British Steel Industry* (1962).

Crossley, D. W., 'The Management of a Sixteenth Century Ironworks', *Econ. Hist. Rev.*, 2nd ser., XIX (1966).

Downes, R. L., 'The Stour Partnership, 1726–36', *ibid.*, III (1950–1).

Erickson, Charlotte, *British Industrialists: Steel and Hosiery, 1850–1950* (1959).

Flinn, M. W., *Men of Iron: The Crowleys in the Early Iron Industry* (1962).

——— 'The Growth of the English Iron Industry, 1660–1760', *Econ. Hist. Rev.*, 2nd ser., XI (1958–9).

——— 'British Steel and Spanish Ore, 1871–1914', *Econ. Hist. Rev.*, 2nd ser., VIII (1955–6).

——— and Birch, A., 'The English Steel Industry before 1856', *Yorks. Bull.*, VI (1954).

Gale, W. K. V., *The British Iron and Steel Industry: A Technical History* (1967).

Hammersley, G., 'The Charcoal Iron Industry and its Fuel, 1540–1750', *Econ. Hist. Rev.*, 2nd ser., XXVI (1973).

Hyde, C. K., 'The Adoption of Coke-Smelting by the British Iron Industry, 1709–1790', *Explorations in Economic History*, X (1972–3).

—— 'Technological Change in the British Wrought Iron Industry, 1750–1815: A Reinterpretation', *Econ. Hist. Rev.*, 2nd ser., XXVII (1974).

—— 'The Adoption of the Hot Blast by the British Iron Industry: A Reinterpretation', *Explorations in Econ. Hist.*, X (1972–3).

Johnson, B. L. C., 'The Foley Partnerships: The Iron Industry at the End of the Charcoal Era', *Econ. Hist. Rev.*, 2nd ser., IV (1951–2).

—— 'The Midland Iron Industry in the early Eighteenth Century', *Business History*, II (1959–60).

McCloskey, D. N., *Economic Maturity and Entrepreneurial Decline: British Iron and Steel, 1870–1913* (Cambridge, Mass., 1973).

—— 'International Differences in Productivity? Coal and Steel in America and Britain before World War I', in McCloskey (ed.), *Essays on a Mature Economy* (1971).

—— 'Productivity Change in British Pig Iron, 1870–1939', *Quarterly Journ. of Econs.*, LXXXII (1968).

Orsagh, T. J., 'Progress in Iron and Steel, 1870–1913', *Comparative Studies in Society and History*, III (1960–1).

Payne, P. L., 'Iron and Steel Manufactures', in Aldcroft (ed.), *The Development of British Industry and Foreign Competition, 1875–1914* (1968).

Raistrick, A., *Dynasty of Iron Founders: the Darbys and Coalbrookdale* (1953; repr. 1970).

—— and Allen, E., 'The South Yorkshire Ironmasters, 1690–1750', *Econ. Hist. Rev.*, IX (1938–9).

Roepke, H. H., *Movements of the British Iron and Steel Industry, 1720–1951* (Urbana, Ill., 1956).

Schubert, H. R., *History of the British Iron and Steel Industry from B.C. c.450 to A.D. 1775* (1957).

Sinclair, W. A., 'The Growth of the British Steel Industry in the Late Nineteenth Century', *Scottish Journ. of Pol, Econ.*, VI (1959).

Straker, E., *Wealden Iron* (1931).

Temin, P., 'The Relative Decline of the British Steel Industry, 1880–1913', in H. Rosovsky (ed.), *Industrialization in Two Systems* (New York, 1966).

Vaizey, J., *The History of British Steel* (1974).

Leather and footwear
Church, R. A., 'Labour Supply and Innovation, 1800–1860: the Boot and Shoe Industry', *Business History*, XII (1970).

—— 'The British Leather Industry and Foreign Competition, 1870–1914', *Econ. Hist. Rev.*, 2nd ser., XXIV (1971).

—— 'The Effect of the American Export Invasion on the British Boot and Shoe Industry, 1885–1914', *Journ. of Econ. Hist.*, XXVIII (1968).

Clarkson, L. A., 'The Organization of the English Leather Industry in the late Sixteenth and Seventeenth Centuries', *Econ. Hist. Rev.*, 2nd ser., XIII (1960–1).

—— 'The Leather Crafts in Tudor and Stuart England', *Agric. Hist. Rev.*, XIV (1966).

Head, P., 'Boots and Shoes', in Aldcroft (ed.), *The Development of British Industry and Foreign Competition, 1875–1914* (1968).

Hillman, H. C., 'Size of Firms in the Boot and Shoe Industry', *Econ. Journ.*, XLIX (1939).

Mounfield, P. R., 'The Footwear Industry of the East Midlands', *East Midland Geographer*, Vols. 3 and 4 (1964–5).

—— 'The Shoe Industry in Staffordshire, 1767–1951', *North Staffs. Journal of Field Studies*, V (1965).

Rimmer, W. G., 'Leeds Leather Industry in the Nineteenth Century', *Thoresby Society*, XLVI, Miscellany 13 (1960).

Sparks, W. L., *The Story of Shoemaking in Norwich* (1949).

Sutton, G. B., 'The Marketing of Ready Made Footwear in the Nineteenth Century: A Study of the firm of C. & J. Clark', *Business History*, VI (1963–4).

Victoria County History, Northamptonshire, II (1906); *Leicestershire*, IV (1958).

Waterer, J. W., *Leather in Life, Art and Industry* (1946).

Woodward, D. M., 'The Chester Leather Industry, 1558–1625', *Lancs. & Chesh. Hist. Soc.*, Vol. 119 (1967).

Mechanical engineering, including water and steam power

Particular reference must be made to the Newcomen Society's *Transactions*, the main source for the technical history of engineering. It is impossible in this space to make even a brief selection from the numerous volumes produced over more than half a century.

Aldcroft, D. H., 'The Performance of the British Machine Tool Industry in the Inter-War Years', *Bus. Hist. Rev.*, XL (1966).

Barton, D. B., *The Cornish Beam Engine* (2nd edn., 1966).

Boucher, C. T. G., *John Rennie, 1761–1821* (1963).

Burn, D. L., 'The Genesis of American Engineering Competition, 1850–1870', *Econ. Hist.*, II (1931), repr. in Saul (ed.), op. cit.

Burstall, A. F., *History of Mechanical Engineering* (1963).

Cardwell, D. S. L., *Steam Power in the Eighteenth Century* (1963).

Church, R. A., 'Nineteenth Century Clock Technology in Britain, the United States, and Switzerland', *Econ. Hist. Rev.*, 2nd ser., XXVIII (1975).

Cule, J. E., 'Finance and Industry in the Eighteenth Century: the Firm of Boulton and Watt', *Econ. Hist.*, IV, No. 15 (1940).

Dickinson, H. W., *A Short History of the Steam Engine* (2nd edn., 1963, with Introduction by A. E. Musson).

—— *James Watt, Craftsman and Engineer* (1936).

—— and Jenkins, R., *James Watt and the Steam Engine* (1927).

—— and Titley, A., *Richard Trevithick* (1934).

Floud, R. C., *The British Machine-Tool Industry, 1850–1914* (1976).

Gribbon, H. C., *The History of Water Power in Ulster* (1969).

Guthrie, J., *A History of Marine Engineering* (1971).

Habakkuk, H. J., *America and British Technology in the Nineteenth Century* (1962).

Harris, J. R., 'The Employment of Steam Power in the Eighteenth Century', *History* LII (1967).

Hills, R. L., *Power in the Industrial Revolution* (1970).

Jenkins, R., *Links in the History of Engineering and Technology* (1936).

Musson, A. E., and Robinson, E., *Science and Technology in the Industrial Revolution* (1969).

—— *James Watt and the Steam Revolution* (1969).

Musson, A. E., 'Joseph Whitworth and the Growth of Mass-Production Engineering', *Bus. Hist.*, XVII (1975).

—— 'Industrial Motive Power in the United Kingdom, 1800–70', *Econ. Hist. Rev.*, 2nd ser., XXIX (1976).

—— Introduction to Dickinson, op. cit., and to W. Pole (ed.), *The Life of Sir William Fairbairn* (1871; new edn., 1970).

Raistrick, A., 'The Steam Engines on Tyneside, 1715–1778', *Newcomen Soc. Trans.*, n.s., XVII (1936–7).

Robinson, E., 'The Early Diffusion of Steam Power', *Journ. Econ. Hist.*, XXIV (1974).

Roe, J. W., *English and American Tool Builders* (1916).

Roll, E., *An Early Experiment in Industrial Organisation, being a History of the Firm of Boulton and Watt, 1775–1805* (1930).

Rolt, L. T. C., *Tools for the Job: A Short History of Machine Tools* (1965).

—— *Isambard Kingdom Brunel* (1957).

—— *Thomas Telford* (1958).

—— *George and Robert Stephenson* (1960).

—— *Thomas Newcomen: The Prehistory of the Steam Engine* (1963).

Rosenberg, N. (ed.), *Great Britain and the American System of Manufacturing* (1968).

Saul, S. B. (ed.), *Technological Change: The United States and Britain in the Nineteenth Century* (1972), including his article on 'The Market and the Development of the Mechanical Engineering Industries in Britain, 1860–1914', *Econ. Hist. Rev.*, 2nd ser., XX (1967).

—— 'The Engineering Industry', in Aldcroft (ed.), *The Development of British Industry and Foreign Competition, 1875–1914* (1968).

—— 'The Machine Tool Industry in Britain to 1914', *Bus. Hist.*, X (1968).

—— 'The American Impact on British Industry, 1895–1914', *ibid*, III (1960).

Scott, J. D., *Vickers: A History* (1962).

Skilton, C. P., *British Windmills and Watermills* (1947).

Steeds, W., *A History of Machine Tools* (1969).

Stowers, A., 'Observations on the History of Water Power', *Newcomen Soc. Trans.*, XXX (1955–7).

Syson, L., *British Water Mills* (1965).

Tann, J., *The Development of the Factory* (1970).

—— 'The Textile Millwright in the Early Industrial Revolution', *Textile History*, V (1974).

Wilson, C., and Reader, W. J., *Men and Machines. A History of D. Napier & Son Engineers, Ltd., 1808–1958* (1958).

Wilson, P. N., 'Water Power and the Industrial Revolution', *Water Power*, Aug. 1964.

—— 'Water-driven Prime Movers', *Chartered Mechanical Engineer*, Jan. 1961.

Motor and aircraft manufactures (including the cycle industry)

Andrews, P. W. S., and Brunner, E., *Life of Lord Nuffield* (1955).

Castle, H. G., *Britain's Motor Industry* (1950).

Caunter, C. F., *The History and Development of Cycles* (1955).

Fearon, P., 'The Formative Years of the British Aircraft Industry, 1913–1924', *Bus. Hist. Rev.*, XLIII (1969).

—— 'The British Airframe Industry and the State, 1918–35', *Econ. Hist. Rev.*, 2nd ser., XXVII (1974). See also the 'Comment' by A. J. Robertson and Fearon's 'Reply', *ibid.*, XXVIII (1975).

Grew, W. F., *The Cycle Industry* (1921).

Harrison, A. E., 'The Competitiveness of the British Cycle Industry, 1890–1914', *Econ. Hist. Rev.*, 2nd ser., XXII (1969).

Higham, R., 'Quantity *vs.* Quality: The Impact of Changing Demand in the British Aircraft Industry, 1900–1960', *Bus. Hist. Rev.*, XLII (1968).

Maxcy, G., and Silberston, A., *The Motor Industry* (1959).

Maxcy, G., 'The Motor Industry', in Cook (ed.), *Effects of Mergers* (1958).

Overy, R. J., *William Morris, Viscount Nuffield* (1976).

P.E.P., *Report on Motor Vehicles* (1950).

Rhys, D., *The Motor Industry: an Economic Survey* (1972).

Saul, S. B., 'The Motor Industry in Britain to 1914', *Bus. Hist.*, V (1962–3).

Walford, E. W., *Early Days in the British Motor Cycle Industry* (1931).

Non-ferrous metals

Barton, D. B., *A History of Tin Mining and Smelting in Cornwall* (1967).

—— *A History of Copper Mining in Cornwall and Devon* (2nd edn. 1968).

Burt, R. (ed.), *Cornish Mining* (1969).

—— 'Lead Production in England and Wales, 1700–70', *Econ. Hist. Rev.*, 2nd ser., XXII (1969).

Chaloner, W. H., 'Charles Roe of Macclesfield (1715–81): an Eighteenth-Century Industrialist', *Lancs. & Chesh. Antiq. Soc. Trans.*, LXII (1950–1), LXIII (1952–3).

Cocks, E. J., and Walters, B., *A History of the Zinc Smelting Industry in Britain* (1968).

Donald, M. B., *Elizabethan Copper: The History of the Company of Mines Royal, 1568–1605* (1955).

—— *Elizabethan Monopolies: The History of the Company of Mineral and Battery Works from 1565 to 1604* (1961).

Earl, B., *Cornish Mining* (1968).

Gough, J. W., *The Mines of Mendip* (1930).

Hamilton, H., *The English Brass and Copper Industries to 1800* (1926; 2nd edn. 1967).

Hamilton-Jenkin, A. K., *The Cornish Miner* (1927; repr. 1972).

Hammersley G., 'Technique or Economy? The Rise and Decline of the Early English Copper Industry, *ca.* 1550–1660', *Bus. Hist.*, XV (1973).

Harris, J. R., *The Copper King. A Biography of Thomas Williams of Llanidan* (1964).

Hatcher, J., *English Tin Production and Trade before 1550* (1973).

Hunt, C. J., *The Lead Miners of the Northern Pennines in the Eighteenth and Nineteenth Centuries* (1970).

Jenkins, R., 'Copper Smelting in England, Revival at the end of the Seventeenth Century', *Newcomen Soc. Trans.*, XXIV (1943–4 and 1944–5).

Kirkham, Nellie, *Derbyshire Lead Mining through the Centuries* (1968).

Lewis, G. R., *The Stannaries: A Study of the English Tin Miner* (1908; repr. 1965).

Lewis, W. J., *Lead Mining in Wales* (1967).

Minchinton, W. E., *The British Tinplate Industry: A History* (1957).

Raistrick, A., *Two Centuries of Industrial Welfare: the London (Quaker) Lead Company, 1692–1905* (1938).

—— and Jennings, B., *A History of Lead Mining in the Pennines* (1965).

Richardson, J. B., *Metal Mining* (1974).

Roberts, R. O., 'Copper and Economic Growth In Britain, 1729–84', *Nat. Library of Wales Journ.*, X (1957).

—— 'Development and Decline of the Copper and other Non-Ferrous Metal Industries in South Wales', *Trans. Hon. Soc. of Cymmrodorion*, 1956, repr. in Minchinton (ed.), *Industrial South Wales, 1750–1914* (1969).

Shaw, W. T., *Mining in the Lake Counties* (1970).

Papermaking and printing

Alford, B. W. E., 'Business Enterprise and the Growth of the Commercial Letterpress Printing Industry, 1850–1914', *Bus. Hist.*, VII (1965).

—— 'Government Expenditure and the Growth of the Printing Industry in the Nineteenth Century', *Econ. Hist. Rev.*, 2nd ser., XVII (1964–5).

Blagden, C., *The Stationers' Company: A History, 1403–1959* (1960).

Clair, C., *A History of Printing in Britain* (1965).

Coleman, D. C., *The British Paper Industry, 1495–1860* (1958).

Handover, P. M., *Printing in London from 1476 to Modern Times* (1960).

Legros, L. A., and Grant, J. C., *Typographical Printing Surfaces* (1916).

Musson, A. E., *The Typographical Association* (1954).

—— 'Newspaper Printing in the Industrial Revolution', *Econ. Hist. Rev.*, 2nd ser., X (1957–8).

Plant, Marjorie, *The English Book Trade* (1939; reprinted 1974).

Shorter, A. H., *Paper Making in the British Isles* (1971).

Thomas, A. G., *The Paper Industry in Scotland, 1590–1861* (1975).

Pottery manufacture

Barton, R. M., *A History of the Cornish China-Clay Industry* (1966).

Bladen, V. W., 'The Potteries in the Industrial Revolution', *Econ. Hist.*, No. I (1926).

Board of Trade, *Working Party Reports: Pottery* (1946).

Forsyth, G., *Twentieth Century Ceramics* (1936).

Green, A. T., and Stewart, G. H. (eds.), *Ceramics: A Symposium* (1953).

Hagger, R. G., *Pottery through the Ages* (1959).

Hillier, B., *Master Potters of the Industrial Revolution: the Turners of Lane End* (1965).

Hower, R. M., 'The Wedgwoods: Ten Generations of Potters', *Journ. of Econ. & Bus. Hist.*, IV (1932).

McKendrick, N., 'Josiah Wedgwood: An Eighteenth-Century Entrepreneur in Salesmanship and Marketing Techniques', *Econ. Hist. Rev.*, 2nd ser., XII (1959–60).

—— 'Josiah Wedgwood and Factory Discipline', *Hist. Journ.*, IV (1961).

Owen, H., *The Staffordshire Potter* (1901).

Rolt, L. T. C., *The Potters' Field: A History of the South Devon Ball Clay Industry* (1974).

Thomas, J., 'The Pottery Industry and the Industrial Revolution', *Econ. Hist.*, No. 12 (1937).

—— *The Rise of the Staffordshire Potteries* (1971).

Victoria County History, Staffordshire, II (1967), articles by R. G. Haggar and J. G. Jenkins on 'Pottery' and 'Ceramic Engineering'.

Warburton, W. H., *The History of Trade Union Organisation in the North Staffordshire Potteries* (1931).

Weatherill, Lorna, *The Pottery Trade and North Staffordshire, 1660–1760* (1971).

Wedgwood, J. C., *Staffordshire Pottery and its History* (1913).

Whiter, L., *Spode: A History of the Family, Factory and Wares from 1733 to 1833* (1970).

Shipbuilding

Buxton, N. K., 'The Scottish Shipbuilding Industry between the Wars', *Bus. Hist.*, X (1968).

Coleman, D. C., 'Naval Dockyards under the Later Stuarts', *Econ. Hist. Rev.*, 2nd ser., VI (1953–4).

Davis, R., 'English Merchant Shipping in the Economy of the Late Seventeenth Century', *ibid.*, IX (1956–7).

—— *The Rise of the English Shipping Industry in the Seventeenth and Eighteenth Centuries* (1962; repr. 1972).

Dougan, D., *The History of North East Shipbuilding* (1968).

Graham, G. S., 'The Ascendancy of the Sailing Ship, 1855–1885', *Econ. Hist. Rev.*, 2nd ser., IX (1956–7).

Grant, Sir Allan, *Steel and Ships: The History of John Brown's* (1950).

Guthrie, J., *A History of Marine Engineering* (1971).

Harley, C. K., 'The Shift from Sailing Ships to Steamships, 1850–1890', in McCloskey (ed.), *Essays on a Mature Economy* (1971).

Jones, L., *Shipbuilding in Britain* (1957).

Kirkaldy, A. W., *British Shipping: Its History, Organisation and Importance* (1914).

Maywald, K., 'The Construction Costs and the Value of the British Merchant Fleet, 1850–1938', *Scottish Journ. of Pol. Econ.*, III (1956).

Moss, M. S., and Hume, J. R., *Workshop of the British Empire: Engineering and Shipbuilding in the West of Scotland* (1977).

Parkinson, J. R., *The Economics of Shipbuilding in the United Kingdom* (1970).

Pollard, S., 'The Decline of Shipbuilding on the Thames', *Econ. Hist. Rev.*, 2nd ser., III (1950–1).

—— 'Laissez-faire and Shipbuilding', *ibid*, V (1952–3).

—— 'British and World Shipbuilding, 1890–1914', *Journ. of Econ. Hist.*, XVII (1957).

Robertson, P. L., 'Technical Education in the British Shipbuilding and Marine Engineering Industries, 1863–1914', *Econ. Hist. Rev.*, 2nd ser., XXVII (1974).

Scott, J. D., *Vickers: A History* (1962).

Smith, E. C., *A Short History of Naval and Marine Engineering* (1938).

Sturmey, S. G., *British Shipping and World Competition* (1962).

Small metal manufactures

Allen, G. C., *The Industrial Development of Birmingham and the Black Country 1860–1927* (1929; repr. 1966).

Ashton, T. S., *An Eighteenth Century Industrialist: Peter Stubs of Warrington, 1756–1806* (1939; repr. 1961).

—— 'The Domestic System in the Early Lancashire Tool Trade', *Econ. Hist.*, I (1926).

—— 'The Records of a Pin Manufactory, 1814–21', *Economica*, V (1925).

Barker, T. C., 'The Seventeenth-Century Origins of Watchmaking in South-West Lancashire', in J. R. Harris (ed.), *Liverpool and Merseyside* (1969).

Church, R. A., 'Nineteenth-Century Clock Technology in Britain, the United States, and Switzerland', *Econ. Hist. Rev.*, 2nd ser., XXVIII (1975).

Court, W. H. B., *The Rise of the Midland Industries, 1600–1838* (1938).

Flinn, M. W., *Men of Iron: The Crowleys in the Early Iron Industry* (1962).

Hey, D., *The Rural Metalworkers of the Sheffield Region: A Study of Rural Industry before the Industrial Revolution* (Leicester Univ., Dept. of Local History, Occasional Papers, Second Series, No. 5, 1972).

Lloyd, G. I. H., *The Cutlery Trades* (1913).

Nokes, B. C. G., 'John English of Feckenham, Needle Manufacturer', *Bus. Hist.*, XI (1969).

Pollard, S., *A History of Labour in Sheffield* (1959).

Robinson, E., 'Eighteenth-Century Commerce and Fashion: Matthew Boulton's Marketing Techniques', *Econ. Hist. Rev.*, 2nd ser., XVI (1963–4).

Roper, J. S., *Early North Worcestershire Scythesmiths* (1967).

Rowlands, Marie B., *Masters and Men in the West Midlands Metalware Trades before the Industrial Revolution* (1975).

Smith, Barbara M. D., 'The Galtons of Birmingham: Quaker Gun Merchants and Bankers, 1702–1831', *Bus. Hist.*, IX (1967).

Textile manufactures

The Bibliography has been divided into sections, dealing with particular industries, but there are some general works, as well as the journal *Textile History*, covering a broader range.

Chapman, S. J., and Ashton, T. S., 'The Sizes of Businesses, Mainly in the Textile Industries', *Journ. of Roy. Stat. Soc.*, LXXVII (1914).

English, W., *The Textile Industry: An Account of the Early Inventions of Spinning, Weaving, and Knitting Machines* (1972).

Harte, N. B., and Ponting, K. G. (eds.), *Textile History and Economic History* (1973).

Tann, J., *The Development of the Factory* (1970).

Woollen and worsted

Allison, K. J., 'The Norfolk Worsted Industry in the Sixteenth and Seventeenth Centuries', *Yorks, Bull.*, XII (1960), XIII (1961).

Bartlett, J. N., 'The Mechanisation of the Kidderminster Carpet Industry', *Bus. Hist.*, IX (1967).

Bowden, P. J., *The Wool Trade in Tudor and Stuart England* (1962).

Chapman, S. D., 'The Pioneers of Worsted Spinning by Power', *Bus. Hist.*, VII (1965).

Clapham, J. H., *The Woollen and Worsted Industries* (1907).

—— 'The Transference of the Worsted Industry from Norfolk to the West Riding', *Econ. Journ.*, XX (1910).

Coleman, D. C., 'An Innovation and its Diffusion: The "New Draperies"', *Econ. Hist. Rev.*, 2nd ser., XXII (1969).

Crump, W. B., *The Leeds Woollen Industry, 1780–1820* (1931).

—— and Ghorbal, G., *History of the Huddersfield Woollen Industry* (1935; repr. 1968).

Deane, P., 'The Output of the British Woollen Industry in the Eighteenth Century', *Journ. of Econ. Hist.*, XVII (1957).

Edwards, J. K., 'The Decline of the Norwich Textiles Industry', *Yorks. Bull.*, XVI (1964).

Friis, A., *Alderman Cockayne's Project and the Cloth Trade* (1927).

Glover, F. J., 'The Rise of the Heavy Woollen Trade of the West Riding of Yorkshire in the Nineteenth Century', *Bus. Hist.*, IV (1961–2).

Gulvin, C., *The Tweedmakers: A History of the Scottish Fancy Woollen Industry, 1600–1914* (1973).

Heaton, H., *The Yorkshire Woollen and Worsted Industries from the Earliest Times up to the Industrial Revolution* (1920: 2nd edn., 1965).

Jenkins, D. T., *The West Riding Wool Textile Industry, 1770–1835* (1975).

Jenkins, J. G., *The Welsh Woollen Industry* (1969).

—— (ed.), *The Wool Textile Industry in Great Britain* (1972).

Lipson, E., *The History of the English Woollen and Worsted Industries* (1921; repr. 1965).

Lloyd-Prichard, M. F., 'The Decline of Norwich', *Econ. Hist. Rev.*, 2nd ser., III (1950–1).

Lowe, N., *The Lancashire Textile Industry in the Sixteenth Century* (1972).

Mann, Julia de L., *The Cloth Industry in the West of England from 1640–1880* (1971).

Mendenhall, T. C., *Shrewsbury Drapers and the Welsh Wool Trade in the Sixteenth and Seventeenth Centuries* (1953).

Pilgrim, J. E., 'The Rise of the "New Draperies" in Essex', *Univ. of Birmingham Hist. Journ.*, VII (1959–60).

Plummer, A., *The Witney Blanket Industry* (1934).

—— *The London Weavers' Company, 1600–1970* (1972).

Ponting, K. G., *A History of the West of England Cloth Industry* (1957).

—— *The Woollen Industry of South-West England* (1971).

Ramsay, G. D., *The Wiltshire Woollen Industry in the Sixteenth and Seventeenth Centuries* (1943; repr. 1965).

Sigsworth, E. M., *Black Dyke Mills* (1958).

—— and Blackman, J. M., 'The Woollen and Worsted Industries', in Aldcroft (ed.), *The Development of British Industry and Foreign Competition, 1875–1914* (1968).

Tann, Jennifer, *Gloucestershire Woollen Mills* (1967).

Unwin, G., 'The History of the Cloth Industry in Suffolk', *Studies in Economic History* (1927; repr. 1966).

Wilson, C., 'Cloth Production and International Competition in the Seventeenth Century', *Econ. Hist. Rev.*, 2nd ser., XIII (1960–1).

Wilson, R. G., *Gentlemen Merchants* (1971).

The cotton industry

Aspin, C., and Chapman, S. D., *James Hargreaves and the Spinning Jenny* (1964).

Blaug, M., 'The Productivity of Capital in the Lancashire Cotton Industry during the Nineteenth Century', *Econ. Hist. Rev.*, 2nd ser., XIII (1960–1).

Board of Trade, *Working Party Reports: Cotton* (1946).

Boyson, R., *The Ashworth Cotton Enterprise* (1970).

Catling, H., *The Spinning Mule* (1970).

Chapman, S. D., *The Early Factory Masters: The Transition to the Factory System in the Midlands Textile Industry* (1967).

—— *The Cotton Industry in the Industrial Revolution* (1972).

—— 'Fixed Capital Formation in the British Cotton Industry, 1770–1815', *Econ. Hist. Rev.*, 2nd ser., XXIII (1970).

Chapman, S. J., *The Lancashire Cotton Industry* (1904).

—— *The Cotton Industry and Trade* (1905).

Cook, P. L., 'The Calico Printing Industry', in Cook (ed.), *Effects of Mergers* (1958).

Daniels, G. W., *The Early English Cotton Industry* (1920).

Edwards, M. M., *The Growth of the British Cotton Trade, 1780–1815* (1967).

Fitton, R. S., and Wadsworth, A. P., *The Strutts and the Arkwrights, 1758–1830* (1958).

Hill, R. L., *Power in the Industrial Revolution* (1970).

Jewkes, J., 'The Localisation of the Cotton Industry', *Econ. Hist.*, No. 5 (1930).

Kirby, M. W., 'The Lancashire Cotton Industry in the Inter-War Years: A Study in Organizational Change', *Bus. Hist.*, XVI (1974).

Lee, C. H., *A Cotton Enterprise, 1795–1840: A History of M'Connel and Kennedy, Fine Cotton Spinners* (1972).

Robertson, A. J., 'The Decline of the Scottish Cotton Industry, 1860–1914', *Bus. Hist.*, XII (1970).

Robson, R., *The Cotton Industry in Britain* (1957).

Rodgers, H. B., 'The Lancashire Cotton Industry in 1840', *Trans. of Inst. of Brit. Geographers*, Vol. 28 (1960).

Sandberg, L. G., 'American Rings and English Mules', *Quarterly Journ. of Econs.*, LXXXIII (1969), repr., in Saul (ed.), *Technological Change* (1970).

—— *Lancashire in Decline* (Columbus, Ohio, 1974).

Shapiro, S., *Capital and the Cotton Industry in the Industrial Revolution* (New York, 1967).

Smelser, N. J., *Social Change in the Industrial Revolution: An Application of Theory to the British Cotton Industry, 1770–1840* (1959).

Taylor, A. J., 'Concentration and Specialisation in the Lancashire Cotton Industry, 1825–1850', *Econ. Hist. Rev.*, 2nd ser., I (1948–9).

Turnbull, G., *A History of the Calico Printing Industry of Great Britain* (1951).

Tyson, R. E., 'The Cotton Industry', in Aldcroft (ed.), *The Development of British Industry and Foreign Competition, 1875–1914* (1968).

Unwin, G., *Samuel Oldknow and the Arkwrights* (1923).

Wadsworth, A. P., and Mann, Julia de L., *The Cotton Trade and Industrial Lancashire, 1600—1780* (1931; repr. 1965).

The linen industry

Gill, C., *The Rise of the Irish Linen Industry* (1925).

Harte, N. B., 'The Rise of Protection and the English Linen Trade, 1690–1790', in Harte and Ponting (eds.), op. cit.

Horner, J., *The Linen Trade of Europe in the Spinning-Wheel Period* (1920).

Rimmer, W. G., *Marshall's of Leeds, Flax Spinners, 1788–1886* (1960).

Warden, A. J., *The Linen Trade, Ancient and Modern* (1864; repr. 1967).

Silk and rayon manufactures

Chaloner, W. H., 'Sir Thomas Lombe and the British Silk Industry', in his *People and Industries* (1963).

Coleman, D. C., *Courtaulds: An Economic and Social History* (2 vols., 1969).

Hague, D. C., *The Economics of Man-Made Fibres* (1957).

Hard, A., *The Story of Rayon* (1944).

Harrop, J., 'The Growth of the Rayon Industry in the Inter-War Years', *Yorks, Bull.*, XX (1968).

Smith, D. M., 'The Silk Industry of the East Midlands', *East Midlands Geographer*, Vol. 3, Part I, No. 17, June 1962.

Warner, F., *The Silk Industry of the United Kingdom: Its Origin and Development* (1921).

Hosiery and lace manufactures

Chapman, S. D., 'The Genesis of the British Hosiery Industry, 1600–1750', *Textile History*, III (1972).

—— 'Enterprise and Innovation in the British Hosiery Industry, 1750–1850', *ibid.*, V (1974).

Erickson, Charlotte, *British Industrialists: Steel and Hosiery, 1850–1950* (1959).

Felkin, W., *History of the Machine-Wrought Hosiery and Lace Manufactures* (1867; centenary edn., 1967, with introduction by S. D. Chapman).

Head, P., 'Putting Out in the Leicester Hosiery Industry in the Middle of the Nineteenth Century', *Trans. Leics. Arch. & Hist. Soc.*, XXXVII (1961–2).

Horn, P. L. R., 'Pillow Lacemaking in Victorian England: The Experience of Oxfordshire', *Textile History*, III (1972).

Nelson, Evelyn G., 'The Putting-out System in the English Framework Knitting Industry', *Journ. of Econ. & Bus. Hist.*, II (1929–30).

Smith, D. M., 'The British Hosiery Industry at the Middle of the Nineteenth Century', Inst. of Brit. Geographers, *Trans. and Papers*, Publication No. 32 (1963).

Thirsk, J., 'The Fantastical Folly of Fashion: the English Stocking Knitting Industry, 1500–1700' in Harte and Ponting (eds.), op. cit.

Varley, D. E., 'An Outline of the History of the Machine-made Lace Trade from 1768 to 1914', Part I of *A History of the Midland Counties Lace Manufacturers' Association, 1915–1958* (1958).

—— *John Heathcoat, 1783–1861. Founder of the Machine-made Lace Industry* (1969).

Wells, F. A., *The British Hosiery and Knitwear Industry: Its History and Organization* (rev. edn., 1972).

Industrial Histories of Regions and Towns

This section includes *general* industrial histories of various regions and towns; many studies of *particular* local industries have been included in the previous section. Selection in this case is especially invidious, because of the immense number and variety of local historical studies. In this limited space, we can only make general reference to the *Victoria County Histories*, the transactions of innumerable local history societies, and the *Industrial Archaeology* series published by David & Charles—all mines of detailed and often invaluable information on local industries. Here we can only select a few special studies, to illustrate the quality of regional and local industrial histories.

Allen, G. C., *The Industrial Development of Birmingham and the Black Country, 1860–1927* (1929; repr. 1966).

Barker, T. C., and Harris, J. R., *A Merseyside Town in the Industrial Revolution: St. Helens, 1750–1900* (1954).

Booker, J., *Essex and the Industrial Revolution* (1974).

Bouch, C. M. L., and Jones, G. P., *A Short Economic and Social History of the Lake Counties, 1500–1830* (1961).

Chalklin, C. W., *Seventeenth Century Kent: A Social and Economic History* (1965).

Chaloner, W. H., *The Social and Economic Development of Crewe, 1780–1923* (1950).

—— 'Manchester in the Latter Half of the Eighteenth Century', *Bull. of John Rylands Library*, Vol. 42 (1959).

Chambers, J. D., *Nottinghamshire in the Eighteenth Century* (1932; 2nd edn. 1966).

—— *The Vale of Trent, 1670–1800* (*Econ. Hist Rev.* Supplement III, 1957).

Church, R. A., *Economic and Social Change in a Midland Town: Victorian Nottingham, 1815–1900* (1966).

Clark, P., and Slack, P., *Crisis and Order in English Towns, 1500–1700* (1971).

Cornwall, J., 'English Country Towns in the 1520s', *Econ. Hist. Rev.*, 2nd ser., XV (1962–3).

Court, W. H. B., *The Rise of the Midland Industries, 1600–1838* (1938).

Davies, C. S. (ed.), *A History of Macclesfield* (1961).

Dodd, A. H., *The Industrial Revolution in North Wales* (1933; 2nd edn. 1951).

Dyer, A. D., *The City of Worcester in the Sixteenth Century* (1973).

Fisher, F. J., 'The Development of London as a Centre of Conspicuous Consumption in the Sixteenth and Seventeenth Centuries', *Trans. Roy. Hist. Soc.*, 4th ser., XX (1948).

George, M. D., *London Life in the Eighteenth Century* (1925; 3rd edn. 1951).

Gill, C., and Briggs, A., *A History of Birmingham* (2 vols., 1952).

Hall, P. G., *The Industries of London since 1861* (1962).

Harris, J. R. (ed.), *Liverpool and Merseyside* (1969). See also Barker and Harris, op. cit.

Hoskins, W. G., *Industry, Trade, and People in Exeter, 1688–1800* (1935).

—— *Provincial England: Essays in Economic and Social History* (1963).

John, A. H., *The Industrial Development of South Wales, 1750–1850* (1950).

Kellett, J. R., 'The Breakdown of Gild and Corporation Control over the Handicraft and Retail Trade in London', *Econ. Hist. Rev.*, 2nd ser., X (1957–8).

Lenman, B., *From Esk to Tweed* (1975).

Lewis, E. D., *The Rhondda Valleys* (1959).

MacCaffrey, W. T., *Exeter, 1540–1640* (Cambridge, Mass., 1958; 2nd edn. 1976).

Marshall, J. D., *Furness and the Industrial Revolution* (1958).

McGrath, P. (ed.), *Bristol in the Eighteenth Century* (1972).

Mee, G., *Aristocratic Enterprise: The Fitzwilliam Industrial Undertakings, 1795–1857* (1975).

Minchinton, W. E. (ed.), *Industrial South Wales, 1750–1914* (1969).

Payne, P. L. (ed.), *Studies in Scottish Business History* (1967).

Pollard, S., *A History of Labour in Sheffield* (1959).

—— 'Barrow-in-Furness and the Seventh Duke of Devonshire', *Econ. Hist. Rev.*, 2nd ser., VIII (1955–6).

Prest, J., *The Industrial Revolution in Coventry* (1960).

Raybould, T. J., *The Economic Emergence of the Black Country: A Study of the Dudley Estate* (1973).

Richards, E., *The Leviathan of Wealth: The Sutherland Fortune in the Industrial Revolution* (1973).

Richardson, K., *Twentieth-Century Coventry* (1972).

Rowe, J., *Cornwall in the Age of the Industrial Revolution* (1953).

Slaven, A., *The Development of the West of Scotland, 1750–1960* (1975).

Smith, D. H., *The Industries of Greater London* (1933).

Stephens, W. B., *Seventeenth Century Exeter: A Study of Industrial and Commercial Development, 1625–1688* (1958).

Tawney, A. J. and R. H., 'An Occupational Census of the Seventeenth Century', *Econ. Hist. Rev.*, V (1934–5).

Trinder, B., *The Industrial Revolution in Shropshire* (1973).

Tupling, G. H., *The Economic History of Rossendale* (1927).

Williams, J. E., 'Whitehaven in the Eighteenth Century', *Econ. Hist. Rev.*, 2nd ser., VII (1955–6).

Wrigley, E. A., 'A Simple Model of London's Importance in Changing English Society and Economy, 1600–1750', *Past & Present*, No. 37 (1967).

Index

This is primarily an index to the various industries dealt with in this book and to their changing forms of organization. So many individuals, firms, processes, areas and places are referred to in the text that to have included all these would have made the index excessively long. Such references can be found fairly easily through the relevant industrial entries.